Literature, Democracy and Transitional Justice
Comparative World Perspectives

LEGENDA

LEGENDA is the Modern Humanities Research Association's book imprint for new research in the Humanities. Founded in 1995 by Malcolm Bowie and others within the University of Oxford, Legenda has always been a collaborative publishing enterprise, directly governed by scholars. The Modern Humanities Research Association (MHRA) joined this collaboration in 1998, became half-owner in 2004, in partnership with Maney Publishing and then Routledge, and has since 2016 been sole owner. Titles range from medieval texts to contemporary cinema and form a widely comparative view of the modern humanities, including works on Arabic, Catalan, English, French, German, Greek, Italian, Portuguese, Russian, Spanish, and Yiddish literature. Editorial boards and committees of more than 60 leading academic specialists work in collaboration with bodies such as the Society for French Studies, the British Comparative Literature Association and the Association of Hispanists of Great Britain & Ireland.

The MHRA encourages and promotes advanced study and research in the field of the modern humanities, especially modern European languages and literature, including English, and also cinema. It aims to break down the barriers between scholars working in different disciplines and to maintain the unity of humanistic scholarship. The Association fulfils this purpose through the publication of journals, bibliographies, monographs, critical editions, and the MHRA Style Guide, and by making grants in support of research. Membership is open to all who work in the Humanities, whether independent or in a University post, and the participation of younger colleagues entering the field is especially welcomed.

ALSO PUBLISHED BY THE ASSOCIATION

Critical Texts
Tudor and Stuart Translations • *New Translations* • *European Translations*
MHRA Library of Medieval Welsh Literature

MHRA Bibliographies
Publications of the Modern Humanities Research Association

The Annual Bibliography of English Language & Literature
Austrian Studies
Modern Language Review
Portuguese Studies
The Slavonic and East European Review
Working Papers in the Humanities
The Yearbook of English Studies

www.mhra.org.uk
www.legendabooks.com

TRANSCRIPT

Transcript publishes books about all kinds of imagining across languages, media and cultures: translations and versions, inter-cultural and multi-lingual writing, illustrations and musical settings, adaptation for theatre, film, TV and new media, creative and critical responses. We are open to studies of any combination of languages and media, in any historical moments, and are keen to reach beyond Legenda's traditional focus on modern European languages to embrace anglophone and world cultures and the classics. We are interested in innovative critical approaches: we welcome not only the most rigorous scholarship and sharpest theory, but also modes of writing that stretch or cross the boundaries of those discourses.

www.legendabooks.com/series/transcript

TRANSCRIPT

1. *Adapting the Canon: Mediation, Visualization, Interpretation*, edited by Ann Lewis and Silke Arnold-de Simine
2. *Adapted Voices: Transpositions of Céline's Voyage au bout de la nuit and Queneau's Zazie dans le métro*, by Armelle Blin-Rolland
3. *Zola and the Art of Television: Adaptation, Recreation, Translation*, by Kate Griffiths
4. *Comparative Encounters between Artaud, Michaux and the Zhuangzi: Rationality, Cosmology and Ethics*, by Xiaofan Amy Li
5. *Minding Borders: Resilient Divisions in Literature, the Body and the Academy*, edited by Nicola Gardini, Adriana Jacobs, Ben Morgan, Mohamed-Salah Omri and Matthew Reynolds
6. *Memory Across Borders: Nabokov, Perec, Chamoiseau*, by Sara-Louise Cooper
7. *Erotic Literature in Adaptation and Translation*, edited by Johannes D. Kaminski
8. *Translating Petrarch's Poetry: L'Aura del Petrarca from the Quattrocento to the 21st Century*, edited by Carole Birkan-Berz, Guillaume Coatalen and Thomas Vuong
9. *Making Masud Khan: Psychoanalysis, Empire and Modernist Culture*, by Benjamin Poore
10. *Prismatic Translation*, edited by Matthew Reynolds
11. *The Patient, the Impostor and the Seducer: Medieval European Literature in Hebrew*, by Tovi Bibring
12. *Reading Dante and Proust by Analogy*, by Julia Caterina Hartley
13. *The First English Translations of Molière: Drama in Flux 1663-1732*, by Suzanne Jones
14. *After Clarice: Reading Lispector's Legacy in the Twenty-First Century*, edited by Adriana X. Jacobs and Claire Williams
15. *Uruguayan Theatre in Translation: Theory and Practice*, by Sophie Stevens
16. *Hamlet Translations: Prisms of Cultural Encounters across the Globe*, edited by Márta Minier and Lily Kahn
17. *The Foreign Connection: Writings on Poetry, Art and Translation*, by Jamie McKendrick
18. *Poetics, Performance and Politics in French and Italian Renaissance Comedy*, by Lucy Rayfield

Literature, Democracy and Transitional Justice

Comparative World Perspectives

❖

Edited by
Mohamed-Salah Omri and Philippe Roussin

LEGENDA
Transcript 19
Modern Humanities Research Association
2022

Published by Legenda
an imprint of the Modern Humanities Research Association
Salisbury House, Station Road, Cambridge CB1 2LA

ISBN 978-1-78188-374-7 (HB)
ISBN 978-1-78188-377-8 (PB)

First published 2022

Copy-Editor: Richard Correll

CONTENTS

ACKNOWLEDGEMENTS

The editors would like to express their gratitude to the individuals and institutions without whom the project would not have been completed. Ali Souleman and Robin Ostle have graciously interviewed and translated Zakaria Tamer. Thanks are due to Agnès Delage (Aix Marseille Université) who was one of the conveners of the conference which resulted in this book. Thanks are due also to Graham Nelson for overseeing the publication process; to Matthew Reynolds for recommending the volume and encouraging bilingual academic publication; to Richard Correll for meticulous copy-editing; and to Mariachiara Leteo for logistical support in organizing the event and for indexing the book. We are grateful to Raihana Omri for granting us permission to use her artwork titled *Satellites # 2* as the cover image. The work is copper etching, drypoint with chine-collé on paper. The piece was inspired by the Tunisian revolution of 2011, exploring the themes of oppression and freedom. We are also grateful to Zakaria Tamer, who took the time and generously engaged with participants and students during the colloquium.

It is our pleasure to recognize support from Centre de recherches sur les arts et les languages (CNRS, EHESS), International Research Network Literature and Democracy (XIXth–XXIst centuries): Theoretical, Historical and Comparative Approaches (CNRS); Maison Française d'Oxford; Modern Humanities Research Center (TORCH); Oxford Comparative Literature and Translation network and St John's College, University of Oxford.

We owe a special debt to the contributors not only for their outstanding contributions but also for their extreme patience with this long publication process.

Oxford, June 2022

NOTES ON CONTRIBUTORS

Carrol Clarkson is Professor and Chair of English at the University of the Western Cape in South Africa. Before coming to UWC, she was Professor and Chair of Modern English Literature at the University of Amsterdam. She has published widely on aesthetics, legal theory, and South African literature and art. Her books include *J. M. Coetzee: Countervoices* (Palgrave 2009; 2nd edn 2013) and *Drawing the Line: Toward an Aesthetics of Transitional Justice* (Fordham University Press, 2014).

Anissa Daoudi is Senior Lecturer in Arabic and Translation Studies at the University of Birmingham. She held a Leverhulme Fellowship for research on sexual violence in Algeria in the Civil War of the 1990s. She also edits a blog on *Sexual Violence at Wartime*. Her publications include: *Cultural and Linguistic Encounters: Arab EFL Encoding and Decoding Idioms* (2011); a special issue on *e-Arabic and Minority Voices in the MENA Region* and essays on the concept of e-Arabic; 'Algerian Women and the Traumatic Decade: Literary Interventions' in the *International Journal of Language and Trauma* (2017); and 'Testimony and Literature as Alternative Transitional Justice in Algeria', *Interventions*, 22 (2020), 1045–64.

Agnès Delage is Professor at Université d'Aix Marseille. She is a member of Centre Aixois d'Etudes Romanes / Telemme: Temps, Espaces, Langages, Europe Méridionale, Méditerranée ; a former member of La Casa de Velázquez (Madrid); a member of GDRI *Literature and Democracy (19th–21st centuries): Theoretical, Historical and Comparative Approaches*, responsible for the project OBERT *Observatoire Européen des Récits du Travail* (Université Aix Marseille). Amongst her publications are: *Escribir la democracia: literaturas y transiciones políticas*, ed. by A.-L. Bonvalot, A. Delage, A.-L. Rebreyend, and P. Roussin (Madrid: Casa de Velázquez, 2017). The main focus of her research is contemporary Spain.

Mohsen Elkhouni is Professor of Social and Political Philosophy at the Institut Supérieur des Sciences Humaines at the University of Tunis El Manar and Institute Director. He is the Lead of the research lab Enlightenments, Modernity and Cultural Diversity. His publications include: *Enlightenment and Critique* (Lattakia, Syria, 2006, 2009) (in Arabic); *Society and Communicative Reason* (Tunis, 2014) (in Arabic) and Co-editor of *University and Society within the Context of Arab Revolutions and New Humanism* (Tunis, 2016) (in English, Arabic and French). He is translator into Arabic of Claude Nicolet's *L'Idée républicaine en France (1789–1924): essai d'histoire critique* (1982) (Bayreuth, 2011). Elkhouni is a frequent commentator on Tunisia in local and Arab media.

Jesús Izquierdo Martín is Professor of Modern History at the Autonomous University of Madrid. He has spent his time in different national and foreign universities questioning the civic uses of the past. He has researched modern uses of some of historical concepts, the social foundations of individual behaviour, the tragic precariousness of personal identity, utopian thinking, or the relationship between history and literature. Currently he is engaged in the study of memory and genocide during Francoism and the transition to democracy, and in the topic of public history. Notable among his publications are *La guerra que nos han contado y la que no memoria e historia de 1936 para el siglo XXI (Postmetropolis)* (2017), and 'El historiador y el desafío posmoderno', in *El reconocimiento de las diferencias. Estados, naciones e identitades en la globalicization*, coord. por Juan Ramón de la Fuente, Pedro Pérez Herrero (2017). Today he co-directs the broadcasting program Contratiempo. Historia y Memoria with a team of good friends.

Chi-Ming Lin has studied in Paris and became a doctor of École des Hautes Études en Sciences Sociales in 1999. Now Professor at the Department of Arts and Design of National Taipei University of Education, he is specialized in the field of theory of image, French contemporary thought, cross-boundary study of arts, and contemporary aesthetics. His recent publications include *Multiple and Tension: On History of Photography and Photographic Portrait* (2013) and the Translator's Introduction to *L'Histoire de la folie à l'âge classique* (2016). He was the Director of National Taiwan Museum of Fine Arts (2018–20). Art critic and curator, he is presently one of the Vice-Presidents of the International Association of Art Critics.

Manuel Loff is a tenured Associate Professor at the Department of History and Political and International Studies, Universidade do Porto (Portugal), coordinator at the Instituto de História Contemporânea (Universidad NOVA de Lisboa) of a research project on Connected Histories: State-Building, Social Movements and Political Economy. He is also an associate researcher at the Centre d'Estudis sobre les Èpoques Franquista i Democràtica (Universitat Autònoma de Barcelona). He has been researching twentieth-century political and social History, Memory Studies, and political securitization in the twenty-first century. Currently he is focused on comparative democratic transitions in the 1970s and 1980s; on twenty-first-century new authoritarian liberalism, the extreme right and neofascism; and on social forms of (re)construction of collective memory on authoritarianism, coloniality and political transitions. He has a column in Lisbon's daily newspaper *Público.*

Annick Louis is a Professor at the Université de Besançon. She specializes in comparative literature of the nineteenth, twentieth and twenty-first centuries, with focus on Latin American and European cultures. Her work proposes an epistemology perspective on literature and social sciences. She has published *Jorge Luis Borges: œuvre et manœuvres* (L'Harmattan, 1997), *Borges face au fascisme 1. Les Causes du présent* (2006) and *Borges face au fascisme 2. Les Fictions du contemporain* (2007). She has also published recently on the relation between narrative and archaeology in *L'Invention de Troie: les vies rêvées de Heinrich Schliemann* (EHESS, 2020), on writing and exploration narrative, in *Homo explorator: Arthur Rimbaud, Lucio V. Mansilla y Heinrich Schliemann* (Garnier/Classiques, 2021), and on the status of the literary discipline, *Sans objet. Pour une épistémologie du littéraire* (Hermann, 2021).

Daniel O. Mosquera is currently Professor of Spanish and Latin American Studies, chair of the Modern Languages and Literatures Dept. and former director of the Latin American and Caribbean Studies Program at Union College in Schenectady, NY. He has published on Latin American colonial historiography and transatlantic studies, blackness and popular culture and politics, trash and eco-politics, and film and cultural studies and cultural theory. He has also directed and co-produced two documentaries on Afro-Colombian (*chocoano*) religious practices and popular culture. He is a published translator and a former member of the editorial board in the *Journal of Latin American Cultural*, where he currently serves as a member of the Advisory Board.

Brendon Nicholls is Associate Professor of Postcolonial African Studies in the School of English, University of Leeds. He is author of *Ngugi wa Thiong'o, Gender, and the Ethics of Postcolonial Reading* (Ashgate, 2010) and *Nadine Gordimer's July's People* (Routledge, 2010). He has published articles in *Modern Fiction Studies, Research in African Literatures, Cultural Critique, Journal of Commonwealth Literatures*, and *English in Africa*. He is a Visiting Research Fellow at Rhodes University, South Africa.

Christian Axboe Nielsen is Associate Professor of History and Human Security at Aarhus University in Denmark. He has worked as an analyst at the International Criminal Tribunal for the Former Yugoslavia and at the International Criminal Court, and has appeared as an expert witness in international and domestic criminal and civil cases, including the trials of Mićo Stanišić, Stojan Župljanin, Goran Hadžić and Radovan Karadžić. His latest book is *Yugoslavia and Political Assassinations* (Bloomsbury/I. B. Tauris, 2020).

Mohamed-Salah Omri is Professor of Modern Arabic and Comparative Literature and Tutorial Fellow at St John's College, Oxford. His publications include: *University and Society within the Context of Arab Revolutions and New Humanism* (with Elkhouni and Guessoumi, 2016); *Confluency (tarafud) between Trade Unionism, Culture and Revolution in Tunisia* (2016); *Nationalism, Islam and World Literature* (2006), and essays on settler colonialism, the Arabic novel and poetry and revolution in Tunisia. He has also published on transitional justice and representations of torture in literature.

Robin Ostle is Emeritus Research Fellow in Modern Arabic at St John's College in the University of Oxford. His recent publications include *Studying Modern Arabic Literature*, edited with Roger Allen (Edinburgh University Press, 2015) and *Modern Literature in the Near and Middle East, 1850–1970* (sole editor), 2nd edn (Routledge, 2016).

Philippe Roussin is Director of Research at CNRS, Centre for research on arts and language (CNRS-EHESS), Paris; Coordinator of the GDRI Literature and Democracy (19th–21st centuries): Theoretical, Historical and Comparative Approaches. His recent publications include: Philippe Roussin and Sebastian Veg (eds), *Démocratie et littérature: expériences quotidiennes, espaces publics, régimes politiques, Communications*, 99 (Seuil, 2016); Per Krogh Hansen, John Pier, Philippe Roussin, and Wolf Schmid (eds), *Emerging Vectors of Narratology* (de Gruyter, 2017); A.-L.

Bonvalot, A.-L. Rebreyend and Ph. Roussin (eds), *Escribir la democracia: literatura y transiciones democraticas* (Casa de Velázquez, 2019); and Catherine Brun and Philippe Roussin (eds), *Post-censure(s), Communications*, 106 (Seuil, 2020).

Ali Souleman is a Professor of Theatre Studies, writer and literary translator. He worked as a Professor of Theatre Studies in the Higher Institute of Dramatic Arts in Damascus 2005–14. He was a CARA Fellow and visiting researcher in St John's College, University of Oxford 2014–16. Currently he is an independent researcher and literary translator based in Oxford. His publications include a book entitled *Zil al-Wardah: Masrah George Schehadé* [The Shadow of the Flower: The Theatre of George Schehadé] (1998) and three translated books, as well as articles and essays on Modern Arabic Drama, in addition to regular contributions and critical reviews to the Arab press since 1995.

Zakaria Tamer is widely considered the most important living Arab short story writer.Born in Damascus in 1931, his first short stories were published in the late 1950s. In 1978, he published the acclaimed *Al-Numur fi al-Yawm al-Ashir* [The Tigers on the Tenth Day]. Tamer was forced to resign from his position at *Al-Ma'rifa* in the late 1980s and moved to the UK where he edited *Al-Naqid* [The Critic] and was culture editor at Riad El-Rayyes publishing house, both of which played very important roles in the development of the Arabic literature. Among his collections are *Nida'a Nouh* [Noah's Summons] (1994); *Sanadhak* [We Shall Laugh] and *IF!* (both 1998); *Al-Hisrim* [Sour Grapes] (2000); *Taksir Rukab* [Breaking Knees] (2002); and *Al-Qunfuth* [The Hedgehog] (2005). His work has been translated into English, Spanish, French, Italian, Russian, German, and many other languages. In 2015, Tamer was awarded the Mahmoud Darwish Award for Freedom and Creativity. Since 2012, he has been writing regularly on his Facebook page *Al-Mihmaz*, which features very short stories and satirical pieces.

Sonia Zlitni-Fitouri is Professor of Francophone and Comparative Literature at the French Department, University of Tunis. She directs the research lab, Intersignes (LR14E501). Among her publications, all in French, are: *Edouard Glissant: pour une poétique de la relation. Limites. Epreuves. Dépassement* (ed.) (2008); *L'Espace dans l'œuvre de Rachid Boudjedra: épuisement, débordement, Préface de Rachid Boudjedra* (Tunis: Sud Editions, 2010); *Pour un art de la relation: processus narratif et restructuration du sujet dans trois romans maghrébins de langue française* (Centre de publications universitaires, 2014); *Littératures francophones et comparées: postures postcoloniales* (ed.) (2018); *Assia Djebar: de l'écrit au cri* (ed.) (2018); *Réinventer la nature: pour une écopoétique des littératures de langue française* (ed.) (2021).

INTRODUCTION

Mohamed-Salah Omri and Philippe Roussin

Transitional justice emerged in the late 1980s and early 1990s, mainly in response to political changes in Latin America and in Central and Eastern Europe. Since these changes were popularly called 'transitions to democracy', people began calling this new multidisciplinary field 'transitional justice'. It has since become one of the key elements of transition policy. Following the trials of former members of military juntas in Greece (1975), Argentina (1983) and Chile (1990), two key milestones marked the rise of transitional justice. The first was the establishment, in 1995, of South Africa's post-apartheid Truth and Reconciliation Commission (TRC), and the second was the creation, in 2002, of the International Criminal Court (ICC), with its headquarters at The Hague. Having become, since the 1990s, one of the major themes of law, transitional justice is implemented through mechanisms of very different natures: permanent criminal courts, mixed or *ad hoc* courts, and even 'para-jurisdictional' bodies. Tools such as trials, truth commissions, reparations, museums and other places of memory have been used either in isolation or in combination. The International Criminal Tribunal for Rwanda, the International Criminal Tribunal for the former Yugoslavia, hybrid courts such as the Special Panel of the Dili District Court, the Extraordinary Chambers of the Courts of Cambodia and the International Criminal Court (ICC), which has universal jurisdiction, are recent examples of these temporary international tribunals. Truth commissions are not jurisdictions but commissions of inquiry aimed at uncovering crimes and human rights violations committed by a government or by non-state actors.

Although transitional justice has become one of the main tools of democratization in the last thirty years, the relationship between transitional justice and democracy is complex. Indeed, there is a wide range of cases where the two do not necessarily overlap. We have democratization without transitional justice — Spain, parts of Central and Eastern Europe, for example; transitional justice without democratization — attempts in Algeria and Morocco, where aspects of transitional justice such as amnesty and reconciliation have been implemented, but democratization has not followed; or in the case of Taiwan, a desire to do justice that comes to light long after the transition to democracy. In addition, there is the danger of over-generalization by which successful cases (parts of Latin America) are taken as models for the idea of transitional justice as a whole, regardless of the specific nature of each national and historical situation. In 2007, according to Kathryn Sikkink and Carrie Booth Walling, who surveyed data on human rights trials for a 26-year period covering 192 countries and territories, 'of the total, 34 countries have used truth commissions, and 49 countries had at least one transitional human rights trial. If we look only at the approximately 84 new and/or transitional countries in the period 1979–2004, well over half of these transitional countries attempted some form of judicial proceeding and more than two-thirds of transitional countries used some transitional justice mechanism.'[1]

The relationship between justice and literature — this 'staging of the human interlocution' where men and women file charges, plead, testify and judge — goes back to ancient times in the Western world. Since the beginnings of rhetoric, *narrative* (*narratio*) has been the main element of judicial rhetoric whose function has been to establish facts and provide evidence in order to answer the question of knowing *what had happened.*

Considerable thought has been put into understanding the linkages between literature, and writing more generally, and authoritarianism based on research on specific case studies in Europe, Latin America and South Africa, in particular. In situations where a society emerges from authoritarian rule and its monopoly on truth claims, everyone feels entitled to their own truth. Writing — and the necessity and the desire for writing — become essential as forms for the representation of rights, making the case for justice, staking truth claims, or arguing counter-claims. Writing is seen as a contribution to the effort to prevent a return to dictatorship. It also testifies to abuses. Writers seek justice in the sense of directing collective remembering, contributing to the construction of a new collective memory, and resisting amnesia.

Testimony and narrative have been at the heart of the various truth and reconciliation commissions. Narratives and the narrative reconstruction of crimes were meant to establish the facts, to contribute to the establishment of the truth as well as to do justice to the sufferings of the victims. They also aimed at getting people to agree on a narrative of the past and articulating new representations of past violence in the public space. At the same time, they brought up the issue of how to rewrite official and manipulated history. More broadly, these narratives raise three questions: 1) How does this literature position itself between what obstructs truth and what authorizes it or makes it possible by giving it a status through narrative shaping or construction? 2) How does literature become a means of exploring the changing social status of truth? 3) How do these writings authorize/expand conceptions of both literature and truth?

With these developments, a literature that addresses these questions was born. It has been defined by the temporalities and stakes of its own and lies outside the walls of transitional justice in the strict sense. Alongside law, literature and art have played an important role within the framework of transitional justice. It was a writer, Ernesto Sabato, who chaired the Comisión Nacional sobre la Desaparición de Personas (CONADEP) which, after the end of the Argentine military dictatorship (1976–83), looked into the fate of tens of thousands of Argentines who had been kidnapped, tortured or murdered by the junta. The commission compiled 50,000 pages of files containing evidence of systematic kidnappings, torture and rape. Its findings and recommendations were published in 1984 in a book called *Nunca Más*.

In Rwanda, from July to August 1998, four years after the genocide which caused the death of 800,000 Tutsis in 1994, a dozen African writers, artists and filmmakers, at the initiative of Nocky Djedanoum and Wole Soyinka, travelled to Rwanda as part of the 'Writing for the Duty of Remembrance' project, visiting scenes of the tragedy, sites of the crimes and sites of memory where the bones of the victims were exposed. They spoke with the survivors and questioned the executioners in order to produce testimonial texts. Returning to Rwanda in 2000, these writers presented their works to the public there.

Since his first documentary film, *Site 2*, which deals with refugee camps in Thailand, Ritty Pahn's cinema has been portraying Cambodia's struggle to heal its wounds after mass killings during the 1975–79 Khmer Rouge regime. In 2002, *S21, the Khmer Rouge Death Machine* (*S21, la machine de mort khmère rouge*), addressed the necessity of remembrance at a time when the process of setting up extraordinary chambers within Cambodian courts was bogged down in disputes between the Cambodian government and the United Nations. His 2016 film *Exile* looks back on the difficult work of mourning the survivors of the Khmer Rouge repression and seeks to represent the image of the dead. In 2018, *Tombs without Names* (*Les Tombeaux sans noms*) evoked the need to offer a burial to the victims of the Khmer Rouge regime.

The salient features and history of intersections between literature, democratization and transitional justice form the focus of the present collection of essays. They explore case studies coming from South Africa, Rwanda, Argentina, Colombia, Portugal, Spain, Algeria, Tunisia, France and Taiwan. While the cases of South Africa and Latin America have already attracted considerable academic attention, less effort has been devoted to Central and Eastern Europe, the Arab World and Asia. The collection devotes attention to the comparative study of literatures written in the wake of violence and on their role in the aftermath of conflicts. It addresses the way literary texts inform broader discourses around transitional justice, historical reckoning, and political and social reconciliation. It also demonstrates how literature has criticized the normativity of 'humanitarian narratives' produced in the context of transitional justice and the ideology of reconciliation or, conversely, how literature has sought to restore, in literary discourse, the ineffable dimension of extreme violence or torture. The essays explore these roles from the perspective of related disciplines and in specific situations. The collection assumes an interdisciplinary vocation and aims to achieve a multi-disciplinary perspective by bringing together scholars from the fields of literary studies, history, politics, law and philosophy, as well as writers and other cultural practitioners.

The volume gathers sixteen contributions, including a conversation with Zakaria Tamer, a prominent Syrian writer. They emerged from the international colloquium, *Literature, Democracy and Transitional Justice* held from 18 to 20 March 2018 at St John's College and the Maison Française d'Oxford. The colloquium was part of the work of the international research network 'Literature and Democracy

(Nineteenth and Twentieth Centuries): Theoretical, Historical and Comparative Approaches' funded by the CNRS in Paris and in collaboration with St John's College, Oxford, and Casa de Velázquez in Madrid, Spain.

The five chapters written originally in French have been translated into English. The publishing series is keen to live up to its ideal of being open to languages beyond English and different practices of academic writing, thus breaking away from the monolingual norm. The book is multilingual, as well, in terms of disciplinary languages, for it combines history, literary studies, philosophy, political theory and interviews. Therefore, the texts are arranged in terms of geography, not along disciplinary lines. Grouping the various contributions by broad cultural area (Latin America, Arab World, Africa, Europe, Asia) sets out a panorama of transitional justice, a geography that spans history beyond the national and linguistic frames. In our view, this direction allows explorations situated in the history and social dynamics of the functions that literature fulfils, such as identifying facts, events and people; literature as pact/contract; as testimony and space for thinking about injustice and justice. All contributions are thoroughly contextualized, rather like case studies. This makes location important. Assembling the studies by geographical area allows for multiple entries to the same socio-political situation. This distribution also shows the global relevance of literature, democracy and transitional justice. At the same time, it allows for specificities to be highlighted, especially since there is no claim to the universality of democracy and transitional justice; rather, both are situational.

Two seminal cases of conflict and transition make up the intervention on Africa. Carrol Clarkson's 'Literacy and Democracy: Transitional Justice in South Africa' underscores the neglected issue of literacy and democracy. Clarkson discusses pivotal moments in South Africa's colonial, apartheid and post-apartheid legacy where the fault line between illiteracy and literacy throws into relief Western cultural presuppositions about writing and democracy, even before a discussion of literature and transitional justice can begin. With reference to the work of Steve Biko, Antjie Krog, Njabulo Ndebele, Willem Boshoff and Zak Yacoob (among others), the chapter examines different ways in which the philosophical preconditions of writing and literacy lead us to reconsider the material stakes of democracy. Brendon Nicholls addresses the aftermath of genocide in literature in his chapter, 'Literature and Transitional Justice after the Rwandan Genocide: Veronique Tadjo's *The Shadow of Imana*'. The travelogue in question (1998) undertakes a quest to memorialize the victims and the atrocities of the Rwandan genocide. However, as her narrative proceeds, Tadjo increasingly encounters the instability of these historical and legal categories. Acts of literary memorialization, Tadjo suggests, are ultimately impossible, given the complexities and ambivalences one encounters when attempting to recover historical truth. The chapter argues that the travelogue points out the practical insufficiencies of transitional justice after the Rwandan genocide while widening the categories of involvement and complicity in atrocity. Structurally, it models transition and reconciles itself to its own destabilized and disrupted foundations. Literature, by implication, offers its readers a performative model of transition, in which reconciliation without truth is possible.

Latin America has witnessed foundational moments in both testimonial literature and protracted conflict and abuse, from Chile and El Salvador to Colombia and Argentina, Peru and Guatemala. In 'Justice transitionnelle et justice civile dans *AntígonaS. Linaje de Hembras* (2001) de Jorge Huertas', published here in both English and French, Annick Louis considers the Argentinian process of transitional justice, which is often considered exemplary. During the period from 1987 to 2002, victims and civil society organized themselves to resist the denial of justice. Some literary texts enacted these claims by revisiting classical texts. The play, *AntígonaS. Linaje de Hembras* by Jorge Huertas, first staged in 2001, joins in the interest in the Greek classic, which enacts a refusal to bury Polynices, the son of Oedipus and Jocasta, and studies the tyrannical figure of Creon. It also prefigures the social and financial crisis of December 2001, which pushed Argentina to the brink of default and resulted in the most dramatic civil unrest for a decade, at the same time showing a liberating dimension. Daniel Mosquera's 'The Irreverence of Bones: Reclaiming Trashed Lives in the Aftermath of Violence in *Adios Ayacucho* (1984) and *Insensatez* (2004)' explores the emblematic connection between the human as 'waste' and violence in the context of transitional justice and memory retrieval. It analyses two fictional narratives: Julio Ortega's *Adios Ayacucho*, the story of a murdered Peruvian indigenous activist leader, whose partial remains return from the dead to travel in search of the missing body parts; and Horacio Castellanos Moya's *Insensatez* [*Senselessness*], which revisits government human rights abuses in Guatemala against indigenous populations from the perspective of a copyeditor hired 'to clean up' the language in the official report. The two narratives bring the 'wasted' to the forefront of reconciliation as a means to decentralize the forensic, anthropological, universalist pretentions of human rights while at the same time advocating for an ethically more inclusive and embodied understanding of social memory.

In Europe after 1945, argues Philippe Roussin in 'Justice, rhétorique judiciaire et reconstruction de la littérature en Europe après 1945 (Céline, Frisch, von Salomon)', literature was reconstructed around a set of moral, ethical and political questions, in the context of the trials of the immediate post-war period (the French purge, the Nuremberg trials in Germany) which mark the birth of international criminal justice and remain an essential reference in the field of transitional justice. This reconstruction takes place through the reconquest of the territory of fiction and the appearance of documents and testimony. Roussin explores three literary works published around 1950 which have in common the explicit form of inquiry, interrogation, investigation and trial: Louis-Ferdinand Céline's *Féerie pour une autre fois* (1952), Max Frisch's *Stiller* (1954), and Ernst von Salomon's *Der Fragebogen* (1951). By contrast, texts that presented themselves as documents or testimonies satisfy this necessity of narrating and this demand for justice.

In Spain, after 1975, a form of hegemonic narrative was constructed according to which democracy was the result of a pact of reconciliation, which allowed the nation to overcome the legacy of a fratricidal war. From this perspective, democracy would have guaranteed a return to normality and to Europe that was previously impossible to achieve. The genocidal logic of the Franco regime was disguised as a simple authoritarian logic. Thus runs the argument put forth by Jesús Izquierdo in 'Unfinished Transition: Spain as a Democracy without Transitional Justice'. The historical actors who published their memoirs contributed to a majoritarian form of collective memorialization in the country. It is a story which is less about the transitional political pact than it is a pact of denial, a post-traumatic consequence of violence. This study explores intellectuals and writers who have contributed to this hegemonic interpretation: Javier Pradera, J. Vidal-Beyneto, Gabriel Celaya, Juan Luis Cebrián, Pedro Laín Entralgo, and Fernando Chueca Goitia. Because justice was not done in reality, literature had to imagine it. Agnès Delage's chapter, 'Démocratie sans justice: les paradoxes de la justice littéraire dans l'œuvre de Javier Cercas', takes the work of Javier Cercas as the starting point to study the construction of an imaginary of literary justice as a substitute for the trial of Franquist crimes. It compares the way in which the documentary novel, especially *Anatomía de un instante* [*The Anatomy of a Moment*] (2009), legitimizes the absence of transitional justice in Spain by imagining it as a democratic peril with works that envisage restorative justice as the foundation of a democratic approach to political violence. One such case is the attempt to experiment with literary fora where victims meet their aggressors away from the public processes of law.

In neighbouring Portugal, unlike most other transitions from dictatorship to liberal-democratic regimes, especially the remaining ones that Samuel Huntington called a 'third wave of democratization', the transitional model met every condition to produce a clear rupture with the authoritarian past. Nevertheless, what emerges from the study of the social and political (re)constructions of the memory of the Portuguese dictatorship (1926–74) over the past four decades is that state policies on these issues drew a very similar picture to those countries in which transition was completely different. Manuel Loff develops this argument in his 'Transitional Justice and Uses of the Past in Post-authoritarian Portugal'. He suggests that public policies on the memory of the authoritarian regime, and especially on the colonial past, can scarcely be taken as 'historical justice'.

Unlike in Spain, and closer to what happened in Nuremberg, the courts took up accountability for human rights abuses in the former Yugoslavia. The United Nations International Criminal Tribunal for the Former Yugoslavia indicted 161 individuals for crimes against humanity, war crimes and genocide. Christian Axboe Nielsen looks into the process in his chapter, 'Voices of Suffering: Maintaining and Disseminating the Voice of Victims after the ICTY'. From the very first conviction of a low-level perpetrator (Duško Tadić) until the final verdicts against highest-ranking perpetrators (Radovan Karadžić and Ratko Mladić), the court transcripts at the ICTY quoted extensively from victims. Without their courageous and often harrowing testimony, it would have been impossible to prove the crimes. In many judgments, the transcript quoted at length from victims, thereby highlighting their humanity as well as the barbarous nature of the criminal acts they suffered. As such, the judgements mark an unwitting but important contribution to the 'humanitarian narratives' that have shaped our understanding of the wars of Yugoslav succession. The focus of the chapter is the use of victim testimony in the cases of Stanislav Galić (siege of Sarajevo), Milomir Stakić (Prijedor), Milan Lukić (Višegrad) and Radovan Karadžić.

Testimonies, whether written or oral, represent key elements in the pervasive abuses that have gone largely unpunished across the Arab World. Sonia Zlitni-Fitouri looks across the Maghreb region through the lenses of French-language Maghrebean narratives (novels and testimonies) that reflect the prison world, its imaginary reconstruction, and the experience of violence or barbaric aggression. Her chapter, 'De l'écriture en souffrance à la pensée de la liberté ou comment "marcher sur l'oubli" ', studies autobiographical novels and testimonies of the 'years of lead' in Morocco such as *Tazmamart, cellule 10* (2000) by Ahmed Marzouki and *La Vie devant moi* by Soukaina Oufkir (2008). It also looks at the texts of the Tunisian Gilbert Naccache, *Qu'as-tu fait de ta jeunesse?* (2009) and *Cristal* (1982), and the novel *Nos silences* (2009) by the Algerian Wahiba Khiari which reports on the violence perpetrated by the jihadists on women. The chapter attempts to show how prison discourse becomes a subversive discourse that may serve to thwart totalitarian state structures. It demonstrates that writing and witnessing become a way of 'walking on oblivion' (Tahar Bekri), of reactivating 'this pathological memory', of moving towards a thinking of freedom.

Anissa Daoudi's chapter, 'Testimonies and Literature as Alternative Transitional Justice in Algeria', zeroes in on Algeria in a discussion of two interrelated elements in relation to the use of testimonies (fictional or personal) to inform us about transitional justice in Algeria in the aftermath of the Civil War (1990s), known as the 'Black Decade'. The first consists of published literary texts that include fictional testimonies such as Assia Djebar's later novels in French, Fadhila Al Farouq's *Taa Al Khajal* [*Female Shyness*] (1998) in Arabic, and Baya Gacemi's testimony *Moi, Nadia, femme d'un émir du GIA* (1998) — all examples of 'écriture d'urgence'. The second element is personal testimonies of victims and survivors of the 1990s narrating their stories at a 'writing workshop' organized by Daoudi in Blida, Algeria, on 1 November 2017 in collaboration with the NGO Djazairouna and Algerian writers. The chapter brings into focus various forms of translation and testimony of sexual violence in particular.

Tunisia is the focus of the chapter 'Writing, Law and Transitional Justice in Tunisia' by Mohamed-Salah Omri. He explores selected testimonies and memoirs by survivors of state repression, including Gilbert Naccache (mentioned above), Belhaj Yahiya, Sassi, Jelassi, Cherni, Ben Mhenni, Fliss and Ben Brik. The chapter extends Omri's previous work on the idea of literary justice and writing about torture into the analysis of key terms associated with functions of literature in traumatic situations, namely, writing about injustice, performing justice, 'proleptic forgiving' and memorialization. One concern of the chapter is the ways in which the revolution of 2011, which led to the liberation of narrative in Tunisia, has affected perceptions of the role of writing during the transition, against the background of the idea of legalism developed in the chapter.

The idea of forgiveness and tolerance in Arab culture is the subject of Mohsen Elkhouni's 'La Tolérance dans la pensée arabo-musulmane, de la Renaissance à nos jours'. According to John Rawls's *Theory of Justice* (1999) and *Political Liberalism* (2005), it would not be possible to approach the issue of tolerance without establishing its link with justice. The link becomes even more essential in a transitional period characterized by conflict. Thus tolerance becomes the objective of democratic transition, as it is currently experienced in parts of the Arab world. The chapter examines the three arguments most frequently advanced in response to the question: 'Is tolerance part of the theoretical and cultural tradition in the Arab world?' It shows that the need for the virtue of tolerance, which has become a fundamental value in democratic systems, is not entirely absent from the Arab philosophical tradition or from literary and religious writings which entertain the dream of a just and tolerant world (Ibn Arabi, Ibn Rushd, Naguib Mahfuz).

Both tolerance and intolerance are the staples of the prominent Syrian writer Zakaria Tamer who was interviewed by Robin Ostle and Ali Souleman in preparation for the colloquium in which the present volume was conceived. Tamer is widely considered the Arab world's most important living short story writer. His work has been translated into English, Spanish, French, Italian, Russian, German and Japanese. Tamer often records the loss of his multi-ethnic society to authoritarian politics and sectarianism. He does so through short narratives that show the precarious lives of regular citizens pitted against brutal injustices and arbitrary denial of freedom.

Not unlike Spain and parts of the Arab world, transitional justice in Taiwan has been a very long process. Chi-Ming Lin's 'Alternative Account, Mourning Family and Transformation into Life: Three Contemporary Artworks Related to the Event of 28 February 1947 in Taiwan' discusses three contemporary Taiwanese artworks in their relation to the emphasis on victims of the event of 1947. 'The Brilliant Post' (2003), by Mei Dean-E, is based on the tragic life of the woodcut print artist, Huang Rong-Can, who was put to death during the period of White Terror in Taiwan. Hsieh Chun-Te's 'The Tears of Danshuei River' (2011) goes back to the banks of Danshuei River where many executions were perpetrated, using staged photography to represent the grief of the victims' families. The short film by the renowned filmmaker Tsai Ming-Liang, *Transformation into Life* (2013), finds its inspiration in the photograph of the dead body of the painter Chen Cheng-po. At the end of the film, Tsai brings Chen back to life and thus, symbolically, makes him live in the memory of the viewer. The comments on and the interpretation of these three contemporary art works aim to understand how art can contribute to the long process of justice in Taiwan.

Looking across the contributions that make up the current volume, one cannot help but notice that metaphors cast a powerful presence as a mode of expression. This is rather fitting in a work about literature and the pain of the self and the other, loss and recovery, absence and presence, silence and speaking/articulation across wide and diverse locations of power, repression and resistance. Here, *naming* is a matter of the utmost importance. Atrocities, genocides and wars often resist naming or, more accurately, are subjected to a battle over names: calling a civil war a collective madness, talking about collective responsibility (*everybody was guilty*), labelling a bloody history *the events* (*al-ahdath*). Sharing blame equally among victims and perpetrators amounts to whitewashing, evading accountability and assigning responsibility. Unsurprisingly, the terms *amnesia* and *erasure* are common among all the chapters. As a response, *naming* takes on crucial role: naming victims, perpetrators (Omri replicates the insistence by the survivors of torture on naming their torturers and inscribing them in their testimonies) and wars (Loff and war without name; the Algerian 'black decade' in Daoudi). Part of this naming process is a process of recovery. Literature, theatre and historical accounts seek to assuage and restore. We need to find the bones and be able to read them as subjects (indigenous bones), Mosquera argues. Jesús Izquierdo speaks about 'walking over dead bodies in Spain'. Naming the disposability of bodies — assassinations, mass graves, genocides... — and narratives — testimonies, eyewitness accounts, writings on the walls of prison cells... — are all closely related.

These studies demonstrate the diversity in the ways transitional justice, particularly truth and reconciliation commissions, have been conceptualized, adapted and implemented. Transitional justice has been variously understood as something foreign and thus viewed as needing domestication through local forms of reconciliation and conflict resolution; a social pact by which conflicts are submitted to transaction, or a manual to be adopted with little say given to local actors. Transitional justice is also about collective memory, collective remembering, creating consensus in a body shattered by violent conflict and disagreement. The chapters also demonstrate the complexity of the relationship between transitional justice and literature. Literature imagines justice, records injustice, but it can also be complicit with oppression. It can participate in changing the social status of truth. On the other hand, when we take testimony as literature, we are stretching how literature itself is conceived. What haunts these transitional narratives is not only the past and its ghosts, but also the future and the shapes it might take: what will return and in what shape?

Note to the Introduction

1. Kathryn Sikkink and Carrie Booth Walling, 'The Impact of Human Rights Trials in Latin America', *Journal of Peace Research*, 44.4 (2007), 427–45; see also Kathryn Sikkink, *The Justice Cascade: How Human Rights Prosecutions Are Changing World Politics* (New York: W. W. Norton, 2011).

PART I

Africa

CHAPTER 1

Literacy and Democracy: Transitional Justice in South Africa[1]

Carrol Clarkson

I

If democracy can be defined as the principle or practice of social equity, then the question of literature — or even more fundamentally, of literacy — in South Africa challenges any assumptions about easy relationships between literature, democracy, and transitional justice. Social practices of writing and reading are connected through a reciprocal anticipation of shared understanding — which is another way of saying that democracy presupposes a shared basic level of literacy, just as literacy itself requires a basic level of democracy before literature has a chance of gaining traction in a process of transitional justice. This cyclical passage through reading, writing, and democracy is an urgent one in South Africa, not least when one takes into account the findings of a recent Progress in International Reading in Literacy Study (PIRLS). Out of fifty countries in the study, South Africa came last, with nearly four out of five Grade Four school children falling below the lowest recognized benchmark for reading literacy. South Africa has eleven official languages, and the level of literacy in some of the African languages is even more sobering: more than 90% of pupils cannot read for meaning in Sepedi and Setswana, and illiteracy in Tshivenda, isiXhosa, Xitsonga, isiZulu and isiNdebele are almost as high.[2]

A colonial legacy and the aftershocks of an apartheid school education system in South Africa open up a chasm between the level of literacy on the one hand and the smooth workings of transitional justice on the other. But the fault line provokes further thought about the parameters of, and assumptions about, literacy and illiteracy in the first place. What counts as 'reading matter'? What is considered worthwhile for children to learn to 'read'? What systems of literacy gain ascendancy over others? And what does this tell us about the cultural contingencies, subjections, extinctions, and arrogations of political power? A striking instance that brings these questions to the fore is the work of nineteenth-century linguists Wilhelm Bleek and Lucy Lloyd, who sought to transcribe the near-extinct Xam languages by means of the Western alphabet — just as they themselves wrestled with their own limited understanding of the drawings/maps/diagrams/symbols of their interlocutors.[3]

My attention in this chapter turns to literature in the ongoing process of transitional justice, even while the material preconditions of writing and reading — of literacy itself — are never far from my considerations. In the discussions to follow I explore selected writings, or, as J. M. Coetzee might put it, the 'literary thinking' of a few prominent writers, artists, and legal theorists in South Africa's transition to democracy.[4]

II

South African writer Njabulo Ndebele opens his collection of essays, *Fine Lines from the Box: Further Thoughts about Our Country* (2007), with an exhilarating scene:

> A turning point in my life occurred when I discovered a treasure trove of banned books in my father's garage. One day, alone at home and bored during the school holidays in the mid-1960s, I began to explore my home. There was that wooden crate at the front right corner of the garage [...]. Inside were many books on music, art, and poetry, and others that I thought my father must have used for his degree studies at the University of the Witwatersrand. But as I got closer to the bottom of the box, my heart leapt with disbelief! Here was *Down Second Avenue* by Ezekiel Mphahlele; and *Road to Ghana* by Alfred Hutchinson; and *Blame Me on History* by Bloke Modisane [...], *Let my People Go* by Albert Luthuli [. . .] and other lesser known books that I do not remember now. Banned books![5]

From this day onwards, the young Ndebele's perceptions begin to change as he imagines a different kind of agency and participation in the political forcefield. The books open up a mind-shifting portal onto the field of reading, writing, thinking, and debating, a portal that the censorship board had attempted to obstruct.[6] What is memorable for Ndebele, the writer, as he relives his boyhood reading of *Down Second Avenue* and *Blame Me on History*, is a shock of recognition, an identification with the characters he reads about — and at the same time, an appreciation that racial oppression in South Africa could not simply be subsumed within a universal abstraction: 'It struck me then that oppressed people were far more complex than the collective suffering that sought to reduce them to a single state of pain'.[7] In their singularity, Ndebele writes, 'these books spoke to me with a directness I had not encountered in many school books about South Africa'.[8] This creative tension between what is shared and what is unique, between what is familiar and what is new, is played out, each time, in cycles of writing and reading.

To read and to write, to speak and to listen: these basic human aesthetic acts were jeopardized as the apartheid government banned books, and imposed its dividing lines between people and the stories they could tell. It would take feats of courage and imagination to cross these lines, opening oneself up to, and listening to, others; committing oneself to different kinds of conversation; shifting one's own sense of exposure to and participation in different fields of engagement. South African-born writer and academic, Stephen Clingman, invites us to think about these margins of exposure, where the stakes were nothing short of the risk and the transformation of a sense of oneself. With specific reference to Nelson Mandela and Afrikaner lawyer and activist, Bram Fischer, Clingman speaks of those brave enough to make the treacherous crossings over legal, political, and racial lines during the apartheid regime: the result was 'a new kind of language, a new syntax made of these connections and contiguities, these forms of expression; a new grammar of identity'.[9] In its banning of books, the apartheid government betrayed its awareness of the threat that reading and writing posed to its ideology of segregation, but despite its efforts, this new 'grammar of identity', in its incipient and transformative stages, can be tracked in several South African novels in the time of its transition to democracy — perhaps most noticeably in the political and ethical charge in the use of the word 'we'.

This collective pronoun is placed under extraordinary semantic strain in novels written at the time of, and shortly after the first democratic elections in 1994 — to the extent that the word 'we' challenges, rather than simply affirms, pre-existing configurations of community, identity, and belonging. I am thinking especially of characters like Treppie Benade in Marlene van Niekerk's *Triomf* ('We, watse stront!' [trans: We, what rubbish!/What shit!]);[10] Refentše and his friends in the tenuous 'we' and 'our' of Phaswane Mpe's *Welcome to Our Hillbrow* ('there are very few Hillbrowans, if you think about it, who were not originally wanderers from Tiragalong and other rural villages, who have come here, as we have, in search of education and work. Many of the *Makwerekwere* you accuse of this and that are no different to us — sojourners, here in search of green pastures');[11] David Lurie in J. M. Coetzee's *Disgrace* ('"This is not how we do things," snaps David, '*We*: he is on the point of saying, *We Westerners*');[12] and Aubrey Tearle in Ivan Vladislavić's *The Restless Supermarket* ('What do I mean by "we"? Don't make me laugh',[13] and 'what did I really mean? Who were "we"? The human race? People of good sense and common decency? The ragtag remnants of the Café Europa? Was it a royal "we"?').[14]

To say 'we' or 'our' usually depends on the sense of a shared and remembered past, and when it is used without qualification or question, it has the effect of affirming a shared present. At the level of representational content, the novels I have just mentioned register a sense of threat to inherited beliefs and communal values — hence the persistence of the challenge to the parameters of 'we' in each novel's *themes*. But at the level of performative event[15] — that is to say, in each instance of the book's being-read — the novel inaugurates a new community; it reconfigures a 'community' of readers. A dynamic tension thus arises: the novels assert a sense of loss, but this assertion of loss can only find expression in an event that moves beyond it. In Jean-Luc Nancy's phrasing, 'Regretting the absence of meaning itself has meaning'.[16] Further, through our recognition that this text constitutes an address to us as potential readers or listeners — which is to say, through the prior fact of the text's *address* (before any internal, thematic content is understood) — *we* are instantiated as addressees, and hence, '*we* are meaning in the sense that we are the element in which significations can be produced and circulate'.[17] This is not to say that an expression of the dissolution of community within the novels themselves finds a cosy resolution the moment these books are read. Nevertheless, all of these authors are attentive to literature's address as it takes effect in a world of readers: part of the work of literature is to lead us to question received parameters of community — and hence of the self.

'[R]eading and writing are two sides of a coin I wish to call *the art of the fine line*', Ndebele writes,[18] and with reference to the delicate balance I spoke of earlier, between the individual and the collective, between the known and the new, Ndebele goes on to describe acts of writing and reading as a process of 'pushing the boundaries of thought in *our* democracy and deepening intellectual engagement'.[19] Ndebele's phrasing marks out a tension between what is innovative, beyond pre-existing thought, pushing the boundaries, and what is familiar, signalled in the 'our' of a present that recognizes, as much as it instantiates, the sense of a shared history. Clingman's reflections on the boundary in *The Grammar of Identity* deepen the conceptual challenge: the 'boundary is also a horizon', writes Clingman,

> a destination never quite reached, like the boundary of the world. The boundary of meaning, then, is a transitive boundary; the transitive is intrinsically connected with meaning; navigation depends on, and creates, the transitive boundary which itself may undergo change. In all these ways the boundary is not a limit but the space of transition.[20]

Ndebele's literary commitment appreciates the way in which the *passage* from writing to reading and writing again opens new horizons, new possibilities for 'thoughtful intervention'. It is an 'antidote to orthodoxy and the comfort zones of populism',[21] but at the same time it creates bonds amongst '*us*', the writers and readers who bear the legacy of words — and worlds — once outlawed: 'This book is a tribute to my father's banned books: imprisoned thought now freely available, challenging *us* to build on the legacy'.[22]

For Clingman, thinkers, writers, and activists within the antiapartheid struggle 'were people who lived the boundary in their lives; they were transitional in every, including the best, sense: making their way from one time towards another'.[23] But if these were 'precarious lives', with all the semantic freight that Judith Butler gives to this phrase,[24] what of *us*, we readers who read those stories now? What assertion and assurances of a communal identity are made in the 'we' reading the transnational fiction Clingman reads and writes about with such poignancy: 'Underlying it all, the figure in the carpet à la Henry James, is the question of identity: of how, emerging within and from a broken world *we* might approach one another to make something more just, more human of it'.[25]

This sense of accountability in becoming *we, the readers*, is played out in the very act of reading the title and subtitle of Ndebele's collection of essays. The front cover of the book reads: *Fine Lines from the Box: Further Thoughts about Our Country*. The 'fine lines' refer to the box of banned books that Ndebele found as a child; 'further thoughts about our country' alludes to the ground-breaking essays Ndebele wrote in the 1980s, which were published together in 1991 under the title *Rediscovery of the Ordinary: Essays on South African Literature and Culture*. The shift from 'South

African' in the subtitle of *Rediscovery of the Ordinary*, to the 'our' in 'our country' of *Fine Lines from the Box*, dramatically insists on a world now shared by writer and reader. Further, the 'our' makes it difficult to sustain a distinction between constative and performative effects of the text: the world spoken *about* is the very one that belongs to the reader, a world animated in each event of reading.

Any use of 'I', 'you' or 'we' — however much these terms are contested at a thematic, constative level — *activates* the reader's complicity in the address as interlocutor and participant in a political contract of cultural recognition. The act of perceiving the material printed letters on a page — the passage through writing and reading — creates a boundary of meaning: a horizon never reached, but one that comes into view thanks to an appreciation of what is shared. To conclude the discussion of Ndebele: the act of reading takes us to an interface of meaning, at once confirming and challenging the boundaries of ourselves by exposing what we, the readers, share.

III

My discussion of Ndebele has broached literature's transformative potential, which is at least in part thanks to its appeal — and challenge — to subjective experience. But if subjective experience is easily associated with literature and the arts, the law (not least since the notorious 'ancient antagonism' between the philosophers and the poets in Plato's *Republic*),[26] is readily accepted as being aligned with the rational pursuit of truth: it is objective, impartial, even blind. What then, of the relationship between literature and the law in a process of transitional justice? Seemingly, they operate along entirely unrelated tracks. But what has attracted my attention in some of the jurisprudence in South Africa's transition to democracy is an active advocacy of the value of affective storytelling in judicial proceedings; a value we would more readily associate with literature and the creative arts. Former Justices Albie Sachs and Zak Yacoob, amongst others, have written in compelling ways about the *literary* art of legal judgement.

For Sachs, judges are the influential storytellers of our age, and the way the story is told is just as important as what is said. The narrative voice of the judge is neither that of an oracular 'pure and detached wisdom',[27] nor is it the predetermining, algorithmic voice of a computer. Instead, the judicial storyteller has the voice of an embodied subject, one 'immersed in and affected by the very processes we deal with'.[28] In an influential paper delivered at the University of the Witwatersrand in 2014, Zak Yacoob takes this idea even further: judging is a human process, and cannot, and should not, be an objective, mechanical process of applying points of law; rather, 'judging is about human beings and therefore it is absolutely essential for a judge to bring his or her subjectivity and his or her own humanity into the judging process'.[29] Citing Benjamin Cardozo's *The Nature of the Judicial Process*, Yacoob goes on to say: 'We may try to see things as objectively as we please. None the less, we can never see them with any eyes except our own'.[30] Judging always happens in a complex human context, and further, Yacoob goes on to say, still citing Cardozo:

> Deep below consciousness are other forces, the likes and the dislikes, the predilections and the prejudices, the complex of instincts and emotions and habits and convictions, which make the man, whether he be litigant or judge.[31]

Judgments are 'storytelling contests' Yacoob boldly claims, and the aim of a trial is not to find the truth, but to establish a case beyond reasonable doubt. Yacoob shocks us out of our assumptions: 'judges never know what the truth is and you can never know at the end of a case whether the judge's conclusion has resulted in a true finding or not'.[32] In Yacoob's disaggregation of 'truth' and 'reasonable doubt', the judge, just like the poet or the artist, offers 'representations' — and is also beset by the doubts and impassioned emotions that make us human.

For Yacoob, human values are not impartial. They tell a story of subjective commitment — of partiality. And these values can also be set into narrative motion as an instrument of political and legal change. The process of legal judgment, or judicial persuasion, in Yacoob's terms, pulls out the stops of storytelling to remind us of and to convince us about the values a society upholds; legal judgements can be activated to alter the narratives a society tells about itself in imagining a more just future.

IV

A further striking example of an attentiveness to the values we associate with the literary arts — values of the individual and the subjective (where one would expect a neutral institutional standard) — is in the official signage at the Constitutional Court in Johannesburg. Garth Walker designed the typeface;[33] he visited the site before the Court was built (it is on the site of the infamous prison complex that was closed in 1983 — the prison where Nelson Mandela was also held),[34] and took his inspiration from the traces of former prisoners' graffiti that he found on the derelict buildings. The official signage is thus evocative of individual handwritings, the embodied materialization of one person's wanting-to-say. The lettering is striking in its unexpected singularity, interrupting the automations of received ideas; speaking to the reader in the language of individual address rather than in the legal stereotype of hierarchical institutional order and state control. The official signage itself is an articulate performative riposte — in writing — to the apartheid regime which incarcerated individuals who would prove, in some instances quite literally, to be the writers of South Africa's Constitution.

In his autobiography, *Long Walk to Freedom*, Nelson Mandela speaks about the oppressions of prison life:

> Prison is designed to break one's spirit and destroy one's resolve. To do this, the authorities attempt to exploit every weakness, demolish every initiative, negate all signs of individuality — all with the idea of stamping out that spark that makes each of us human and each of us who we are.[35]

These handwritten 'signs of individuality' go even further still: when the original eleven Constitutional Court judges were inaugurated, they each wrote the words,

"PRO PATRIA"

FIG. I.I. 'Pro Patria'. A poem that Willem Boshoff wrote in protest against compulsory military conscription during the apartheid years.

'Human Dignity, Equality and Freedom', in their own hand, and each in one of South Africa's eleven official languages. The writings were cast in concrete and are now part of the lintel above the main entrance door of the Court. The graffiti-signage and the handwriting of the judges authorize the foundational principles of the Constitution: despite the extent of apartheid's atrocities, that human spark of individual liberty would not be stamped out. The handwriting in Sesotho is that of former justice, Zak Yacoob, who is blind. In their unregulated spiritedness the letters of the word *seriti* prance across the lintel in celebration of human freedoms and idiosyncrasies. *Seriti:* dignity, integrity, the singular shadow that you cast, the legacy that you leave behind.

V

One of the artists whose work is represented at the Constitutional Court is that of word artist Willem Boshoff, whose ethically and politically charged works first came into prominence in the late 1970s. Boshoff experiments with the materiality of works and the ambiguous borderlands in which they operate: the visual and the verbal; seeing and reading; perceiving and understanding; English and other indigenous languages in South Africa — some of which are now extinct. His works challenge assumptions about social and political hierarchies, contingencies and contiguities, inviting the reader-viewer to imagine a differently ordered society.

In *KYKAFRIKAANS* (*LOOKAFRIKAANS*), a slim volume of poetry published in 1980, the poems are printed, or shall we say painted, with a typewriter.[36] Typewritten letters are arranged in different shapes across the page, sometimes forming readable words or syllables or sentence fragments, but in many instances the letters overlap, making it difficult to discern meaningful words at all. In the discussion to follow, I briefly consider two of these poems: 'Pro Patria' and 'Verskanste Openbaring' [Hidden Revelation].

The regimented words in 'Pro Patria', 'links regs links regs' [left right left right], march in five vertical rows of footprints from the bottom to the top of the page. But these words themselves are interrupted by scraps and shards of other words, some in English, some in Afrikaans, for example, 'sky' 'die' 'breek' [break]. We also find some other fragments of words that are difficult to make sense of at all. The thoughts, and individuality, and mystery of each person intimated in the word fragments may indeed be broken by the military regime, but the 'signs of individuality', to borrow Mandela's phrasing again, are never entirely obliterated, even as the military binary of 'left right' is relentlessly bawled out.

In 'Verskanste Openbaring' [Concealed Revelation], Boshoff explores the idea of human attempts at understanding, and treats language as a screen that obscures the meanings it seeks to bring to light. This poem takes as its medium the text of the Book of Revelation, the last chapter of the Bible. Boshoff typed a page of text, put the same sheet back into the typewriter, and continued typing layers and layers of the text of Revelation on the same page. The trouble is, the more words of Revelation you have, the more obscure they become, and in the end you can only make out a

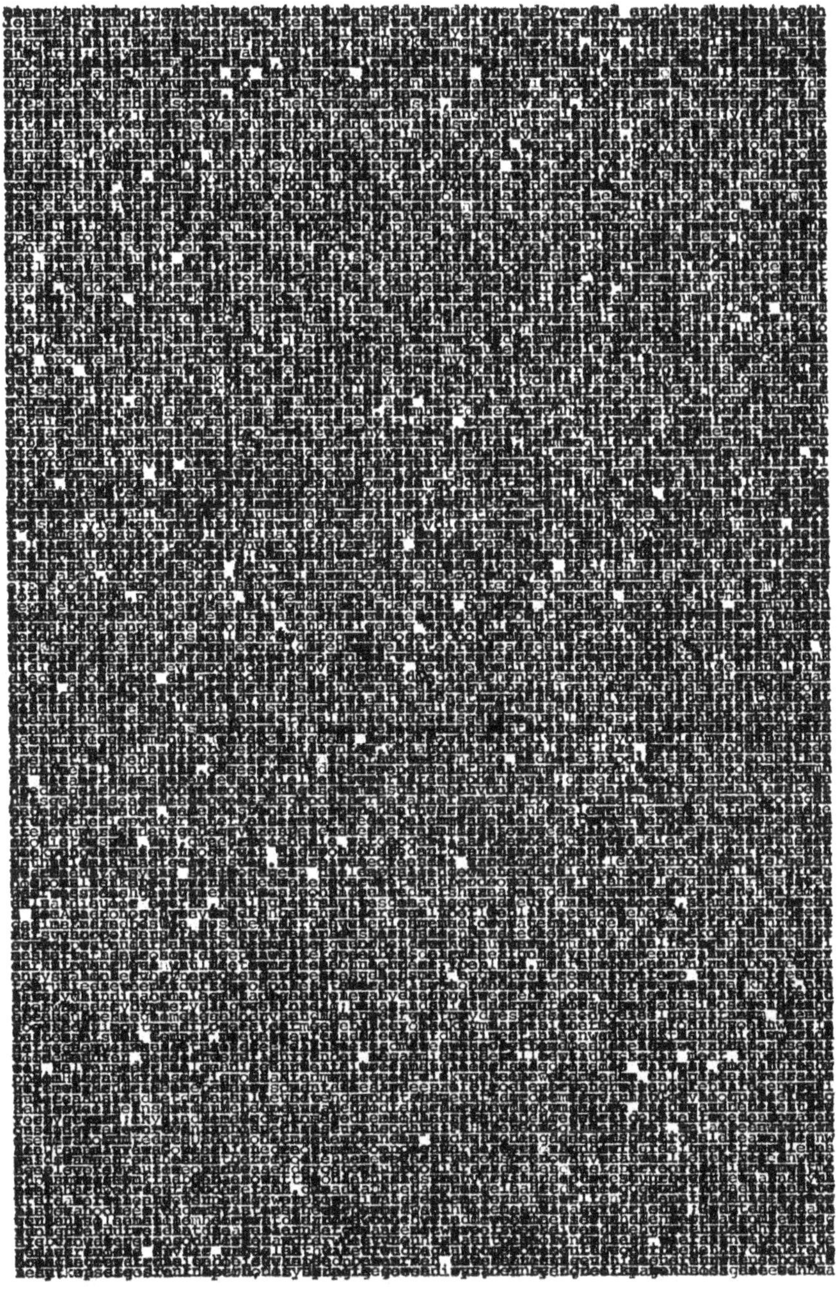

FIG. 1.2. Willem Boshoff, 'Verskanste Openbaring' [Concealed Revelation]

few letters here and there. The little white dots are where the spaces between the words coincide in all the layers of text. In one of our many conversations, Boshoff explained to me that these spaces are little bright stars shining through the dark obscurities of language; it is in the spaces between words that we sometimes see the light, and understand better.

The poems in *KYKAFRIKAANS* — and other works in Boshoff's corpus as a whole — highlight the ethical and political risk of complacently privileging one kind of knowing, one kind of human interaction, over another: reading over looking; speech over silence; logic over affect; sight over touch; English over the other ten official languages in South Africa. Boshoff's work invites us to imagine other modes of expression, other fields of sensory perception, and hence other ways of thinking and imagining a more just future. This brings me, finally, to a reflection on the term 'aesthetics' and the value of an attentiveness to literature and the other arts in a time of transitional justice.

VI

In ancient Greek philosophy, *aesthesis* refers to 'lived, felt experience, knowledge as it is obtained through the senses'.[37] One of the meanings of 'aesthetics' (dating back to 1803) is 'the science of the conditions of sensuous perception' (*OED*). In what ways is a social setting calibrated, so that some people (or other animals, or things) are seen, or heard, or valued as significant, while others are not? What does it take to recalibrate the settings, so that what has been unseen, or unheard, or devalued before, can now be perceived as worthy of attention? It is in this context that we appreciate that aesthetic discussions could be useful in thinking through questions of social justice.

In his influential work *The Politics of Aesthetics*, Jacques Rancière speaks in specific terms of 'aesthetic acts' as 'configurations of experience that create new modes of sense perception and induce novel forms of political subjectivity'.[38] I take an aesthetic act to be any event, or an encounter with a work, a text, a painting, that brings about a different *perception* of one's standing in relation to others. In what ways, and under what conditions do these aesthetic acts lead to a different way of perceiving the relation between the actual and the possible, say, or to a radically different appreciation of what counts as perceptible, or intelligible or legitimate in a social order? In her seminal paper on the African philosophy *ubuntu*, former Constitutional Judge Yvonne Mokgoro foregrounds the integral role of *perception* in political thought: *ubuntu* is a 'world view' 'a determining factor *in the formation of perceptions* which influence social conduct'.[39] What interests me is the context in which certain artworks, or poems, or novels — or even a legal judgement, or the signs on a building — by creating a new field of perception, have the potential to bring about shifts in the way a society delineates itself in terms of what it *perceives* to be significant, or readable, or even noticeable at all.

An aesthetic understanding brings us back to our senses: it draws attention to the nuances of different modes of representation, enabling us to think and question and recalibrate our perceptions of what is salient, legitimate or meaningful. A shift in our modes of representation affects the material field of what can be seen, or heard, or read — opening up the potential for different perceptions of what counts and what matters.

Notes to Chapter 1

1. My sincere thanks to Mohamed-Salah Omri for inviting me to present this paper at the colloquium in Oxford, and to contribute to this volume.
2. See the PIRLS website, and useful summaries of the survey results in Dave Chambers, '80% of Grade 4s Can't Read, Literacy Survey Reveals', *Times Live*, 12 May 2017, <https://www.timeslive.co.za/news/south-africa/2017-12-05-80-of-grade-4s-cant-read-literacy-survey-reveals/> and Thando Khubeka, '78% of Grade 4 Pupils in SA are Illiterate — Study', *Eyewitness News*, 12 May 2017, <http://ewn.co.za/2017/12/05/78-of-grade-4-pupils-in-sa-are-illiterate-study>. In September 2018, Parliament's Constitutional Review Committee recommended that South African Sign language become the country's 12th official language. See Law for All, blog at <https://www.lawforall.co.za/sign-language-south-africa/> [accessed 29 July 2019].
3. See for instance the preface of *Specimens of Bushmen Folklore* where Bleek and Lloyd are obliged to come up with a staggering array of diacritical marks to render in written form the /Xam narratives related by //kabbo, Dia!kwain and others. At the same time, the drawings, marks, lines, and circles produced by the /Xam challenge ordinary Western modes of 'reading'. Wilhelm Bleek and Lucy Lloyd, *Specimens of Bushmen Folklore,* Facsimile Reprint (Cape Town: Struik, 1968).
4. J. M. Coetzee, 'On Literary Thinking', *Textual Practice*, Special Issue 30@30: The Future of Literary Thinking, ed. by Peter Boxall and Michael Jonik, 30.7 (2016), 1151–52.
5. Njabulo Ndebele, *Fine Lines from the Box: Further Thoughts about Our Country*, ed. by Sam Raditlhalo (Cape Town and Johannesburg: Umuzi, 2007), p. 9.
6. For an extended account of literary censorship in South Africa, see Peter McDonald, *The Literature Police: Apartheid Censorship and its Cultural Consequences* (Oxford: Oxford University Press, 2009).
7. Ndebele, *Fine Lines*, p. 10.
8. Ndebele, *Fine Lines*, p. 10.
9. Stephen Clingman, 'Looking from South Africa to the World: A Story of Identity for our Times', *Safundi* (2013), 1–20 (p. 5).
10. Marlene Van Niekerk, *Triomf* (Cape Town: Queillerie, 1994), p. 43.
11. Phaswane Mpe, *Welcome to Our Hillbrow* (Pietermaritzburg: University of Natal Press, 2001), p. 18. 'Makwerekwere' is a pejorative term for a black person who is not South African.
12. J. M. Coetzee, *Disgrace* (London: Secker and Warburg, 1999), p. 202.
13. Ivan Vladislavić, *The Restless Supermarket* (Cape Town: David Philip, 2001), p. 6.
14. Vladislavić, *The Restless Supermarket*, p. 154. I discuss the use of the word 'we' more fully in Chapter 7 of Carrol Clarkson, *Drawing the Line: Toward an Aesthetics of Transitional Justice* (New York: Fordham University Press, 2014).
15. I am relying here on the distinction between constative and performative uses of language as set out by John L. Austin, *How to Do Things with Words* (Oxford: Oxford Paperbacks, 1965).
16. Jean-Luc Nancy, *Being Singular Plural*, trans. by Robert Richardson (Stanford, CA: Stanford University Press, 2000), p. 1.
17. Nancy, *Being Singular Plural*, p. 2, emphasis in the original.
18. Ndebele, *Fine Lines*, p. 10, Ndebele's emphasis.
19. Ndebele, *Fine Lines*, p. 11, my emphasis.
20. Stephen Clingman, *The Grammar of Identity: Transnational Fiction and the Nature of the Boundary* (Oxford: Oxford University Press, 2009), p. 22.
21. Ndebele, *Fine Lines*, p. 11.
22. Ndebele, *Fine Lines*, p. 11, my emphasis.
23. Clingman, *Looking from South Africa*, p. 7.

24. Judith Butler, *Precarious Life: The Power of Mourning and Violence* (New York: Verso, 2004).
25. Clingman, *Looking from South Africa*, p. 8, my emphasis.
26. Plato, *The Republic*, trans. by Desmond Lee, 2nd edn (London: Penguin, 2003).
27. Albie Sachs, *The Strange Alchemy of Life and Law* (Oxford: Oxford University Press, 2009), p. 270.
28. Ibid.
29. Zak Yacoob, 'Judicial Persuasion', paper presented at the Wits Institute for Social and Economic Justice, 7 August 2014 and transcribed by Tracey Calmeyer, p. 12. <https://archive.org/details/JusticeZakYacoob7.8.14>.
30. Benjamin Cardozo, *The Nature of the Judicial Process* (New York: Dover, 2005), p. 9, cited in Yacoob. Zak Yacoob himself is blind, and so his references to Benjamin Cardozo's *The Nature of the Judicial Process* take on a special resonance.
31. Cardozo, *Judicial Process*, p. 163.
32. Yacoob, 'Judicial Persuasion', p. 10, my emphasis.
33. Garth Walker, Archives, <http://10and5.com/2015/03/12/archives-garth-walker-design-spanning-three-decades/>.
34. For a concise history of the site and the building of the Constitutional Court see the Constitutional Court Art website, <http://ccac.org.za/>.
35. Nelson Mandela, *Long Walk to Freedom* (London: Abacus, 1995), p. 463.
36. Willem Boshoff, *KYKAFRIKAANS* (Johannesburg: Pannevis, 1980). Examples of the poems in *KYKAFRIKAANS* can be found on the artist's website, <https://www.willemboshoff.com/>.
37. *The Continental Aesthetics Reader*, ed. by Clive Cazeaux (London and New York: Routledge, 2000), p. xv. For an extended discussion of aesthetics see Clarkson, *Drawing the Line*.
38. Jacques Rancière, *The Politics of Aesthetics*, trans. by Gabriel Rockhill (London: Continuum, 2004), p. 9.
39. Yvonne Mokgoro, 'Ubuntu and the Law in South Africa', *Buffalo Human Rights Review*, 4 (1998), 15–23 (p. 15), my emphasis.

CHAPTER 2

❖

Literature and Transitional Justice after the Rwandan Genocide: Véronique Tadjo's *The Shadow of Imana*

Brendon Nicholls

The role of literature in concretizing memory after mass political violence is well known. Véronique Tadjo's *The Shadow of Imana: Travels in the Heart of Rwanda* undertakes a quest to memorialize the victims and the atrocities of the Rwandan genocide. The Rwandan genocide of 1994 entailed the massacre of between 500,000 and 810,000 mainly Tutsi victims.[1] An estimated 19% of the Hutu male adult population (or 367,000 men) were involved in perpetrating the atrocities.[2] Well-known as the blunt facts of the genocide may be, the intricacies and complexities of legal and historiographic processes in the aftermath are less secure. For example, the difficulties of evidence gathering are obvious when you are missing 800,000 witnesses and when you have 367,000 perpetrators. As Tadjo's narrative proceeds, it increasingly encounters the instability of received legal and historical categories. Acts of literary memorialization, Tadjo suggests, are ultimately impossible, given the nuances and ambivalences that one encounters when attempting to recover genocide's historical truth.

My argument follows five stages. First, I argue that Tadjo turns to literature to model global human complicity with murderous and violent impulses. In this way, literary allusion in *The Shadow of Imana* allows readers to encounter unbidden and repudiated intertextual voices working through ourselves. Tadjo resolves our universal capacity for genocide, and our literary complicity with violence, by destabilizing the truth claims of her narrative and by arranging her narrative in the form of overlapping or co-implicated stories. Truth, or something like it, accrues between flawed perspectives. Second, I demonstrate the challenges that have beset transitional justice in Rwanda in the three legal institutions presiding over genocide cases: the International Criminal Tribunal for Rwanda, the national courts, and the community courts or *gacacas*. Third, I argue that *The Shadow of Imana* engages with these institutional challenges directly, but offers literature as a space in which neither truth, nor singular perspectives are necessary. As such, literary narrative does not require the same confirmatory guarantees as the criminal courts. For this reason, literature may moot the *possibility* of transitional justice in its own internally constructed fictional world. Fourth, *The Shadow of Imana* assumes that literature can do what the law cannot. Specifically, Tadjo's formal arrangement of related fragments or vignettes, and her introduction of overtly fictional chapters in the middle of the book, allow her to model transitional, restorative and reparative justice within fiction. Since fiction can introduce new 'facts' into the known and can sustain contradictory possibilities, it can accomplish more than the minimal legal standards of evidence and processes of prosecution, testimony and judgment. Finally, I show that Tadjo widens the category of the legal person to include the idea of justice for the dead and she construes genocide as a normative environment, not an exceptional event. I conclude that *The Shadow of Imana* models transition structurally and reconciles itself to its own destabilized and disrupted foundations by augmenting and layering a prior story. Literature, by implication, offers its readers a performative model of transition, in which reconciliation without truth is possible.

Literature and Complicity

As critics have noticed, *The Shadow of Imana* destabilizes its own generic categories, moving between travel narrative, short story, folktale, memoir, eye-witness account, historical documentary, among others. Zoe Norridge states that the text is 'manifestly literary: it has a complex structure organized along conceptual rather than chronological lines, contains imaginary pieces alongside actual testimony and draws on poetic language and imagery to explore the legacies of the genocide.'[3] While Norridge's claim is suggestive and useful, no one has yet identified how narrative form is a response to the conceptual problems of recounting and responding to genocide. The basic structure of the book is that there are two long sections bookending it — the First Journey and the Second Journey — which purport to be non-fictional travelogue. The middle portion contains four long sections, three of which are clearly fictional and one of which may or may not be fiction. The travelogue sections of The First Journey and The Second Journey contain multiple vignettes, which generally take their names from either the site or place being described, or the vocation or name of the person being described or giving testimony. Collectively, these vignettes produce a mosaic or a series of fragments that stage visits to place and encounters with noteworthy individuals. While the book relies upon the myth of travel and its concomitant discovery of story, the transitional role of fiction in the middle of the book means that Tadjo is doing something unusual with travel narrative. Encounter stages story, which stages transitional consciousness.

The Shadow of Imana was a commissioned text. It was 'written under the auspices of the "Rwanda: écrire par devoir de mémoire" (Rwanda: writing as a duty to remember) project, run by the organizers of Fest'Africa, an annual festival of Africa based in Lille'.[4] In 1998, ten African writers were invited to take up writing fellowships in Rwanda and to reflect upon the memory of the genocide.[5] There was a subsequent conference 'in Rwanda in May–June 2000'.[6] These institutional bases for writing are significant, because Tadjo's introductory paragraph displays self-reversing qualities, as if she is initially ill at ease with the duty of starting to say something:

> It had long been my dream to go to Rwanda. No, 'dream' is not the right word. I had long felt a need to exorcise Rwanda. [...] I was starting from a particular premise: what had happened there concerned us all. It was not just one nation lost in the dark heart of Africa that was affected. To forget Rwanda after the sound and the fury was like being blind in one eye, voiceless, handicapped. It was to walk in darkness, feeling your way with outstretched arms to avoid colliding with the future.
>
> Of course, I did not consciously think this. I just wanted to go to Rwanda because I needed to.[7]

In this passage, we see a compulsion to visit Rwanda because of a dream, then an exorcism, then an unelaborated need. The organizing voice is self-revising. It undermines any immediate claim to a relationship with Rwanda. However, Tadjo does assert explicitly literary affiliations. The dark heart of Africa uncomfortably references Conrad's *Heart of Darkness*,[8] and 'the sound and the fury' alludes to Shakespeare's *Macbeth*.[9] Likewise, Tadjo's original French subtitle 'Voyages jusqu'au bout de Rwanda' evokes Louis-Ferdinand Céline's *Voyage au bout de la Nuit* [*Journey to the End of the Night*].[10] This matrix of literary allusion suggests that Tadjo's obligations are as strongly literary as they are humanitarian, but I would suggest that her intertexts invite questioning. How do we reconcile 'writing as a duty to memory' with our own memories of Conrad's atrociously genocidal Kurtz (who famously exclaims 'Exterminate all the brutes!') with Shakespeare's murderer Macbeth who discounts the importance of life just when justice for his own crimes is about to arrive, or with Celine's intensely dislikeable protagonist Ferdinand Bardamu, who suggests that our greatest human depths are to be discovered in war and illness?

I think that such discomforting literary affiliations are part of Tadjo's point. Elsewhere in the book, Tadjo claims that Rwanda is universal not because it makes a claim on everyone's moral sense, but because we are all potential perpetrators of genocide. Genocidal violence, for Tadjo, is constitutive. 'Rwanda is inside me, in you, in all of us', she insists,[11] a claim underscored by Sister Agatha late in the book: '"Hatred lies dormant in all of us."'[12] Likewise, literature ventriloquizes voices to which none of us might wish to adhere but which its readers nevertheless internalize. As readers, we are obliged to accommodate disquieting literary voices (like Kurtz, like Macbeth, like Bardamu) that we might otherwise prefer to repudiate. Citation 'is a mark of non-self-identity',[13] but it is also inscribed in literary readers, operating them silently from within. If Tadjo is right to suggest that all of us, any of us, are capable of committing genocide and participating in its atrocities, then perhaps we are being invited to entertain an analogy between our unacknowledged capacity to commit massacre and the unbidden thoughts and the unwelcome identifications of which all literary readers are composed. Literary allusion allows Tadjo to layer and complicate the genocide and its effects, relaying our readerly understandings via the genocidal contexts and affects from which we initially believe ourselves to be separate.

We are told that the Rwandan government's misinformation about the genocide and its desire to eliminate Tutsis and political opponents 'passed all understanding'.[14] This is, of course, an allusion to Philippians 4. 7, in which Paul faces execution and instructs the Philippians to seek out 'the peace of God, which transcends all understanding'. But the biblical allusion also recurs as a part-resolution to T. S. Eliot's contemplation of post-war Europe in 'The Waste Land', in which 'death had undone so many'.[15] We might say that Tadjo's citation of these two texts synthesizes the genocidal context of mass murder by execution. In fact, *The Shadow of Imana* explicitly refuses Eliot's shoring of the fragments of culture against his ruin after the mass slaughter of World War I. Eliot's cultural fragment is precisely what implicates Tadjo's readers in genocide. Eliot's 'shantih', or the 'peace that surpasses understanding',[16] becomes unpeaceful in its submission to new, murderous, connotations, not least the false comforts of 1994 Rwandan misinformation campaigns. *The Shadow of Imana* repurposes even our most reassuring cultural reference points, such as Philippians and 'The Waste Land', in order to model our contemporary complicity with injustice.

Tadjo has her first encounter with Rwanda outside of its national borders — via a South African car guard who is a Rwandan refugee. She initially hopes that 'Post-apartheid South Africa might perhaps be able to offer some answers to my questions, especially in relation to the problem of reconciliation on a national scale'.[17] At the time of her writing, South Africa had recently conducted its Truth and Reconciliation Commission, so Tadjo is explicitly measuring comparable possibilities for transitional justice in a Rwandan context. As Russell West-Pavlov astutely comments, 'This gesture is more than one of mere historical parallels or genealogies. Far more, it is imagined as an entanglement or an intertwining of the two countries' histories of trauma, so that the core of one history can be found in the other.'[18] Reconciliation here is bifurcated across geographical space. The logic is of mutually contaminating conditions, of imbricated traumas, not of facile comparison.

Tadjo's subsequent journey to Rwanda initially presents itself as a travelogue. We are privy to the fact that the quickest route from South Africa to Rwanda is Johannesburg–Paris–Brussels–Kigali, that the narrator loses her luggage on the Paris–Brussels leg, that she is not insured, that she has no visa and must surrender her passport to the Rwandan Ministry of National Security.[19] In short, Tadjo destabilizes her own status as privileged outsider, as witness, by foregrounding her trivial travelling setbacks. Once in Kigali, Tadjo implicates the reader in genocide by positioning it as a form of species memory that we all retain somewhere in our psyche: 'We have to remember that time of endless night, return to that time of the great terror, the time when humans, face to face with their great destiny, had not yet discovered their humanity.'[20] Tadjo extends this idea to undercut the primacy of language in both testimony and narration, since expression and affect contain more truth: 'The truth is revealed in people's eyes. Words have so little value. You need to get under people's skins. See what is inside.'[21] Paradoxically, intelligibility and understanding take the form of wounding. Getting under people's skins is an invasive act, especially when words have already been discounted as an avenue for doing so. Tadjo is again problematizing the idea of separability between the *genocidaire*, the victim and the witness. The witness too is a symbolic participant in the crime, excavating people's insides by getting under their skins. In short, the banality of evil, and its commonplace perpetration, mean that empathic understanding and violation become indistinguishable states.

Rwandan Transitional Justice and its Challenges

I posit that Tadjo is led to such paradoxes and contradictions by the material difficulties of 'doing justice' to Rwanda. So many victims did not live to tell what happened, meaning that the possibilities for narrative itself were vastly diminished. The staggering numbers of the accused overwhelmed state institutions and resources leading, again, to an insufficiency of narrative. For these reasons and others, the aftermath of the Rwandan genocide presents considerable challenges to the ideals of transitional justice. Three legal institutions have handled this aftermath. First, the International Criminal Tribunal for Rwanda was established in 1995 by UN Security Council Resolution 955 in order to prosecute acts of genocide, crimes against humanity and other serious violations of international humanitarian law. Presiding in Arusha, Tanzania, the Tribunal made the genocide internationally visible and remedied, to some extent, the previous failure of the international community to intervene during the massacre. But the International Tribunal was beset by inefficiency due to its very diligence and its high standards of proof. By 2009, the tribunal had completed 50 trials, with another 11 trials in progress and 14 accused still in detention awaiting trial. The second legal institution to handle the aftermath of the genocide was the Rwandan national court system. Prosecutions began in 1996, and by 1999, 1800 cases had been prosecuted.[22] Unlike the International Criminal Tribunal for Rwanda, the death sentence was passed occasionally, with executions taking place until 1998.[23] This led to the perception that justice for the high-ranking officers and officials who ordered the killings was more lenient than that dispensed to the low-ranking defendants who carried out those orders. However, 125,000 accused languished in prisons that were built to house only 50,000 inmates.[24] Even with prosecutions at the rate of six hundred per year it would have taken over a century to process the outstanding criminal trials. In January 2001, the Rwandan government inaugurated the traditional community court system of the *gacaca* to preside over two phases of justice — information gathering and prosecution. Prosecutions began in August 2006, and by December 2006, 51,649 cases had been tried — at a rate of 10,000 per month.[25] A year later, in December 2007, as many as a million cases had been tried according to some estimates.[26]

The *gacaca* courts were conceived in order to offer a communal and participatory form of justice, with the idea of strengthening Rwandan democracy. While the *gacaca* system was much more efficient than the International Criminal Tribunal and the national courts, it was beset by numerous shortcomings. Firstly, the *gacaca* courts never traditionally tried criminal cases — they tried 'property matters, such as inheritance and family law issues'.[27] Secondly, *gacacas* never traditionally imposed prison sentences.[28] In their original form, they were designed to integrate offenders back into the community and to restore harmonious relations. Therefore, *gacacas* were traditionally communal, rehabilitative and restorative, but they might now impose a retributive punishment of up to thirty years.[29]. Thirdly, in their recent incarnation, *gacacas* have often relied upon untrained, illiterate judges; moreover, the accused is compelled to answer questions but is prohibited from having a counsel for the defence.[30] As such, *gacacas* are open to claims of corruption and unfair breaches of international standards for due process. To understand the scale of the *gacaca* enterprise, compare Rwanda's '700 judges and magistrates, of whom fewer than 50 had any formal legal training'[31] prior to 1994 with the (scaled back number of) 170,000 judges required for the second, streamlined, iteration of the *gacaca* courts in 2004.[32] Moreover, *gacacas* have been accused of being a government political instrument — trying Hutu accused while ignoring accusations against Tutsi perpetrators among the Rwandan Popular Front.[33]

These three legal institutions evidence the sheer challenge of administering transitional justice in situations of mass perpetration, especially in an impoverished country like Rwanda that is also attempting to reconstruct its democracy and its civil and political institutions. The simple scale and complex intricacy of the challenge faced by transitional justice mean that it can only be implemented in practice when some of its founding ideals or standards (of proof or of fairness) are compromised.

The Shadow of Imana and Transitional Justice

Véronique Tadjo is well aware of these shortcomings of transitional justice in Rwanda. *The Shadow of Imana* engages with them directly. In the vignette 'Travelling Court Martial at Ntongwe', she describes the defendant, Edouard Mujyambere's claim that he has been subject to 'false testimonies so as to take his father's house from him, after his father died during the war',[34] but when he gives instructions to a girl, '[those] close by are watching wide-eyed'. Tadjo does not adjudicate in such moments, but measures supposedly false charges against the possibility of witness intimidation, all set against the glacial pace of a trial beset by delays. Likewise, in a vignette titled 'Section for Those Condemned to Death or Life Imprisonment', Tadjo records verbatim a prisoner's sense of injustice:

> '[One] prisoner cannot testify in another's defence. Only those who survived the genocide may testify. It's a betrayal created between the courts and the genocide survivors. And what about those who killed, but also saved lives? The courts should take that into account. Why is there no follow up when someone appeals? Where are the copies of the judgements?'
>
> [...]
>
> 'The witnesses for the prosecution are living in our homes and taking our possessions. The judges are among the genocide survivors. How can they judge our case impartially?'[35]

There is a powerful critique here of impediments to the defendant's right to a fair trial, including a radical delimitation of the supportive testimony that he or she might muster, the fact that no records of the judgments are kept, and the fact that appeals are not heard promptly, if at all. Even with lowered burdens of proof (since the defence is impeded and evidence available to the court is disproportionately weighted in favour of the prosecution), the national courts are still highly inefficient. Procedural injustices are structural — for instance, an innocent person might languish in prison waiting for an appeal hearing.

The Shadow of Imana also questions the institution of the *gacacas*:

> The Gacaca means a return to traditional justice. How did the ancestors judge? How did they mete out punishment? Traditional customs are being revived in the face of this emergency. Solutions for the present must be sought in the past.
>
> [...]
>
> Did the ancestors know the crime of genocide?[36]

Tadjo's probing of the foundations of the *gacaca* system is pointed, because she is aware of widespread feelings that neither the *gacacas*, nor the national courts, nor the international criminal tribunal succeeded in bringing about a truly national reconciliation. Because criminal prosecutions are adversarial, they risk reopening old conflicts and reawakening violent political impulses. But in a more complicated way, the provision for *gacacas* opened up the problem of retroactivity within Rwandan jurisprudence. To define penalties for genocidal acts in law, the Rwandan legislature had to refer itself to crimes (for example, murder or rape) as they were defined by pre-genocide legislation — for example in the Rwandan Penal Code of 1977 and various international instruments, including the Geneva Convention of 1949. Neither the Penal Code, nor the international instruments prescribed a specific penalty for explicitly *genocidal* acts. The difficulty was that Organic Law no. 40/2000 (26 January 2001), which established the *gacaca* courts, had to apply 'penalties from the Penal Code to acts prohibited elsewhere than in the Code',[37] thus possibly contradicting the legal principle of '*nulla poena sine lege* [no punishment without law]'.[38] Tadjo's questioning of whether the ancestors knew the crime of genocide is not simply speculation about whether primordial human presences comprehended the primordial scene of species murder; it is also a question about how *gacacas* may mobilize tradition without a secure legal precedent for dealing with genocide's exceptional status. Tadjo's repeated assertion that genocide pre-dates our humanity, and is sustained in species memory, introduces an ambivalence into the legal principle of 'no punishment without law'. In short, she suggests that perpetrators are being tried for what we all remember, but the law does not. In applying itself to human questions, the law is destined to overlook pre-human atrocity.

Additionally, Tadjo is sensitive to the intricacies that led ordinary people to become perpetrators. For instance, in an account of Thérèse's son Isaac, the narrator offers an unattributed observation: 'the militia were taking young people by force and making them fight and kill: "If you do not kill, we will kill you. If you do not kill them, they will kill you."'[39] There is a double compulsion here, in which one cannot do other than kill. Without choice or intention, complications are introduced into *mens rea* — the guilty frame of mind necessary for the defendant to be held responsible for his or her *intentional* criminal act. Tadjo offers a deep-seated critique of the flawed evidential premises of the criminal law. The law assumes the reliability of testimony: the witness is typically sworn to 'tell the truth, the whole truth, and nothing but the truth'. However, this assumption of truthful testimony is radically undercut by Thérèse herself, who says, '"The Rwandan people are a nation of liars. They never tell the truth to anyone."'[40] Like the Cretan paradox, there is no way that this statement could logically be true. Thérèse, a Rwandan, could not possibly be telling the truth when saying that all Rwandans lie. If all Rwandans lie, they are plausibly not Rwandans at all, to the extent that they share the defining characteristic of Cretans. The conventional resolution to the Cretan paradox, while logical, does not work in the context of penal justice either. Thérèse may be lying in saying that all Rwandans lie, even though her statement would be truthful to her own lie. Imagining one Rwandan who tells the truth, thus allowing Thérèse's statement to be false, is cold comfort given the sheer scale of unprocessed genocide testimony. Moreover, if lying is, perversely, a unifying factor between Rwandan prosecutor, Rwandan counsel for the defence, Rwandan judge, perpetrator, victim and witness, then the possibility of robust legal adjudication is remote.

In the vignette called 'The Lawyer from Kigali', Tadjo complicates legal axioms even further. She describes an unnamed lawyer who 'comes from another African country'.[41] His double structure of origination — from Kigali, from another country — destabilizes the boundary between the outsider and the insider. The lawyer claims that 'no one will ever really be able to understand what has happened here. Trying too hard to rationalise, you get lost in false truths'.[42] Even if not all Rwandans are liars, contrary to the 'false truths' just claimed in Thérèse's self-validating statement, the logical processes of deduction and proof succumb to the efforts involved in rational comprehension. Truth, it seems, is the first casualty of justice. Moreover, the lawyer's views on the International Criminal Tribunal for Rwanda and the Rwandan national court system are imparted via a curious formulation:

> You feel that what he would like to say is: 'They have all the time in the world and can afford to have lofty sentiments about their work. Meanwhile, however, Rwandan prisoners are rotting in the cells of run-down and overcrowded prisons. One hundred and thirty thousand prisoners! Even the United States does not have so many. If you calculate that a thousand prisoners, maximum, can be tried in a year, how many years are we looking at?'[43]

There is a spiral of attribution in this passage. The 'you' (an implied reader) has opinions that, once examined, revert back to a female 'I' — the narrator — disguised as a 'he' — the lawyer from Kigali. Additionally, there is a fraught line between legal opinion and fiction. The thoughts are attributed by the narrator to us, indicating what we feel the lawyer would like to say. So the narrator attributes to readers a feeling that readers cannot yet have, because the reading process is linear and we have not yet finished reading the sentence. In a state of readerly ignorance, we are made to impute a statement to the lawyer that he would like to express, but cannot. We might like to impute it, but we cannot yet either. Moreover, the lawyer's justification for being in Rwanda ('If [Rwandans cannot get themselves out of this], why am I here?'[44] closely mirrors Tadjo's own justification for writing after visiting Nyamata and Ntarama Church: 'If we are absolutely nothing, why take the trouble to write?'[45] In this moment, the book is collapsing its own quite careful gender demarcations and speaking positions, complicating its own perspectives on genocide and its aftermath. It is as if the parallel between lawyer and narrator opens up the possibility that writing and justice may be kindred projects in *The Shadow of Imana*.

In a subsequent section, called simply 'The Writer', Tadjo fictionalizes her own previous sentiments about genocide (in the introductory paragraph of *The Shadow of Imana*), but via a *male* writer: 'We must understand the real meaning of genocide, violence accumulated over the years. [...] The writer pushes people to listen to his voice, in an attempt to exorcise the buried memories.'[46] We find another act of self-distancing here. The female narrator's opinion *prior to travelling* is focalized by a male writer encountered *while travelling*. The female narrator's initial sentiments and statements (about exorcizing Rwanda) are subject to the male writer's incremental recombination (exorcizing buried memories). Of course, the male writer also exorcizes the female narrator's buried memories of her own former opinion. In other words, previous elements of the narrative are folded into later sections, and become subject to a differential progression. In this way, the book is transitioning its reader through a narrative process of fact-finding, and then rewriting it according to circumstantial testimony.

Literary Justice in Excess of the Law

Such moments of self-distancing might lead us to consider the unreliability of Tadjo's narrator, although this would be too simple. Dissembling, Tadjo's narrator may paradoxically become truly 'Rwandan' and eminently faithful to her material. I suggest that Tadjo is using fiction's possibilities to accomplish what courts of law cannot. Fiction offers something in excess of the law. Fiction may hold alternative, contradictory evidence equally in play, may redistribute the perspective of testimony in the interest of accumulating approximate story, may alter material evidence after the fact. In this way, the writer, like the lawyer, may be 'from Kigali' in a complex, post-foundational, indigenizing move. *The Shadow of Imana* gives clues to its own narrative method in an account of orphaned children:

> If you push them to talk, to speak of their former life, they retreat further into lies, lies that shield them against the cruelty of adults. They will tell you what you want to hear.
>
> It is only at night, when darkness has fallen, that occasionally you will hear a few snatches of the truth. The fragments of their stories overlap with each other, and finally, a picture emerges.[47]

Like the children, Tadjo is compelled to speak, as part of her wider commitments to the project 'Rwanda: Écrire Par Devoir de Mémoire' [Rwanda: Writing as a Duty to Remember]. The picture that emerges in the overlapping stories of the children may not be truth as such, but it is at least a coherent picture, an approximate representation. Likewise, Tadjo aspires to co-implicate discovered testimony with the instabilities of fiction, with the aim of coalescing something like a common *gestalt*.

There is a key staging post at the end of Tadjo's first journey. The penultimate section relays an urban legend and the vignette is titled 'In Kigali, They Tell the Following Story'. In this urban legend, a widow returns to her home after the genocide. She falls very ill. Her neighbour, who has killed her son, nurses her and they fall in love. The narrator proceeds to problematize the status of this story and to probe its instabilities:

> We do not learn [...] if the man knows that the woman knows of his crime. We do not know how he came to be so involved with her. Does he know that she probably has AIDS?
>
> Is this a true story? Was it made-up to discourage inter-ethnic marriages? Was it to show how murderers are still mingling with the general population and that the do-gooders of today are perhaps yesterday's killers?
>
> Should we condemn this woman's love? Is the man redeemed by it?[48]

A few things interest me in this urban legend. First, Tadjo discovers a story in Kigali and this becomes the immediate precedent for her own explicitly fictional narratives in the middle of the book. Second, the story told in Kigali models reconciliation between perpetrator and survivor, but seemingly without any factual guarantees or defined outcomes. The reconciliation may be deadly if the woman has AIDS. Reconciliation may therefore tip into indirect retribution. Thirdly, the story is impossible to adjudicate, given that it may have a manipulative social use to discourage inter-ethnic marriages. Fourthly, Tadjo concludes the vignette with the observation: 'This love was born of death. Death is its beginning and its end. Death is love, the connection.'[49] The final sentence, in the French original, resolves the narrative tangles of urban legend by recourse to the confirmations of homophone: 'La mort est l'amour, le lien'. The instability of the story and its resolution in homophonic echoes lead Tadjo towards 'thinking from the place of death' in the fictional middle sections. She wants to include the dead in her considerations of what justice looks like.

Tadjo's descriptions of genocide memorials suggest that at stake in the dead and how we treat them is our own humanity. At Nyamata church, only the victims who could be identified were buried. The unidentified 'are there, to bear witness, and will have no burial'.[50] Those who remain unburied do so because the living will not desecrate their memory by burying them anonymously. They remain to attest to their own secret, former lives. But the fact that they remain unburied means that 'these dead are screaming still'.[51] There is a paradox between ethical and respectful non-burial (which refuses to dehumanize the dead) and unjust non-burial (which also refuses to humanize them). The upshot of this paradox is that the dead's humanity persists in remnants:

> But the stench of death has become unbearable. Particles from the massacre are floating in the air. The dead point an accusing finger at the living who are still making use of them. The dead want to return to the earth. They rise up in protest. They want to melt into the earth.[52]

The protest of the dead is their airborne stench, a remnant of their decrepit vitality. Their desire to return to the earth or to melt into it is also the desire to finally dissipate the unbearable aftermath of atrocity. To the extent that the stench of death is a form of physical memory, it is also implicitly a repulsive memory. This very visceral account of Nyamata does not mean that Tadjo is disrespecting the dead. Instead, I would argue that she is suspicious of all forms of memory because she sees the genocidal impulse itself as deriving from an atavistic and not wholly forgotten human past. For this reason, Tadjo is critical of the folkloric traditions of heroic violence stored in the Rwandan landscape, because she views these as recurrent, foundational motivations for genocide:

> Who can say what makes up the memory of a whole nation? What images carpet its unconscious mind? Who can know what slaughter, hidden behind the centuries gone by, is even now sculpting the future of a nation?[53]

Tadjo identifies that narrative (of heroic killing) may persist as memory, in which those long dead have bequeathed genocide to the living. Given the dangers of reactivating such memories, justice for the dead is a tricky project. Doing right by the dead always has to happen in an absence of guarantee, and fiction is suited to this project. Fiction's co-ordinates establish possible and often plausible worlds, but they must be set out in a narrative progression that is devoid of confirmation. If fiction does not require proof or confirmation, this frees it to take a step beyond the obligations of the law.

'The Wrath of the Dead' is the first in the sequence of middle sections of the book, each of which is fictional. The mode of telling changes from first person to third person, evacuating the narrator's eye-witness account. In 'The Wrath of the Dead', Tadjo thinks about what justice might resemble for the dead. The dead are unrestful, we are told, outraged at having their lives cut short. The resolution to this haunting, to this disquiet of the dead who abide, is to bring in a soothsayer, who instructs the survivors of genocide that 'only the living can bring the dead back to life':[54]

> It is the dead themselves who are asking us to go on living, to resume our activities, to speak again those words they can no longer say themselves. [...] The dead will be reborn in every fragment of life, however small, in every word, in every action, however simple it may be.[55]

Justice for the dead, for the non-subject, requires the living to fulfil all of the potential in life that was denied to the dead. One fulfilment might be to continue to speak what the dead cannot (as fiction does). In other words, Tadjo considers what justice might mean for the spirit-subject, who is not a subject of law or a legal 'person' in any orthodox sense. The dead cannot become bearers of rights or responsibilities and yet they may still demand justice in excess of the law from the living.

The next fictional section is titled 'His Voice'. Isaro, the widow of a suicide, arranges to meet a man whose voice sounds like her former husband, Romain. We learn that Romain has committed suicide because he has likely perpetrated the murder of Nkuranya's family. The man Isaro is meeting is later revealed to be Nkuranya. So 'His Voice' is shared by both Romain the perpetrator and Nkuranya the survivor. Isaro is prompted by her grief to restore relations with a survivor who, like her, has lost his family. The voice of the dead and the voice of the living are purposefully blended in this story to allow the restoration of the social after genocide. The soothsayer in 'The Wrath of the Dead', who asserts that the dead should be 'reborn in every fragment of life',[56] is a proleptic (prophetic) device, prefiguring Nkuranya's resolution to carry 'memories of them in us and let those memories become part of our daily lives'.[57] Isaro's realization that Nkuranya has 'penetrated the secrets of her soul'[58] means that we have a possible nascent love relationship between two survivors whose involvement is a little like the protagonists in 'In Kigali, They Tell the Following Story'. Story, like the sign 'Kigali', moves. Moreover, Isaro is responsible for Romain's suicide. When Romain asks Isaro if she trusts in his innocence, she lies: '"Of course I do. I wouldn't be with you if I didn't."'[59] Isaro's lie plays out like Thérèse's claim. If the statement is true and Romain has killed, he knows that their relationship is terminal. If the statement is false and Isaro knows that Romain knows she is lying, then Isaro believes that Romain has killed. Either way we have an inescapably logical double-bind leading to Romain's suicide. In short, Tadjo begins to incrementally combine the previous elements of narrative in this overtly fictional story, testing the parameters of the possible in order to probe new forms of perpetration (Isaro prompting Romain's suicide), victimhood (Nkuranya losing his family), and reconciliation (between the voices of the dead perpetrator and the living survivor, between the bereaved Isaro and the bereaved Nkuranya).

In the next section, titled 'Anastase and Anastasie', we receive what must be a fictional account of a similarly named brother, Anastase, and sister, Anastasie. The gender transitions that we first saw at work between the female narrator and the unnamed male Writer are now resumed to allow a consideration of the proximity of the perpetrator rapist and his sister, the victim. Anastase and Anastasie's minor differences in name are counterposed to the gulf of gender violence that separates them when Anastase rapes Anastasie. The account must be fictional because we gain access to the consciousness of Anastasie during and after the rape, but she is long-dead due to the genocide by the time of the story's telling. Anastasie experiences the rape as her 'first death',[60] in common with many of the women raped during the genocide:

> One form of 'dying' that is strongly associated with the genocide of the Tutsi in Rwanda, is the experience of being raped. Mujawayo (196–97) notes that during a study performed by an association for women in Rwanda, focusing on the 'taboo' topic of rape, it was found that eighty per cent of the female survivors had been raped and more than half of them infected with AIDS. Although a word for this crime had not existed in this society before the genocide, the term *kubohoza*, to 'liberate' through violence (*libérer*, 195), became a common word

> for it, because of its use by perpetrators: 'We have liberated those Tutsi women, we have liberated those arrogant ones...' (196).[61]

Rape as a weapon of genocide is closely twinned with another weapon — killing — but rape is an inescapably gendered weapon. Anastasie's experience of rape leaves her wanting to 'disappear into oblivion, sail gently along, let herself be carried away by the underground stream'.[62] This sentiment foreshadows the passage several years later of the genocide victims thrown into rivers in order that the Tutsi or 'Watussi' might be returned to North Africa from whence colonial myth fantasized that the Tutsi had first come.[63] We are told that Anastasie does not know how she is ever 'going to be able to get up' or to 'face other people' after her rape, as if she is already symbolically dead.[64]

During her far more sparsely detailed 'second death', Anastasie overcomes such questions. She and other Hutu moderates take a stand for several weeks, fighting off militias that want to massacre her Tutsi neighbours. Anastasie dies at some point late in April 1994 when the resistance eventually succumbs. The relationship between Anastasie's first (fictional) and second (possibly real) death is significant. Tadjo has inserted a fictional rape prequel into a received genocide history in order that Anastasie's heroic fight and death (unjust in themselves) serve as a just outcome in overcoming the deadening effects of a previous sexual outrage committed against her. Anastasie's death becomes an opportunity to reconsider her previously possible life in fiction. Because literature is not bound to be truthful, it is able to imagine possible retroactive justices in which a second death is an afterlife that surmounts the conditions of the first death. Since Anastasie has been brought 'back to life' after her first death, we are permitted a very faint hope that her second death is neither absolute, nor final. Moreover, it is clear that as a Hutu woman who has been subject to rape, Anastasie skews the propagandized framing of Hutu-on-Tutsi rape as *kubohoza*. In a subtle twist, Anastasie is 'liberated' from the deadening effects of her rape through anti-militia violence, which itself aims to liberate Tutsi and Hutu moderate men and women from Hutu extremist perpetration.

Genocide as Environment

In Tadjo's most radically imaginative moments, she devolves humanity to nonhuman actors. For instance, when Isaro and Nkuranya first meet, their conversation is continually disrupted by a bee. It is only at the second meeting, when reconciliation seems more likely, that they may speak without interruption. Tadjo's implicit logic is that all of humanity is capable of genocide. Therefore, true humanity exists in a prior state, a proto-human state before we became aware of our humanity and its genocidal potentials. By extension, the nonhuman world of environment, insect and animal is a repository or placeholder for our common, lapsed proto-humanity. Consolate, whose mother is imprisoned indefinitely, has a smile with 'the taste of mango' and 'the curve of her buttocks [evokes] an earthly scented love'.[65] Because her mother's eyes have screened off the past, Consolate finds comfort in the blissful feeding of a cat's first litter of kittens. The cat's animal mothering in the present substitutes for the lost human mother of Consolate's own past — a mother whose own acts as perpetrator may have voided her memory of proto-humanity. Visiting Nyamata Church, the site of approximately 35,000 deaths, Tadjo observes: 'Driver ants criss-cross the red earth. What do they remember of the genocide?'[66] This is a complex speculation. First, driver ants would have been among those species picking clean the bones 'in the open, among the tall grasses'.[67] Memory for driver ants, therefore, might be felt at the sensorium of nourishment, not observation or reflection. Second, the short life-span of the driver ant would make memory trans-individual, experienced not by insect 'participants' or 'witnesses' to the scene, but instead in the aggregate gains (or losses) of the ant colony during the genocide and its aftermath. Ant memory is distributed in species energies, according co-existent insects the life that genocide does not accord to its victims.

On the road to Butare, Tadjo asserts 'in the distance the hills are making love to the sky. And their silent groans create those clouds you see.'[68] Here, the vapours constituting clouds are the breaths of groaning lovers — land and sky. But there is a second figurative order in which the telekinetic groans of hill and sky utter their progeny, clouds, into being — just as *The Shadow of Imana* utters the claims of the dead into being in 'The Wrath of the Dead' or unifies the perpetrator (Romain) and the victim (Nkuranya) through similarities of voice. Tadjo extends her metaphor to landscape, claiming 'The hills are so green, so fertile. Terraced crops descend like giant staircases.'[69] Landscape in this passage becomes a site of humane inhabitation, much like a terraced, multi-storey house. And yet, subtending this habitable landscape is the latent potential for violence: 'The seeds of violence have always existed, buried in the ancestral land. With the seasons they germinated and propagated, poisongrass invading the countryside.'[70] The humane and habitable scene of agriculture, we might say, threatens to become the uncannily human and violent theatre of war. As Tadjo is aware, the implements of farming converted easily during the genocide into weapons of slaughter, so that even her narratorial present is subtended by the possibility of violence: 'Armed soldiers are marching along the verges of the path. We pass a line of peasant farmers going to the fields. One of them is carrying an axe.'[71] Framed by the repressive forces of the state, the farmer's axe is a tool seemingly out of keeping with the sowing or reaping of a harvest. It points to latent genocidal uses from another temporality. Those uses unsettle because they cannot quite be disclosed in this moment. A similar complicity is accorded to the gorillas of the Volcano National Park, who have a 'beauty that passes our understanding',[72] in words that mimic the earlier descriptions of Rwandan government misinformation. Tadjo asks the same question about the gorillas that she will later ask about the ancestors: 'Do the great apes know what happened at the foot of the mountains?'[73] In short, genocide becomes an environment, not simply reducible to human actors. Its origins are both ancient and insinuated into our present. Its effects are both all too human and distributed beyond our species into the landscape.

Conclusion

The Shadow of Imana voices some of the practical insufficiencies of transitional justice after the Rwandan genocide, while widening the categories of involvement and complicity in atrocity. The ambit of complicity unmistakably includes us, Tadjo's literary readers. Moreover, Tadjo uses the possibilities of fiction to model the idea of a restorative justice for the dead (in 'The Wrath of the Dead'), thinks about how the possibilities of fiction might allow for a retroactive reading of justice via genocide ('Anastase and Anastasie'), and draws attention to acts of reconciliation that risk exonerating perpetrators ('There is a Story They Tell in Kigali'). Tadjo suggests that the instability of story and the vexed truth-status of fiction are uniquely comparable to genocidal aftermaths. Given her claim that we are all possible perpetrators in theory, Tadjo is using fiction to transition us from ignorant outsiders into conscious insiders. Since the narratives within *The Shadow of Imana* develop within the ambit of influence of their immediate predecessors and overlap, Tadjo's second visit to Rwanda becomes visible as an incremental recombination of the narratives comprising the first visit. Structurally, then, *The Shadow of Imana* models transition and reconciles itself to its own destabilized and disrupted foundations by augmenting and layering prior story. Literature, by implication, offers its readers a performative model of transition, in which reconciliation without truth is possible.

Notes to Chapter 2

1. Amaka Megwalu and Neophytos Loizides, 'Dilemmas of Justice and Reconciliation: Rwandans and the Gacaca Courts', *African Journal of International and Comparative Literature*, 18.1 (2010), 1–23 (p. 1).
2. Megwalu and Loizides, 'Dilemmas of Justice and Reconciliation', p. 2.
3. Zoe Norridge, *Perceiving Pain in African Literature* (Basingstoke: Palgrave, 2013), p. 139.
4. Norridge, *Perceiving Pain*, pp. 138–39.
5. 'As an organized tour of a country that is not a popular tourist destination, the visit bore some resemblance to a specialist package holiday.' Nicki Hitchcott, 'Travels in Inhumanity: Véronique Tadjo's Tourism in Rwanda', *French Cultural Studies*, 20.2 (2009), 149–64 (pp. 152–53).
6. Norridge, *Perceiving Pain*, p. 139.
7. Véronique Tadjo, *The Shadow of Imana: Travels in the Heart of Rwanda*, trans. by Véronique Waverley (Oxford: Heinemann, 2002), p. 3. Véronique Tadjo, *L'Ombre d'Imana: voyages jusqu'au bout du Rwanda* (Arles: Actes Sud, 2000).
8. Joseph Conrad, *Heart of Darkness* [1899] (New York: St. Martins, 1996), p. 171.
9. William Shakespeare, *Macbeth*, ed. by Frank Kermode (Boston, MA: Houghton Mifflin, 1974), Act v, Scene 5.
10. Louis-Ferdinand Céline, *Journey to the End of the Night*. 1932. trans. by Ralph Manheim (New York: New Directions, 1983).
11. Tadjo, *Shadow of Imana*, p. 37.
12. Tadjo, *Shadow of Imana*, p. 116.
13. Spivak notes that '[quotation] in Derrida is a mark of non-self-identity: the defining predication of a woman, whose very name is changeable.' See Gayatri Chakravorty Spivak, 'Displacement and the Discourse of Woman', in *Displacement: Derrida and After*, ed. by Mark Krupnick (Bloomington: Indiana University Press, 1983), pp. 169–95 (p. 171).
14. Tadjo, *Shadow of Imana*, p. 32.
15. T. S. Eliot, *Collected Poems* (London: Faber, 1936), p. 65.
16. Eliot, *Collected Poems*, pp. 79, 86 n. 433.

17. Tadjo, *Shadow of Imana*, p. 3.
18. Russell West-Pavlov, '"Regardez la vie reprendre": Futurity in Véronique Tadjo's *L'Ombre d'Imana / The Shadow of Imana*', *Tydskrif vir Letterkunde*, 51.2 (2014), 114–29 (p. 122).
19. Tadjo, *Shadow of Imana*, pp. 6–8.
20. Tadjo, *Shadow of Imana*, p. 9.
21. Tadjo, *Shadow of Imana*, p. 11.
22. Megwalu and Loizides, 'Dilemmas of Justice and Reconciliation', p. 3.
23. Lars Waldorf, 'Mass Justice for Mass Atrocity: Rethinking Local Justice as Transitional Justice', *Temple Law Review*, 79.1 (2006), 1–87 (p. 46).
24. Megwalu and Loizides, 'Dilemmas of Justice and Reconciliation', p. 3.
25. Megwalu and Loizides, 'Dilemmas of Justice and Reconciliation', p. 4.
26. Ibid.
27. William A. Schabas, 'Genocide Trials and Gacaca Courts', *Journal of International Criminal Justice*, 3 (2005), 879–95 (p. 891).
28. Megwalu and Loizides, 'Dilemmas of Justice and Reconciliation', p. 4.
29. Waldorf, 'Mass Justice for Mass Atrocity', p. 54.
30. Coel Kirkby, 'Rwanda's Gacaca Courts: A Preliminary Critique', *Journal of African Law*, 50.2 (2006), 94–117 (pp. 108–09).
31. Schabas, 'Genocide Trials and Gacaca Courts', p. 883.
32. Schabas, 'Genocide Trials and Gacaca Courts', p. 894.
33. Phil Clark, 'Hybridity, Holism, and Traditional Justice: The Case of the Gacaca Courts in Post-Genocide Rwanda', *George Washington International Review*, 39 (2007), 765–837 (p. 806).
34. Tadjo, *Shadow of Imana*, p. 94.
35. Tadjo, *Shadow of Imana*, pp. 99–100.
36. Tadjo, *Shadow of Imana*, p. 97.
37. Jacques Fierens, 'Gacaca Courts: Between Fantasy and Reality', *Journal of International Criminal Justice*, 3 (2005), 896–919 (p. 907).
38. Fierens, 'Gacaca Courts', p. 906.
39. Tadjo, *Shadow of Imana*, p. 22.
40. Tadjo, *Shadow of Imana*, p. 20.
41. Tadjo, *Shadow of Imana*, p. 23.
42. Ibid.
43. Tadjo, *Shadow of Imana*, p. 24.
44. Ibid.
45. Tadjo, *Shadow of Imana*, p. 17.
46. Tadjo, *Shadow of Imana*, p. 27.
47. Tadjo, *Shadow of Imana*, p. 63.
48. Tadjo, *Shadow of Imana*, p. 37.
49. Tadjo, *Shadow of Imana*, p. 37. Ulrika Kistner comments, somewhat obtusely: 'At the point at which it becomes clear that all pretensions of the realist narrative break down [...] the heterodiegetic narrator intervenes to hollow out any notion of a proairetic-hermeneutic kernel of the would-be narrative, and to prevent the closure of the story around a single point of semi-symbolic convergence.' Ulrika Kistner, 'Commemoration and Counter-Memory: "The Genocide Series"', *South African Historical Journal*, 62.4 (2010), 619–33 (p. 627).
50. Tadjo, *Shadow of Imana*, p. 12.
51. Tadjo, *Shadow of Imana*, p. 12.
52. Tadjo, *Shadow of Imana*, p. 16.
53. Tadjo, *Shadow of Imana*, p. 19.
54. Tadjo, *Shadow of Imana*, p. 45.
55. Tadjo, *Shadow of Imana*, pp. 45–46.
56. Tadjo, *Shadow of Imana*, p. 46.
57. Tadjo, *Shadow of Imana*, p. 57.
58. Tadjo, *Shadow of Imana*, p. 58.
59. Tadjo, *Shadow of Imana*, p. 55.

60. Tadjo, *Shadow of Imana*, p. 66.
61. Anna Marie de Beer and Elisabeth Snyman, 'Shadows of Life, Death and Survival in the Aftermath of the Rwandan Genocide', *Tydskrif vir Letterkunde*, 52.1 (2015), 113–30 (p. 117).
62. Tadjo, *Shadow of Imana*, p. 63.
63. Tadjo, *Shadow of Imana*, p. 22.
64. Tadjo, *Shadow of Imana*, p. 66.
65. Tadjo, *Shadow of Imana*, p. 28.
66. Tadjo, *Shadow of Imana*, p. 13.
67. Tadjo, *Shadow of Imana*, p. 12.
68. Tadjo, *Shadow of Imana*, p. 17.
69. Tadjo, *Shadow of Imana*, p. 18.
70. Tadjo, *Shadow of Imana*, p. 19.
71. Ibid.
72. Tadjo, *Shadow of Imana*, p. 81.
73. Tadjo, *Shadow of Imana*, p. 83.

PART II

Latin America

CHAPTER 3

Transitional Justice and Civil Justice in *AntígonaS. Linaje de Hembras* (2001) by Jorge Huertas

Annick Louis

Launched immediately after the last dictatorship ended (1976–83), the process of democratization in Argentina is characterized by the alternation of moments of justice and others marked by amnesty.[1] *AntígonaS. Linaje de hembras*, a play by Jorge Huertas,[2] was written in 2001, during the period of the first amnesties, toward the end of Carlos Menem's presidential term (1989–99). The work articulates the classical Greek plot into a series of human rights movements that include what Ana Longoni calls 'visual politics,' a tradition of political mobilization that aims to denounce those responsible for crimes during the dictatorship that went unpunished.[3]

George Steiner had already pointed out Western literature's fascination with *Antigone*;[4] however, his reflections do not concern Latin America, where the play is the object of particular interest. There are in fact some thirty versions in the twentieth century, among them *Antígona Vélez* (1951) by Leopoldo Marechal.[5] Since the last dictatorship, the essence and the meaning of Antigone have radically changed in Argentina; if there is no trace of significant adaptations during that period, after it ends they are particularly numerous. To the well-known *Antígona furiosa* (1986) by Griselda Gambaro, one should add: *La cabeza en la jaula* (1987) by David Cureses; the novel *El cementerio del tiempo* (1990) by Federico Peltzer; *In memoriam Antigonae* (1999) by Rómulo Pianacci; *Golpes a mi puerta* (1988) by Juan Carlos Gené; *Antígona... con amor* (2003) by Hebe Campanella; *Antígona ¡no!* (2003) and *Una mujer llamada Antígona* (2011) by Yamila Grandi; and *Antígona 1–11–14 del Bajo Flores* (2014) by Marcelo Marán. The hypotheses put forward to explain such interest shown on this continent generally evoke the political context, and highlight a series of elements: the prohibition of burying the dead, which is equated with an impossibility of doing so; the figure of the dictator Creon; and the guilt and shame experienced by those who did not react, accepting a compromise with power.[6] To better understand the appeal that the classical play exerts, we can recall some figures: the 30,000 known *desaparecidos* (i.e. victims of forced disappearance) during the last dictatorship, and the 1,300 bodies uncovered, of which only 800 have been identified. Despite the trials and the convictions that have ensued since 2003, the year in which the amnesty laws were revoked, those responsible for the illegal repression refuse to indicate where the bodies are located.[7] Nevertheless, Huertas's play presents another characteristic that relates to the contemporary Argentine context: the promotion of the female identity of Antigone. Indeed, to the political crimes denounced are added the crimes committed against women — the femicides (*femicidios*).[8] Let us also recall some figures, as femicides steadily rose until 2016: in 2013, 295 women were murdered; in 2014, 277; in 2015, 286; in 2016, 226. Today in Argentina, a femicide is committed every thirty hours. Thus, Huertas's play associates political crimes with crimes against women (civil and gender crimes), while inscribing a double anticipative dimension in the play, as the trials against the military responsible for repression resumed only in 2003, and movements against femicide appeared in the last decade. *AntígonaS. Linaje de hembras* therefore draws a parallel between the demand for justice for the victims of the last dictatorship and that of civil justice for women, which thus acquires the dimension of transitional justice. Civil justice in the context of femicide is elevated to the rank of transitional justice, and femicide presented as genocide.

The Argentine Voices of Antigone

The first performance of *Antígonas. Linaje de hembras* was given not in Argentina, but in Greece, in 2001, at the First International Festival of Ancient Greek Theatre of Kalamata. After touring in Pylos and Athens, it was played in September 2002 at the La Plata Argentine Theater, again under the direction of Roberto Aguirre. In November 2002, the play was staged in the Auditorium Jorge Luis Borges of the National Library of Buenos Aires. In November 2002, the text was published by Biblos, with a preface by Leandro Pinkler (philosopher and specialist in ancient Greek culture from the University of Buenos Aires), and Mauricio Kartun, who is currently one of the most important playwrights in the country, authored another preface. In October 2007, the play was performed at Villa María, Córdoba. As we can see, *AntígonaS* appeared on prestigious circuits, but not the most important ones in the country, and its performances were sporadic. The originality of the staging aroused admiration and enthusiasm among theatre specialists as all the roles were played by women, with the exception of that of Creon;[9] in addition, it presents itself as a musical where tango energizes the scenes, and the refinement of the costumes suggests a particularly enchanting aesthetics of movement. Another version was staged, also under the direction of Roberto Aguirre, where all the characters were played by male actors except for Antigone.[10] In both cases, the place occupied by music and the staging borrowed from the dancing show, refer to the current conceptions of the Greek classical theatre; they highlight the fact that tragedy was a choral and dance performance tightly bound to the community.[11]

The play preserves most of Sophocles' classical scenes. It re-enacts the episode of the meeting between the sisters, the announcement of the prohibition issued by

Creon, the presence of Haemon and Tiresias, and the lamentation of Antigone as she is condemned. But these scenes are recontextualized in the Argentina of the time, although there is no precise temporal indication. Despite a recognizable narrative, several elements are modified, including the title, which introduces the plural of the name and the subtitle that explains the title, and evokes a communitarian character. The epigraph from Homero Manzi offers an interpretation of the piece as a work rather than of its content/meaning: 'Estoy lleno de voces y colores. Unas veces / recogidos en el sonambulismo de la marcha; / otras, inventados tras mi propia soledad' [I am full of voices and colours. Sometimes / recovered in the walking of somnambulism; / other times, invented after my own solitude]. Its function is to propose a definition of the aesthetics of the piece, as the words 'recogido' [recovered] and 'inventados' [invented] may be interpreted as a synthesis of the play. It also alludes to the work of rewriting different discourses in the play.

Nevertheless, one of the main differences with Sophocles' tragedy is the structure of Jorge Huertas's play. *AntígonaS* is organized into nineteen scenes, or stage fragments, whose structure, genre, and length vary, the more lyrical moments being in free verse. The external structure of the classical tragedy — preface, alternation of *stasimons* and episodes — is thus replaced by a succession of fragments; the plot is fragmented, and its development interrupted by moments not directly linked to the main action. These fragments, which lack apparent coherence, incorporate a series of varied topics, breaking away from the Aristotelian unity of action and its development according to the principles of necessity and plausibility. Through this means, Huertas inserts issues alien to Sophocles but which are familiar to the Argentine audience. The piece thus presents itself as a kind of pastiche of quotations and references where the identification of references and allusions — which show different degrees of explicitness — will depend on the skill and cultural background of each spectator; this technique raises the essential question of the constitution of a community with blurred borders, to which the play is directly addressed, and with which it enters in communion.

A further modification is where the action unfolds. The identity of the city of Buenos Aires is affirmed through the mention of a series of places: the 'Plaza de Mayo' is thus renamed 'Ágora de Mayo' (p. 24), where the 'Didascalias' places the action on the outside of the play. The 'Río de la Plata' and the 'Plaza de Mayo' appear as spaces that condense the country, and simultaneously, the river appears as the space where burial is refused to the dead, where the new Polynices, drowned in the 'death flights' are evoked directly (p. 43). The River, which is 'hecho de tiempo' [made of time] (p. 23), embodies the bestiality for the city, and is the source of the contamination due to the crimes it conceals unwittingly. This is one of the most interesting aspects of the play — the relationship between the absence and the omnipresent of the dead (the 'disappeared'): the body of Polynices is in the middle of the city rotting, but it also lies at the bottom of the river; it is everywhere — like the bodies of the dead. Much emphasis is placed by Huertas on the location (there are more than forty direct or indirect allusions to the city), and the fact that the city is transformed into a character: the space is familiar to the Argentine reader but at the same time it is made strange and alien to the reader/spectator. The city is corrupt, nauseating, the air and the river reek of death. From the opening, the audience is confronted with the problem: 'La patria está muriendo' [The fatherland is dying] (p. 21). Initially we do not know to whom to attribute this apocalyptic scenario, but it quickly appears as a consequence of the silence maintained on the crimes committed, a silence the women exhort the city to break, while the concertina urges a reaction. In Sophocles' *Antigone*, the destruction of the city appears only at the end; in Huertas's play, on the contrary, it is present from the outset, though with more intensity at the end. The question of the moment in which the piece takes place is more complex; it seems to correspond to the moment of its writing, because, as we will see, there are many references to episodes and characters of Argentine history and various facts up to the 1990s.

If the play depicts the main characters of Sophocles' tragedy, some are modified, and we also note the introduction of characters referring to Argentina, the main one being the river (Río de la Plata), which does not interact with the other characters, but introduces a lyrical tone. The river is the witness of what is going on in the city, it reports on crimes committed since its foundation — it is older than the city and has known 'el mundo sin que existiera gente' [the world before people existed] (p. 23). Another character related to Argentina is the 'Embalsamada Peregrina' [the errant embalmed woman], obviously referring to Eva Perón (1919–1952), as her corpse, which had been embalmed, was kidnapped after the coup d'état of 1955, and disappeared for thirty years. Some of Eva's speeches are also quoted in the play. The story of Evita's corpse echoes the situation of the *desaparecidos*, and becomes the emblem of a dead deprived of burial (pp. 37, 46–47); the bandoneon, silent witness, questioned by the chorus, can be identified with the public. We also notice that the chorus of the ancients of Thebes is replaced by a female chorus, evoking the 'Madres de Plaza de Mayo' [Mothers of May Square] (p. 51). Should the chorus, then, be regarded as a character or not? In the case of Huertas, it seems that indeed it is, since its members appear more as a set of individualities than as a chorus. As for Tiresias, his identification through his representation and his comments to Jorge Luis Borges (who was already dead at the time the play was written) introduces a different function; because if, in Sophocles' work, Tiresias' revelations change Creon's attitude, leading him to reverse the punishment imposed on Antigone, in Huerta's play that is not the case. With the exception of the Bandoneon and the River, the interventions of the characters are articulated from this collective presence-voice which is the chorus of females, certainly the most complex character, as in the Greek tragedy.

Sense and Communion with the Community

In *AntígonaS*, the referent is constructed from a saturation of references to history, culture, Argentine literature. But the origin of these references is not explicit. It is through them that the play establishes a form of complicity and communion with the spectator. These references include names and titles — from musicians, singers, and composers of tango lyrics, such as Alfredo Gobbi (p. 20), J. D'Arienzo (p. 71), Aníbal Troilo (pp. 20, 71), Osvaldo Pugliese (p. 70), Roberto Goyeneche (p. 20), Enrique Santos Discépolo (p. 20), Enrique Cadícamo (p. 71). As stated, there is also a series of references to the city of Buenos Aires (pp. 24, 30), but also to historic national characters: the 'gauchos' (pp. 25, 29), the African Americans who fought in the Independence Wars (p. 25); and, as already mentioned, the 'Embalsamada Peregrina' and Tiresias-Borges. A series of more or less explicit allusions to Argentine history concerns 'death flights' (pp. 26, 31, 43), and the Falklands War (pp. 60, 61). A typical Argentine vocabulary also helps to anchor the play in this context, such as: 'pichicatero' [drug addict] (p. 21), 'guachos' [orphans] (p. 21); 'piropo' [compliment] (p. 29), and the use of 'vos' (pp. 64, 69). An example of the mode of referring to Argentine characters is: 'A Discepolín pedíle las alas y el aliento / A un dios Polaco, azul y pichicatero' [Ask Discepolín wings and energy / To a Polish god, blue and drugged] (p. 21). 'Discepolín' refers to Enrique Santos Discépolo (1901–1951), one of the most important tango lyric authors and singer; the 'Polish god' referring to Roberto Goyeneche (1926–1994). As for Argentine history, here are two examples of how it fits into the play: the phrase 'muchachos vencidos bajo un manto de neblina' [young boys defeated in a cloak of fog] (p. 26), is a reference to the Falklands War that opposed Argentina to the UK in 1982. The verse 'Nosotras las chinitas catamarqueñas' [We, the Indian mixed from Catamarca] (p. 59) refers to the murder of María Soledad Morales, a young woman victim of a sexual orgy, in 1990, in which the sons of political leaders were implicated. The play also presents a series of intertextual references in the form of various citations of literary texts, advertisements, and political speeches such as that of Eva Perón on the occasion of the adoption of women's suffrage on 23 September 1947 (p. 28), fragments of Videla's speeches (p. 46), tango lyrics (p. 62), and other musical lyrics (p. 36).

The tragedy by Sophocles thus constitutes the axis of the work, but Huertas's play is saturated with references to Argentine texts and other discourses. Among the literary texts let us cite: 'Esa mujer' [That Woman] by Rodolfo Walsh (1966) (p. 37); 'Historia del guerrero y la cautiva' [History of the Warrior and the Captive] (p. 55) and 'El simulacro' [The Mirage] by Borges (pp. 54, 57), as well as the 'Two English Poems' also by Borges (p. 53), 'Buenos Aires' (1963) (p. 54), 'Poema Conjetural' [The Conjectural Poem] (p. 55). We also find references to Hernández's *Martín Fierro*, a canonical work of Argentine literature (p. 22). Many tango lyrics (sometimes slightly altered) come from 'Mi noche triste' [My sad night] by Pascual Contursi (p. 57), 'Papá Baltasar' [Father Baltasar] (p. 26), 'Sur' (p. 69) and 'Malena' by Homero Manzi (1907–1951), and 'Naranjo en Flor' [Orange Blossom] by Homero Expósito (p. 41). Among the advertisements to be found are ones for the soaps *Lux* and *Palmolive* (p. 46). My hypothesis about these references, which raise the question of the spectator's ability to decipher and understand of the play, is that the fact of having preserved the main moments of the classical tragedy allows its comprehension, beyond the level of deciphering references to Argentine history and culture. The rewriting thus acquires a specific meaning, because if the plot were not previously known to the public, the fragmentary character of the text could undermine its understanding. Thus, these references conduct a phagocytosis of the text of Sophocles, and forge a tight link to the Argentinean spectator, establishing a form of communion, in which the theatrical show becomes an intense community experience.

Legality and Gender

In Huertas's play, the conflict between Antigone and Creon takes on a new dimension that is barely alluded to by Sophocles, that of a gender conflict. In Sophocles, the character of Antigone has characteristics considered as masculine for the time and distant from the traditional model of woman, even though in her final tirade she returns to a more traditional role and expresses her regret at dying without having been married and having had children. The conflict between the sexes appears through the generational conflict between Creon and Haemon (Sophocles, *Antigone*, Third episode, Scene 1): Creon begins by discrediting the influence of a woman compared to that of the father, then he accuses his son of making himself the champion of a woman, and of being her slave. Creon's invectives take a turn that discredits women and any form of female authority.

In Huertas's *AntígonaS* the generic opposition is accentuated: all women facing abusive power and finding themselves in a situation of rebellion are Antigones, and Antigone is all these women, who are the mothers, the wives and the daughters of the dead. But — and this is one of the most ambivalent aspects of the play — if they rebel against the power of men, they are just as much the victims as their accomplices. In a particularly interesting moment of the play, the well-known sentence that incarnated indifference toward state violence under the last Argentine dictatorship is used in connection with femicide: 'Corifeo: ¿Vas a matar a Antígona? / Coro: Por algo será. Por algo será' [Coryphe: Are you going to kill Antigone? / Chorus: There must be a reason. There must be a reason] (p. 44).

In Sophocles, the opposition between the law of the city and the law of the gods structures the conflict; in Huertas's play, the law of the city is a more secret, specific, demanding law that binds Antigone to history: by opposing Creon she also counters the abuse of power that characterizes the history of the country — a masculine power. Here too, Creon is carried away by 'hubris' — in ancient Greece, the concept was not limited to the field of the religious, but was also used in the political, moral and social fields. From Homer to Aristotle, 'hubris' not only means arrogance, pride or an inability to admit human limitations, but also implies that the actions undertaken dishonour others, are an affront to justice, that they bring disaster not only on the individual who committed the fault, but also on the family, and on society as a whole (as we can see in *The Persians* of Aeschylus). The catastrophe that threatens the city is usually due to the conduct of a hero in the Greek world, while in Huertas's play it is linked to a male abuse of power throughout the history of the country. Huertas rewrites Argentine history using this parameter: the classical conflict of contrasting wills takes place in this scenario and introduces a tension alien to the tragedy. Antigone's role, and the women's role as a chorus, is to urge rebellion against the omnipotence of the tyrant, who destroys the city and its inhabitants, and to emphasize the responsibility of man (the masculine) in political life. A direct relationship is established between the misfortunes suffered by the city and the atrocities committed by the tyrant; the hubristic conduct of Creon and his allies is the cause of the final catastrophe, which threatens to destroy the city and transform it into a wasteland. The play ends thus: the fragment 'Peste y enigma' [Plague and Enigma] concentrates images of an apocalypse, which, for us today, announces the economic crisis of December 2001, with its end-of-the-world upheaval. The destruction in this drama engages the participation of the River, which brings to the surface the atrocities committed by man: the sea disgorges the dead, following the model of Revelation: 'Y el mar entregó los muertos que había en él; y la muerte y el Hades entregaron los muertos que había en ellos; y fueron juzgados cada uno según sus obras' [And the sea gave up the dead that were in it; and death and Hades gave up the dead that were in them; and they were judged according to their works].[12] In Huertas's play, in the end, the River returns the corpses, in a ferocious gesture devoid of rationality.

The final apocalypse results from the conduct of Creon, which is inserted in a series of crimes, one of which is the femicide (pp. 39, 40, 49–50, 67). Creon jeopardizes the stability of the city: his delirious acts transform the city into a place where the balance is upset; not because of the choice to remain faithful to a law (the one of the city), but as a form of abuse of tyrannical power. Creon acts as if he were God and, as we have seen, he expresses himself with sentences borrowed from the Argentine dictators, Videla in particular (pp. 35, 40, 45). Creon is a tyrant blinded by an inordinate fanaticism and by his devotion to Buenos Aires, possessed by a megalomaniac feeling that leads him to believe himself the custodian of a divine power whose mission is to save Buenos Aires, to the detriment of its inhabitants, an existence shaped by an incessant process of destruction and renewal. His arrogance rises to unexpected heights; despite the warnings of Tiresias, he cannot spot his mistakes: 'La ciudad sufre su locura' [The city suffers his madness] (p. 54). Creon does not change his mind at the end, despite the suicide of his son and his wife, rather, he indulges his delirium, and it is this delirium of redemption that puts in jeopardy the power and the very existence of Buenos Aires — as Antigone states. However, Creon imposes his law, and wants to cleanse the city of all opposition: 'Antes que la familia está la Patria. Antes que los seres queridos está la ciudad' [The fatherland comes before the family. The city comes before the loved ones] (p. 30).

Nevertheless, if on the one hand there is a close link between the inordinate pride of those who have power and the disasters that threaten the city, on the other hand, we do not know from where or from whom the punishment comes or whether this catastrophe corresponds to a divine will. If the images reinforce the association with the biblical text, and thus inscribe a religious conception of Revelation, it is not clear that this catastrophe is orchestrated by the will of a god (or gods) angry at the violence of men — whereas, as we have seen, Creon grants himself the status of God. Faced with the absence of any explicit reference or hint concerning the one to whom responsibility can be attributed, one thinks rather of an uprising of nature, against the atrocities committed by men, and a reaction to the arrogant and disrespectful attitude against them. We can say, to conclude, that if there is a divinity, it is nature, which attends through the Rio to the spectacle of men pitted against one another. The enigma introduced by the last fragment of the work, which also brings a scenario of despair, recalls the enigma of Oedipus, and the survival of the city; in Huertas's play, the enigma posed is that of the future of the homeland: to the absence of justice throughout history for the victims of political violence is added the absence of justice regarding violence against women. The history of the city, which, according to the Argentine tradition, merges with the history of the country, unfolds in a circularity that leads to a hopeless apocalypse. History is neither linear nor cyclical, but an incessant process of destruction and renewal, which nevertheless leads to the final destruction of the city, according to Hesiod and Solon. Huertas makes men responsible for the misfortunes of the city — men and women: the Argentine Creon's abuse of power and the passivity of the citizens.

This is one of the aspects in which Huertas's play most departs from Sophocles: it reverses the mythological saga of the Labdacids by making the beginning of the history of Oedipus — the enigma of the Sphynx and the plague of Thebes — the end of Argentine history: after the suicide of Haemon and Eurydice, a new form of Sphynx appears in the River, and vomits the *desaparecidos*, which in turn prompts an outbreak of the plague. The plague in Huertas's play, unlike the tragedy, is not a sign sent by the Gods who can repair the hero's suffering or expulsion. The water is contaminated, the enigma and the plague are reinstalled at the end and expose the impurity of the contamination by the bodies without burial, which abuses and hurts the women in particular. The final series of questions remains unanswered.

The last scene, assumed by the women's chorus, summons lamentation and prayer, as an omen and a sentence, an invocation to save the city from the monster that devours its children. The last words of the Coryphaeus broaden the context of the tragic conflict and pose it as an existential enigma of a people. The last lines of the play — 'Que será de la reina del Plata / que será de mi tierra querida' [What will become of the Queen of Silver / What will become of my beloved homeland] (p. 72) — bring back the strength and conflict of the classic tragedy, the genre that explored the tensions of the *polis* and allowed the *polis* to think about itself.

Transitional Justice and Civil Justice

As we said, one of the specificities of Huertas's play is the parallel drawn between political violence (historical) and violence against women (femicide). The society represented appears to be divided into men and women, and the sexual crime presents itself as a weapon, in a country which, in the context of the trials of those responsible for crimes against humanity committed under the last dictatorship, has considered granting a specific legal figure to such crimes. The opposition between executioners and victims here includes that between men and women, without exclusivity.

The anticipatory dimension of the play is played out on several levels. On the one hand, the demand for justice and the final apocalypse, since from 2003 the trials of the leaders of the dictatorship will resume; on the other hand, the end of 2001 was marked by an economic crisis that shook the whole country. Note that the play attributes this apocalypse to the lack of justice either for the political victims or for those of femicide, thus establishing a link between the ultra-liberal austerity plans and lack of respect for human rights in Argentina. The idea that only justice can save the city and the country acquires a utopian dimension that becomes anticipatory in retrospect. In this sense we can understand the play as an attempt to describe what we can call 'transitional injustice'. The play anticipates the new forms of politics that we are facing today, because our traditional categories are being challenged and new forms of power, whose political identity is not yet quite defined, are emerging. This is the case in Argentina with the emergence of women's rights movements: the fight to legalize abortion, the demand for new legislation, and the recognition of violence against women. In Argentina, social demands and the context of poverty give a specific meaning to this struggle because the conditions are quite different from the ones European countries experienced when they witnessed these kinds of demand for justice. We notice that the events carried out in this context often have the Congress and the Congress Square as their epicentre, while May Square is often relegated to a second rank; the choice of this space translates the projection toward the demand for change in the jurisdiction of the country.

Finally, I would like to recall the question posed by Adam Rosenblatt in *Digging for the Disappeared*:[13] do the dead have rights? or should the work of exhumation of the victims of state violence or mass crimes be carried out exclusively in the name of the rights of families, communities, society (social justice)? In Huertas's play the final apocalypses seems to originate in a kind of revolt of nature, cluttered by corpses. The River returns the bodies, as if they ended up claiming justice for themselves and might stand up as an autonomous legal instance.

Notes to Chapter 3

1. The first trial of the leaders of the military dictatorship took place between 22 April and 14 August 1985, with sentences handed down on 9 December 1985. The set known as 'impunity laws' consists of four moments: the 'Laws of Self-Amnesty N. 22.924' pronounced by the military dictatorship in 1983; the 'Final Point Law' of 1986; the 'Law of Due Obedience' of 1987, issued under the government of Alfonsín; and, finally, a set of ten laws designed to amnesty

those responsible for crimes during the dictatorship who had already been tried, promoted between 1989 and 1990 by Carlos Menem. In 2003, under the presidency of Néstor Kirchner, systematic trials of those responsible for the repression resumed.

2. Jorge Huertas's career is as varied as it is productive; a psychologist (UCA), he is also the author of novels and plays, a theatre teacher, and a director. See <http://www.autores.org.ar/sitios/jhuertas/>.
3. Ana Longoni, 'Introducción', in *El siluetazo*, ed. by Gustavo Bruzzoni and Ana Longoni (Buenos Aires: Adriana Hidalgo, 2008).
4. George Steiner, *Antigones* (New Haven, CT, and London: Yale University Press, 1996), pp. ix, 121.
5. Pilar Hualde, 'Mito y tragedia griega en la literatura iberoamericana', *Cuadernos de filología clásica*, 22 (January 2012), 185–222.
6. María Gabriela Rebok, *La actualidad de la experiencia de lo clásico y el paradigma de Antígona* (Buenos Aires: Biblos, 2013); Rómulo E. Pianacci, *Antígona: una tragedia latinoamericana* (Irvine, CA: Gestos, 2008); Moira Fradinger, 'An Argentine Tradition', in *Antigone on the Contemporary World Stage*, ed. by Erin B. Mee and Helene P. Foley (Oxford: Oxford University Press, 2011), pp. 67–145; *The Returns of Antigone: Interdisciplinary Essays*, ed. by Tina Chanter and Sean D. Kirkland (Albany, NY: Albany State University Press, 2014).
7. *Restos humanos e identificación: violencia de masa, genocidio y el 'giro forense'*, ed. by Elisabeth Ansttet, Sévérine Garibian and Jean-Marc Dreyfus (Buenos Aires: Miño y Dávilas, 2017).
8. Moira Fradinger, 'Making Women Visible: Multiple Antigones on the Colombian Twenty-first Century Stage', in *The Oxford Handbook of Greek Drama in the Americas*, ed. by Kathryn Bosher et al. (Oxford: Oxford University Press, 2018).
9. Moira Soto, 'Una mina inagotable', *Página 12* (Buenos Aires), 13 June 2003; Carlos Pacheco, 'Antígona: una mujer que parece ser eterna', *La Nación* (Buenos Aires), 7 July 2003; Juan Ramón Seia, 'El poder engendra toda muerte', *Crítica* (Villa María), 23 October 2007.
10. *AntígonaS, linaje de hembras* (Todos Hombres), play dir. by Roberto Aguirre (Teatro de Repertorio, Melo 1756, Florida, Provincia de Buenos Aires, Argentina, 2014).
11. Claude Calame, *La Tragédie chorale: poésie grecque et rituel musical* (Paris: Les Belles Lettres, 2017).
12. Revelation 20. 13.
13. Adam Rosenblatt, *Digging for the Disappeared: Forensic Science after Atrocity* (Palo Alto, CA: Stanford University Press, 2014).

CHAPTER 4

❖

Justice transitionnelle et justice civile dans *AntígonaS. Linaje de Hembras* (2001) de Jorge Huertas

Annick Louis

Entamé immédiatement après la fin de la dernière dictature (1976–83), le processus de démocratisation argentin se caractérise par l'alternance de moments de justice et d'autres marqués par des amnisties.[1] *AntígonaS. Linaje de Hembras* [*AntigoneS. Lignée de femelles*] pièce de théâtre de Jorge Huertas,[2] écrite en 2001, pendant la période des premières amnisties, vers la fin du mandat présidentiel de Carlos Menem (1989–99), articule, au récit classique, une série de mouvements en défense des droits humains: les 'politiques visuelles', dans les termes de Ana Longoni, destinés à dénoncer les responsables de crimes pendant la dictature restés impunis.[3] Une tradition de mobilisation politique qui s'inscrit dans la pièce de Huertas.

George Steiner s'était déjà interrogé sur la fascination qu'exerce *Antigone* dans la littérature occidentale,[4] mais ses questionnements ne concernent pas l'Amérique Latine, où la pièce fait l'objet d'un intérêt particulier, puisqu'on compte au moins une trentaine de versions au XX siècle, parmi lesquelles se trouve la célèbre *Antígona Vélez* (1951) de Leopoldo Marechal.[5] En Argentine, depuis 1976, l'essence et le sens d'Antigone semblent avoir changé radicalement; si on n'a pas de trace d'adaptations marquantes sous la dictature, après elles sont particulièrement nombreuses: à la célèbre *Antígona furiosa* (1986) de Griselda Gambaro, viennent s'ajouter: *La cabeza en la jaula* (1987) de David Cureses, le roman *El cementerio del tiempo* (1990) de Federico Peltzer, *In memoriam Antigonae* (1999) de Rómulo Pianacci, *Golpes a mi puerta* (1988) de Juan Carlos Gené; *Antígona... con amor* (2003) de Hebe Campanella; *Antígona ¡no!* (2003), *Una mujer llamada Antígona* (2011) de Yamila Grandi; *Antígona 1–11–14 del Bajo Flores* (2014) de Marcelo Marán. Les hypothèses avancées pour expliquer l'intérêt du continent, évoquent généralement le contexte politique, et soulignent une série d'éléments: l'interdiction d'enterrer les morts qui est assimilée à une impossibilité de le faire; la figure du dictateur Créon; la culpabilité et la honte de ceux qui n'ont pas réagi, acceptant un compromis avec le pouvoir.[6] Afin de mieux saisir l'attrait que la pièce classique exerce, on peut rappeler quelques chiffres: à celui connu de 30,000 disparus pendant la dernière dictature, il faut rajouter le moins connu de

1300 corps retrouvés, parmi presque 800 ont été identifiés. Malgré les procès et les condamnations qui se sont succédé depuis 2003, moment de la révocation des lois d'amnisties, les responsables de la répression refusent d'indiquer les lieux où se trouvent les corps.[7]

Néanmoins, la pièce de Huertas présente un autre élément qui renvoie au contexte argentin contemporain, la mise en avant de l'identité féminine d'Antigone, car aux crimes politiques dénoncés viennent s'ajouter les crimes commis contre les femmes — les féminicides (los *femicidios*).[8] Rappelons également quelques chiffres: les *féminicides* étaient en augmentation en Argentine jusqu'à 2016. Voici les données des dernières années: en 2013, 295 femmes ont été assassinées; en 2014, 277; en 2015, 286; en 2016, 226. Aujourd'hui, toutes les trente heures, un *féminicide* est commis en Argentine. La pièce de Huertas associe ainsi les crimes politiques et les crimes contre les femmes (des crimes civils), tout en inscrivant une dimension doublement anticipatoire dans la pièce, puisque les procès contre les responsables de la répression sous la dictature reprendront à partir de 2003, et les mouvements actuels contre le féminicide. *AntígonaS. Linaje de hembras* met donc en parallèle la demande de justice pour les victimes de la dernière dictature et celle de justice civile pour les femmes, qui acquiert ainsi la dimension d'une justice transitionnelle. La justice civile dans le cadre du féminicide est élevée au rang de justice transitionnelle, et le féminicide présenté comme un génocide.

Les Voix argentines d'Antigone

La première de *AntígonaS. Linaje de hembras* n'a pas eu lieu en Argentine, mais en Grèce, en 2001, au Premier festival International de théâtre grec ancien de Kalamata; après des tournées à Pylos et Athènes, elle se produit en septembre 2002, au Théâtre argentin de La Plata, toujours sous la direction de Roberto Aguirre; en novembre 2002, elle est représentée à l'Auditorium Jorge Luis Borges de la Bibliothèque Nationale de Buenos Aires. En novembre 2002 le texte est publié par la maison d'édition Biblos, avec une préface de Leandro Pinkler (philosophe et spécialiste de la culture grecque ancienne de l'Université de Buenos Aires), et de Mauricio Kartun qui est aujourd'hui un des auteurs de théâtre les plus importants du pays; en octobre 2007, la pièce a été jouée à Villa María, Córdoba. Comme on peut le voir, *AntígonaS* a intégré des circuits prestigieux, mais pas les plus importants, même s'ils n'ont rien de marginal, et sa présence sur la scène est sporadique. L'originalité de la mise en scène première a suscité de l'admiration et de l'enthousiasme chez les spécialistes de théâtre, car tous les rôles étaient joués par des femmes, à l'exception de celui de Créon;[9] de plus, elle se présente comme un spectacle musical où le tango anime les scènes, et le travail des costumes propose une esthétique mouvante particulièrement attrayante. Une autre version fut jouée où tous les personnages étaient représentés par des hommes à l'exception d'Antigone, aussi sous la direction de Roberto Aguirre.[10] Dans les deux cas, la place qu'occupent la musique et la mise en scène proche du spectacle dansant, renvoient aux conceptions actuelles du théâtre classique grec, qui soulignent la tragédie comme performance chorale et dansante, tout comme le rapport étroit des représentations à la communauté.[11]

La pièce conserve la plupart des scènes de Sophocle: elle reprend l'épisode de la rencontre entre les sœurs, l'annonce de l'interdiction de Créon, la présence d'Hémon et de Tirésias, la lamentation d'Antigone au moment où elle est condamnée. Mais ces scènes sont recontextualisées dans l'Argentine de la période, sans qu'il y ait, pourtant, d'indication temporelle précise. Malgré un récit reconnaissable, un certain nombre d'éléments sont modifiés, parmi lesquelles, le titre, qui introduit le pluriel du nom et le sous-titre qui explique le titre, et évoque un caractère communautaire; l'épigraphe de Homero Manzi, qui propose une interprétation de la pièce en tant qu'œuvre plus que de son contenu: 'Estoy lleno de voces y colores. Unas veces / recogidos en el sonambulismo de la marcha; / otras, inventados tras mi propia soledad' [Je suis rempli de voix et de couleurs. Parfois / cueillis dans le somnambulisme de la marche; / d'autres, inventés par moi dans ma propre solitude]. Sa fonction est de proposer une définition de l'esthétique, puisque les mots 'recogido' [réuni] et 'inventados' [inventés] peuvent être lus comme une synthèse de la pièce, et font allusion au travail de reprise de différents discours de l'œuvre.

Néanmoins, la structure de la pièce de Jorge Huertas constitue un des éléments qui l'éloignent le plus de la tragédie de Sophocle: elle s'organise en 19 scènes, ou fragments scéniques, à la structure, le ton et la longueur variés, qui assument, dans les moments les plus lyriques, la forme de poèmes en vers libre. La structure externe de la tragédie classique — préface, alternance de stasimons et d'épisodes — est donc ici remplacée par une succession de fragments, l'histoire est fragmentée, et son développement est interrompu par des moments qui ne sont pas directement liés à l'action principale. Ces fragments qui manquent de cohérence apparente incorporent une série de thèmes autres, rompant avec l'unité d'action aristotélicienne et son développement en fonction des principes de nécessité et vraisemblance; par ce biais Huertas insère des problématiques étrangères à Sophocle mais qui sont familières au spectateur/lecteur argentin. La pièce se présente donc comme une sorte de pastiche de citations et de renvois où l'identification des références et les allusions — qui montrent différents degrés d'explicitation — dépendra de la compétence et du bagage culturel de chaque spectateur/lecteur — , ce qui pose la question essentielle de la constitution d'une communauté aux frontières floues, mais à laquelle la pièce s'adresse directement, et avec laquelle elle entre en communion.

Une autre modification est le scénario où se déroule l'action: Buenos Aires, dont l'identité est affirmée à travers la mention d'une série de lieux (p. 24), comme la Place de Mai, rebaptisée 'Ágora de Mayo', où la Didascalie du début situe l'action. Le Rio de la Plata et la Plaza de Mayo apparaissent comme des espaces qui condensent le pays, et, simultanément, le Fleuve apparaît comme l'espace du refus d'enterrer les morts, là où reposent de nouveaux Polynice, noyés dans les 'vols de la mort' évoqués directement (p. 43); le Fleuve, qui est 'hecho de tiempo' (fait de temps, p. 23), est devenu pour la ville l'incarnation de la bestialité, et la source de la contamination en raison des crimes qu'il occulte malgré lui. Il s'agit d'une des zones les plus intéressantes de la pièce — le rapport entre l'absence et l'omniprésente des morts (disparus): le corps de Polynice est au milieu de la ville en train de pourrir, mais il est aussi au fond du fleuve, il est partout — comme les corps des morts. L'accent est mis sur le lieu de l'action par Huertas (il y a plus de quarante allusions à la ville, directes ou indirectes) et la ville transformée en personnage; l'espace est familier pour le lecteur argentin mais en même temps il est rendu étrange et étranger au lecteur/spectateur; la ville est corrompue, nauséabonde, l'air et le fleuve empestent la mort. Dès l'ouverture, le spectateur est confronté au problème: 'La patria está muriendo' [La Patrie est en train de mourir] (p. 21). Un scénario apocalyptique qu'on ne sait à quoi attribuer au départ, mais qui, rapidement, apparaît comme conséquence du silence sur les crimes commis, que les femmes exhortent à rompre, alors que le bandonéon appelle à réagir. Dans *L'Antigone* de Sophocle la thématique de la destruction de la ville apparaît uniquement à la fin de l'œuvre; chez Huertas, en revanche, elle est présente dès le départ, mais revient avec davantage d'intensité à la fin. La question du moment où se déroule la pièce est plus complexe; il semble correspondre au moment de sa rédaction, car, comme on le verra, on trouve de nombreuses références à des épisodes, des personnages de l'histoire argentine et des faits divers allant jusqu'aux années 1990, alors qu'aucune indication temporelle précise n'est donnée.

Si la pièce met en scène les personnages principaux de la tragédie de Sophocle, certains sont modifiés, et on constate également l'introduction de personnages renvoyant à l'Argentine: le Río de la Plata, qui n'interagit pas avec les autres, mais donne lieu à des moments de lyrisme; le fleuve est 'hecho de tiempo' [fait de temps], témoin de ce qui se passe dans la ville, rend compte des crimes commis depuis sa fondation, et a connu 'el mundo sin que existiera gente' [le monde avant qu'il existe des gens] (p. 23); la 'Embalsamada Peregrina' [l'embaumée errante], qui renvoie à Eva Perón (1919–1952), une identité affirmée par la reprise de ses discours et par l'histoire du cadavre de Evita qui, avait été embaumé, et qui fut séquestré en 1955 à la suite du coup d'état connu sous le nom de 'Revolución Libertadora', et dont pendant presque vingt ans on a ignoré où il se trouvait. L'histoire du cadavre de Evita fait écho à la situation des disparus, et devient l'emblème d'un mort sans sépulture (pp. 37, 46–47); le bandonéon, témoin muet, interpelé par le chœur, peut être identifié au public. Remarquons aussi la substitution du chœur d'anciens thébains par le chœur de femelles, dans lequel s'inscrivent les Mères de la Place de Mai (p. 51). Reste la question de s'il faut considérer le chœur comme des personnages ou pas; dans le cas de Huertas, il semble que oui, puisque ses intégrantes apparaissent davantage comme un ensemble d'individualités que comme un Chœur. Quant à Tiresias, son identification à travers sa représentation et ses propos à Jorge Luis Borges (déjà mort au moment de l'écriture de la pièce) introduit une modification de fonction, car chez Sophocle les révélations de Tirésias déterminent le changement d'attitude de Créon qui essaie de revenir sur le châtiment imposé à Antigone, alors que chez Huertas, ce n'est pas le cas. A l'exception du Bandonéon y du Río les interventions des personnages s'articulent à partir de cette présence-voix collective qui est le chœur de femelles, le personnage le plus complexe, comme dans la tragédie grecque.

Sens et communion avec la communauté

Dans *AntígonaS* le référent se construit à partir d'une saturation de références à l'histoire, la culture, la littérature argentine, mais l'origine de ces références n'est pas explicitée; c'est à travers ces nombreux renvois que la pièce établit une forme de complicité et de communion avec le spectateur.

Parmi ces renvois, on trouve des noms et des titres — de musiciens, de chanteurs et d'auteurs de paroles de tango, tels que Alfredo Gobbi (p. 20), J. D'Arienzo (p. 71), Aníbal Troilo (pp. 20, 71), Osvaldo Pugliese (p. 70), Roberto Goyeneche (p. 20), Enrique Santos Discépolo (p. 20), Enrique Cadícamo (p. 71). Comme nous l'avons dit, il y a aussi une série d'allusions à la ville de Buenos Aires (pp. 24, 30), mais aussi à des personnages de l'histoire du pays, les 'gauchos' (pp. 25, 29), les noirs (p. 25) et, déjà mentionnés, la 'Embalsamada Peregrina' et Tirésias-Borges. Une série d'allusions plus ou moins explicites à l'histoire argentine concerne les 'vols de la mort' (pp. 26, 31, 43), la Guerre des Malouines (pp. 60, 61). Un vocabulaire typiquement argentin contribue à ancrer la pièce dans ce contexte, tel que: 'pichicatero' [drogué], 'guachos' (p. 21); 'piropo' (p. 29), l'emploi du tutoiement (pp. 64, 69). Un exemple du mode de renvoie à des personnages argentins est: 'A Discepolín pedíle las alas y el aliento / A un dios Polaco, azul y pichicatero' [Demande a Discepolín les ailes et le temps / A un Dieu Polonais, bleu et drogué] (p. 21) — 'Discepolín' renvoyant a Enrique Santos Discépolo (1901–1951), un des plus importants compositeurs de tango et milonga, et chanteur; le 'Dios Polaco' étant une allusion à Roberto Goyeneche (1926–1994), ainsi appelé en raison de ses origines. Quant à l'histoire argentine, voici deux exemples de la façon dont elle s'inscrit dans la pièce. L'expression 'muchachos vencidos bajo un manto de neblina' [Jeunes hommes vaincus sous un manteaux de brouillard] (p. 26) qui renvoie à la Guerre des Malouines qui opposa l'Argentine à l'Angleterre, et de déroula entre le 2 avril–20 juin 1982. Le vers 'Nosotras las chinitas catamarqueñas' [Nous, les métisses d'indien, de Catamarca] (p. 59) convoque le cas de María Soledad Morales, une jeune femme droguée et victime d'une orgie sexuelle, puis assassinée, en 1990. La pièce présente également une série de références intertextuelles sous la forme de citations diverses de textes littéraires, de publicités, de discours politiques comme celui d'Eva Perón à l'occasion de l'obtention du vote féminin le 23 septembre 1947, transcrit textuellement (p. 28), et des fragments de discours de Videla (p. 46), de paroles de tango (p. 62), de musique (p. 36).

La tragédie de Sophocle constitue donc l'axe de l'œuvre, mais la pièce est saturée de références à d'autres textes. Parmi les textes littéraires cités se trouvent 'Esa mujer' de Rodolfo Walsh (1966) (p. 37); 'Historia del guerrero y la cautiva' (p. 55) et 'El simulacro' de Borges (pp. 54, 57), ainsi que les poèmes: 'Two English Poems' de Borges (p. 53), 'Buenos Aires' 1963 (p. 54), 'Poema Conjetural' (p. 55); on trouve également des références au *Martín Fierro* de Hernández, ouvrage canonique de la littérature argentine (p. 22). De nombreuses paroles de tango (parfois légèrement modifiées) venant de 'Fueron tres años' de Juan Pablo Marin, 'Mi noche triste' de Pascual Contursi (p. 57), 'Papá Baltasar' (p. 26), 'Sur' (p. 69), 'Malena' de Homero Manzi (1907–1951), 'Naranjo en Flor' de Homero Expósito

(p. 41). Parmi les publicités, il faut mentionner celle des savons *Lux* et *Palmolive* (p. 46). Mon hypothèse concernant ces renvois ou références, qui posent la question du déchiffrement et de la compréhension de la pièce, est que le fait d'avoir conservé les principaux moments de la tragédie classique permet sa compréhension, au-delà du niveau de déchiffrement des références à l'histoire et la culture argentines; la réécriture acquiert donc un sens particulier, car si l'intrigue n'était pas connue préalablement du public, le caractère fragmentaire du texte pourrait attenter contre sa compréhension. Ainsi, ces renvois phagocytent le texte de Sophocle, et tissent un lien étroit au spectateur argentin, une forme de communion, dans laquelle le spectacle théâtral devient une expérience communautaire intense.

Légalité et genre

Dans la pièce de Huertas le conflit entre Antigone et Créon prend une dimension nouvelle qui est à peine insinuée chez Sophocle: celle d'un conflit de genre. Chez Sophocle, le personnage d'Antigone a des caractéristiques considérées comme masculines pour l'époque et éloignées du modèle traditionnel de femme, même si dans sa tirade finale elle revient à un rôle plus traditionnel et exprime le regret de mourir sans s'être mariée et avoir eu des enfants. Le conflit entre sexes apparaît à travers le conflit générationnel entre Créon et Hémon (Sophocle, *Antigone*, Troisième épisode, scène 1): Créon commence par discréditer l'influence d'une femme par rapport à celle du père, puis accuse son fils de se faire le champion de la femme, et d'en être l'esclave. Les insultes de Créon prennent une tournure qui discrédite la femme, et visent l'absence de reconnaissance d'une autorité féminine possible.

Dans *AntígonaS* de Huertas, l'opposition générique est accentuée, toutes les femmes qui font face à un pouvoir abusif et se trouvent en situation de rébellion sont Antigone, et Antigone est toutes ces femmes, qui sont les mères, les épouses, les filles des morts; mais, et c'est là un des aspects les plus ambivalents de la pièce, si elles se rebellent contre le pouvoir des hommes, elles en sont tout autant les victimes que leurs complices. Dans un moment particulièrement intéressant, la célèbre phrase qui exprimait l'indifférence envers la violence d'état sous la dernière dictature argentine est réutilisée pour faire référence au féminicide: 'Corifeo: ¿Vas a matar a Antígona? / Coro: Por algo será. Por algo será' [Coriphée: Tu vas tuer Antigone? / Chœur: Il y a bien une raison. Il y a bien une raison] (p. 44).

Chez Sophocle, l'opposition entre la loi de la ville et la loi des dieux organise le conflit; chez Huertas, la loi de la ville est une loi plus secrète, spécifique, exigeante qui lie Antigone à l'histoire: en s'opposant à Créon, elle le fait aussi à l'abus du pouvoir qui caractérise l'histoire du pays — un pouvoir masculin. Créon est, ici aussi, emporté par la 'hybris'; comme on le sait, dans la Grèce antique, le concept ne se limite pas au terrain du religieux, mais est également utilisé dans le domaine politique, moral et social; d'Homère à Aristote, il ne signifie pas uniquement arrogance, orgueil ou incapacité de reconnaître ses limitations, mais implique aussi que les actions entreprises déshonorent les autres, sont un outrage à la justice, amènent le désastre sur une famille, et non pas seulement sur l'individu qui a commis la faute, et aussi sur la société toute entière (comme dans *Les Perses* d'Eschyle). La catastrophe qui menace la ville est généralement due à la conduite d'un héros dans le monde grec, alors que chez Huertas elle est liée à l'abus masculin du pouvoir tout au long de l'histoire du pays; Huertas réécrit l'histoire de l'Argentine à partir de ce paramètre: le conflit classique de volontés se déroule dans ce scénario et introduit une tension étrangère à la tragédie. Le rôle d'Antigone et des femmes — sous la forme du chœur — est d'appeler à réagir contre la toute-puissance du tyran, qui détruit la ville et ses habitants, et de souligner la responsabilité de l'homme (le masculin) dans la vie politique. Un rapport direct est établi entre les malheurs dont la ville souffre et les atrocités commises par le tyran; la conduite hybristique de Créon et ses alliés est la cause de la catastrophe finale, qui menace de désintégrer la ville et de la transformer en un terrain vague. C'est ainsi que se termine la pièce; le fragment 'Peste et énigme', concentre les images d'une apocalypse, qui, pour nous aujourd'hui, annonce la crise de décembre 2001, avec son bouleversement de fin du monde. La destruction dans ce drame engage la participation du Rio, qui ramène à la surface les atrocités commises par l'homme: la mer recrache les morts, sur le modèle de l'Apocalypse: 'Y el mar entregó los muertos que había en él; y la muerte y el Hades entregaron los muertos que había en ellos; y fueron juzgados cada uno según sus obras' [Et la mer rendit les morts qui étaient en elle; et la mort et l'Hadès rendirent les morts qui étaient en eux; et ils furent jugés selon leurs œuvres].[12] Chez Huertas, à la fin de la pièce, le Fleuve rend les corps reçus, en un geste féroce et dépourvu de rationalité.

L'apocalypse finale résulte de la conduite de Créon, qui s'insère dans une suite de crimes parmi lesquels se compte le féminicide (pp. 39, 40, 49–50, 67). Créon met en péril la stabilité de la ville, ce sont ses actes délirants qui transforment la ville en un lieu où l'équilibre est rompu, non pas en raison du choix de rester fidèle à une loi (celle de la ville) mais comme une forme d'abus de pouvoir tyrannique: Créon se prend pour Dieu et, comme on a vu, il s'exprime à partir d'expressions empruntées aux dictateurs argentins, Videla en particulier (pp. 35, 40, 45). Créon est un tyran aveuglé par un fanatisme démesuré et par sa dévotion pour Buenos Aires, possédé par un sentiment mégalomane qui le pousse à se croire le dépositaire d'un pouvoir divin, dont la mission est de sauver Buenos Aires, *au détriment* de ses habitants, une existence modelée par un processus incessant de destruction et de renouvellement. Son arrogance et son orgueil atteignent des dimensions insoupçonnées, malgré les avertissements de Tirésias, il ne peut voir ses erreurs ('La ciudad sufre su locura' [La ville souffre de sa folie] (p. 54)). Créon ne change pas d'avis à la fin, malgré le suicide de son fils et de sa femme, il affirme son délire, et c'est ce délire de rédemption qui met en péril le pouvoir et l'existence même de Buenos Aires — tel que l'affirme Antigone; mais Créon impose sa loi, et veut nettoyer la ville de toute opposition: 'Antes que la familia está la Patria. Antes que los seres queridos está la ciudad' [La Patrie se place avant la famille. La ville avant les êtres aimés] (p. 30).

Néanmoins, si d'un côté, il existe un lien étroit entre l'orgueil démesuré de ceux qui ont le pouvoir et les désastres qui menacent la ville, d'un autre côté, on ne sait pas d'où ni de qui vient le châtiment ou si cette catastrophe répond à une volonté divine. Si les images accentuent l'association au texte biblique, et donc inscrivent une conception religieuse de l'Apocalypse, il n'est pas évident que cette catastrophe soit orchestrée par la volonté d'un dieu (ou des dieux) en colère par la violence des hommes — alors que, comme on a vu, parallèlement Créon s'octroie le statut de Dieu. Face à l'absence de toute référence explicite ou d'allusion concernant celui à qui on peut attribuer la responsabilité, on pense plutôt à un soulèvement de la nature, contre les atrocités commises par les hommes, et à une réaction face à l'attitude orgueilleuse et irrespectueuse contre eux. Nous pouvons dire pour conclure que s'il y a une divinité, c'est la nature, qui assiste à travers le Rio au spectacle des hommes qui s'affrontent. L'énigme introduite par le dernier fragment de l'œuvre qui apporte aussi un scénario de désespoir, rappelle l'énigme d'Œdipe, et la survie de la ville; chez Huertas, l'énigme posée est celle de l'avenir de la patrie: à l'absence de justice tout au long de l'histoire pour les victimes de violence politique s'ajoute l'absence de justice concernant la violence faite aux femmes. L'histoire de la ville qui, selon la tradition argentine, se confond avec l'histoire du pays, se déploie en une circularité qui débouche sur une apocalypse sans espoir. L'histoire n'est ni linéaire ni cyclique, mais un processus incessant de destruction et de renouvellement, qui mène néanmoins à la destruction finale de la ville; suivant Hésiode et Solon, Huertas rend les hommes responsables des malheurs de la ville — les hommes et non pas les femmes — les abus de pouvoir du Créon argentin et la passivité des citoyens.

Il s'agit là d'un des aspects où la pièce de Huertas s'écarte le plus de Sophocle: il inverse la saga mythologique des Labdacides en faisant du début de l'histoire d'Œdipe — l'énigme du Sphynx et la peste de Thèbes — la fin de l'histoire argentine, car c'est après le suicide d'Hémon et d'Eurydice qu'une nouvelle Sphynx apparaît dans le Fleuve, et vomit les morts disparus et réduits au silence, amenant la peste. La peste chez Huertas, à différence de la tragédie, n'est pas un signe envoyé par les Dieux qui peut réparer la souffrance ou l'expulsion du héros; l'eau est contaminée, l'énigme et la peste se réinstallent à la fin de la pièce, et mettent à nu l'impureté de la contamination des corps sans sépulture, qui insulte et blesse surtout les femmes. La série de questionnements finale reste sans réponse.

La dernière scène, prise en charge par le chœur de femmes, convoque la lamentation et la prière, comme un présage et une sentence; une invocation à sauver la ville du monstre qui dévore ses enfants. Les derniers mots du Coryphée élargissent le cadre du conflit tragique, et le posent en énigme existentiel d'un peuple. Les vers sur lesquels se ferme la pièce — 'Que será de la reina del Plata / que será de mi tierra querida' [Qu'adviendra-t-il de la reine du Plata / qu'adviendra-t-il de ma terre aimée] (p. 72) — ramènent la force et le caractère conflictuel de la tragédie classique; le genre qui a permis d'explorer les tensions de la *polis*, et à la polis de s'interroger elle-même.

Justice transitionnelle et justice civile

Une des spécificités de la pièce de Huertas est donc la mise en parallèle entre la violence politique (historique) et la violence faite aux femmes (féminicide). La société représentée apparaît comme étant divisée en hommes et femmes, et le crime sexuel se présente comme une arme, dans un pays qui, dans le cadre des procès faits aux responsables de crimes contre l'humanité commis sous la dernière dictature, a envisagé d'accorder une figure légale spécifique à celui-ci. L'opposition bourreaux/victimes englobe ici celle entre hommes et femmes, sans pour autant se limiter à celle-ci.

La dimension anticipatoire de la pièce se joue sur plusieurs niveaux. D'une part, la demande de justice et l'apocalypse finale, puisque dès 2003 les procès contre les responsables de la dictature reprendront, d'autre part la fin de l'année 2001 fut marquée par un crash économique qui bouleversa l'ensemble du pays. Notons que la pièce attribue cette apocalypse à l'absence de justice envers les victimes politiques et celles de féminicide, mettant ainsi en rapport les économies ultralibérales et absence de respect des droits humains en Argentine. L'idée que seule la justice peut sauver la ville et le pays acquiert une projection utopique qui devient anticipatoire en raison des événements ultérieurs. En ce sens nous pouvons comprendre la pièce comme une tentative de décrire ce que nous pouvons appeler 'l'injustice transitionnelle'. La pièce anticipe les nouvelles formes du politique auxquelles nous sommes confrontés aujourd'hui où nos catégories traditionnelles éclatent et de nouvelles formes de pouvoir émergent, qui ont une identité politique pas encore tout à fait définie. C'est le cas en Argentine avec l'émergence des mouvements pour les droits des femmes: la lutte pour légaliser l'avortement, la demande de nouvelles législations et reconnaissance de la violence faite aux femmes. On ne peut que souligner l'écart qui existe avec ce que les pays européens ont connu, en raison de leurs revendications sociales et du contexte de pauvreté que connaît le pays. Les manifestations réalisées dans ce cadre ont souvent pour épicentre le Congrès et la Place du Congrès, alors que la Place de Mai est souvent reléguée à un deuxième plan, un choix de cet espace traduit la projection vers la demande d'un changement dans la juridiction du pays.

Pour finir, je voudrais renvoyer au travail de Adam Rosenblatt, *Digging for the Disappeared*,[13] où celui-ci pose la question: est-ce que les morts ont des droits? ou est-ce que le travail d'exhumation des victimes de violence d'état ou de crimes de masse doit se faire exclusivement au nom des droits des familles, des communautés, de la société (justice sociale)? Dans la pièce de Huertas l'apocalypse finale semble avoir pour origine une sorte de révolte de la nature, encombrée par les cadavres: le fleuve rend les corps, comme si ceux-ci finissaient par réclamer justice par eux-mêmes et pouvaient s'ériger en instance juridique autonome.

Notes to Chapter 4

1. Le premier procès à l'encontre des chefs du gouvernement militaire se déroula entre le 22 avril et le 14 août 1985, les sentences furent prononcées le 9 décembre 1985. L'ensemble connu sous le nom de 'lois d'impunité' est constitué de quatre moments: la 'Lois d'auto-amnistie N. 22.924' prononcée par la dictature militaire en 1983; la 'Loi de point final' de 1986, et la 'Loi de

l'Obéissance due' de 1987, émises sous le gouvernement d'Alfonsín, et un ensemble de dix lois destinées à amnistier les responsables de crimes sous la dictature qui avaient été jugés, promues entre 1989 et 1990 par Carlos Menem. En 2003, sous la présidence de Néstor Kirchner des procès systématiques aux responsables de la répression ont repris.

2. Jorge Huertas, *AntígonaS. Linaje de Hembras* (teatro) (Buenos Aires: Biblos, 2002). Le parcours de Jorge Huertas est aussi varié que productif; psychologue (UCA), reçu en 1972, il est aussi auteur de romans, de pièces de théâtre, enseignant de théâtre, et directeur. Voir: <http://www.autores.org.ar/sitios/jhuertas/>.
3. Ana Longoni, 'Introducción', in *El siluetazo*, édité par Gustavo Bruzzoni and Ana Longoni (Buenos Aires : Adriana Hidalgo, 2008), pp. 5–60.
4. George Steiner, *Antigones* (New Haven, CT, et Londres: Yale University Press, 1996), pp. ix, 121
5. Pilar Hualde, 'Mito y tragedia griega en la literatura iberoamericana', *Cuadernos de filología clásica*, 22 (Janeiro 2012), 185–222.
6. María Gabriela Rebok, *La actualidad de la experiencia de lo clásico y el paradigma de Antígona* (Buenos Aires: Biblos, 2013); Moira Fradinger, 'An Argentine Tradition', in *Antigone on the Contemporary World Stage*, édité par Erin B. Mee et Helene P. Foley (Oxford: Oxford University Press, 2011), 67–145; *The Returns of Antigone: Interdisciplinary Essays*, édité par Tina Chanter and Sean D. Kirkland (Albany, NY: Albany State University Press, 2014).
7. *Restos humanos e identificación. Violencia de masa, genocidio y el 'giro forense'*, édité par Elisabeth Ansttet, Sévérine Garibian, Jean-Marc Dreyfus (Buenos Aires: Miño y Dávilas, 2017).
8. Moira Fradinger, 'Making Women Visible: Multiple Antigones on the Colombian Twenty-first Century Stage', in *The Oxford Handbook of Greek Drama in the Americas*, édité par Kathryn Bosher et al. (Oxford: Oxford University Press, 2018).
9. Moira Soto, 'Una mina inagotable', *Página 12*, Buenos Aires, 13 juin 2003; Carlos Pacheco, 'Antígona: una mujer que parece ser eterna,' *La Nación*, Buenos Aires, 7 juillet 2003; Juan Ramón Seia, 'El poder engendra toda muerte', *Crítica*, Villa María, 23 octobre 2007.
10. *Antígonas, linaje de hembras* (Todos Hombres), dir. par Roberto Aguirre (Teatro de Repertorio, Melo 1756, Florida, Provincia de Buenos Aires, Argentina, 2014).
11. Claude Calame, *La Tragédie chorale: poésie grecque et rituel musical* (Paris: Les Belles Lettres, 2017).
12. L'Apocalypse, 20. 13.
13. Adam Rosenblatt, *Digging for the Disappeared: Forensic Science after Atrocity* (Palo Alto, CA.: Stanford University Press, 2014).

CHAPTER 5

❖

The Irreverence of Bones: Reclaiming Trashed Lives in the Aftermath of Violence in *Adios Ayacucho* (1984) and *Insensatez* (2004)

Daniel Mosquera

Our social edifice is permeated by multiple layers of belief regarding the granting or revoking of humanity based on perceived contamination or potential for disposability. When we learn of political realities that label people as undesirable, subject to persecution, brutality, or removal, depictions are infused often with trash-related meanings of pollution and dirt. That in the context of economic inequality and repressive regimes and behaviours a *semantics* of waste and purging emerges not only to justify but also to chart cartographies of exception and terror is a well-known fact in the history of human rights abuses. In its modern manifestation, this process of transferal is engrained and exacerbated in societies in which market-based economics and despotic governments join forces to forge the course of national existence. Hence, as we realize that approaches to transitional justice rely on remnants and on bringing back to life and back into social and legal memory the material and symbolic residue left behind on the heels of systemic discarding and ostracism, we must grasp this crucial process from the perspective of salvaging and forensic inquiry prevalent in truth commissions. Our principal tendency is to frame and perceive processes of memory recovery temporally from legal, forensic, archaeological, and ethnographic and ethno-historical viewpoints, mostly in the assembly of legalized narratives — collecting pieces, bones, testimonies, and any other traces deemed valuable in the pursuit of truth and also in individual and social restoration. In addition, the collection of data and its elucidation are designed to aid in the ability to formulate agendas and acts of reconciliation. Literature has contributed to these methods in a parallel but also divergent way, having often no precise role to play in legal terms and little to add when legitimating the demands truth claims pose on the public search for justice, with some notable but also at times conflicting concessions in the Latin American context.[1]

From a plural perspective of transitional justice mechanisms and their expanding scope, literary voices acquire salience as more situations of systemic brutality are put creatively to the transitional justice test. Here, I would like to explore the emblematic connection between the human as waste and violence in the context of transitional justice and memory retrieval by analysing two fictional narratives inspired by historical events in Peru and Guatemala. The first one is Julio Ortega's *Adios Ayacucho* [*Good Bye Ayacucho*] (1986),[2] the story of the Peruvian indigenous farmworker and activist leader, Alfonso Cánepa, whose body is tortured, burned, and cut up but whose partial remains return from the ditch where they were thrown and travel to the capital city Lima to demand the recovery of the lost parts of his dead body in order to be whole again. The second narrative is Horacio Castellanos Moya's *Insensatez* [*Senselessness*] (2004),[3] a novel revisiting government human rights abuses against indigenous populations in Guatemala from the perspective of a copy-editor hired, for pay, to make more legible and 'clean up' the testimonies and inquiries gathered in the official report. As I argue, these two stories are in some way also about waste and cleansing, and interpellate society as a whole and truth commission processes in particular by calling attention to the proximity between discards and humanity in the context of embedded structures of neglect and disposability that confront society with the production and recovery of its own waste. As conjured in these stories, retrieval of remains addresses an endemic viciousness that has a long and complex pedigree in Latin America since colonial times and that goes beyond defined periods of violence. It also acknowledges forms of subjectivity, culture, and memory formation amid indigenous populations that have been long discarded as atavistic and discordant with modernity, a material culture excess in need of eradication.

While reflecting on the challenges that airing a country's 'dirty laundry' represents for truth commissions, in a time and context when and where humanity's plural worth must also be recognized, these two narratives decentralize the universalist and particularist pretentions of human rights by expanding subjective and ontological frameworks and advocating, in divergent ways, for an ethically more inclusive and embodied understanding of social memory. Both stories combine fiction with what we might term the lettered archive — contemporary legal, journalistic, and historiographical material related to ongoing processes of memory recovery; both appeal to irony and irreverence, destabilizing the epistemological gravitas that frames so much output on human rights abuses; and, finally, as hybrid texts inspired by documented realities of genocide, both stretch the limits of language and representation by engaging, and engaging with, various cultural patterns and disruptions.

Coupling the meanings of waste with truth commission and reconciliation work might seem anomalous. If we consider how a *semantics* of waste tints to a visible degree the expurgation that often undergirds repressive realities of dehumanization, we might reach a different conclusion. In contemporary English, for example, the word 'undesirable' shares a sinister yet pragmatic and symbolic space with programmes and acts of prophylaxis. Spanish and Portuguese have developed their own semantic formations applicable to different circumstances when downgrading the human, pairing it with detritus and lack of worth in various contexts of pollution and rejection. As in English, all manners of sayings and pragmatic prognoses abound in both languages. I would like to focus more on the manner in which the stories approach the presence of indigenous people in the search for recognition and restitution rather than on the aesthetic choices representative of such disruptions. In an attempt to highlight the salvaging of indigenous humanity during periods of transitional justice within which this humanity is summoned back into public consciousness, the need to foster a different set of affective dispositions becomes paramount. In this reading, what appears as derisive and, by some measure and readings, as cynical or disenchanted, can also operate as a mechanism of cognitive dissonance. I would prefer to think of this propensity as a vital dislocation of the limits imposed on the process of seeking justice and resolution by the rationality most truth commission practices epitomize. One might consider such strategies as operating in a similar fashion.

Adios Ayacucho accomplishes this in different ways, first by starting from the point of view of fragmentation and the impossibility of being heard — or even perceived as complete — under existing social and jurisdictive norms. The main character, Cánepa, begins his story by anticipating the moment of interpellation of the polis, the capital where political power is concentrated, as the time of his own restoration becomes a prescient goal. '"I came to Lima to recover my corpse." That's how I'd start my speech upon arrival.'[4] Once he is able to get his partial body out of the ditch and back to his hometown, Quinua, the mutilated indigenous leader reaches the police station to confront the sergeant about the forged charges that — as he recalls — led to his torture and subsequent killing. The sergeant immediately recognizes him and replies, without looking at him, 'Don't play the fool... you're a dangerous terrorist.'[5] The dismissal prompts Cánepa to recall the process of torture and discarding of his body, ending with an analogy that will haunt the rest of the story: 'That same policeman, before nearing the ditch that would become my grave, filled my belly with dried hay while laughing, as if I were a doll bound *only to be discarded*'.[6] The story then follows the trek of Cánepa's partial remains to Lima relying on a picaresque, road journey structure. Along the way, he meets different archetypal characters that span the spectrum of social actors comprising, at the time, Peruvian society: an anthropologist, who follows him almost until the end of the story and whose epistemological and certified authority is constantly under scrutiny; different social actors active in the reality of violence, from members of the Peruvian Maoist insurgent group Sendero Luminoso to state forces represented by soldiers and police; and various indigenous and other Peruvian participants and spectators.

Once in the city, Cánepa ends up mixing with beggars and other characters associated with sidelined, lumpen underclasses, invisible or discarded subjects of the modern city unable to be heard, and seen only in the context of criminalization, as he reaches the country's political and elite epicentre. Up to this point, everyone he meets on the way questions his ability to speak based on his fractional, decrepit appearance. To most, he is ghastly, an anomaly that needs to be either hidden or buried, as waste often is, situations that prompt Cánepa constantly to manoeuvre his way out of permanent restraint, rejection, or outright disappearance. After all, Cánepa is not only dead but his body is also *not complete*. Although he manages at the end of the story to interpellate Fernando Belaúnde Terry — at the time the real president of the nation — in front of the Municipal Palace, Cánepa receives no response from him; he is nearly twice lynched by police forces, and is ultimately saved by another downgraded character, Petiso.

Unsuccessful in getting his discarded bones back or receiving any type of response, Cánepa decides with Petiso's help to desecrate the sepulchre of the Spanish Conquistador Francisco Pizarro located in the nearby cathedral; he appropriates some of those bones to replace his own missing ones, and settles down to rest, declaring himself finally whole. The many ironies implicit in this transaction and completion of the body and the negation of a wholesome indigenous totality — as the final solution to reintegration and inclusiveness — further cement our perception of systemic displacement and violent desecration within the Peruvian body politic and its social and political imagination.

A second strategy of disruption becomes manifest in the story by referencing Andean, pre-Hispanic structures of memory formation related, among others, to folk musical culture, burial practices, and social healing, all cultural features highlighted in the well-known theatre adaptation of the story by the Peruvian theatre ensemble Yuyachkani (a Quechua word meaning 'I am thinking; I am remembering').[7] Although both the novel and the theatre adaptation indicate the impossibility of restoration under existing (modern) cultural and institutional norms, the story still positions indigenous culture as a site of interpellation and repossession of the self. This recovery is suggested as ineluctably emetic in nature. Not only does violence render the human body segmented and stained but its reintegration also seems, in light of a deep-rooted contempt for indigenous life, almost insurmountable. We must note that the resurfacing of evidence in the guise of abandoned bones, narrated from the perspective of the aggrieved, disfigured subject, emerges incomplete as well but meets a recognition whose historical sum is demanded before the law. How long we follow Cánepa's tragic journey impacts our ability to understand and feel the historical debasement of his life. Regardless of whether it is through narrative or images, as Susan Sontag reminds us in *Regarding the Pain of Others*, the question of length of exposure might not necessarily solve the problem of shift in perception, however.[8] In the end, as she concludes, we might not discern the pain of others; we cannot really imagine it.[9] Finally, addressing a history of centuries of marginalization, dispossession, and disposability demands, in *Adios Ayacucho*, a place in the process of truth-seeking that seems hard to accommodate within transitional justice strictures. In other words, to recover the bones we need first to be able to identify and be inclined to discern and read them, not only as forensic and subjective traces of the humanity of the individual who is part of a body politic. Sadly, indigenous bones represent in our minds, until today, mostly archaeological signs.

Just as *Adios Ayacucho* starts with the pronouncement of a partial body whose missing remains were dispensed with and disappeared, violently discarded, Castellanos Moya's opening in his novel *Insensatez* is concerned with fractured cognition and the psychology of dispossession.[10] 'I am not complete in the mind,' reads the narrator, as he sits to examine the hundreds of pages in the commission's report he has been tasked to edit and clean up (make legible), coming across a translated testimony from a Mayan indigenous witness who saw and survived the carnage that Guatemalan soldiers inflicted on his entire family. However, our attempts to grasp the selective but persistent testimony and the fictional editor's task of ordering the various reports are also affected by his cynicism and erratic obsessions and destabilized by his world-weariness and personal, sexual compulsions. Most of his language relates to justice, to the institutions that impart it; and to the social actors that activate it. This language appears followed recurrently by the phrase 'so-called', rendering the narrator's mediation as a corrector, but also as the lettered filter into indigenous subjectivity and memory retrieval, partial and unstable. Similarly, his propensity to try to find analogies for what is in fact indescribable, forces him to admit metaphoric partiality, as the phrase 'as if' becomes a recurrent syntactic motif as well. The whole novel fluctuates between his thoughts about the testimonies and reports, his fascination with lyrical patterns of indigenous thought he finds compelling and of literary value, and his almost psychosomatic, misogynistic, and carnal shifting fixations.

Mostly for these reasons, some of the more negative evaluations of Castellanos Moya's work have underlined concrete layers of cynicism as an unproductive aesthetics, a sort of failed mediation, because cynicism comes to dominate the narrative perspective.[11] As I mentioned earlier, however, we can also approach the threshold of such irreverence and cynicism into memory retrieval and 'trashed' indigenous subjectivity from a different angle, one in which we as readers see ourselves also implicated, facing an unexpected dissonance, perhaps no different in scope from the conflicted feelings we face when confronting that which has been discarded but comes back to haunt us. The narrator wants us and other characters in the novel to recognize an unsettling indigenous alterity while partaking indirectly of its centuries-old trashing. He wants us to be, as he himself becomes, transfixed by the peculiar cathartic language, by its non-Spanish linearity and grammar, cadence, and recurring imagery. At the same time, he is aware of the value these pronouncements might have when made 'legible' in truth commission reports and, particularly, in the report he is in the process of editing:

> ... [they were] forceful phrases uttered by indigenous people for whom the events they were describing meant unearthing their most painful memories, but also entering in a therapeutic stage when confronting the past... How they themselves recognized in those testimonies that looked like concentrated pain capsules, the phrasing of which had such resonance, a force, and depth that I had jotted down several of them in my personal notebook...[12]

Mesmerized by the language in the testimonies and mistrustful of all institutions, the narrator moves between the seat of the Guatemalan Archbishopric, where he is asked to labour, between adjacent bars where he drinks and daydreams, a few other places where he indulges his sexual fantasies and neurotic proclivities, and his apartment, where he gives free rein to his physical and seductive adventures. Starting to feel persecuted amidst a climate of silencing pro-human rights voices, he withdraws at the end of the novel to an isolated spiritual retreat in the countryside belonging to the Archbishopric in order to finish his editorial task. Moving between entertaining external machinations and, perhaps, real persecution, and increasingly fearful for his life, he then flees the retreat and finds refuge at a cousin's house in a Swiss city during carnival time. There, he is unable to disengage his mind from the testimonies and he discovers, through an e-mail sent to him by one of his friends in Guatemala, that the Monsignor overseeing the retrieval and organization of testimonies had been assassinated after making public the report he himself had helped to correct.

In my analysis of this novel, I'd like to focus on a few words used in strategic locations, which relate to this inquiry into waste and humanity in the context of political repression. The two words are 'orear' [to freshen, to air out][13] and 'basurear'[14] or 'basura' [literally to turn into trash, or trash, respectively]. When the narrator imagines indigenous recollection as a therapeutic or cathartic process, the analogy he uses to identify this process refers to airing out 'bloodthirsty ghosts that stalked [indigenous peoples'] dreams.' In this instance, cleansing is related to indigenous psychic memory. Later on, as he expects to receive a first payment for his editorial work, which he notices is delayed, he goes into a paroxysm insulting the person he holds responsible for the oversight: 'Did he think that he could treat me like garbage as he pleases? Didn't he notice that I was not just another one of those hung-up ['acomplejados'] Indians he was used to dealing with?'[15] This pronouncement is revealing of one of the underlying stereotypical assumptions about indigenous peoples and the perception of their humanity as one of downgraded, disposable value, whose character is subordinate. We soon also learn of the narrator's apathy to aspects of his task and to the humanitarian motives and institutional and ideological context that advance it, even though he is captivated by the vivid contrast between indigenous language and suffering. From the beginning, there is a defiance that puts him at odds with the ethical, moral, and political assumptions of the truth commission and of the anticipated reverence its objectives almost mandate in its reception. The narrator's chronic cynicism and contradictions, both of which become part of his self-reflexive, almost scornful mental reactions and personal crises, reveal disillusionment and a deep ambivalence about coming into contact with a subjective universe that has been rejected as a matter of culture but is now, to him, lyrically proximate. As narrated in the testimonies, the stench of death, systemic and practised, is to him replete with magnificence. Yet his need to rescue indigenous subjectivity in the testimonies is selective and predicated on his own necessities as a writer. He fluctuates between, on the one hand, the recognition that the epistemological structure within which he functions and through which the massacred memory of the Mayan people is to be rescued is inadequate and, on the other, the necessity to highlight the existence of a trace that is either impenetrable or unrecognized, but which has to be brought back to public awareness.

As the protagonist finds himself persecuted while working in the country home, he hides behind a trash container, the 'only place where [he] could hide without his pursuers and guards finding [him]'.[16] It is at this precise point, supposing his own demise and possible disappearance in a country where such events, under a dictatorship, had become routine, that he declares his 'preoccupation that the hundreds of testimonies [under his care] could get lost' but realizes that more copies existed in his friend's and the Archbishopric's computers. In the midst of frantic fear, he pulls out the notebook where he had been copying the phrases from the testimonies that most struck him as profound, and once again returns to a fragment he has copied during the last days: 'In that pestilent semi-darkness behind the trash container, I was able to decipher, lightening my wait, a text that said *that the name of the dead be erased so that they become free, and we have no [more] problems*, which made evident that even some of the Indian survivors did not want to recover their memory but to perpetuate oblivion'.[17]

Able to migrate to the Swiss enclave, cradle of the institutional and also mythological narratives of international human rights, and to stay at a cousin's home, our narrator seeks his own purging, his own restitution, 'to heal from the psychic and emotional aggression to which [he felt he] had been subjected while once and again correcting the report...'.[18] There, he ponders his own psychological fragmentation, fearful of confronting his own memory of the one thousand one hundred pages he has corrected, and remembers a testimonial phrase whose anomalous grammatical structure leads him to believe it is a reflection of a shattered psyche, and to speculate that his, too, might be damaged. 'For me to remember was to live again the nightmarish testimonies I read so many times.' It is here, near the novel's conclusion, that his memory of two fragments emerges declaring 'they were people like us, towards whom we felt fear' and 'we all know who the assassins are',[19] as the narrator becomes more and more inebriated. His expression of hopeless rage towards the criminals (he even believes he saw the face of one of the generals pursuing him before he left Guatemala) turns into a final, impotent cry of accusation in the midst of carnival. The novel ends with a mixture of sex (his cousin ends up in the apartment with a Dutch woman) and an email from one of his friends in Guatemala revealing that Monsignor had just been assassinated in his parish home, his head utterly smashed with a brick, after having made public the report. The narrator ends with his friend's words: 'Everyone is fucked. Be thankful that you left.'[20] The word in Spanish is 'cagado', literally a reference to the human as excrement, a comparison to one of the lowest metaphoric deployments announcing (and often justifying) human degradation.

The narrator-as-editor's initial response, of feeling throughout his exposure to the Guatemalan genocide overwhelmed and imperilled by both the carnage of a wasted humanity and the awe such absurd extremes produce in him, is echoed at the end of the novel, as the mixture of mundane, carnal matters and the vivid disposal of life underscores, taunts, and modulates the mounting denunciation.

The counterpoint between cultivated disparagement and the quotidian, systemic degradation of humanity, as documented through the indigenous testimonies, drives the narrative and propels the need to confront the violent past, to retrieve not just the lives that have been discarded but the circumstances that led to the violence explicit in the act's justification.

⋆ ⋆ ⋆ ⋆ ⋆

In her essay 'Alien to Modernity: The Rationalization of Discrimination', Jean Franco takes to task Mario Vargas Llosa and layers of the projects of truth and reconciliation commissions because of the persistent discrimination that she sees permeating their discourse about indigenous peoples.[21] Franco argues that we tend to concentrate the meaning of ethnic cleansing around the bodily erasure of the person or the community, as a sort of methodical annihilation dotted by festering bouts of violence; but that we forget that cleansing is a much deeper, more complex historical process that also takes into account cultural erasure as the price that must be paid to cross the threshold of modernity.[22] The recognition that the search for, and institution of, modernity has relied for centuries on a persistent exclusion and rejection of indigenous populations, among others, inspired stories like the ones I have examined here. The methodical and often extreme dehumanization at the hands of violent agents, propelled by long-standing prejudice, emerges in both stories in a grotesque, absurd, and tragic kind of humour that gestures back to the system that produces it. In *Insensatez*, the narrator, believing that 'the army had forced half of the population [in Guatemala] to murder the other half',[23] concludes by shouting at the ghost of one of the generals, amidst a public that doesn't understand him, 'We all know who the murderers are!'[24] Cánepa in *Adios Ayacucho* attempts not just to interpellate the system that maims and murders him, but does so in a way that declares, as well, that society is in some ways also responsible for such acts of dehumanization.[25]

As Gay Hawkins explains in her book *The Ethics of Waste*, waste always 'gestures back to the economy that produced it',[26] an economy that bespeaks industrial, moral, and psycho-social dimensions of community and self. Jean Franco's critique of the political philosophy partially responsible for upholding the downgrading of indigenous humanity echoes this view indirectly.[27] In her assessment, 'while the Peruvian Commission went to extraordinary efforts to publicize its findings and confront Peru with its violent past, the society it scrutinized was already undergoing an intense process of change in which discrimination was the undertow'.[28] This undertow carried with it an accumulated backdrop of rejected values the Commission identified but of which it could only scratch the surface. One could argue that much in colonial relations has been predicated on the conservation and increase of such undertows, as Franz Fanon and others have clearly argued in their analyses. As Julio Ortega explains in one of his interviews, physical and epistemic violence produces a deep alienation and uprooting that disrupt existing orders and cycles, leaving confusion among the people.[29] I believe that literature has helped unearth aspects of this confusion by disrupting prevailing paradigms for explanation, where laughter and irony also become expressions of defence against the toughness of reality; as well, perhaps, as — to recall Susan Sontag's meditations — instruments through which remembering can also become an ethical, partial act for reconciliation.[30]

Notes to Chapter 5

1. Notable novelists like Ernesto Sábato (National Commission on the Disappeared, 1983–84) and Mario Vargas Llosa (Presidential Commission on the Ayacucho massacre, 1983) were invited to participate, for instance, and with conflicting results, in the work of truth commissions in their respective countries. What's more, the prominence of the much-studied 'dictator novel' as a distinctive sub-genre within Latin American letters reveals that scrutinizing the deep contradictions of societies under dictatorship is in Latin America almost a regional compulsion.
2. Julio Ortega, *Adios, Ayacucho* (Philadelphia, PA: Ishi Publications, 1986).
3. Horacio Castellanos Moya, *Insensatez* (Madrid: Tusquets Editores, 2004).
4. Ortega, *Adios, Ayacucho*, p. 9. All translations are mine, unless otherwise noted.
5. Ibid, p. 4
6. Ibid, p. 4, my italics.
7. A new edition of *Adios, Ayacucho* published by Fondo de Cultura Económica (Colección Tierra Firme) in 2018 incorporates, as a comparative but also archival extension, the script of the play produced by Yuyachkani.
8. Susan Sontag, *Regarding the Pain of Others* (New York: Farrar, Straus, and Giroux, 2003).
9. Sontag, p. 125.
10. Castellanos Moya, *Insensatez*.
11. See Beatriz Cortez, who concludes that such aesthetics of cynicism represents in the end a 'failed project'; Beatriz Cortez, *Estética del cinismo: pasión y desencanto en la literatura centroamericana de posguerra* (Guatemala: F & G Editores, 2010), p. 26.
12. Castellanos Moya, *Insensatez*, p. 30.
13. Ibid, p. 30.
14. Ibid, pp. 38–39.
15. Ibid, p. 38.
16. Ibid, p. 143.
17. Ibid, p. 144.
18. Ibid, p. 149.
19. Ibid, pp. 150–55.
20. Ibid, p. 155.
21. Jean Franco, 'Alien to Modernity: The Rationalization of Discrimination', *A contracorriente: A Journal of Social History and Literature in Latin America*, 3.3 (2006), 1–16.
22. Franco, 'Alien to Modernity', p. 4.
23. Castellanos Moya, *Insensatez*, p. 151.
24. Ibid, p. 155.
25. Ortega, *Adios, Ayacucho*.
26. Gay Hawkins, *The Ethics of Waste* (Oxford: Rowman & Littlefield, 2006), p. vii.
27. Franco, 'Alien to Modernity', pp. 2, 13
28. Ibid, p. 16.
29. Héctor Turco, 'Adios Ayacucho: una novela de Julio Ortega', *Retablo*, 20 June 2009 (interview), <http://retabloayacuchano.blogspot.com/2009/07/adios-ayacucho-una-novela-de-julio.html>, [accessed 2 March 2018].
30. Sontag, *Regarding the Pain of Others*, p. 115.

PART III

Europe

CHAPTER 6

❖

Justice, Judicial Rhetoric, and the Reconstruction of Literature in Post-1945 Europe (Céline, Frisch, von Salomon)

Philippe Roussin

The links between justice and narrative literature stretch back to ancient times. Within the Western tradition, these connections were first formalized and codified within rhetoric, which, as we know, distinguishes between three types of discourse: epideictic rhetoric, which praises or blames, and deals with the present; deliberative (or political) rhetoric, for debating the fate and future of the City, and thus relates to the future; and judicial rhetoric, for use during trials at court. Judicial rhetoric seeks to establish the facts that occurred, and to ascertain their course and how they were linked; it bears on the circumstances of actions, and on the intentions of the agents involved. Its purpose is to accuse and to defend. It deals with the past and makes particular use of narrative (in rhetorical treatises, the lengthiest discussions about narration are in parts about judicial rhetoric). Within judicial rhetoric, narrative serves to answer the question of knowing what happened. It sets out facts, or, if they are obscure or controversial, offers a way of establishing them. It consists in saying everything that may throw light on them, or on everything which would imply that they occurred, irrespective of whether they caused any damage or harm, and irrespective of any importance one may wish to attach to them. Narrative is not only used to present facts and actions, but also to categorize them, indicating from what point of view and in which light they are to be considered.

In post-1945 Europe, with the Nuremberg trials and the trials to purge collaborators in France, the connection between literature, judicial rhetoric, and justice was seen in a new light, and acquired renewed topicality. Literature was flooded with questions of truth, facts, and responsibility for what had happened during the Second World War, thus venturing onto the terrain of law, justice, and ethics. In order to describe and try to gauge the meaning of these close connections between justice, judicial rhetoric, and post-1945 literature, I will be drawing on three literary works published almost simultaneously, at the very beginning of the 1950s, in Germany, France, Switzerland: Ernst von Salomon's *Der Fragebogen* (Germany, 1951, published in the United States as *The Questionnaire*, and in Britain as *The Answers*), Louis-Ferdinand Céline's *Féerie pour une autre fois* (France, 1952, published in English as *Fable for Another Time*), which I will dwell on in greater detail, and Max Frisch's *Stiller* (Switzerland, 1954, published in English as *I'm Not Stiller*). Each draws on a different genre. Ernst von Salomon's is comprised of the author's answers to the official canvass of 131 questions drawn up by the Americans at the end of the war to catch former Nazis in an infallible net of countless questions. It is autobiographical in nature. Céline's work belongs to the genre of self-fiction, which he uses to manipulate and rewrite history for revisionist ends, as we shall see. *Stiller* is a fictional narrative made up of Stiller's 'notes in prison', followed by a 'postscript by the prosecutor'. It seeks to establish and understand deeds and actions during the recent war attributed to Stiller, who refuses to recognize the identity — his identity — that he is called upon to answer for before the courts.

Each of these books faced and, in its own manner, confronted the question of judgement and responsibility, of how the responsibility for telling what had happened was linked to the possibility of so doing. Each author was involved in explaining and justifying, each in their own manner in the light of their personal experience. Ernst von Salomon, a former member of the German *Freikorps* who was closely associated with the conservative revolution, enjoyed great success as a writer as a young man during the Weimar Republic. He went on to oppose the Nazis and disappeared from the public eye, having published nothing since 1933. In *Der Fragebogen*, he uses the American questionnaire to recount his own life and to denounce both the Nazis and the victors. The work was perceived as an ambitious, ambiguous, and impenitent book. It became a bestseller and one of the most discussed books in the immediate post-war period in Germany. Céline is the only one of the three to have been indicted after the war. In June 1944 he fled Paris for Germany, then Denmark. He was investigated for collaboration, put on trial in France, and convicted *in absentia* in 1950. *Féerie pour une autre fois* is the first book Céline brought out in France on returning from his exile in Denmark, after his conviction and subsequent amnesty in 1951. The situation of the Swiss writer Max Frisch differed from that of Céline and von Salomon, since he was in no way targeted personally by the questions being asked by the justice system in the wake of the Second World War.

These works share a certain number of characteristics, of which I will list five. All three works unfold against the backdrop of the trials immediately after the war, explicitly in the case of von Salomon and Céline, implicitly in that of Frisch. They all borrow from the discursive model of judicial rhetoric. All three take an interrogation as their declared matrix. They are built on the same schema of succeeding questions and answers, an agonistic dialogue. Above and beyond the original and personal answers each provide, all three also address a further question, each in its own manner, once again: that of literature and fiction's right to exist in the wake of the Second World War, and the conditions for this existence.

While these three works all choose to use judicial rhetoric, they do so for very different, not to say opposing, literary and ideological projects. For von Salomon and Frisch, it was a matter of using the dramatization judicial rhetoric accommodated to devise an autonomy for literature and find a place for fiction in the aftermath of the war. For Céline, on the other hand, it was a matter of mobilizing literature and its stylistic, poetic, and rhetorical resources to turn these back against post-war justice, against its principles and rulings, including that against Céline himself.

In *Der Fragebogen*, as in *Stiller*, the narrative is presented as the response to a set of questions. Unlike the Americans who came up with the questions, the narrator is sceptical of the idea that any truth might issue from them:

> This questionnaire is not the first to occupy me, I have already encountered a certain number of questionnaires of the same kind or of similar nature. [...] Even during the period between 30 January 1933 and 6 May 1945, [...] I had many questionnaires before my eyes, and I can state that I always read them attentively. [...] Reading all these questionnaires has invariably produced the same effect on me, has produced a certain number of feelings, the first and strongest of which is a penetrating sense of unease. [...] How is one to understand the existence of this questionnaire other than as a modern attempt to incite me to examine my conscience? [...] The Allied Military Government [...] sent this questionnaire to my home, starting immediately and abruptly, like an investigating magistrate in front of a criminal, with an onslaught of 131 questions. Coldly and tersely, it demands of me nothing less than the truth. [...] The abundant questions require abundant answers. [...] The way this questionnaire proceeds ignores the defense; but precisely because nobody knows what it is driving at, no one can ascertain that its methods do not conceal the unforeseen possibility of bringing forth the truth. I wish to serve this possibility in the hope that many others will be similarly tempted, with the quantity of answers generating a quality of description about what happened in our country which is approximately true. But then the questions in this questionnaire are not addressed to my conscience, but to my memory![1]

Stiller's notes in prison express similar doubts and questions:

> So they want me to tell them my life story. Nothing but the plain, unvarnished truth. A pad of white paper, a fountain pen with ink that I can have refilled whenever I like at the expense of the state, and a little good will — what's going to be left of truth when I get at it with my fountain pen? And if I just stick to the facts, says my counsel, we will get truth in the corner. [...] Where could truth escape to if I write it down?[2]

In Frisch and von Salomon, the narratives apparently agree to engage with the judicial genre's game of exchange and argumentation, each text overtly presenting itself as an answer to a set of questions; yet as they progress, they seem to lose sight of the initial reasons occasioning them (establishing the facts, acknowledging responsibility or an identity, and reaching a truth). To judicial rhetoric's finite game of alternating statements, seeking to reach an end and thus a conclusion enabling a judgement to be issued, these literary narratives oppose the principle of incompletion and uncertainty. This provides a way of indicating that narrative is not discourse about a past composed of finite questions, nor is literature discourse about closed questions. In response to the judicial issue of justifying speech or a given utterance, these works answer that any literary or fictional narrative inevitably lacks justification. They emphasize that narrative does not have to supply a reason for narrative, any more than it has to prove anything at all.

Despite taking the form of a reply, *Stiller* and *Der Fragebogen* evade the finite game of questions and answers. While taking judicial rhetoric as their discursive model, they oppose the singular and incomplete version of events inherent to narrative to the finite and ordered nature of any discourse targeting truth and judgement; they tell of the lack of closure of any singular discourse. Confronted with the enjoinder to speak the truth, the imperative to be sincere or obtain a confession, as posited by the judicial genre on which they are modelled, they reconstruct a place for narrative, a place that is distinct from that which the court holds for judicial discourse.

They thus enable literature and fiction to exist once again in the mismatch that they, as narratives, open up vis-à-vis the question: the length of the answer provided is disproportionate to the brevity of the question asked. Thus on being adjured to state his nationality, von Salomon provides an answer running over thirty pages explaining why he is Prussian, not German. An autobiography cannot be contained within the official canvas afforded by 131 questions. The literary response inevitably overflows the limits of the answer to the question asked by the justice system. Literature is thus comprised of excess in comparison to the question. It is both an inadequate and a disproportionate response. *Stiller* and *Der Fragebogen* take the matrix of judicial rhetoric to say afresh that a literary response is incommensurable with the judicial question, to express the inevitable and growing distance of the narrative from the questions to which it owes its existence. In exceeding the closed game of accusation and defence, of questions and answers, these works pave the way to a freedom and autonomy for literature in the aftermath of the war, opening up the space of fiction. By staging the discrepancy between the answer and the question, they also raise the issue of the incompatibility between private discourse and public discourse.

Céline's use of the forms of judicial rhetoric to serve fiction in *Féerie pour une autre fois* is guided by an entirely different logic. As of 1944 and the end of the German occupation of France, against the backdrop of purges and the attendant judicial investigations, the French literary field was recomposed around a set of moral and ethical issues; these issues, centred around the great judicial division into *facta* and *verba*, pertained to the author's responsibility, his or her right to err, together with the very status of literature. In 1944 France, writers and journalists who had collaborated could be tried and found guilty of conniving with the enemy and harming the state's external security (based on articles 75 and 86 of the French Penal Code). Additionally, the ordinance of 26 August 1944 introduced a sentence of *dégradation nationale* [being stripped of rank] for all those guilty of *indignité nationale* [national disgrace]: this applied to the publication of articles, pamphlets, or books in favour of the enemy, of collaboration with enemy, of racism, or of totalitarian doctrines.[3] In response to those who voiced surprise that writers could be put on trial, and who countered calls for justice with the need to heal fractures at whatever cost, Sartre answered that an author's status as a *magister* brought with it a responsibility. In October 1945, in his presentation to the new journal, *Les Temps Modernes*, he wrote:

> All writers of bourgeois origin have known the temptations of irresponsibility: for a century, it has been a traditional aspect of a career in letters. [...] Today things have reached the point where we have seen writers, who were blamed or punished for having lent their pen to the Germans, appear painfully surprised. 'What? Is what one writes a form of commitment?' they say. We do not want to be ashamed of writing, and we do not want to spout empty words.[4]

Sartre thus indicated that there was no reason for literature to stand exempt from the morals and conception of what was right which applied to an individual's and a society's ordinary life. There could be no exceptional status. In *Qu'est-ce que la littérature?*, one of the lessons he drew from the war was that literature had a social responsibility, together with a moral and political function. Moving from aesthetic to moral and political concerns after 1945, from the issue of contingency to that of freedom, he held that the freedom to write was nothing without the freedom of citizens, and that literature could not go hand in hand with all regimes.

Céline was one of the writers to be regularly denounced in the Resistance movement's underground press for having contributed to collaborationist newspapers, for his public stances under German occupation, and for his antisemitic pamphlets written before and during the war, between 1937 and 1941. In June 1944 he was forced to flee Paris, and after spending time with the colony of French exiles and collaborators who had joined the French head of state, Philippe Pétain, in Sigmaringen, in Germany, he reached Denmark in March 1945. In April 1945, the French courts found him guilty of treason and conniving with the enemy. He was arrested in Copenhagen in December 1945, where he was imprisoned and hospitalized, before being released, but not extradited, in June 1947, and convicted *in absentia* by the French courts in February 1950, sentenced to one year in prison and declared a national disgrace. On being amnestied in 1951, he returned to France, where he published *Féerie pour une autre fois* in 1952. This novel was an initiative to exculpate and rehabilitate its author and to reopen his trial.

The writing of the novel coincided with the years when the author was under judicial investigation. Céline worked on *Féerie pour une autre fois* at the same time as he was preparing his legal defence. He started writing the novel in 1946, in his Danish prison, in parallel with the memoranda of defence he was putting together for his legal counsel. There were many close, not to say inextricable, links between the literary material and the legal material. It would seem that the literary text and his defence were initially one and the same. Having read the unusually numerous successive versions of the text (there were nearly ten), one may say that the novel was entirely extracted and built from the legal material, which he then needed to rearrange and fictionalize. It may be viewed as a vast excrescence from the memoranda of defence, and read as an immense work to rejig, edit, and rewrite the legal material, not only for literary ends but also so as to refute, exculpate, and justify.

As of late 1945, Céline started to respond to the various charges and accusations brought against him, in a series of memoranda, letters, and factums he prepared for his counsel and which were written for the court. He set out a certain number of arguments which emerge virtually unchanged (other than stylistically) in his novel. Against accusations presenting him as an antisemitic *propagandist*, he sought to define himself as a *writer.* Céline knew exactly what he was doing by this: it was important for him to be judged as a *writer*, rather than as a journalist or pamphleteer, for purge courts made a distinction between journalists, who had lent or sold their pen to the enemy, and writers who, while having published in journals, had used their talent for strictly 'literary' ends. The sentences applicable to 'journalists' were therefore stiffer than those applicable to 'writers'. Confronted with a legal system which judged collaborators as having betrayed the mother country, he pointed out that he was a former combatant who had been wounded during the First World War, presenting himself as a patriot and pacifist. To counter the charges against his antisemitic stances during the occupation, he sought to present his pamphlets as texts written and published *before* the war. This argument was made so that he would be judged for a crime of opinion, not for having encouraged antisemitic persecution in occupied France.

The many preparatory versions of the work enable us to follow the hesitations step-by-step, the successive adjustments in a rewriting which sought to present the accused in a better light than in the court cases, to exonerate him of all responsibility, to sidestep the problem of guilt and, ultimately, transform the accused into a victim. The first draft of the novel was written in prison in March 1946, scribbled down in the school notebooks Céline filled between answering the accusations brought against him, as indicated by the lists of names and brevity of the sentences jotted down in telegraphic style. These seem guided by the need to prevent his forgetting, to recall events, and at the same time driven by the urgent need to be able to provide responses to the questions asked during interrogations by the Danish police, to which the text alludes repeatedly. The various stages in the legal proceedings (with the sequence of statements specific to each moment: the categorizing of the facts, the investigation, the bringing of charges, the case for the prosecution, the defence, then the verdict, amnesty, and overruling of this judgement in December 1951) are present in all the versions which, from 1946 to 1952, were written at the same time as investigations were proceeding for the trial. Each version presents and constitutes the witness statements, declarations, and testimonies which were reworked, revised, and corrected by the writer standing trial.

The text of *Féerie pour une autre fois*, published in 1952, is posterior to the author's trial and thus occurs in its *aftermath.* It is intended as a counter-trial calling for the judgement against him to be declared iniquitous. Céline explicitly goes over the collaboration trials which had occupied the public sphere since France had been liberated, calling on literary and public opinion as his witness. While making extensive use of the discursive form of judicial rhetoric, the narrative of *Féerie pour une autre fois* deflects it from its purpose and turns it back against itself. It is not legal testimony. Its objective is not to establish facts; on the contrary, it seeks to render the reality of facts unrecognizable, and the reasons for the judgement iniquitous or incomprehensible. Thus the incipit explicitly proclaims:

> The horror of reality! All places, names, characters, situations set forth in this novel are imaginary! Absolutely imaginary! No relationship whatsoever with any reality![5]

The narrative drains judicial rhetoric of its meaning, pushing it towards a rhetoric devoid of purpose, transforming it into a discursive machine, a game, a masquerade even. Thus ridiculed, this rhetoric enables the novelist to convey the accused's point of view from his own chosen terrain, that of literature, against the judges and the thing judged.

It is this rehashing, displacement, and scrambling of judicial rhetoric that enables the writer both to deny the accusations against him, and to undertake a veritable rewriting of history. This perverted rhetoric enables Céline to play with the legal charges brought against him, with the facts being judged, with the past, with history, with historical truth. Coming in the aftermath of the trial, the book allows Céline to bring about a change in tone. The narrative has shifted from the dynamic of defence to that of accusation. Carnivalesque self-fiction allows everything that is forbidden in court: it authorizes all changes in place, all swapping of roles; it enables the counsel for the defence to become that for the prosecution, transforming the accused into the accuser, turning the culprit into a victim.

The case set out by *Féerie pour une autre fois* targets the exceptional courts set up during the purge in France, their way of functioning, and the difficulties they encountered in categorizing crimes and infringements. Céline draws on the arsenal available to Vichy supporters, to those standing trial, and to supporters of reconciliation, taking up the argument that the severity of the applicable sentences is disproportionate to the minor nature of the infringements committed. He protested vigorously against his conviction. Among the indictments brought against him, he singled out those for which he knew he was innocent. He exaggerated the charges brought against him to the point of making them implausible, such as, for instance, Sartre's accusation of treachery and venality in *Portrait de l'antisémite* in December 1945.[6] Hyperbolic distortion of certain accusations enabled him to deny other more established facts, and, ultimately, to plead not guilty to the crimes he stood accused of: 'In what domain precisely have I collaborated with the enemy? Antisemitism? No [...]. Propaganda? No. So in what?' (defence memorandum, 6 November 1946). The case for the defence shaded progressively into a case for the prosecution.

Mikhail Bakhtin's dialogism teaches us that any narrative, far from being the totality it seems to present, is in fact constituted in relation to some other, always possible narrative; further, it is not distinct from the alternative it constitutes in relation to this other narrative, which it suspends and interrupts. The narrator of 1952 knows that for his *version* of history to be accredited, he has to situate his discourse among other discourses, state how it is linked to them, he needs to enter into contention and compete with other narratives: the accounts by those who had survived the camps, the testimony heard in other courts in France and elsewhere, the crime reports covering the purge trials, the accounts of those he calls the 'victors', and so on. The accused accuses while at the same time rejecting these other witnesses and their accounts, putting forward the idea that the history to which they bear witness did not take place:

> And Buchenwald? Drat!... — You haven't been there either. [...] It's no worse than Auschwitz! It's not much alongside Dora! You've never been to Dora! I never wanted anyone to go there![7]

He puts forward the revisionist argument that the account to which survivors bear witness is incompatible with the fact that they *survived*. What the narrative of *Féerie pour une autre fois* confronts and opposes is, precisely, all the words and testimony from the trials and camps, received as proof in the courts.

Just as Céline had gone over his defence memoranda, he went through the text of his novel before handing it over to his publisher. On the typescript, he *crossed out* the names of the Nazi camps which had appeared in the early versions of his texts, replacing them with the banal names of several German towns: 'Dora' became 'Cassel' in the final text of the work published in 1952, 'Buchenwald' was changed to 'Lünebourg', 'Auschwitz' was replaced by 'Augsbourg', while 'Dachau' disappeared behind 'Claunau'.[8] The narrative thus provides a largely imaginary and unrecognizable geography of Germany. Run-of-the-mill German town names replace those which had come to symbolize the camps, and which had received great publicity on being liberated. In thus removing the camps' names, Céline's writing performs the verbal equivalent of the Nazis' dismantling and destruction of the installations on evacuating the death camps. To act in defence of the accused, who claims to be innocent, the narrative cannot do other than deform and rewrite history. The formidable language machinery of *Féerie* is assembled by sidestepping the past, resulting in an *account under erasure* as presented in the final text.

The narrative of *Féerie* is rhythmed by the alternation between questions and answers. Despite this continual interplay with the trial form, it does not seek to establish what is right and what is not, or decide who is right and who is wrong. It seeks to go over the head of and against the judges, addressing a public and a readership it endeavours to set up in judgment of the solely verbal performance by the writer. It takes judicial rhetoric, a means for administering proof, and deflects it towards a goal detached from its entire purpose — namely establishing facts. Eloquence is passed off as skilful jousting, engendering all the artifices and means of convincing. The duel between defence counsel and prosecutor plays a sizeable part. It accentuates the theatrical, playful, and agonistic dimension, for it seeks to reduce the reality and significance of the trial to mere role-playing. This is why the narrator can take up several positions, play several contradictory roles, take in turn the place of the accused and of the accuser, the defence and the prosecutor. He responds using the terms of the attack. He addresses judge and reader at the same time. He asks questions which he answers himself; he raises objections he immediately refutes. He thus gives full rein to the 'archaic' aspect of the trial, which, as Johan Huizinga notes in *Homo ludens*, transpires whenever 'it is not the meticulously deliberated juristic argument that tips the balance, but the most withering and excoriating invective. The agon in this case consists almost exclusively in the endeavour of each party to exceed the other in choice vituperation.'[9] And indeed, *Féerie pour une autre fois* offers many examples of choice vituperation, directed against those Céline terms the 'illusionists of history' ('prestidigitateurs d'Histoire').[10]

Céline's novel raises several difficult problems, stemming from the relationship the text builds up between fiction and self-fiction, literature and justice, history and historical revisionism. Its singularity resides in the very pronounced and constantly maintained inner tension between a literary *game* seeking to ridicule justice and transform it into an object of laughter — to strip it of all significance and all exemplary and historical value — and the *reality* of the trials (the trial of the author, the post-war trials in France, and the trials of Nazi war criminals in Germany) as the place where justice is dispensed. The narrative does not here serve the enterprise of justice, nor does it seek any truth. It mixes judicial rhetoric with fiction. Unlike Max Frisch and Ernst von Salomon, Céline refuses all knowledge of how the law, justice, and the post-war trials in France and Europe helped shape a new historical conscience.

Notes to Chapter 6

1. Ernst von Salomon, *The Answers to the 131 Questions in the Allied Military Government 'Fragebogen'*, trans. from the German by Constantine Fitzgibbon (London: Putnam, 1954), pp. 3–8.
2. Max Frisch, *I'm Not Stiller* [1954], translated from the German by Michael Bullock (London: Penguin, 1961), p. 15.
3. See Gisèle Sapiro, *La Guerre des écrivains* (Paris: Fayard, 1999); on legislation during the purge, see Henry Rousso, *Vichy: l'événement, la mémoire, l'histoire* (Paris: Gallimard, 2001), pp. 489–677, and Marc-Olivier Baruch (ed.), *Une poignée de misérables: l'épuration de la société française après la Seconde Guerre mondiale* (Paris: Fayard, 2003).
4. Jean-Paul Sartre, 'Présentation des *Temps modernes*' [October 1945], in *Situations II* (Paris: Gallimard, 1975), p. 209. Translated by Adrian Morfee.
5. Louis-Ferdinand Céline, *Fable for Another Time*, translated from the French by Mary Hudson (Lincoln: University of Nebraska Press, 2003), p. xxxvii.
6. Jean-Paul Sartre, 'Portrait de l'antisémite' [December 1945], in *Situations II*, pp. 254–85; see Louis-Ferdinand Céline, *Féerie pour une autre fois I*, in Id., *Romans IV*, p. 94, my translation.
7. Louis-Ferdinand Céline, *Féerie pour une autre fois I*, in Id., *Romans IV*, version C, August–November 1948, pp. 870–71, my translation.
8. Louis-Ferdinand Céline, *Féerie pour une autre fois I*, in Id., *Romans IV*, p. 31, p. 32 and p. 66.
9. J. Huizinga, *Homo ludens: A Study of the Play-Element in Culture* (Abingdon: Routledge and Kegan Paul, 1949), pp. 158–72.
10. Louis-Ferdinand Céline, *Féerie pour une autre fois I*, in Id., *Romans IV*, p. 66, my translation.

CHAPTER 7

Justice, rhétorique judiciaire et reconstruction de la littérature en Europe après 1945 (Céline, Frisch, von Salomon)

Philippe Roussin

Les liens entre la justice et la littérature narrative sont anciens. Au sein de la tradition occidentale, ils ont été une première fois formalisés et codifiés dans le cadre de la rhétorique. Celle-ci, on le sait, distinguait trois grands genres de discours: le genre épidictique, qui traite du présent, loue et blâme, le genre délibératif (ou politique) qui permet de débattre du sort et de l'avenir de la cité et porte donc sur le futur et le genre judiciaire. Mobilisé dans l'enceinte du tribunal à l'occasion des procès, le genre judiciaire vise à établir les faits qui ont eu lieu, à connaître leur déroulement et leur enchaînement; il porte sur les circonstances des actions, comme sur les intentions des agents qui y ont pris part. Il a pour fonction d'accuser et de défendre. Traitant du passé, il fait particulièrement appel au récit (c'est dans les parties réservées à la rhétorique judiciaire des traités de rhétorique que l'on trouve les plus longs développements consacrés à la narration). Le récit, dans le cadre de la rhétorique judiciaire, a pour fonction de répondre à la question de savoir ce qui s'est passé. Il expose les faits et sert à les établir quand ils sont obscurs ou controversés. Il consiste à dire tout ce qui peut les éclairer ou tout ce qui donnera à entendre qu'ils se sont produits, qu'ils soient cause de dommage ou de préjudice, qu'ils aient eu ou non l'importance qu'on veut leur prêter. Le récit sert non seulement à présenter les faits et les actions mais aussi à les qualifier: il indique de quel point de vue et sous quel jour il faut les considérer.

Après 1945, en Europe avec les procès de Nuremberg, en France avec les procès de l'Epuration, les liens entre la littérature, la rhétorique judiciaire et la justice ont connu une nouvelle actualité et sont apparus sous un jour nouveau. Les questions de la vérité, des faits et de la responsabilité de ce qui s'était passé pendant la seconde Guerre mondiale ont envahi la littérature tandis que la littérature s'avançait sur le terrain du droit, de la justice et de l'éthique. Pour décrire et essayer d'approcher le sens de cette proximité de la justice, de la rhétorique judiciaire et de la littérature après 1945, je m'appuierai sur trois œuvres littéraires qui ont paru au tout début des années 1950, presque en même temps, en Allemagne, en France et en Suisse: *Le Questionnaire* d'Ernst von Salomon (Allemagne, 1951), *Féerie pour une autre fois* de Louis-Ferdinand Céline (France, 1952), texte sur lequel je m'attarderai plus particulièrement, et *Stiller* de Max Frisch (Suisse, 1954). Les trois textes relèvent de genres littéraires différents. Le livre d'Ernst von Salomon est constitué des réponses fournies par l'auteur au canevas officiel de 131 questions élaboré par les Américains pour prendre les anciens nazis dans la nasse infaillible d'innombrables questions, à la fin de la guerre. Il est de nature autobiographique. L'œuvre de Céline appartient au genre de l'autofiction, qui devait servir à son auteur autant à fictionnaliser l'expérience vécue qu'à manipuler et à réécrire l'histoire, à des fins révisionnistes, on le verra. *Stiller* est un récit fictionnel fait des 'notes de Stiller en prison', suivi d'une 'postface du procureur'. La narration cherche à connaitre et à établir ce qu'avaient été, pendant la guerre qui venait de s'achever, les faits et les gestes de Stiller, qui refusait de reconnaître l'identité — la sienne — dont la justice lui demandait de répondre.

Ces trois œuvres faisaient face et étaient, chacune à leur manière, confrontées à la question du jugement et de la responsabilité, du lien entre la responsabilité et la possibilité de dire et de raconter ce qui s'était passé. Chacun des trois auteurs était engagé dans cette entreprise d'explication et de justification, de manière particulière et compte tenu de son expérience personnelle. Ancien des corps francs allemands et proche de la Révolution conservatrice, Ernst von Salomon est un écrivain qui avait connu très jeune un grand succès à l'époque de la République de Weimar. Opposé aux nazis, il s'était fait oublier et n'avait rien publié après 1933. Dans *Le Questionnaire*, il se sert du canevas du fameux questionnaire américain pour raconter sa propre vie et dénoncer les nazis aussi bien que les vainqueurs. L'œuvre est perçue comme un livre d'impénitence, ambitieux et ambigu. Devenu un bestseller, le livre sera l'un des plus discutés de l'immédiat après-guerre en Allemagne. Céline est le seul des trois auteurs à avoir été inculpé par la justice de l'après-guerre. Il a fui Paris en juin 1944 pour l'Allemagne puis le Danemark, il est poursuivi par la justice de l'Epuration, qui instruit son procès en France et qui le condamnera en 1950 par contumace. *Féerie pour une autre fois* est le premier roman que l'auteur fait paraître en France, à son retour d'exil au Danemark, après son jugement et l'amnistie dont il a bénéficié en 1951. La situation de Max Frisch, écrivain suisse, est différente de celle de Céline et d'Ernst von Salomon: il n'est aucunement, visé, à titre personnel, par les questions alors posées par la justice au sortir de la seconde guerre mondiale.

Ces œuvres ont en commun un certain nombre de traits. J'en relève cinq. Toutes trois ont pour arrière fond les vagues de procès de l'immédiate après-guerre, de manière explicite chez Ernst von Salomon et chez Céline et implicite, chez Frisch. Elles empruntent toutes au modèle de discours qui est celui de la rhétorique judiciaire. Elles ont toutes trois pour matrice déclarée la forme de l'interrogatoire. Elles sont construites sur le même schéma de la succession d'une question et d'une réponse, d'un dialogue de type agonistique. Au delà des réponses particulières et originales qu'elles fournissent, les trois œuvres affrontent encore, chacune à leur manière, une autre question: celle du droit à exister pour la littérature et la fiction, au sortir de la seconde guerre mondiale, et des conditions de cette existence.

Dans ces trois œuvres, le choix de la même rhétorique judiciaire devait être mis au service de projets littéraires et idéologiques très différents sinon opposés. Chez von Salomon comme chez Max Frisch, il s'agissait d'inventer et de trouver, à partir de la dramatisation que permettait la rhétorique judiciaire, une autonomie de la littérature et une place pour la fiction au sortir de la guerre. Chez Céline, il était plutôt question de mobiliser la littérature et les ressources littéraires (stylistiques, poétiques, rhétoriques), pour les tourner et les faire jouer contre la justice de l'après-guerre, contre ses principes comme ses jugements, y compris celui qui concernait au premier chef l'écrivain.

Dans *Le Questionnaire* comme dans *Stiller*, le récit se donnait pour la réponse à un ensemble de questions. Que des questions ainsi posées et des réponses qui leur étaient apportées puisse découler une vérité, cette idée des rédacteurs américains du questionnaire devait susciter le scepticisme du narrateur:

> Ce questionnaire n'est pas le premier qui m'occupe, j'ai déjà eu affaire à un certain nombre de questionnaires du même genre ou d'un caractère semblable. [...] Même à l'époque comprise entre le 30 janvier 1933 et le 6 mai 1945, [...] j'ai eu devant les yeux de nombreux questionnaires et je puis certifier que je les ai toujours lus attentivement. [...] La lecture de tous ces questionnaires a, chez moi, invariablement produit le même effet: elle a provoqué un certain nombre de sensations dont la première — et la plus forte — était celle d'un malaise pénétrant. [...] Comment comprendre l'existence de ce questionnaire sinon comme une tentative moderne de m'inciter à un examen de conscience? [...] Le Gouvernement Militaire Allié [...] m'envoie le questionnaire à mon domicile et commence tout de suite et brusquement, comme un juge d'instruction devant un criminel, par un flot de 131 questions. Froidement et sèchement, il exige de moi rien moins que la vérité. [...] L'abondance des questions requiert l'abondance des réponses. [...] La procédure de ce questionnaire ignore la défense, mais précisément parce que personne ne sait où il veut en venir, personne ne peut affirmer que ses méthodes ne cachent pas la possibilité imprévue de faire apparaître toute la vérité. Je veux servir cette possibilité dans l'espoir que beaucoup d'autres se laisseront tenter comme moi, afin que de la quantité de réponses résulte la qualité d'un tableau approximativement vrai de ce qui s'est passé dans notre pays. Mais alors les questions de ce questionnaire ne s'adressent pas à ma conscience, mais à ma mémoire![1]

Les notes écrites en prison par Stiller faisaient état de doutes et d'interrogations semblables:

> Il faut que je raconte! Que je raconte la vérité de ma vie, rien que la pure et simple vérité! Un bloc de papier blanc, un stylo et de l'encre que je peux faire renouveler à tout moment aux frais de l'Etat avec, de plus un peu de bonne volonté: elle n'aura pas d'autre choix la vérité, si je la confie à ma plume! Et si je m'en tiens simplement et convenablement aux faits, estime mon avocat, nous aurons au moins cerné la vérité [...] Comment échapperait-elle si je la consigne par écrit?[2]

Alors même qu'il semblait accepter d'entrer dans le jeu de l'échange et de l'argumentation du genre judiciaire et qu'il se présentait, ostensiblement, comme une réponse à un ensemble de questions, le récit, chez Frisch et chez von Salomon, devait, à mesure qu'il se développait, perdre de vue les motifs premiers qui en étaient la cause et l'origine (l'établissement des faits, la reconnaissance d'une responsabilité ou l'aveu d'une identité, l'obtention d'une vérité). Au jeu fini des tours de parole du discours de la rhétorique judiciaire visant à parvenir à une fin et à une conclusion et à permettre d'énoncer un jugement, le récit littéraire opposait ainsi un principe d'inachèvement et d'incertitude. C'était par là indiquer que le récit n'était pas un discours portant sur le passé de questions finies et que la littérature n'était pas non plus un discours portant sur des questions fermées. A la question, posée par la justice, de la justification de la parole ou de tel énoncé, ces œuvres répondaient par l'inévitable défaut de justification de tout récit, littéraire et fictionnel. Elles soulignaient que le récit n'avait pas à donner la raison du récit et qu'il n'avait pas non plus à faire preuve de quoi que ce soit.

En même temps que ces récits se donnaient la forme d'une réponse, *Stiller* et *Le Questionnaire* se dérobaient au jeu fini des questions et des réponses. Tout en prenant pour modèle discursif la rhétorique judiciaire, ils opposaient la version singulière et inachevée des faits qu'était tout récit à la finitude et à l'ordre d'un discours visant la vérité et le jugement, et ils disaient l'absence de clôture de tout discours singulier. Face à l'injonction de vérité, à l'impératif de sincérité ou à l'obtention de l'aveu posé en principe par le genre judiciaire qui leur servait de modèle, ils reconstruisaient un lieu pour le récit, distinct du lieu que le tribunal pouvait être pour le discours judiciaire.

Ils faisaient exister à nouveau la littérature et la fiction dans l'écart qu'ils creusaient ainsi, en tant que récits, par rapport à la question: la longueur de la réponse fournie était disproportionnée par rapport à la brièveté de la question posée. C'est ainsi que, mis en demeure de décliner sa nationalité, Salomon fournissait une réponse de trente pages pour expliquer pourquoi il était prussien et non pas allemand. L'autobiographie ne pouvait être contenue dans les limites d'un canevas officiel de 131 questions. La réponse littéraire débordait inévitablement les limites de la réponse à la question posée par la justice. La littérature était ainsi faite d'un excès par rapport à la question. Elle était une réponse à la fois disproportionnée et inadéquate. *Stiller* et *Le Questionnaire* se saisissaient de la matrice de la rhétorique judiciaire pour dire, à nouveaux frais, l'incommensurabilité de la réponse littéraire et de la question judiciaire, la distance inévitable et croissante du récit par rapport aux questions auxquelles il devait son existence. Débordant le jeu fermé de l'accusation et de la défense, des questions et des réponses, ces œuvres permettaient de retrouver une liberté et une autonomie de la littérature au sortir de la guerre et lui ouvraient l'espace de la fiction. En mettant en scène l'inadéquation de la réponse par rapport à la question, elles soulevaient également le problème de l'incompatibilité du discours privé et du discours public.

La manière dont Céline devait mettre les formes de la rhétorique judiciaire au service de la fiction dans *Féerie pour une autre fois* obéissait à une tout autre logique.

A partir de 1944 et de la fin de l'Occupation allemande, le champ littéraire s'était reconstruit et réorganisé, en France, dans le cadre de l'Epuration et de la justice de l'Epuration, autour d'un ensemble de questions morales et éthiques qui engageaient, à travers la grande division juridique entre *facta* et *verba*, la responsabilité de l'écrivain, son droit à l'erreur et le statut même de la littérature. Dans la France de 1944, les écrivains et les journalistes qui avaient collaboré pouvaient être mis en accusation et condamnés pour intelligence avec l'ennemi et atteinte à la sûreté extérieure de l'Etat (sur la base des articles 75 et 86 du Code pénal). L'ordonnance du 26 août 1944 instaurait, en outre, une peine de dégradation nationale pour tous ceux qui s'étaient rendus coupables d'indignité nationale: elle visait le fait d'avoir publié des articles, des brochures ou des livres en faveur de l'ennemi, de la collaboration avec l'ennemi, du racisme ou des doctrines totalitaires.[3] A ceux qui s'étonnaient que l'on juge des écrivains et qui opposaient alors à la justice le souci d'apaisement à tout prix, Sartre devait répondre que la responsabilité de l'écrivain était un attribut du magistère qu'il exerçait. En octobre 1945, dans sa présentation de la nouvelle revue *Les Temps Modernes*, il écrivait:

> Tous les écrivains d'origine bourgeoise ont connu la tentation de l'irresponsabilité: depuis un siècle, elle est de tradition dans la carrière des lettres [...] Aujourd'hui les choses en sont venues à ce point que l'on a vu des écrivains, blâmés ou punis parce qu'ils ont loué leur plume aux Allemands, faire montre d'un étonnement douloureux. 'Eh quoi? disent-ils, ça engage donc, ce qu'on écrit?' Nous ne voulons pas avoir honte d'écrire et nous n'avons pas envie de parler pour ne rien dire.[4]

Sartre indiquait ainsi qu'il n'existait aucune raison pour que la littérature s'exempte des morales et des conceptions du bien qui avaient cours dans la vie ordinaire des individus et des sociétés. Il ne pouvait y avoir pour elle de statut d'exception. Dans *Qu'est-ce que la littérature?*, il faisait de la responsabilité sociale de la littérature et de sa fonction morale et politique, une leçon de la guerre. Passant, après 1945, des préoccupations esthétiques à des préoccupations morales et politiques, de la problématique de la contingence à celle de la liberté, il soutenait que la liberté d'écrire n'était rien sans la liberté du citoyen et que la littérature ne pouvait s'accompagner de tous les régimes.

Céline figurait parmi les écrivains régulièrement dénoncés par la presse clandestine de la Résistance pour sa participation aux journaux de la collaboration, pour ses prises de position publiques sous l'occupation allemande et pour ses pamphlets antisémites écrits avant et pendant la guerre, entre 1937 et 1941. Il devait fuir Paris, dès juin 1944, et rejoindre le Danemark en mars 1945, après avoir fait partie de la colonie des exilés et collaborateurs français regroupés en Allemagne, à Sigmaringen, autour du chef de l'Etat français, Philippe Pétain. En avril 1945, la justice française devait l'inculper de trahison et d'intelligence avec l'ennemi. Arrêté à Copenhague en décembre 1945, emprisonné, hospitalisé puis élargi en juin 1947, mais non extradé, il était condamné par contumace, par la justice française, en février 1950, à un an de prison et déclaré en état d'indignité nationale. Amnistié en 1951, il devait revenir en France et publier, en 1952, *Féerie pour une autre fois*. Le roman se voulait une entreprise de disculpation et de réhabilitation de l'auteur en même temps qu'une réouverture de son procès.

L'écriture du roman devait coïncider avec les années d'instruction du procès de l'auteur. Céline a, en effet, travaillé à *Féerie pour une autre fois* en même temps qu'il préparait sa défense en justice. Il avait commencé de rédiger le roman, en 1946, dans sa prison danoise parallèlement aux mémoires en défense qu'il constituait alors pour son avocat. Les liens entre la matière littéraire et la matière juridique étaient nombreux et étroits, sinon inextricables. A l'origine, texte de défense et texte littéraire semblent, d'ailleurs, n'avoir fait qu'un. On peut dire, après avoir lu les versions successives du texte, inhabituellement nombreuses (près de dix), que le roman a été comme entièrement dégagé, extrait de et construit à partir de la matière juridique qu'il devait ensuite réarranger et fictionnaliser. On peut le considérer comme une gigantesque excroissance des mémoires en défense et le lire comme un immense travail de montage et de déplacement, de réécriture de la matière juridique à des fins non seulement littéraires mais aussi à des fins de réfutation, de disculpation et de justification.

Dès la fin de 1945, Céline a commencé de répondre aux différentes charges et accusations retenues contre lui, dans un ensemble de mémoires, de lettres et de factums qu'il rédigeait pour son avocat et qui étaient destinés à la justice et à ses juges. Il y développait un certain nombre d'arguments, qui devaient se retrouver, presque inchangés sinon stylistiquement, dans le roman. Face aux accusations qui le présentaient comme un *propagandiste* antisémite, il entendait se définir comme un *écrivain*. Céline savait parfaitement ce qu'il faisait en revendiquant une telle identité. Il était important pour lui de pouvoir être jugé comme *écrivain* et non comme journaliste ou publiciste: la justice de l'Epuration distinguait, en effet, entre les journalistes, qui avaient été engagés, avaient prêté ou vendu leur plume à l'ennemi, et les écrivains qui, tout en ayant publié dans les revues, s'en étaient tenus à un usage strictement 'littéraire' de leur talent. Les peines encourues par les 'journalistes' étaient plus sévères que les peines encourues par les 'écrivains'. Face à une justice qui jugeait les collaborateurs comme des traîtres à la Patrie, il rappelait sa qualité d'ancien combattant et de blessé de la première Guerre mondiale, et il se présentait comme un patriote et comme un pacifiste. Contre les charges visant ses prises de position antisémites pendant l'Occupation, l'accusé s'efforçait de présenter ses pamphlets comme des textes écrits et publiés avant-guerre. L'argument devait lui permettre d'être jugé pour délit d'opinion et non pour encouragement à la persécution antisémite dans la France Occupée.

Les nombreuses versions préparatoires de l'œuvre permettent de suivre, pas à pas, les tâtonnements et les ajustements successifs d'un travail de réécriture qui visait à présenter l'accusé sous un meilleur jour que ne le faisait la justice, à l'exonérer de toute responsabilité, à contourner et à éviter le problème de la culpabilité et à transformer, finalement, l'accusé en une victime. Ecrite en prison en mars 1946, notée dans ces cahiers d'écolier que l'écrivain noircit alors, entre deux réponses aux accusations portées contre lui, la première esquisse du roman, comme le montrent les listes de noms et la brièveté des phrases rédigées en style télégraphique qu'elle contient, semble guidée par le besoin de lutter contre l'oubli et de se remémorer les événements, en même temps qu'elle paraît commandée par la nécessité et l'urgence de pouvoir fournir les réponses aux questions posées lors des interrogatoires de la police danoise auquel le texte ne cesse de faire allusion. Les différentes étapes de la procédure judiciaire (avec l'enchaînement des discours propres à chacun de ses moments: qualification des faits, instruction, accusation, réquisitoire, plaidoirie, verdict, amnistie et cassation de ce jugement en décembre 1951) se retrouvent dans toutes les versions qui, de 1946 à 1952, s'écrivent en même temps que progresse l'instruction du procès. Elles livrent et constituent ainsi autant de témoignages, de déclarations et de dépositions remaniés, revus et corrigés par l'écrivain accusé.

Postérieur au procès de son auteur, le texte de *Féerie* publié en 1952, intervient dans un *après coup*. Il se veut un contre-procès appelant à la révision d'un jugement que l'auteur qualifie d'inique. Il revient explicitement sur les procès de la collaboration qui ont occupé l'espace public depuis la Libération et en appelle à l'opinion publique et littéraire qu'il prend à témoin. Si le récit de *Féerie pour une autre fois* investit et mobilise bien, à son profit, la forme discursive de la rhétorique judiciaire, il en use, en fait pour la détourner de sa finalité et la retourner contre elle-même. Il n'est pas un témoignage en justice, il n'a pas pour objet l'établissement des faits. Il vise, au contraire, à rendre méconnaissable la réalité des faits et incompréhensibles ou iniques les raisons du jugement. Ainsi l'incipit proclame-t-il explicitement

> l'horreur des réalités! Tous les lieux, noms, personnages, situations, présentés dans ce roman sont imaginaires! Absolument imaginaires! Aucun rapport avec aucune réalité![5]

Le récit vide la rhétorique judiciaire de son sens, il tend à la changer en une rhétorique sans objet, à la transformer en une simple machine de discours voire en un jeu et une mascarade. Ainsi, tournée en ridicule, cette rhétorique permet au romancier de faire valoir le point de vue de l'accusé depuis le terrain qu'il s'est choisi, celui de la littérature, contre les juges et contre la chose jugée.

C'est ce jeu de reprise, mais aussi de déplacement et de brouillage, de la rhétorique judicaire qui permet à l'écrivain de nier les faits qui lui sont reprochés mais aussi de se livrer à une véritable entreprise de réécriture de l'Histoire. Cette rhétorique travestie permet de jouer avec les charges portées contre l'auteur par la justice, avec les faits jugés, avec le passé et avec l'histoire et la vérité historique. Dans l'après coup que le livre constitue par rapport au procès, Céline a, en outre, changé de ton. Le récit est passé de la dynamique de la défense à celle de l'accusation. L'autofiction carnavalesque permet tout ce que le tribunal interdit: elle autorise tous les changements de places et de rôles; elle permet à l'avocat de se muer en procureur, elle transforme l'accusé en un accusateur, et elle fait de celui qui était coupable une victime.

Le plaidoyer de *Féerie pour une autre fois* vise les tribunaux d'exception de la justice de l'Epuration, leur fonctionnement, les difficultés rencontrées par cette justice pour qualifier les délits et les crimes. Dans l'arsenal où les vichyssois, les accusés des procès et les partisans de la réconciliation nationale puisent pour refuser les mises en jugement, Céline reprend à son compte les arguments de l'incohérence et de la disproportion entre la légèreté des délits commis et la sévérité des peines encourues. Il s'insurge contre l'incrimination retenue contre lui. Parmi les chefs d'accusation dont on le poursuit, il reprend surtout ceux pour lesquels il se sait innocent. Il grossit les charges retenues contre lui au point de les rendre invraisemblables: il en est ainsi de la trahison ou de la vénalité dont Sartre l'accuse en décembre 1945 dans son *Portrait de l'antisémite*.[6] La déformation et la distorsion hyperboliques de certaines des accusations lui servent à nier d'autres faits plus avérés et, finalement, à plaider non coupable pour les crimes qu'on lui impute: 'Dans quel domaine ai-je précisément collaboré avec l'ennemi? L'antisémitisme? Non [...] La propagande? Non — Alors?' (Mémoire en défense, 6 novembre 1946). Le plaidoyer devient progressivement un réquisitoire.

Le dialogisme de Mikhaïl Bakhtine enseigne que, loin d'être la totalité dont il présente l'apparence, tout récit se constitue, en fait, par rapport à un autre récit toujours possible, qu'il ne se distingue pas de l'alternative qu'il constitue par rapport à cet autre récit, qu'il suspend et vient interrompre. Le narrateur de 1952 sait que, pour faire accréditer sa *version* de l'histoire, il lui faut situer son discours parmi les autres discours, dire la nature des liens qu'il entretient avec eux, entrer en concurrence et lutter avec d'autres narrations: témoignages des rescapés des camps, dépositions entendues dans d'autres tribunaux en France et à l'étranger, chroniqueurs judiciaires des procès de l'Epuration, récits de ceux qu'il nomme les 'vainqueurs', etc. L'accusé porte ici accusation en même temps qu'il récuse ces autres témoins et leurs récits, avançant l'idée que l'histoire dont ils témoignent n'aurait pas eu lieu:

> Et Buchenwald flûte alors?... — Vous y avez pas été non plus [...] C'est pas pire qu'Auschwitz! c'est peu de chose à côté de Dora! Vous y fûtes jamais à Dora! j'ai jamais voulu que personne y aille![7]

Il avance l'argument révisionniste de l'incompatibilité entre le récit dont ils témoignent et leur qualité de *survivant*. C'est bien à l'ensemble des mots et des témoignages venus des procès et des camps et qui ont été reçus comme preuves dans l'enceinte des tribunaux que la narration de *Féerie* se confronte et s'affronte.

De même qu'il avait fait contrôler ses mémoires en défense, Céline contrôle le texte de son roman au moment de le remettre à l'éditeur. Sur la version dactylographiée, il efface et *rature* les noms des camps nazis qui figuraient dans les premières versions de son texte et leur substitue les noms banals de plusieurs villes allemandes: 'Dora' devient 'Cassel' dans le texte final de l'œuvre publiée en 1952, 'Buchenwald' est changé en 'Lünebourg', 'Auschwitz' disparaît sous 'Augsbourg', et 'Dachau' derrière 'Claunau'.[8] Le récit nous livre ainsi une géographie en grande partie imaginaire et méconnaissable de l'Allemagne. Les noms anodins et indifférents de villes allemandes sont substitués aux toponymes devenus les symboles des camps, qui avaient fait l'objet de la plus grande publicité au moment de leur libération. Lorsqu'elle barre et efface ainsi les noms des camps, l'écriture de Céline devient l'équivalent verbal du démantèlement et de la destruction des installations des camps de la mort au moment de leur évacuation par les nazis. Pour pouvoir être à décharge, le récit de l'accusé qui se veut innocent ne peut faire autrement que de déformer et de réécrire l'histoire. La formidable machine de langage de *Féerie* est aussi une construction d'esquives, qui permet d'aboutir à l'*histoire sous ratures* que le texte final donne à lire.

Le récit de *Féerie* est rythmé par l'alternance des questions et des réponses. Jeu constant avec la forme du procès, il ne vise pourtant pas à établir ce qui est le droit et ce qui ne l'est pas ni à décider qui a raison et qui a tort. Il choisit de s'adresser, par delà ses juges et contre eux, à un public et à un lectorat qu'il entend faire juge de la seule performance verbale de l'écrivain. D'un moyen au service de l'administration de la preuve qu'est la rhétorique judiciaire, il fait un but, détaché de l'établissement des faits qui en était la raison d'être. L'éloquence passe sous le signe du concours d'habileté qui permet tous les artifices et tous les moyens de convaincre. Elle laisse une large part à la joute verbale entre avocat et procureur. Elle en accentue le caractère théâtral, ludique et agonique parce qu'elle entend réduire la réalité et la portée du procès à celle d'un simple jeu de rôles. C'est à cette condition qu'il devient possible au narrateur d'investir plusieurs positions, de jouer plusieurs rôles contradictoires. Il occupe tour à tour les places de l'accusé et de l'accusateur, de la défense et du procureur. Il répond dans les termes de l'attaque. Son destinataire est en même temps un juge et un lecteur. Il pose des questions auxquelles il répond lui-même; il soulève des objections qu'il réfute aussitôt. Il fait aussi jouer à plein la dimension 'archaïque' du procès, cette dimension 'archaïque' qui, écrit Johan Huizinga dans *Homo ludens*, se manifeste chaque fois que 'ce n'est pas l'argument juridique le mieux pesé qui est décisif, mais l'outrage le plus violent et le plus pertinent': 'la lutte réglée consiste ici à peu près entièrement à l'emporter sur l'adversaire par des discours outrageants bien composés'.[9] *Féerie pour une autre fois* offre, de fait, maints exemples de ces discours outrageants, que Céline oppose à ceux qu'il nomme les 'prestidigitateurs d'Histoire'.[10]

Le roman de Céline pose nombre de problèmes difficiles, dont l'origine et les causes sont à chercher dans le jeu, complexe et jamais innocent, des rapports noués dans le texte entre fiction et autofiction, littérature et justice, histoire et révisionnisme historique. Sa singularité tient à la tension interne très forte et constamment maintenue entre un *jeu* littéraire visant à ridiculiser la justice, à la transformer en un objet de rire — à lui faire perdre toute signification et toute valeur exemplaire et historique — et la *réalité* des procès (procès de l'auteur, procès de l'après-guerre en France, procès des criminels de guerre nazis en Allemagne) comme lieu de la justice rendue. Le récit n'est ici ni au service de l'entreprise de la justice ni de la recherche d'une quelconque vérité. Il mélange la rhétorique judiciaire et la fiction. Et il instrumentalise cette dernière à des fins idéologiques. Céline, à la différence de Max Frisch et d'Ernst von Salomon, ne voulait rien savoir de la manière dont le droit, la justice, les procès de l'après-guerre en France et en Europe contribuaient à donner forme à une nouvelle conscience historique.

Notes to Chapter 7

1. Ernst von Salomon, *Le Questionnaire* [1951], traduit de l'allemand par Guido Meister (Paris: Gallimard, 1993) pp. 8–11.
2. Max. Frisch, *Stiller* [1954], traduit de l'allemand par Eliane Kaufholz-Messmer (Paris: Grasset, 1991), p. 19.
3. Voir Gisèle Sapiro, *La Guerre des écrivains* (Paris: Fayard, 1999); sur la législation de l'Epuration, Henry Rousso, *Vichy: l'événement, la mémoire, l'histoire* (Paris: Gallimard, 2001), pp. 489–677 et, sous la direction de Marc-Olivier. Baruch, *Une poignée de misérables: l'épuration de la société française après la Seconde Guerre mondiale* (Paris: Fayard, 2003).
4. Jean-Paul Sartre, 'Présentation des *Temps modernes*' [octobre 1945], in *Situations II* (Paris: Gallimard, 1975), p. 209.
5. Louis-Ferdinand Céline, *Féerie pour une autre fois I*, in Id., *Romans IV* (Paris: Gallimard, Bibliothèque de la Pléiade, 1993), p. 7.
6. Jean-Paul Sartre, 'Portrait de l'antisémite' [décembre 1945], in *Situations II*, pp. 254–85 (p. 277); voir Louis-Ferdinand Céline, *Féerie pour une autre fois I*, in Id., *Romans IV*, p. 94.
7. Louis-Ferdinand Céline, *Féerie pour une autre fois I*, in Id., *Romans IV*, version C, août-novembre 1948, pp. 870–71.
8. Louis-Ferdinand Céline, *Féerie pour une autre fois I*, in Id., *Romans IV*, p. 31, p. 32 et p. 66.
9. J. Huizinga, *Homo ludens, essai sur la fonction sociale du jeu* (Paris: Gallimard, 1972), pp. 131–49.
10. Louis-Ferdinand Céline, *Féerie pour une autre fois I*, in Id., *Romans IV*, p. 66.

CHAPTER 8

Unfinished Transition: Spain as a Democracy without Transitional Justice[1]

Jesús Izquierdo

My main aim in this chapter is to offer an explanation for/interpretation of the absence of mass grave exhumations from the Civil War by the Spanish state. This lack is a reflection of a specific transitional justice approach based solely on political reconciliation and so devoid of values and principles of justice. This absence proves the long influence of Francoism on Spanish democracy, and this influence was reflected in a redemptive narrative about our recent past in which the dictatorship played a crucial role.

'Let the dead bury their dead'

This command ('Que los muertos entierren a los muertos') was published in *El País* newspaper on 20 January 1977 and the article was written by Javier Pradera, one of the most notorious figures at that moment because of his anti-Francoist activism. A similar heading, 'May the dead bury their dead of the past' ('Que los muertos entierren a los muertos del pasado'), appeared six years later in the same newspaper, in an editorial piece most likely written by Pradera.[2] The years between the publication of these two articles include some of the historic events that have been introduced into Spanish cultural memory as a constituent milestone of the historic object called 'Spanish Transition'. Among these events are the first General Elections held since the Civil War, the signing of the Moncloa Pacts, the approval of the 1978 Spanish Constitution, the failed Coup d'état of 23 February 1981 (F-23), and the overwhelming victory of one of the political parties the Franco Regime had banned, the Socialist Party (PSOE). If Pradera's command helped to create the historic event that is the Spanish Transition it is because of its metaphorical meaning (understood as an unfamiliar use of the words); its capacity to institute the hegemonic relationship that was established between the present and the recent past during the immediate post-Francoist period and its ability to articulate the collective memory of all Spaniards, discrediting other alternative memories and defending the political culture of Spain's current democracy.

The *El País* articles use language in a performative way with the objective of ethically establishing the frontiers between past and present. The writer uses a stereotyped counterpoint between the dead, who are the symbol of what is already known and does not deserve to be repeated, and the living, who incarnate the values which have to be promoted, precisely because they do not belong to the past. Nevertheless, the rhetorical exercise of building the past initiated by Pradera reaches its full potential when the author describes that past as an undesirable place, a 'cataclysm', a dead place, closed, without a current interest for a present that now appears as an exalted event.

Seen from this perspective, the two articles are important examples of a type of narrative that became dominant during the post-Franco years and which still has an immense rhetorical power to create identities not interested in transitional justice. These are a type of post-traumatic narrative that some scholars, especially those interested in the relationship between a violent past and the ways it is represented through history, call redemptive narratives. Their themes are based on the secular account of a biblical composition that sequences three emblematic movements: Expulsion from Paradise, History and Redemption. In terms of laicism, the redemptive narrative goes through a beginning, development and ending. This ending must be considered as an end. This end, according to the historian Dominick LaCapra, is 'an echo of the beginning on a higher level of sense and meaning'.[3] The ending means improvement but, above all, it means closure.

The Transition was built as a historical climax based on a narrative so explicitly redemptive that, sometimes, it did not hide the biblical roots of its tapestry, as can be seen in Javier Pradera's sentences. It echoes the gospel of Saint Luke (9. 60) where Jesus, on his pilgrimage to Jerusalem, denied the request of a man to bury his father because he believed that to do so would distract from their higher mission of enunciating the 'Kingdom of God' on earth. Secularized, the texts signed by Pradera have a messianic meaning: a collective messiah is called upon to start an urgent salvation of the injustices perpetrated by the former generation. Moreover, the former social utopias can be avoided because the old generation is precisely the one guilty of the civil war. According to the *dictum* 'let the dead bury their own dead', the recent past is the sublimation of what is negative, which operates as a counterpoint to highlight the moral consumption of the present. It is, overall, the territory where the ancestors live and where they are only expected to bury themselves along with their former utopias, full of violence and blunders.

This proposal was inspired by the understanding of sources (news, articles, editorials or letters to the editor) published in *El País* newspaper between 1976 and 1986 about the Civil War and the damage it caused during the process of political change. I avoided exploring what we knew specifically as literature or cinema made during those years. Moreover, I have chosen to extend my observation up to 1986 because that year was the fiftieth anniversary of the conflict and the first commemoration celebrated during the post-Francoist Regime in which it was possible to verify the progressive reification of the redemptive narrative.

El País newspaper has been selected as a source because it is considered one of the media directly responsible for the creation of the public post-Francoist space and, consequently, of the specific relationship Spaniards have developed with the past since the death of the dictator. Unlike other media, *El País* introduced itself in 1976 as a media not influenced by the past. The newspaper strove for an investment in the future, which allowed it to extend its influence beyond elites and political parties and to reach a citizenship that was changing after years and years of suffering a dictatorship.[4]

Democracy as Redemption

'The civil war was an evil, and its fruits were bad... only on the overcoming of the past, of all the past, it is possible to construct the present.'

The former director of *El País* newspaper, Juan Luis Cebrián, contributed to consolidate the line between the past and the present that was hegemonic during the post-Francoist Spain.[5] Since then, this way of understanding the present as a locked achievement and the past as a disaster, was recreated in the Madrid newspaper even by ex-Francoist scholars like Pedro Laín Entralgo, who often wrote in the pages of *El País*. The redemptive narrative, structured like the biblical triad 'Expulsion from Paradise', 'History' and 'Redemption', started taking a secularized shape in the form of Civil War, Francoism and Transition. The account described Spain during the Second Republic and the Civil War as the place where backwardness and irrationality dwelled. Namely the 'pretty savage Spain', 'the strained and red necked Spain of the 1930s', 'of passions that stopped us from reasoning' and that gave rise to the 'major disaster of 1936', an 'uncivil war', a 'collective failure', the 'fratricidal war'. Namely 'our unfortunate Spanish war', the 'terrible massacre', the 'atrocious tragedy', from which it was only possible to redeem oneself through a 'maturing process' or a 'rationalization process' that developed into a 'really consolidated democracy', meaning the liberal parliamentary democracy of 1978.[6]

Within this redemptive narrative, the period of 1976–82 is represented as a successful closure. This understanding is not in conformity with the accumulative notion of time common in the philosophies of evolution. The redemptive narrative aims to domesticate the events teleologically with a comforting account, precisely because it gives an end to one of the misery-based histories — namely the Civil War — and announces the start of a new history, now redeemed — that is, the history of the 1978 Democracy. The redeemer bias of the narrative not only appears at its end; it is also evident in how the actors of the narrated history are labelled. It is illustrative that in that respect there is near complete absence of the victim concept to address those who played a role on the stage of the Civil War or in Francoism. Only a dozen articles, editorials or letters to the editor about the history prior to the Transition refers to 'victims of Franco'. This lack is all the more striking given how accustomed we have become to 'victimized societies' nowadays. However, can there be victims in an event — the Civil War, for example — which is plotted as a sort of 'Expulsion from Paradise'? The characters in this narrative are different:

they are victorious, defeated, deceased and dead. They are implicitly or explicitly guilty because the redeemer sense of narrative moves them away from focus as victims and, at the same time, shows them as guilty of a huge catastrophe resulting from their own 'wrath', 'Cainism', 'moral immaturity', 'brutality', 'dogmatism and sectarianism', 'irrationality', 'passions'; in a word, the result of their reprehensible and guilty 'violence'.[7]

Already in 1976 the scholars Chueca Goitia and Julián Marías wrote, in different articles, about the absence during the 1930s of any 'restrained Spaniard' and on the collective distribution of fault, which according to them, demanded 'a huge general confession of each Spaniard'.[8] The same year, two readers sent letters to the editor, in which the first said 'a whole generation was guilty, because they were all wrong', while the second one blamed that generation for living 'the absurdity of an unnecessary war'.[9] The avoidance of the victim concept and the emphasis on the collective distribution of fault was repeated throughout the decade. Another writer for the newspaper, the historian Carlos Seco Serrano, advised in 1985: 'in the wake of the huge catastrophe of 1936 both parties had their faults; and those faults were evident on the climate of hate which preceded'.[10] This advice to the new generation was epitomized in *El País* when it described the Civil War as a 'collective failure' or a 'fratricidal war' which set an example as 'sobering tragedy'.

Nevertheless, in all that period the term *reconciliation* was determinedly seen as a saving concept: it was understood as a period of discontinuity from which it was expected a new history would be created that could define the past as a purely negative counterpoint. The Civil War became something completely noxious. Already in 1979, in an interview with one of the most famous hispanists of that period, the British historian Hugh Thomas, suggested the Civil War was the marker between a doomed past and a reconciled present: in the narrative of the new Spain the conflict operated as 'making differences'.[11] Antonio Tovar made this idea more explicit, in a 1983 article where the command 'thy past be done' was included': 'For the new generations to see the Civil War as a distant historical episode, it is necessary for the actors to reconcile'.[12]

Returning to how the actors of the redeeming narrative were labelled, it was as important to identify those guilty for the Expulsion from Paradise as those messiahs who contributed to the collective salvation. It is within this textual framework that the Francoist reformers and the democratic political opposition found a proper niche to build, with the help of many professional historians, a glorious narrative identity. A new account is constructed as a stereotyped counterpoint to those who incarnated alternative social projects in the 1930s, now labelled, at best, as utopian projects. At the head of the saviour group should have been placed the monarchy, which had reserved for itself the highly important role of closing the hardship history and consummating the beginning of a new era. Juan Carlos I not only had 'symbolically completely healed the scars of the old Cainist wounds', he had also 'found out how not to repeat the atrocious 1936 genocide'. The newspaper also emphasized the fact that 'the long and sometimes conflicted moral maturing process' linked 'our present with the democratic and liberal tradition of our past'.[13]

Trauma, what Trauma?

The redemptive hegemonic account imposed its narrative consistency, trying to escape from the still existing pain among Spaniards: a pain that would end as soon as the opening of the new history would close the past and the Transition and, consequently, its outcome. The relationship established between the past and the present in the hegemonic narrative is emblematic of the denial that the redemptive account created around the initial trauma from which they originated. The narrative elevates the overcoming of the original event, the Civil War, but does not address the traumatic consequences and daily breakdowns that took place after the failed attempt of a Coup d'état in 1936, and especially, the social reorganization developed through the 'systematic' use of fear during almost four decades of Francoist genocide. Indeed, we can speak about genocide if we consider the Francoist fear not as an excess inside an authoritarian order but as an inherent element of a regime that applied a systematic plan to transform the social group, including those who belonged or gave support to the victorious side.[14]

The redemptive narrative represents a necessary event for the teleological review with which the narrative ends. A chapter of tribulations resulting from the Cain or the guilty actions of Spaniards in the 1930s could be understood as a long period of the systematic use of violence or menace by the Francoism with the aim of reorganizing social relationships in that period. It could be said that Spain became, especially during the 1940s and the1950s, some sort of concentrated network, some sort of panoptic menace of a fear, which slowly showed on those who were directly affected by the repression.[15]

Amongst numerous defeated people, the repressive politics of Francoism produced, in a micro political level, violent marks that were not consistent. Therefore, those affected did not have a sense of their own identity, and as a result they questioned — or denied — their own previous existence. This is where it is sensitive to trace the traumatic origin of the redemptive narrative: if the non-daily menace or application of violence worked traumatically, it was because it settled in the unconscious in a way that could not be explained by a consistency in the plot of one's own life. So, the use of fear or intimidation during Francoism created a type of person who remained silent about the violence suffered or made that suffering alien, as if it had been suffered by someone else. They denied a sense of the impact of their past actions or an understanding of the social and political practices which made them a victim of Francoist repression.

Thus, the first years of the Francoism era created a wide group of anguished Spaniards, in the Freudian sense of losing their frames of intelligibility from the moment the violent transformation of social links began. And this violent transformation created traces of painful experience which, settled in the unconscious, could not be narrated, that is, recalled. The psychoanalytical *dictum*, what cannot be remembered cannot be forgotten, is of particular relevance here. Because it cannot be forgotten it is expressed through different types of compulsion, of unconscious non-verbal action, the most common expression of which is to insistently remain silent because of a feeling of powerlessness, and because of a lack of perception of a past life.

But the violent redesign of the relationships which existed previous to the Civil War did not only affect the defeated; some of the victorious saw their pre-conflict meaning of life fall to pieces, as the consistency of their personal continuum broke down. The identity narrative of many of those who fought against the Second Republic was also shocked by the reorganization that the terrorist regime had created as result of the conflict, and its violent ways of seeing the world unsettled the structure of the self — making them also deny their past actions. Seen from that perspective, it suffices to say that the Francoist genocide is the key to understanding the making of a 'denying deal' amongst a significant number of Spaniards.[16] It was an unconscious and social deal, an intergenerational deal that collectively suppressed the memory of what could potentially jeopardize the current interpersonal agreements.

The denying deal was a necessary condition for destroyed memories to appear in a conscious plane. The understanding of the Civil War as a collective madness, typical of the redemptive narrative of the first post-Francoist era, was a paradigmatic case which also nurtured the symbolic reaffirmation of Francoism through representing practices whose aim was to destroy the social relationships previous to the Civil War. Such a narrative aimed at dismantling the memory of those relationships and worsening the loss of memory of those past actions by those who, in an inter-subjective way, recognized themselves in the framework of those relationships. If memory is the presence of absence in the conscious or in the unconscious, the emptiness left by those relationships and projects of the 1930s was filled with presences of disruptive madness.

The understanding of 'Victory' as a way of legitimizing and justifying events such as the Coup d'état of 1936 and the subsequent repression is a kind of narrative, an abettor which, even if it didn't exclude in any way the reference to the original event — imagined as 'Glorious National Movement' — did not represent it as a traumatic. On the contrary: the first Francoist era created a narrative which stressed even more the devastation of many of the defeated, the destruction of the memory of the social links that provided them with a consistent identity, extinguishing the ability of a person to recall memories and to narrate them.

The denying deal updated itself during Francoist 'developmentalism', a period when there was not as much repression compared to the previous one. It was through the 1960s, in a context where the middle class grew, the rural exodus increased, where the new mass consumption appeared, of economic growth and of new legitimacy of the regime based on its efficiency, when a huge part of the generation of baby boomers agreed on creating social frameworks for the memory of the Civil War. For the new social classes, the 1930s did not even have the same meaning that the first Francoism period (1939–59) gave to them, where the Civil War was represented as an exalted fight in the defense of an eternal Spain against communist internationalism. The war, the whole war, was then interpreted as a collective madness, filled with passionate and radical people.[17]

The Mythical Dimension of a Redemptive Narrative

In the past few decades, there has been a huge historiography production and a huge drive for memorialization that has tried to disrupt the hegemonic narrative of the Transition from two perspectives: historical studies and memory narratives. The former has tried to criticize the belief that 'we are all guilty'. This emanated from the differences between, on one side, those guilty of defending the Second Republic and Democracy and, on the other side, of those who perpetrated the failed Coup d'état of 1936 and the Francoist fascism and genocide. To stress democratic memory has been the main aim of some of these studies.[18] The latter did a commendable job, especially from the second half of the 2010s, vindicating the 'lesser human' victim concept of those who had suffered from reprisals at the hands of Francoism. The movement comes from the civil society and it has increasing power to determine the political agenda on the Spanish violent past. There were also political decisions capable of shaking the pillars of that narrative which have been taken. For example, the parliamentary condemnation of Francoism in 1999 and the approval of the Law of Historical Memory in 2007 both have contributed to the spreading of the victim concept.

The spreading of the concept of victim could contribute to the disruption of the redemptive narrative, even if it is only because it could possibly be capable of creating an analytical distance from the current 'guilty' concept, a crucial notion in the consistency of its plot. Although, what could, possibly, be happening is that the use of the notions of 'Civil War victims' or 'Francoism victims' may be exacerbating a victimization feeling that makes the creation of a necessary therapeutic space for treating psychological wounds more difficult. It is necessary to insist on the psychoanalytical idea which claims that not forgetting does not necessarily imply recalling. Retrieving historic memory implies providing actions to narrate personal and collective experiences, organizing memory traces giving them meaning. I mean, it implies creating alternative narrative ways even if they do sometimes relapse into victimization or nostalgia.

The relationship of a huge number of Spaniards with the Civil War had a very obvious historical dystopian residue during the first post-Francoist period and on the pages analysed of ten years of *El País*, when the alleged redemption of the transitional narrative did not appear to be guaranteed for those actors who created it or endorsed it. This form of utopian thought, according to which what is possible is undesirable, emerged from the fictitious prospect of the return of a nonsensical past susceptible to a new Civil War. It is very possible that this negative prospect has contributed to the demobilization of the Transition's social wave of protests, whose origins date back to the second half of the 1950s. It has provided the creation of a markedly conservative political culture with a stake in democracy since the 1970s, as long as this democracy equals public order. And it has contributed to the discrediting of the utopist legacy of the 1930s and of the alternative thinking which started during the Transition.

Most likely the Cainistic dystopia is no longer important for Spaniards once its enabling conditions — the uncertainty of the open political process after Franco's death — has disappeared, especially after the failed Coup d'état of 1981. Although the redemptive narrative of the Transition included from the start a chapter about the return to Hell, this chapter slowly shrank as soon as the democracy of the 1978, as we know it today, was instituted. The more we collectively fell under the spell of the idea of completion the less intense was the menacing feeling of the return to a past that, for decades, was understood as a foreign and irrational place.

No wonder, then, that in the last thirty years, the appeal made to know about the past that should not repeat itself has become less important while another epistemological appeal, born during the first post-Francoist era (as it is written on the pages of the Madrid newspaper), has become dominant. Knowing the recent past has become a requirement to recall our ancestors' nonsense, the collective madness which we, modern Spaniards, have been saved from by inaugurating a new history of an allegedly bloodless process (the Transition) which has led to another citizen culture and democratic institutions that, without regrets, can also set an example to the whole world.

The ideology of nonsense keeps on concealing the original denial deal, validating and justifying the subjective devastation perpetrated by the Francoist genocide and stopping the trauma formulation. If there are no previous identities to formulate, there are no social projects to retrieve from the past. Beyond the political pact made to uncover the responsibilities for our traumatic past, the cultural memory in Spain denies the war trauma and the genocide, in which one's own experience is silenced or alienated or in which the social desensitization towards the suffering of others dominates.[19] For this memory, the recent past has been undoubtedly judged at the same time that history has conveniently been trapped in an engrossed present which, if it could change any political institution or citizen praxis, it would do it without considering the past utopias, because those where ruined by violence and nonsense.

Like any other historical narrative, the redemptive narrative formulated during the post-Francoist period has a mythical dimension, as it has an internal consistency, a plot, that is ultimately self-referential.[20] In Spain the main issue is to deal with the end of a recent past and the start of a new history determined by some sort of historical philosophy based on the inevitable modernization of the citizenship. For some decades we have created a self-centred subjectivity with that utopia which projected our deepest desire to bury the past beyond a bunch of democratic institutions that we sublimated as a counterpoint of those that we have buried with their violent authors. We haven't realized that our inability to improve our citizenship status is related to the resilience of that narrative.

A modest proposal to escape from increasingly playing the victim issue that we had in the past and have in the present might be found in the historical thought of the German philosopher Walter Benjamin.[21] Indeed, his redemptive understanding of history has to be picked up because it is far from consummation and takes into consideration the hopes of the defeated. The victims who were judged as outdated utopians by the victorious, should be considered as projects capable of re-updating and can be an inspiration as the opposite to the idea that the post-

Francoist victorious history is the only possible history. The victims of the past would recover their first form as dissidents and fighters, to remind us that history is open; that it is an arborescence of alternatives where new forms of emancipation can mark the future but also it means new catastrophes could happen, like the one we are currently living through. It is when we can expect such disastrous possible results that we have to go against fundamentalism, dig out the dead, recover their old hopes and formulate a critical thought that can allow us to escape from the dangerous illusion of completion.

We must face the epistemological limits of a redemptive narrative, politically created even beyond historians. These limits determine a way of thinking about transitional justice as political reconciliation without proper truth and justice for the victims of recent past. But without demand of justice, of social reparation, without real transitional justice beyond political reconciliation... only genocide and victims remain under the graves of this country: Spain.

Notes to Chapter 8

1. This paper is inspired by a former text published in Spanish with formal and content changes: Jesús Izquierdo Martín, '"Que los muertos entierren a sus muertos": narrativa redentora y subjetividad en la España postfranquista', *Pandora*, 12 (2014), 43–63. The final English version was written by Núria Canalda Moreno and revised by Geoff Drea. I deeply appreciate their collaboration.
2. 'Los hijos de los vencedores', *El País*, 20 January 1977, and 'Paz a los muertos,' *El País*, 20 July 1983.
3. Dominick LaCapra, *Escribir la historia, escribir el trauma* (Buenos Aires: Nueva Visión, 2005), p. 167.
4. On the relation between media and the building of democracy in Spain, see Rafael Quirosa-Cheyrouze y Muñoz (ed.), *Prensa y democracia: los medios de comunicación en la transición* (Madrid: Biblioteca Nueva, 2009).
5. Juan Luis Cebrián, 'El final de una Guerra', *El País*, 9 January 1977.
6. *El País*, 11 May 1976, 17 July 1977, 6 May 1978, 1 February 1983, 4 January 1981, 11 July 1981, 24 November 1978, 27 July 1980 and 2 September 1980.
7. *El País*, 1 October 1977, 24 November 1978, 12 September 1981, 20 December 1982 and 11 November 1972.
8. *El País*, 11 May and 28 June 1976.
9. *El País*, 10 August and 28 August 1976.
10. 'España, historia inmediata', *El País*, 29 August 1985.
11. *El País*, 20 January 1979
12. *El País*, 14 January 1983.
13. 'El sello de la reconciliación', *El País*, 24 November 1978.
14. Antonio Míguez Macho, *La genealogía genocida de franquismo: violencia, memoria e impunidad* (Madrid: Abada, 2014); and Juan Miguel Baquero Zurita, *El país de la desmemoria: del genocidio franquista al silencio interminable* (Madrid: Roca, 2019).
15. Carlos Hernández de Miguel, *Los campos de concentración de Franco: sometimiento, tortura y muerte tras las alambradas* (Barcelona: Ediciones B, 2019).
16. See *Violencia de Estado y psicoanálisis*, ed. by Janine Puget and René Kaës (Buenos Aires: Centro Editor de América Latina, 1991), p. 177.
17. Pablo Sánchez León and Jesús Izquierdo Martín, *La guerra que nos han contado y la que no* (Madrid: Postmetrópolis, 2017).
18. Manuel Pérez Ledesma, 'La Guerra Civil y la historiografía: no fue posible el acuerdo', in *Memoria de la guerra y del franquismo*, ed. by Santos Juliá (Madrid: Taurus, 2006), pp. 101–33.

19. See Pedro Piedras Monroy, *La siega del olvido: memoria y presencia de la represión* (Madrid: Siglo XXI, 2012).
20. This mythical dimension of historical narratives was proposed by Northrop Frye, *Myth and Metaphor: Selected Essays, 1874–1988* (Charlottesville: University Press of Virginia, 1991).
21. Redemption as openness, and not as closure of history, is the main thesis of Walter Benjamin. See Michel Löwy, *Walter Benjamin: aviso de incendio* (Buenos Aires: Fondo de Cultura Económica, 2002).

CHAPTER 9

❖

Democracy without Justice: The Paradox of Literary Justice in the Work of Javier Cercas

Agnès Delage

Since Argentina first paved the way, back in 1983, transitional justice has taken many different forms. Yet Spain holds a unique place, being one of the few democracies in the world to remain deliberately on the sidelines of the international movement identified as 'the justice cascade'.[1] Indeed, the crimes committed under the Franco dictatorship, from 1939 to 1975, have never been examined by the courts, and a segment of Spanish culture has developed a discourse legitimizing this fact on the grounds that this is what undergirds Spanish democracy. Hence certain jurists note that, since the 2000s, Spain has ceased to be an archetypal model of negotiated, peaceful democratic transition, instead displaying all the symptoms of the perverse effects wrought by a democratization process without justice and a 'symbolic victory of impunity in the face of democracy'.[2] In a recent work, published in 2018, Anja Mihr, a specialist in international law, notes that the absence of transitional justice in Spain has indirectly compounded current weaknesses in its democracy with consequences for its 'poor democratic performance':

> Spain is a case that shows that consolidation can occur even without large-scale vetting or lustration, without trials or commissions of inquiry, and with the lowest level of atonement thinkable, namely by way of amnesty laws, reparations and memorials. However, this low level of Transitional Justice often coincides with low-level regime performance and led to many haunting unconsolidated pockets in Spain which have cost many people's lives and hampered vivid participation by society in building a stronger trust in institutions.[3]

The purpose of this chapter is to show how a major sector in Spanish culture, especially contemporary literature, participates in a social construction that justifies impunity on the grounds that it safeguards democracy, and paradoxically criminalizes the very idea of transitional justice. It analyses how Javier Cercas, currently one of his generation's internationally best-known authors, engages with the Spanish national media, via opinion pieces in *El País*, and with the European literary scene, in order to depict transitional justice as a threat to democracy. His documentary novel *Anatomía de un instante* (2009) [*The Anatomy of a Moment* (2011)] was brought out at a particularly sensitive moment in Spain, shortly after the Zapatero government had passed the memorial laws, in 2007. These triggered an unprecedented attempt to overcome the blockages within a democracy in which crimes committed under Francoism had not been examined by the courts, over thirty years after the dictator's death in 1975.

In October 2008, Judge Baltasar Garzón claimed his court was competent to rule on crimes committed under Francoism, and hence to investigate 114,226 cases of disappearance, drawing on the legal framework provide by crimes against humanity.[4] Shortly after, in 2009, Javier Cercas published *Anatomía de un instante*, a vast documentary enquiry into the military coup of 23 February 1981.[5] The book returns to the origins of democracy-building in Spain, precisely at the moment when transitional justice did not take place. The narrator builds up a complex narrative legitimization of the collective building of a democracy without justice. It was shortly after the removal of Judge Garzón, on 28 November 2008, putting — to date — a definitive end to any judicial proceedings into the dictatorship's crimes, that Cercas opted for the hybrid form of a non-fiction novel to set out an argument whose eminently paradoxical nature needs to be fully gauged: Cercas posits the absolute democratic need for justice, while at the same time asserting that the absence of any actual transitional justice is absolutely necessary in Spain.

Anatomía de un instante thus seeks to oppose a rigorous 'counter-history' to national and international criticism of the Spanish model of transition and to Garzón's attempted judicialization; in so doing, it seeks to operate a vast narrative relegitimization of the fully democratic need for there to be no transitional justice in Spain. The narrator thus addresses the hypothesis of a transitional justice which never took place in Spain, refuting it *in abstracto* as an 'apocalypse of democracy'.[6] The legal adage *Fiat justitia et pereat mundus* is used to underpin the authority of a narrative device which claims to identify the exercise of transitional justice as a major peril for democracy.

This study therefore examines the work of Javier Cercas, and the genre of contemporary non-fiction more generally, as a public intervention in contemporary pan-European democratic debate.[7] In 2016 Javier Cercas was awarded the European Book Prize, promoting the democratic values underpinning the European Union, for another docu-fictional work, *El impostor* (2014) [*The Impostor* (2017)].[8] Yet this docu-fictional enquiry into the imposter Enric Marco uses the theme of imposture to formulate a radical criticism of the inflation of the 'memory business', drawing directly on the problematic theses of the American polemicist Norman Finkelstein. In criticizing contemporary misuses of memory, as allegorized by the feigned deportee, Enric Marco, Cercas once again asserts that transitional justice is now impossible in Spain, the time for justice having been and gone. How are we to situate, historically and politically, this dogmatic denial, this narrative annulment of the possibility of exercising transitional justice in Spain, within a body of investigative documentary literature driven precisely by the desire to 'dispense literary justice'? How are we to analyse Cercas's position in the light of the democratic values to which he lays claim, and for which prestigious literary, academic, and political institutions lionize him?

A Particularity of the Spanish Literary Field: Literary Justice as a Symbolic Substitute for Non-existent Transitional Justice

In an international context in which judicialization processes are central to a return to democracy, Spain is currently on the sidelines. After Franco's death in 1975, and confronted with the, at times, conflicting demands between justice and civil and political peace, the country opted for democratization and reconciliation without any judicial examination of human rights abuses by the Franco regime from 1939 to 1975. Its transition was hence without transitional justice, or rather without several of the main aspects in which transitional justice is currently grounded. Transitional justice, it will be remembered, combines judicial and non-judicial procedures, in which punitive justice, which identifies those responsible and issues penal sanctions, is combined with restorative or reparative justice. The steps taken in Spain were solely in the domain of reparative justice, with collective compensation (for those left disabled and for former republican soldiers, while trade unions organizations recuperated their assets and certain orphans were granted pensions). These were supplemented by other similar measures under the 2007 laws on historical memory. Hence Spain has become a rarity in international law since — Mozambique apart — it is the only democratic country not to have judicialized mass crimes committed by the former regime and to persist in upholding democracy without justice.[9]

It is worth recalling that these were mass crimes: 150,000 people disappeared under Francoist repression, along with 50,000 victims of republican terror, with only 20,000 bodies of the former having thus far been exhumed, placing Spain just behind Cambodia in terms of the number of non-identified disappeared people.[10] The scale and systematic nature of political repression have been revised upwards by the latest historical reappraisals, with Carlos Hernández estimating in 2019 that one million prisoners were interned in 296 concentration camps.[11] In 2018 Neus Roig published a study of the system under which children were taken from their families, placing the number at 300,000 cases over the dictatorship as a whole.[12]

As of the 2000s and with the development of a citizen movement calling for the identification of those who had disappeared under the dictatorship, certain scholars working on Spanish memory sought to give voice to the vanquished by reporting on crimes not covered by law and hence unidentified by society. Documentary novels and works giving voice to the victims have carved out a unique literary space in Spanish democracy, in which the treatment of memory has generated a discursive stage comparable to truth commissions.

Many authors have followed this path, such as Manuel Vázquez Montalbán, Alfons Cervera, Dulce Chacón, Rafael Chirbes, Benjamin Prado, and Isaac Rosa, all extensively studied by literary historians.[13] However, the theme of memory and the associated publishing boom have had a neutralizing and agglutinating effect. Authors adopting totally opposed approaches to memory have been lumped together in a 'memory generation', transforming documentary novels into the symbolic forum for literary justice and democratic debate. Thus authors such as Javier Cercas, Andrés Trapiello, Ignacio Martínez de Pisón, Antonio Muñoz Molina, and Juan Manuel de Prada produce narratives which, above and beyond their many formal similarities, partake in a system of democratic values grounded in the public literary justification of the absence of actual justice in Spain. The issue of transitional justice is illuminating, for it sets this generation of authors apart: despite taking polarized positions on the absence of justice in present-day Spanish democracy, they all present their texts as a form of 'literary justice'.

This literary treatment of the aspiration for justice has produced a highly singular position, namely a fully democratic commitment to democracy without justice. The full extent of the following contradiction needs to be appreciated: the symbolic stage of literary justice legitimizes the non-judicialization of crimes committed under the dictatorship. Certain present-day Spanish authors, the most prominent being Javier Cercas, endeavour in their 'fictionless novels' to provide documentary evidence giving literary form to the fundamental incompatibility between transitional justice and Spanish democracy, thereby authorizing it. In their quest for a truth conveyed by non-fiction, such works develop phantasmatic forms of literary justice building up a counter-imaginary of restorative justice.

Is this documentary literature capable of fully restoring memory and dispensing justice on the literary stage, while at the same time asserting that democracy is radically incompatible with justice in Spain?

The Literary Legitimization in Cercas's Works of How Spanish Democracy is as a Matter of Principle Incompatible with Traditional Justice

This theme is central to Javier Cercas's work, and one he has constantly revisited since his first bestseller, *Soldados de Salamina* (2001) [*Soldiers of Salamis* (2003)], through to *Anatomía de un instante* (2009) [*The Anatomy of a Moment* (2011)], and his recently published documentary novel *El monarca de las sombras* (2017) [*Lord of All the Dead* (2019)]. Cercas uses the hybrid form of non-fiction to bear witness and hence operate restorative literary justice — not for the victims of Francoism, but rather for the model of transition without justice and for the historical individuals democracy has reputedly expunged from the picture, notably soldiers who fought for the fascist cause.

This stance of literary justice is thus diametrically opposed to the initial path taken in the 2000s, when docu-fictional literature first appeared, restoring the voices of those who were victims of Franco's dictatorship. In the name of a salutary revision to mythologies about the resistance and to stereotypes developed during the Transition about the heroism of the Second Republic, Cercas's works called for a more total, more complex, and more democratic memory of the Civil War and post-Francoist transition. Yet this supposedly subversive and critical 'literary justice' in fact serves to justify the existing state of affairs, the status quo of collective memory, together with family memories of fascism. Particularly in *Anatomía de un instante*, the self-fictional narrator embarks on a considerable undertaking, namely sitting in narrative judgement over the Transition. By using the 1981 coup as the touchstone for this pivotal period, Cercas shows that justice would have been an apocalypse of democracy in early 1980s Spain, and that democracy without justice was fully democratic precisely because of its imperfections, hence a goal to strive for. In *El monarca de las sombras*, in 2017, the narrator focuses on the memories of his own family to do justice not for the victims of fascism in Spain, but for a paradoxical victim, namely his great uncle, Manuel Mena, who died in 1938 at the age of nineteen in the Battle of the Ebro. He is presented as a young fascist soldier who was himself a victim of fascism, and a 'triple loser' in the Civil War.

This operation of 'literary justice' is thus presented as bringing greater democratic depth, as a matter of public deliberation about hegemonic or confiscated versions of history. We need to analyse the narrative procedures via which the poetics of 'literary justice', grounding itself in democratic values, exhibit and neutralize the issue of actual justice.

Anatomía de un instante and Sophistry, or How to Provide Literary Justification for Holding that Justice Imperils Democracy

With *Anatomía de un instante*, which met with great international success in 2009, Cercas placed the issue of transitional justice at the heart of a 500-page-long documentary enquiry into the attempted military coup of 23 February 1981. In addition to depicting the coup, Cercas's self-fictional narrator paints a vast canvas through which the legitimacy of democratization without justice in Spain is grounded in sophistry.

One of the threads running through the lengthy enquiry of *Anatomía de un instante* is the adage *Fiat justitia et pereat mundus*, initially taken by Max Weber from Kant (in the latter's *Doctrine of Right*). In Cercas's text it becomes a sort of legal principle, on which the narrator erects the following argument: the duty of justice, taken as a categorical imperative, would, in a sort of apocalypse of justice, result in wrong being done in the name of sovereign good.

> Es cierto que no se hizo del todo justicia, que no se restauró la legitimidad republicana conculcada por el franquismo ni se juzgó a los responsables de la dictadura ni se resarció a fondo y de inmediato a sus víctimas, pero también es cierto que a cambio de ello se construyó una democracia que hubiese sido imposible construir si el objetivo prioritario no hubiese sido fabricar el futuro sino — *Fiat justitia et pereat mundus* — enmendar el pasado.[14]
>
> [It is true that justice was not fully done, that the legitimacy of the republic was not restored, nor was it possible to judge those responsible for the dictatorship or to make immediate and thorough reparations to its victims, but it is also true that in exchange, a democracy was built that would have been impossible to build if the priority objective had not been to fabricate the future but rather — *Fiatjustitia et pereat mundus* — to amend the past.]

This short passage may be used to look in detail at how Cercas's narrative subverts the logical principle of non-contradiction, to assert that it is just and democratic to build a democracy without justice. *Anatomía de un instante* depicts the absence of judicialization of state crimes as both a democratic flaw, and, at the same time, as the prime precondition enabling Spanish democracy.

The narrator's argument opens on an initial statement ('es cierto' [it is true]) listing four historically attested democratic flaws of the Transition: there was no justice, the regime of the Second Republic was not restored, Francoist leaders were not indicted, and victims were not defended. This is followed by a second adverse statement ('pero también es cierto' [but it is also true]) asserting that 'se construyó una democracia', Spain is a democracy.

However, this dual series of attested facts leads to a final retroactive hypothesis (in the unreal past tense 'hubiese sido imposible' [it would have been impossible]) manufacturing an unwarranted causality: there was no justice and Spain is a democracy, therefore, it is because there was no justice that Spain is a democracy. This is a clear instance of sophist reasoning, 'cum hoc ergo propter hoc', in which correlation (between two phenomena that are in fact independent) is taken to imply causation.

The adage *Fiat justitia et pereat mundus* then leads into depiction of a democratically virtuous forgoing of a desire for justice, defined in terms of totalitarian abuse:

> Durante aquellos años todos deseaban evitar a cualquier precio el riesgo de repetir la salvaje orgía de sangre ocurrida cuarenta años atrás, y todos transmitieron ese deseo a una clase política que era sólo su reflejo. No era un deseo heróico, sediento de justicia (o de apocalipsis); era sólo un valeroso y razonable deseo burgués y la clase política lo cumplió, valerosa y razonablemente.[15]
>
> [During those years everyone wanted to avoid at any price the risk of repeating the savage orgy of bloodshed that had occurred forty years earlier, and everyone transmitted that desire for a political class that was only its reflection. It was not a heroic, justice-thirsty (or apocalyptic) desire; it was only a courageous and reasonable bourgeois desire, and the political class fulfilled it, courageously and reasonably.]

The 'thirst' for justice is thus presented by Cercas as an irrational disruption of the body politic, and the forgoing of justice as a collective triumph, requested by the people, of political rationality over an unbridled passion for truth.

Javier Cercas and the Ethic of Responsibility: The Democratic Heroization of Those Who Managed to Wholly Forgo Justice

Additionally, Cercas's text portrays the three heroes of the coup of 23 February (Santiago Carrillo, Manuel Gutiérrez Mellado, and Adolfo Suárez) as democratic heroes forgoing the heroism of justice viewed, as just seen, as an apocalypse of pacified democratization. Cercas thereby borrows his entire line of reasoning from Max Weber, who had used the same Latin quotation, *Fiat justitia et pereat mundus*, to criticize Kantian political rationalism in the context of the Weimar Republic.

Cercas detaches himself from the historical context to Weber's thought, retaining only what enables his text to legitimize, for all political actors, the sacrificing of morality in the name of political responsibility, endowed with its own specific logic and called by the narrator Weberian 'political reason'.

Hence in *Anatomía de un instante*, the ambitious young Francoist Adolfo Suárez, the old Francoist Gutiérrez Mellado, and the old communist Carrillo are portrayed as men who assumed the forgoing of transitional justice as a shared commitment to a Weberian 'ethic of responsibility', underpinning, for Cercas, the very definition of the necessary regulation of political violence within a democracy. These three historical characters thus become heroes of democracy in *Anatomía de un instante*, that is, heroes of 'political reason' in the Weberian meaning of the term, thus acting as the historical and narrative embodiment of the need to uncouple democratization from transitional justice.

Yet it should be noted that in *Anatomía de un instante*, as in his public pronouncements, Cercas never challenges the actual principle of transitional justice. In 2008, when the magistrate Baltasar Garzón was removed from his position after an enquiry was opened into Francoist crimes, Cercas immediately signalled his support for Garzón, on 17 October 2008, declaring 'Olé por Garzón' the day after the latter was charged by the Supreme Court for exceeding his powers. Yet this unequivocal statement of support was taken from an article published several months earlier, under the title 'La tiranía de la memoria',[16] arguing that any judicial investigation into Francoist crimes was materially impossible. Additionally, referring to the Zapatero government's 2007 laws on 'recuperating historical memory', which occasioned to Garzón's initiative, Cercas denounced state action via the memory law as a form of political tyranny, together with 'la creciente inclinación a escribir la historia desde el punto de vista exclusivo de las víctimas' [the growing tendency to write history solely from the viewpoint of the victims].

Cercas subsequently expressed his full support for Garzón in another article in *El País*, published under the title 'Un respeto'.[17] He stated that there had been crimes against humanity and a Francoist project of totalitarian extermination: 'un plan sistemático de exterminio que sembró España de cadáveres y de campos de concentración' [a systematic plan of extermination that sowed Spain with corpses and concentration camps].

But Cercas immediately associated this 'verdad salvaje' [harsh truth] with a series of statements asserting transitional justice was impossible in 2008 Spain:

> la verdad es que no sabemos a quién puede exigirle responsabilidades penales; de acuerdo: parece materialmente imposible juzgar hechos ocurridos hace setenta años; de acuerdo.[18]
>
> [The truth is that we do not know who can be held criminally accountable; agreed: it seems materially impossible to judge events that occurred seventy years ago; agreed.]

In this article, Cercas explicitly sides with Garzón's push to judicialize Francoist crimes from a moral point of view ('la íntima satisfacción'), while bluntly stating it is materially impossible. His public position is therefore far removed from that of other authors, who drew on their international prestige to weigh in and defend the legal validity of Garzón's investigations. It should be noted that in 2009 a manifesto article entitled 'La impunidad del franquismo' was published, again in *El País*, at the initiative of the Nobel prize-winning author José Saramago and co-signed by

Spanish magistrates calling for punitive proceedings to be opened into Francoist crimes against humanity: 'perseguir y castigar los más graves atentados contra la humanidad' [to pursue and punish the most serious offences against humanity].[19] This article noted that transitional justice proceedings were not only wholly feasible legally in Spain in 2009, but had been increasingly called for over recent years by the highest regulatory bodies in international law urging the Spanish state to stop shirking its international legal obligations in this matter.

Comparing Cercas's position in 2008 with that of Saramago in 2009, on the same issue of Garzón's steps to open judicial enquiries into Francoist crimes, show Cercas's public stance to be based on a paradox, too, adhering unreservedly to a form of justice elsewhere said to be materially impossible in Spain.

Conversely, other Spanish authors adopted positions far more favourable to actual justice as opposed to a form of justice eliciting primarily theoretical and ethical respect. Manuel Rivas, for example, referred to democracy being 'amputated' by the lack of transitional justice.[20] Yet in the literary imaginary of writers, even those committed to defending victims' rights, justice is often associated with vengeance. The novelist Francisco Casavella, interviewed in 2009 about his sweeping depiction of memory in *El día de Watusi*, declared even more explicitly that the construct of literary justice was tied to ideas of vengeance: 'toda novela se escribe para vengarse' [all novels are written to take revenge].[21] This brings out the lasting presence in Spain of a culture producing insufficient general adherence to transitional justice, assimilating the latter to political violence and a threat to democracy. Perceptions of actual and even literary justice, seeking not to reconcile but to designate and punish the guilty, are thus broadly associated in Spain with collective vengeance, even by authors closely linked to movements defending the rights of victims of Francoism.

Prominent intellectual figures have helped entrench in Spanish public debate the idea that meting out punitive justice would signify the end of Spanish democracy and amount to an act of political violence without precedent since the end of the dictatorship. Writing in *El País* in 2000, the historian Javier Tusell described the sentences handed down by the Argentine courts to the leaders of Videla's regime as nothing short of 'purges'.[22] Ten years later, in 2010, the Spanish historian Santos Juliá, a specialist in the Transition, criticized calls for transitional justice in Spain thirty-five years after Franco's death as a 'creciente argentinización de nuestra mirada al pasado' [a growing Argentinization of our view of the past].[23] He uses the neologism 'Argentinization' to designate calls for a form of justice that would not be solely restorative but also potentially punitive, for, after many twists and turns and the repeal of the Full Stop amnesty laws, Argentina resumed judicial proceedings in 2010, resulting in 800 people being put on trial. For Santos Juliá, quoting Javier Cercas on this matter, were Francoism to be put on trial in Spain, any ruling could only have moral, not penal force. Justice could take literary but in no case penal form without thereby imperilling democracy.

These examples bring us back to Cercas, showing how others share his public and literary stance against transitional justice and his denunciation of it as an apocalypse of democracy. Transitional justice is still extensively repudiated by particularly influential sectors of literature and the humanities, with a major impact on Spanish public opinion. The correlation between Cercas's literature of historical investigation and scholarship by certain Spanish historians needs to be appreciated if we are to understand how the public legitimization of democracy without justice is built up conjointly in Spain by literature, the media, and historical scholarship. It should be noted that Santos Juliá cited Cercas in his article denouncing the Argentinization of Spain in its quest for transitional justice, referring his readers to an article by Cercas in *El País* entitled 'La puñetera verdad [the bloody truth], also published in 2010.[24] This press article provided the matrix for Cercas's latest novel, *El monarca de las sombras*, published in 2017. As was already the case in *Soldados de Salamina* in 2001, journalistic writing operates as a kind of *avant-texte*, as a democratic testing ground for non-fiction. In this 2010 article, Cercas told the story of his maternal great-uncle, Manuel Mena, a young Falangist who died on the Ebro front in 1938, aged nineteen, transcribing to a new plane the dichotomy between 'political reason' and 'moral reason' discussed above in relation to the 2009 text, *Anatomía de un instante*.

Javier Cercas and Spanish Literary Justice Today: Restoring Spanish Fascism's 'moral reason' in 2017

In *El monarca de las sombras*, published in 2017, the documentary enquiry of the fictionless novel switches focus to fascism's 'moral reason', restoring it via the operation of literary justice. The narrator of *El monarca de las sombras* conducts a meticulous documentary enquiry into his maternal great-uncle's involvement with fascism, lifting what he presents as the final taboo in present-day Spanish democracy. How may one democratically assume one's fascist past, that of one's family and of Spain, which lived under a National-Catholic dictatorship for over forty years? Cercas's book condemns support for fascism from a political point of view, denying it any 'political reason', in the terminology deployed earlier in *Anatomía de un instante*. The narrator attributes political and democratic legitimacy solely to the Second Republic.

Yet this family ego-history also paves the way for the moral rehabilitation of exactly the same engagement with fascism, following the logic of restorative literary justice.[25] For in *El monarca de las sombras*, Cercas constructs a counter-narrative to oppose the international *doxa* about transitional justice as conducted from the viewpoint of the republican victims of Francoism. The narrator extends the status of victims of Francoism, applying it to Francoist soldiers who gave their lives for a political cause, despite the latter not being grounded in democratic 'political reason'.

The narrative thereby seeks to lift a taboo: not that surrounding the Francoist crimes, still unjudged in 2017, but of a supposed 'memoricide' committed by democracy against a generation of fascists who deserve political condemnation but moral rehabilitation. The main device running through *El monarca de las sombras* is a moral allegory borrowed from the *Iliad*, in which the convinced young fascist soldier Manuel Mena is compared to Achilles (enabling attentive readers to infer that the narrator Javier Cercas is no less than Homer). In addition to being heroized as a second Achilles, Manuel Mena, Javier Cercas's great-uncle, is also associated with the main character in a short story by Danilo Kis, 'To Die for One's Country Is Glorious' (in *The Encyclopaedia of the Dead*). These two intertexts, Homer and Kis, provide a way of recasting the meaning of the young man's death, transcending the error of political reason and the 'justice or injustice' of his engagement with fascism:

> Hablo en serio: no juzgamos a Aquiles por la justicia o la injusticia de la causa por la que murió, sino por la nobleza de sus actos, por la decencia y por la valentía y la generosidad con que se comportó. ¿No deberíamos hacer lo mismo con Manuel Mena?
>
> Nosotros no somos griegos antiguos, David.
>
> Pues a lo mejor deberíamos serlo, en esto como en tantas cosas. Mira, Manuel Mena estaba políticamente equivocado, de esto no hay duda, pero moralmente... ¿tú te atreverías a decir que eres mejor que él? Yo no.[26]
>
> [I am serious: we do not judge Achilles by the justice or injustice of the cause for which he died, but by the nobility of his actions, by the decency, bravery and generosity with which he behaved. Should we not do the same with Manuel Mena?
>
> — We are not ancient Greeks, David.
>
> — Well, maybe we should be, in this as in so many things. Look, Manuel Mena was politically wrong, of this there is no doubt, but morally... would you dare to say that you are better than him? I would not.]

The entire documentary narrative of *El monarca de las sombras* seeks to demonstrate historically that the young Manuel Mena's engagement with fascism was grounded in a legitimate form of moral reason. Cercas explores his own family history to compose a tomb, a narrative monument, a memory of and engagement with fascism which claims to be fully democratic and critical. But it should be borne in mind that this type of literary justice presenting itself as a democratic normalization of offences against the memories of the vanquished, while indeed taking democratically into account opposed memories of the Civil War, only does so at the cost of methodically neutralizing the very contemporary issue of the 'justicia o injusticia' of judicial responsibilities pertaining to fascism in Spain.

Lastly, to identify Manuel Mena as a triple loser, the narrator deliberately falsifies the political perspective, particularly regarding social history.

One may thus wonder what the novelist's own regime of responsibility might be, especially as Cercas claims his documentary enquiries have the status of a 'third truth'.[27]

Conclusion

It is important to appreciate the full extent of the 'blind spot' built up by Cercas's work around transitional justice for Francoist crimes, for it draws on a highly complex literary imaginary of literary justice to methodically invert the historically assigned roles of victims and culprits. Historical figures embodying fascism, who could well be indicted in hitherto non-existent transitional justice proceedings, are positioned as victims on the judicial pseudo-stage of non-fiction, as Cercas rehabilitates them through a retrospective and analeptic literary justice, while generally criticizing the excesses of an 'era of victims and witnesses'. This inversion, these logical reversals involve a sophistical argument sustaining the hybrid narrative form of the fictionless novel which plays incessantly with the perpetual reversibility of fact and fiction.

Thus literature is involved in producing a collective imaginary traversing Spanish society and transcending political divides, though Cercas persists in presenting himself as a centre-left intellectual and convinced Europeanist. It should be noted that the Spanish experimentation with democracy without justice has long been untenable on the international stage. The EU (as of 2006) and the UN (as of 2014) have officially called on the Spanish state to depart from the 1977 amnesty law which is no longer compatible with international law, asking it to launch judicial proceedings into Francoist crimes. No Spanish governing party has ever given any effective response to these official injunctions. Recently, on 19 March 2019, the PSOE voted with the right-wing PP and Ciudadanos parties against a proposed reform to the amnesty law tabled by Podemos and independentist parties. It is thus currently impossible at the national level to question the model of democratization without justice in Spain, for such view does not enjoy enough support, not even among the Spanish left, despite demands by citizens' memory movements, certain sectors of the press, and public opinion — demands which are relayed by international bodies.

Javier Cercas's work thus exemplifies the profound aporia regarding social democracy without justice in Spain, which, despite its evident flaws, still legitimizes itself as full democratization. In deliberately establishing a tension between narrative regimes and historical responsibilities, he claims to be producing a supremely democratic literary form continually relaunching public debate and deliberation about versions of history viewed as hegemonic. Indeed, Cercas devoted the lecture series he gave at St Anne's College, Oxford in 2015 to theorizing the hybrid form of the fictionless novel as a democratic form, subsequently published in 2016 as an essay under the title *El punto ciego*. The blind spot that Javier Cercas claims to explore via his documentary fiction is promoted as the quintessential democratic viewpoint, that of perpetual deliberation.

However, one may construct an analytical viewpoint on this 'blind spot' and show that it is a literary device to draw a narrative veil, effectively building the discursive preconditions in which transitional justice is presented as impossible in present-day Spanish democracy. As Luisa-Elena Delgado rightly remarks, part of contemporary Spanish literature, especially Cercas's work, partakes in a general regime in which Spanish democracy is normalized through fiction.[28] For Cercas, and for other authors of his generation, documentary fiction is a way to authorize and validate the absence of transitional justice as a democratic normality. But Cercas thereby constructs a 'blind spot', meaning this justice continues to be unthinkable and unrepresentable for most people in Spain, always being portrayed and imagined as a form of vengeance, hence perpetually held at bay as an apocalypse capable of imperilling present-day democracy. Cercas's work thus shows the extent to which literature, while indeed asserting its democratic capacity to 'do justice', may at times work to imperil the very idea of the legitimacy of actual justice.

Notes to Chapter 9

1. Kathryn Sikkink, *The Justice Cascade: How Human Rights Prosecutions Are Changing World Politics*, The Norton Series in World Politics (New York: W. W. Norton, 2011).
2. Jean-Pierre Massias, 'Politique, politisation et justice transitionnelle', *Les Cahiers de la Justice*, 3.3 (2015), 343–51. See also Rafael Escudero, 'Road to Impunity: The Absence of Transitional Justice Programs in Spain', *Human Rights Quarterly*, 36.1 (2014), 123–46.
3. Anja Mihr, *Regime Consolidation and Transitional Justice: A Comparative Study of Germany, Spain and Turkey* (Cambridge: Cambridge University Press, 2018), p. 339.
4. Javier Álvarez Chinchón, *El tratamiento judicial de los crímenes de la Guerra Civil y el franquismo en España: una visión de conjunto desde el Derecho Internacional*, Cuadernos Deusto de derechos humanos, 67 (Bilbao: Universidad de Deusto, 2012).
5. Javier Cercas, *Anatomía de un instante* (Madrid: Mondadori, 2009).
6. Javier Cercas, *Anatomía de un instante* (Barcelona: Debolsillo, 2011) p. 110.
7. Agnès Delage, *Le Roman historien: littérature, histoire et imaginaires démocratiques dans l'œuvre de Javier Cercas*, Habilitation à Diriger des Recherches (unpublished thesis, Université de Grenoble, 2017).
8. Lucía Abellán, 'Javier Cercas recibe el Premio al Libro Europeo por "El impostor"', *El País*, 8 December 2016.
9. Kora Andrieu and Geoffroy Lavau, *Quelle justice pour les peuples en transition? Démocratiser, réconcilier, pacifier* (Paris: PUPS, 2014).
10. Paul Preston, *El Holocausto español* (Barcelona: Debate, 2011).
11. Carlos Hernández de Miguel, *Los campos de concentración de Franco: sometimiento, tortura y muerte tras las alambradas* (Madrid: Ediciones B, 2019).
12. Neus Roig, *No llores que vas a ser feliz: el tráfico de bebés en España, de la represión al tráfico (1936–1966)*, (Barcelona: Ático de libros, 2018).
13. David Becerra Mayor, *La guerra civil como moda literaria* (Madrid: Editorial Clave Intelectual, 2015).
14. Javier Cercas, *Anatomía de un instante* (Barcelona: Debolsillo, 2011), p. 432.
15. Javier Cercas, *Anatomía de un instante*, p. 110.
16. Javier Cercas, 'La tiranía de la memoria', *El País*, 2 January 2008.
17. Javier Cercas, 'Un respeto', *El País*, 16 October 2008.
18. Ibid.
19. José Saramago, 'La impunidad del franquismo', *El País*, 16 September 2009. The co-signatories with José Saramago were the Spanish magistrates: José Jiménez Villarejo, ex presidente de la Sala Segunda del Tribunal Supremo; Enrique Gimbernat Ordeig, catedrático de Derecho Penal; Javier Moscoso del Prado y Muñoz, ex fiscal general del Estado; Luis Guillermo Pérez, secretario general de la Federación Internacional de Derechos Humanos, and Hernán Hormazábal Malaree, catedrático.
20. 'España es una democracia amputada. Ya no tiene sentido discutir quién debía haber ido a la cárcel, pero la gente debe saber que un torturador como Billy el Niño sigue campando y que nunca hubo una comisión de la verdad. Hemos visto en televisión campos de concentración nazis, pero no franquistas, que hubo.' Manuel Rivas, 'España es una democracia amputada', *El País*, 27 November 2015.
21. Francisco Casavella, 'Entrevista a Francisco Casavella: "La vida real es un sustituto de lo que tú inventas"', *Revista Quimera*, 303 (2009), 22–29.
22. Javier Tusell, '¿Fue modélica la Transición a la democracia?', *El País*, 2 November 2000.
23. Santos Juliá, 'Duelo por la República española', *El País*, 25 June 2010.
24. Javier Cercas, 'La puñetera verdad', *El País*, 6 June 2009.
25. I have examined the problems raised by Cercas's position on memories of European fascism in: Agnès Delage, 'Le Monarque des ombres: Javier Cercas peut-il sauver le soldat fasciste?', A.O.C. <https://aoc.media/critique/2018/10/17/monarque-ombres-javier-cercas-sauver-soldat-fasciste/>.
26. Javier Cercas, *El monarca de las sombras*.
27. I have recently presented the results of this line of enquiry during the 2019 Memory Studies

Associations Conference: session VI Thursday, 27 June, The Construction of the Italian Memory of Fascism through Cultural Representations. Agnès Delage (Universidad Aix Marsella) 'Javier Cercas y la postmemoria del fascism: ¿Memorialización, invención o falsificación?'

28. Luisa-Elena Delgado, *La nación singular: fantasías de la normalidad democrática española (1996–2011)* (Barcelona: Siglo XXI, 2014).

CHAPTER 10

❖

Démocratie sans justice: les paradoxes de la justice littéraire dans l'œuvre de Javier Cercas

Agnès Delage

Dans les multiples configurations qu'ont pu prendre les processus de justice transitionnelle depuis la voie ouverte par l'Argentine en 1983, l'Espagne occupe une place tout à fait singulière. L'état espagnol, est en effet l'une des seules démocraties au monde qui se trouve aujourd'hui volontairement en marge d'un mouvement international identifié comme 'the justice cascade'.[1] Une partie de la culture espagnole a construit un discours qui légitime comme fondement de la démocratie une absence complète de judiciarisation des crimes commis pendant la dictature franquiste, de 1939 à 1975. De ce fait, certains juristes remarquent que l'Espagne a cessé depuis les années 2000 d'être le modèle archétypal d'une transition démocratique négociée et pacifique, pour présenter aujourd'hui tous les symptômes des effets pervers d'un processus de démocratisation sans justice et d'une 'victoire symbolique de l'impunité face à la démocratie'.[2] La spécialiste du droit international Anja Mihr dans un ouvrage récent, publié en 2018, observait que l'inexistence d'une justice transitionnelle en Espagne avait un impact direct sur les fragilités actuelles de la démocratie et sur 'une faible performance démocratique':

> Spain is a case that shows that consolidation can occur even without large-scale vetting or lustration, without trial or commissions of inquiry, and with the lowest level of atonement thinkable, namely by way of amnesty laws, reparations and memorials. However, this low level of Transitional Justice often coincides with low-level regime performance and led to many haunting unconsolidated pockets in Spain which have cost many people's lives and hampered vivid participation by society in building a stronger trust in institutions.[3]

L'objet de cette étude est de montrer comment aujourd'hui un secteur important de la culture espagnole et tout particulièrement de la littérature contemporaine participe à la construction sociale de la justification de l'impunité comme garantie de démocratie et à la criminalisation paradoxale de l'idée même de justice transitionnelle. L'objet de cette étude vise à analyser comment Javier Cercas, qui est actuellement l'auteur espagnol le plus connu de sa génération sur le plan international, intervient à la fois sur la scène médiatique nationale, par ses articles d'opinion publiés dans *El País*, et sur la scène littéraire européenne pour assimiler la justice transitionnelle à un péril démocratique. Le roman documentaire *Anatomie d'un instant* paru en 2009, a ainsi été publié dans un contexte particulièrement sensible en Espagne, peu après que l'approbation de lois mémorielles du gouvernement Zapatero en 2007 ait déclenché une tentative inédite pour dépasser le blocage d'une démocratie sans judiciarisation des crimes du franquisme, plus de trente ans après la mort du dictateur en 1975.

Dès octobre 2008, le juge Baltasar Garzón s'était déclaré compétent pour mettre en jugement les crimes du franquisme, et pour instruire les 114.226 cas de disparitions dans le cadre d'une qualification pénale comme crimes contre l'humanité.[4] Javier Cercas a publié peu après, en 2009, *Anatomie d'un instant*, qui est une vaste enquête documentaire consacrée au coup d'état militaire du 23 F 1981.[5] Il s'agissait d'un retour aux origines de la construction démocratique de l'Espagne, précisément au moment où la justice transitionnelle n'a pas eu lieu, et le narrateur élaborait une légitimation narrative complexe de la construction collective d'une démocratie sans justice. Peu après le dessaisissement du juge Garzón, le 28 novembre 2008, qui a mis un terme jusqu'à aujourd'hui à toute procédure judiciaire concernant les crimes de la dictature, le romancier a choisi la forme hybride du roman sans fiction pour développer un argumentaire dont il faut mesurer le caractère éminemment paradoxal. Javier Cercas postule en effet l'obligation démocratique absolue de la justice, tout en attestant simultanément la nécessité absolue d'une absence de justice transitionnelle effective en Espagne.

Anatomie d'un instant se positionne alors comme un roman sans fiction qui vise à opposer une 'contre-histoire' rigoureuse aux critiques nationales et internationales du modèle transitionnel espagnol et à la tentative de judiciarisation portée par B. Garzón, pour opérer une vaste relégitimation narrative de la nécessité pleinement démocratique de l'absence de justice transitionnelle en Espagne. Le narrateur aborde ainsi au cours de son récit l'hypothèse d'une justice transitionnelle qui n'a jamais eu lieu en Espagne et il la réfute *in abstracto* comme une 'apocalypse démocratique'.[6] L'adage juridique *Fiat justitia et pereat mundus* est utilisé dans cette non-fiction historique consacrée au coup d'état militaire du 23 F 1981 pour fonder en autorité un dispositif narratif qui prétend identifier l'exercice de la justice transitionnelle comme un péril démocratique majeur.

Mon travail interroge donc l'œuvre de Javier Cercas, mais aussi plus généralement le genre de la non-fiction contemporaine, dans sa dimension d'intervention publique dans le débat démocratique contemporain, à l'échelle européenne.[7] Pour un autre récit docu-fictionnel, *L'Imposteur*, publié en 2014, Javier Cercas a reçu en 2016 le prix du livre de la Commission Européenne, qui promeut les valeurs démocratiques qui fondent l'Union Européenne.[8] Pourtant, cette enquête docu-fictionnelle consacrée au faussaire Enric Marco utilisait la thématique de l'imposture pour formuler une critique radicale de l'inflation d'un 'memory business', directement inspirée des thèses problématiques du polémiste américain Norman Finkelstein. Javier Cercas, critiquant les abus de mémoire contemporains allégorisés par le faux déporté E. Marco, affirmait à nouveau que la justice transitionnelle était désormais impossible en Espagne, car le temps de la justice était désormais révolu. Comment situer historiquement et politiquement ce parti-pris d'annulation narrative de l'exercice de la justice transitionnelle en Espagne, dans une littérature d'investigation documentaire qui ambitionne justement de 'faire justice littéraire'? Comment analyser la position de Javier Cercas du point de vue des valeurs démocratiques que cet auteur revendique et pour lequel des institutions littéraires, scientifiques et politiques prestigieuses le légitiment?

En situant avec précision dans le champ culturel espagnol la position à la fois littéraire et publique de Javier Cercas sur la question de la justice transitionnelle, nous pouvons voir comment une œuvre littéraire docu-fictionnelle investit le genre paradoxal de la non-fiction pour une opération de légitimation non moins paradoxale: fonder en validité historique, sociale et politique la démocratie sans justice, du point de vue même d'une exigence de démocratie.

Une spécificité du champ littéraire espagnol: la justice littéraire comme substitut symbolique d'une justice transitionnelle absente

Dans un contexte international qui a placé les processus de judiciarisation au centre des dispositifs de retour à la démocratie, l'Espagne occupe désormais une place tout à fait marginale, parce qu'entre les exigences parfois opposées de la justice et de la paix civile et politique, la transition démocratique espagnole a opté après la mort de Franco en 1975 pour une démocratisation et une réconciliation sans aucune judiciarisation des atteintes aux droits de l'homme commises par le régime franquiste entre 1939 et 1975. Une transition donc qui est *de facto* sans justice transitionnelle ou plutôt sans plusieurs des principaux volets qui fondent la justice transitionnelle actuelle. Je rappelle que la justice transitionnelle combine des procédures judiciaires et non-judiciaires et que la justice punitive, celle qui identifie les responsables et édicte des sanctions pénales, se combine à une justice dite restaurative, une justice réparatrice. En Espagne, les seules mesures prises ont été limitées au secteur de la justice réparatrice, avec des indemnisations collectives dès 1982 (mutilés, anciens militaires républicains, biens restitués à des organisations syndicales, pensions versées à certains orphelins), élargies à d'autres mesures de ce type à partir des lois de mémoire historique de 2007. De ce fait, l'Espagne est devenue un *hapax*, une singularité dans le droit international car, avec le Mozambique, elle est aujourd'hui le seul pays démocratique à n'avoir pas engagé de judiciarisation des crimes de masse commis par le régime antérieur et à continuer aujourd'hui à défendre une démocratie sans justice.[9]

Il s'agit en effet de crimes de masse dont il faut rappeler la magnitude: près de 150.000 personnes disparues pour les victimes de la répression franquiste (et 50.000 pour les victimes de la terreur républicaine), et seulement 20.000 corps exhumés à l'heure actuelle, ce qui place à l'échelle mondiale l'Espagne juste après le Cambodge du point de vue du nombre de disparus non identifiés.[10] La répression a fait l'objet de réévaluations historiques très récentes: l'ampleur et le caractère systématique de la politique de répression de masse ont été revus à la hausse très récemment. Carlos Hernández a estimé en 2019 l'incarcération d'un million de prisonniers dans 296 camps de concentrations.[11]

A partir des années 2000 et avec le développement d'un mouvement citoyen qui demandait l'identification des disparus de la dictature, une partie de la littérature mémorielle espagnole s'est assignée la mission de rendre la parole aux vaincus et de porter témoignage de crimes non qualifiés du point de vue pénal et de ce fait non identifiés dans la société. Le roman documentaire et la restitution de la voix des victimes ont ouvert un espace littéraire inédit dans la démocratie espagnole, dans lequel le travail de mémoire a élaboré une scène discursive proche des commissions de vérité.

Les auteurs qui se sont inscrits dans cette démarche sont très nombreux: Manuel Vázquez Montalbán, Alfons Cervera, Dulce Chacón, Rafael Chirbes, Benjamin Prado, Isaac Rosa et ils sont aujourd'hui très bien étudiés par les historiens de la littérature.[12] Cependant la thématique mémorielle et le caractère massif de ce phénomène éditorial de 'memory boom' ont produit un effet agglutinant et neutralisateur. Des auteurs aux partis-pris mémoriels pourtant tout à fait opposés sont intégrés à cette 'génération de la mémoire' qui a transformé le roman documentaire en scène symbolique de justice littéraire et en espace de débat démocratique. Or, des auteurs comme Javier Cercas, Andrés Trapiello, Ignacio Martínez de Pisón, Antonio Múñoz Molina, Juan Manuel de Prada produisent des récits qui, en dépit d'une grande proximité formelle, se trouvent inscrits dans un système de valeurs démocratiques fondé sur la justification littéraire publique de l'absence de justice effective en Espagne. La question de la justice transitionnelle devient à cet égard très éclairante, car elle fonctionne comme un thème discriminant pour aborder toute cette génération d'auteurs qui revendiquent des écritures relevant toutes de la 'justice littéraire' et qui développent pourtant des positions radicalement clivées sur la question de l'absence de justice dans la démocratie espagnole actuelle.

Dans une partie du champ littéraire espagnol, la littérarisation de l'ambition de justice a en effet produit un positionnement très singulier: un engagement qui se définit comme pleinement démocratique en faveur d'une démocratie sans justice. Il faut alors mesurer l'ampleur de la contradiction suivante: la scène symbolique de justice littéraire légitime l'absence de judiciarisation des crimes de la dictature. Certains auteurs espagnols actuels, et en tout premier lieu Javier Cercas, entreprennent en effet de littérariser et d'autoriser, grâce au parti-pris d'attestation documentaire qui est celui du 'roman sans fiction,' une incompatibilité fondamentale entre la justice transitionnelle et la démocratie espagnole, pour développer des formes fantasmatiquement substitutives de justice littéraire, en élaborant un contre-imaginaire de la justice restaurative dans la quête de vérité portée par la non-fiction.

Cette littérature documentaire peut-elle pleinement restaurer la mémoire et faire justice sur la scène du roman, tout en affirmant l'incompatibilité radicale de la justice et de la démocratie en Espagne?

La légitimation littéraire d'une incompatibilité de principe entre démocratie espagnole et justice transitionnelle chez Javier Cercas

Ce thème est en effet central dans l'œuvre de Javier Cercas et il ne cesse de se reformuler depuis son *bestseller* inaugural publié en 2001, les *Soldats de Salamine*, jusqu'à *Anatomie d'un instant* en 2009 et enfin avec la parution récente, en février 2017 d'un roman documentaire, *Le Monarque des ombres*. Javier Cercas utilise la forme hybride de la non-fiction pour porter témoignage et donc pour faire œuvre de justice littéraire restaurative, non pas pour les victimes du franquisme, mais pour le modèle de transition sans justice et pour des sujets historiques qui auraient été invisibilisés par la démocratie: notamment, les soldats engagés pour la cause fasciste.

Il s'agit donc d'un parti-pris de justice littéraire qui se trouve diamétralement inversé par rapport au postulat initial des années 2000, lorsque la littérature docu-fictionnelle s'est imposée pour restaurer les voix des victimes de la dictature franquiste. Au nom de la révision salutaire des mythologies résistancialistes et des stéréotypes que la Transition a accumulé au sujet de l'héroïsme de la IIe République, Javier Cercas revendique dans son œuvre une mémoire plus totale, plus complexe et plus démocratique de la Guerre Civile et de la transition post-franquiste. Pourtant, la 'justice littéraire' prétendument subversive et critique sert à justifier ce qui existe déjà, un *statu quo* de la mémoire collective, aussi bien que de la mémoire familiale du fascisme. Dans *Anatomie d'un instant*, tout particulièrement, le narrateur auto-fictionnel se lançait dans une entreprise considérable: faire justice narrative à la Transition. En utilisant le coup d'État de 1981 comme la pierre de touche de cette période charnière, Javier Cercas révélait que la justice aurait été une apocalypse démocratique dans le contexte espagnol de l'époque et que la démocratie sans justice était certes imparfaite, mais de ce fait pleinement démocratique, toujours à conquérir. Dans *Le Monarque des ombres*, en 2017, le narrateur prend cette fois-ci pour objet sa propre mémoire familiale, pour faire justice, non pas aux victimes du fascisme en Espagne, mais à une figure de victime paradoxale. Son grand-oncle, Manuel Mena, mort à 19 ans lors de la bataille de l'Ebre en 1938 est en effet présenté comme un jeune soldat fasciste, lui-même victime du fascisme et 'triple perdant' de la Guerre Civile.

Cette entreprise de 'justice littéraire' se présente donc comme un approfondissement démocratique, qui mettrait en délibération publique les versions hégémoniques ou confisquées de l'histoire. Il est important d'analyser quels sont les procédés narratifs qui permettent à la poétique de la 'justice littéraire' d'exhiber et de neutraliser la question de la justice effective, en se fondant sur des valeurs démocratiques.

Anatomie d'un instant et la logique du sophisme: comment justifier littérairement la justice comme un péril démocratique?

Avec *Anatomie d'un instant* tout d'abord, qui a connu un succès international très important en 2009, la question de la justice transitionnelle se retrouve placée au centre d'une vaste enquête documentaire de 500 pages consacrée au coup d'Etat militaire du 23 F 1981. Au-delà du coup d'Etat, le narrateur auto-fictionnel

Javier Cercas compose une grande fresque qui fonde narrativement la légitimité de la démocratisation sans justice espagnole avec des procédés qui relèvent d'une argumentation sophistique.

L'un des fils conducteurs de la longue enquête menée dans *Anatomie d'un instant* est l'adage suivant: *Fiat justitia et pereat mundus*, qui est une sentence initialement empruntée à Kant (extraite de la *Doctrine du droit*) par Max Weber. Elle devient dans le récit de Cercas une sorte de principe de droit, sur lequel le narrateur construit l'édifice de l'argumentation suivante: le devoir de justice, entendu comme un impératif catégorique, entraînerait le pire au nom du souverain bien, dans une sorte d'apocalypse juste.

> Es cierto que no se hizo del todo justicia, que no se restauró la legitimidad republicana conculcada por el franquismo ni se juzgó a los responsables de la dictadura ni se resarció a fondo y de inmediato a sus víctimas, pero también es cierto que a cambio de ello se construyó una democracia que hubiese sido imposible construir si el objetivo prioritario no hubiese sido fabricar el futuro sino –*Fiat justitia et pereat mundus*– enmendar el pasado.[13]

Ce court passage permet d'analyser dans le détail comment l'écriture de Javier Cercas subvertit narrativement le principe logique de non-contradiction, pour affirmer qu'il est juste et démocratique de construire une démocratie sans justice. *Anatomía de un instante* qualifie en effet l'absence de judiciarisation des crimes d'État à la fois comme un défaut de démocratie et en même temps, comme la principale condition de possibilité de la démocratie espagnole.

La démonstration du narrateur s'ouvre en effet sur une première assertion ('es cierto,' il est vrai) qui enregistre quatre manquements démocratiques de la Transition attestés historiquement: pas de justice, pas de restauration du régime de la IIe République, pas d'inculpation de responsables franquistes, pas de défense des victimes. Puis vient une deuxième assertion adversative ('pero también es cierto'), qui affirme 'se construyó una democracia', l'Espagne est une démocratie.

Cette double série de faits attestés débouche pourtant sur une hypothèse finale rétro-active (dans l'irréel du passé 'hubiese sido imposible') qui fabrique une causalité indue: il n'y a pas eu de justice et l'Espagne est une démocratie, donc, c'est parce qu'il n'y a pas eu de justice que l'Espagne a pu être une démocratie. Il s'agit alors bien là d'un sophisme, connu comme 'cum hoc ergo propter hoc' (ceci à cause de cela), qui établit un lien de causalité entre deux phénomènes effectifs pourtant indépendants.

La sentence *Fiat justitia et pereat mundus* ouvre ensuite dans le récit la mise en scène d'un renoncement vertueusement démocratique à un désir de justice qui est défini par ailleurs en termes d'abus totalitaire:

> Durante aquellos años todos deseaban evitar a cualquier precio el riesgo de repetir la salvaje orgía de sangre ocurrida cuarenta años atrás, y todos transmitieron ese deseo a una clase política que era sólo su reflejo. No era un deseo heroico, sediento de justicia (o de apocalipsis); era sólo un valeroso y razonable deseo burgués y la clase política lo cumplió, valerosa y razonablemente.[14]

Le désir 'assoiffé' de justice est donc présenté par Cercas comme un dérèglement irrationnel du corps politique et le renoncement à la justice comme le triomphe collectif, demandé par le peuple, de la raison politique sur la passion déréglée et fanatique de la vérité.

Javier Cercas et l'éthique de la responsabilité: l'héroïsation démocratique de ceux qui ont su renoncer totalement à la justice

Par ailleurs, dans son récit, Cercas représente les trois héros du coup d'Etat du 23 F (Santiago Carrillo, Manuel Gutiérrez Mellado et Adolfo Suárez) comme des héros démocratiques du renoncement à l'héroïsme de la justice conçue comme on vient de le voir comme une apocalypse de la démocratisation pacifiée. Javier Cercas emprunte alors l'intégralité de son raisonnement à Max Weber. Le sociologue allemand avait utilisé la même citation latine, *Fiat justitia et pereat mundus* pour critiquer le rationalisme politique kantien dans le contexte de la République de Weimar.

Le narrateur Javier Cercas rappelle ainsi que, dans la perspective du sociologue allemand, la justice relève pour Weber de la sphère du politique, dans une 'éthique de la responsabilité', qui s'opposait à une 'éthique de la conviction', dans laquelle la norme juridique s'appliquerait *in abstracto*, sans prise en compte des conséquences. Javier Cercas réalise alors un parcours philosophique et strictement anhistorique qui part de Platon et passe par Montaigne pour convoquer ensuite dans le détail l'essentiel de la théorie sociologique wéberienne du pouvoir. Cet exposé synoptique de la théorie de la responsabilité le délie cependant de tout ce qui constituait le socle político-historique de la pensée de Max Weber, lié à son propre engagement politique, qui l'avait conduit à être l'un des fondateurs du Parti Démocrate au lendemain de la défaite allemande de 1918. Javier Cercas se délie de ce contexte historique de la pensée wéberienne pour ne retenir que ce qui lui permet de légitimer dans son récit chez tout acteur politique un sacrifice de l'éthique morale au nom d'une responsabilité politique, dotée d'une logique propre, appelée par le narrateur 'raison politique' wébérienne.

De la sorte, très concrètement, dans le récit de *Anatomie d'un instant*, le jeune franquiste ambitieux Adolfo Suárez, le vieux franquiste Gutiérrez Mellado et le vieux communiste Carrillo sont figurés comme les hommes qui ont assumé en Espagne le renoncement à la justice transitionnelle comme un engagement commun dans une 'éthique de la responsabilité' wéberienne, qui fonde pour Cercas la définition même de la nécessaire régulation de la violence politique en démocratie. Ces trois personnages historiques deviennent de ce fait dans *Anatomía de un instante* des héros de la démocratie, c'est-à-dire des héros de la 'raison politique', au sens wéberien du terme, qui incarnent historiquement et narrativement la déliaison nécessaire entre démocratisation et justice transitionnelle.

Il faut toutefois remarquer que Javier Cercas, dans *Anatomie d'un instant*, tout comme dans ses prises de position publiques ne conteste jamais le principe même de la justice transitionnelle. Lorsque le juge Baltasar Garzón a été dessaisi en 2008 de ses fonctions à l'occasion de l'ouverture d'une enquête sur les crimes du franquisme,

Javier Cercas a immédiatement manifesté son soutien au juge, dès le 17 octobre 2008, le lendemain même de sa mise en accusation par le Tribunal Suprême. Il a ainsi déclaré: 'Olé por Garzón', 'chapeau / bravo Garzón'. Cette déclaration sans équivoque de soutien était pourtant intégrée à une tribune publiée plusieurs mois auparavant, dont le titre était 'La tiranía de la memoria',[15] qui affirmait qu'une telle action en justice était matériellement impossible. Par ailleurs, se référant aux lois dites de 'récupération de la mémoire historique' de 2007 du gouvernement Zapatero, qui étaient à l'origine de l'initiative du juge Garzón, Javier Cercas dénonçait l'action de l'État en matière de loi mémorielle comme une tyrannie politique, ainsi que 'la creciente (inclinación a escribir la historia desde el punto de vista exclusivo de las víctimas)'. La tendance de plus en plus marquée à écrire l'histoire du point de vue des victimes.

Par la suite, Javier Cercas a exprimé pleinement son soutien au juge Garzón, dans une autre tribune de *El País*, intitulée 'Un respeto'.[16] Il affirmait l'existence de crimes contre l'humanité et d'un projet franquiste d'extermination totalitaire: 'un plan sistemático de exterminio que sembró España de cadáveres y de campos de concentración'.

Mais cette 'vérité sauvage' ('verdad salvaje') était immédiatement associée par Javier Cercas à une série d'affirmations qui accréditaient que la justice transitionnelle était *de facto* impossible en Espagne en 2008:

> la verdad es que no sabemos a quién puede exigirle responsabilidades penales; de acuerdo: parece materialmente imposible juzgar hechos ocurridos hace setenta años; de acuerdo.

Dans cette tribune, Javier Cercas prenait position explicitement pour l'entreprise de judiciarisation menée par Garzón d'un point de vue moral ('la íntima satisfacción'), mais il entérinait également son impossibilité effective. Son positionnement public est de ce fait très éloigné de celui d'autres auteurs, qui ont utilisé tout leur prestige international pour peser dans les débats et défendre la validité juridique effective de l'entreprise du juge Garzón. Il faut ainsi rappeler que le Prix Nobel de Littérature José Saramago a eu l'initiative en 2009 d'une tribune-manifeste, elle aussi publiée dans *El País* et intitulée 'La impunidad del franquismo', co-signée avec des magistrats espagnols pour demander l'ouverture d'un processus de justice punitive à l'encontre des crimes contre l'humanité du franquisme: 'perseguir y castigar los más graves atentados contra la humanidad'.[17] Ce texte rappelait que du point de vue du droit, un processus de justice transitionnelle était non seulement parfaitement envisageable en Espagne en 2009, mais qu'il était de plus fortement réclamé depuis plusieurs années par les plus hautes instances de régulation du droit international, qui recommandaient à l'État espagnol de cesser de se soustraire aux obligations juridiques internationales en la matière.

La comparaison de la position de Javier Cercas en 2008 et de José Saramago en 2009, sur la même question du processus judiciarisation des crimes du franquisme entamé par le juge Garzón permet de comprendre que la posture d'adhésion publique de Javier Cercas repose elle aussi sur un paradoxe: l'adhésion sans réserve à une justice par ailleurs postulée comme matériellement impossible en Espagne.

D'autres écrivains espagnols ont en revanche pris des positions beaucoup plus engagées en faveur d'une justice effective et non pas d'une justice qui mériterait essentiellement un respect théorique et éthique. Manuel Rivas a par exemple parlé d'une 'démocratie amputée' par l'absence de justice transitionnelle.[18] Pourtant, dans l'imaginaire littéraire d'écrivains engagés pour la défense des droits des victimes, la justice reste souvent associée à la vengeance. Le romancier Francisco Casavella, interrogé en 2009 sur sa grande fresque mémorielle *El día de Watusi* déclarait de manière encore plus explicite que l'imaginaire d'une justice littéraire avait à voir avec la vengeance: 'toda novela se escribe para vengarse', tout roman est écrit pour se venger.[19] De la sorte, on peut mesurer la permanence d'une culture qui produit en Espagne un déficit collectif d'adhésion à la réalité de la justice transitionnelle, par l'assimilation de celle-ci à une violence politique et à un péril démocratique. Les imaginaires d'une justice effective et même d'une justice littéraire, qui ne viseraient pas à réconcilier, mais bien à désigner et punir les coupables, sont donc globalement associés en Espagne à la vengeance collective, même chez les auteurs les plus proches des mouvements de défenses des droits des victimes du franquisme.

Des figures intellectuelles de premier plan ont contribué à installer durablement dans le débat public espagnol l'idée qu'une justice punitive effective signifierait la fin de la démocratie espagnole et constituerait une violence politique sans précédent depuis la fin de la dictature. En 2000, l'historien Javier Tusell avait qualifié dans une tribune de *El País* les jugements réalisés en Argentine contre les responsables du régime de Videla comme de véritables 'purges'.[20] Dix ans plus tard, en 2010, l'historien espagnol Santos Juliá avait aussi critiqué la formulation d'une demande de justice transitionnelle en Espagne trente-cinq ans après la mort de Franco, comme une 'creciente argentinización de nuestra mirada al pasado'.[21] Une croissante 'argentinisation de notre regard sur le passé'. Par le néologisme 'd'argentinisation' le célèbre historien de la Transition désignait une demande de justice qui n'est pas exclusivement restaurative mais qui pouvait être punitive, puisqu'en 2010, après bien des aléas et la révocation de la loi d'amnistie de *Punto final*, les processus judiciaires avaient repris en Argentine et permis de juger 800 accusés. Or, pour l'historien Santos Julia, qui citait à ce propos l'écrivain Javier Cercas, si jugement du franquisme il devait y avoir en Espagne, celui-ci ne pourrait être que moral, et en aucun cas pénal. La justice peut être éventuellement littéraire, mais elle ne doit pas être pénale, sous peine de faire périr la démocratie.

Ces exemples me permettent de revenir à Javier Cercas, en montrant que son positionnement à la fois public et littéraire contre la justice transitionnelle et sa réfutation comme apocalypse démocratique ne sont pas strictement individuels. Le déni de justice transitionnelle est encore largement dominant, dans des secteurs particulièrement influents du champ littéraire et des sciences humaines qui ont un grand impact dans l'opinion publique espagnole. La corrélation entre la littérature d'investigation historique de Javier Cercas et une partie de l'historiographie savante espagnole doit d'ailleurs être soulignée, pour comprendre comment se construit la légitimation publique de la démocratie sans justice en Espagne entre le champ littéraire, l'espace médiatique et l'historiographie. Remarquons ainsi que Javier Cercas, était cité par Santos Juliá dans sa tribune contre l'argentinisation d'une

Espagne en quête de justice transitionnelle. Le prestigieux historien renvoyait à un article publié par Javier Cercas dans *El País* intitulé 'la puñetera verdad' (la putain de vérité) publié également en 2010.[22] Ce texte journalistique est devenu la matrice du dernier roman de Javier Cercas, publié en 2017, *El monarca de las sombras*. Comme c'était déjà le cas dans *Soldats de Salamine* en 2001, l'écriture journalistique opère comme une sorte d'avant-texte, de laboratoire démocratique de la non-fiction. Dans cet article de 2010, Javier Cercas racontait l'histoire de son grand-oncle maternel, Manuel Mena, jeune phalangiste de 19 ans mort sur le front de l'Ebre en 1938 et il prolongeait sur un nouveau plan la dichotomie entre 'raison politique' et 'raison morale' que j'ai étudiée pour *Anatomía de un instante* en 2009.

Javier Cercas et la justice littéraire aujourd'hui: la restauration de la 'raison morale' du fascisme espagnol en 2017

Dans *El monarca de las sombras*, publié en 2017, c'est désormais la 'raison morale' du fascisme qui fait l'objet de l'enquête documentaire dans le roman sans fiction et d'une processus de restauration par la justice littéraire. En effet, le narrateur de *El monarca de las sombras* mène une minutieuse enquête documentaire sur l'engagement fasciste de son grand-oncle maternel, pour lever ce qu'il considère être le tabou ultime de la démocratie espagnole contemporaine. Comment assumer démocratiquement un passé fasciste, qui est celui de sa propre famille et celui de l'Espagne qui a vécu plus de quarante ans de dictature national-catholique? Javier Cercas condamne dans son récit l'engagement fasciste d'un point de vue politique: il lui dénie ce qu'il appelait déjà dans *Anatomie d'un instant*, toute 'raison politique'. La seule légitimité politique et démocratique est attribuée par le narrateur à la IIe République.

Toutefois, le récit d'égo-histoire familiale ouvre simultanément à une réhabilitation morale de ce même engagement fasciste, dans une logique de justice littéraire restaurative.[23] Concrètement, dans *El monarca de las sombras*, Javier Cercas élabore un contre-récit qui s'opposerait à la *doxa* internationale de la justice transitionnelle menée du point de vue des victimes républicaines du franquisme. Le narrateur étend en effet en le statut de victimes du franquisme aux soldats franquistes qui ont donné leur vie pour une cause politique qui n'était pourtant pas fondée en 'raison politique' démocratique.

Le récit entend donc ici lever un tabou qui n'est pas celui des crimes du franquisme, toujours non-jugés en 2017, mais d'un prétendu mémoricide commis par la démocratie, à l'encontre d'une génération de fascistes qui doivent être condamnés politiquement mais réhabilités moralement. Le fil rouge de *El monarca de las sombras*, est ainsi une allégorie morale empruntée à l'*Iliade*, qui compare le jeune soldat fasciste convaincu Manuel Mena à Achille (le lecteur attentif peut déduire qu'implicitement, le narrateur Javier Cercas ne serait rien moins qu'Homère). Manuel Mena, le grand-oncle fasciste de Javier Cercas est héroïsé sous les traits un second Achille, mais aussi associé au personnage principal d'une nouvelle de Danilo Kis 'Il est glorieux de mourir pour la patrie' (publiée dans 'L'Encyclopédie des morts'). Ces deux intertextes, Homère et Kis, permettent de resignifier dans le récit le sens de la mort du jeune homme, bien au-delà de l'erreur de la raison politique, au-delà de 'la justice ou l'injustice' de l'engagement fasciste:

> Hablo en serio: no juzgamos a Aquiles por la justicia o la injusticia de la causa por la que murió, sino por la nobleza de sus actos, por la decencia y por la valentía y la generosidad con que se comportó. ¿No deberíamos hacer lo mismo con Manuel Mena?
>
> Nosotros no somos griegos antiguos, David.
>
> Pues a lo mejor deberíamos serlo, en esto como en tantas cosas. Mira, Manuel Mena estaba políticamente equivocado, de esto no hay duda, pero moralmente.... ¿tú te atreverías a decir que eres mejor que él? Yo no.[24]

Tout le récit documentaire dans *El monarca de las sombras*, cherche à attester historiquement la démonstration de la légitimité de la raison morale de l'engagement fasciste du jeune Manuel Mena. Javier Cercas entre dans sa propre histoire familiale pour composer un tombeau, un monument narratif, à une mémoire de l'engagement fasciste qui se revendique pleinement démocratique et critique. Mais il faut rappeler que ce type de justice littéraire qui s'exhibe comme une normalisation démocratique et des abus de mémoires des vaincus réalise certes bel et bien une prise en compte démocratique des mémoires opposées de la Guerre Civile, mais au prix d'une neutralisation méthodique de la question très contemporaine de la 'justicia o injusticia' du point de vue des responsabilités judiciaires du fascisme en Espagne.

Enfin, pour pouvoir identifier Manuel Mena comme un triple perdant, le narrateur fausse volontairement la perspective historique, du point de vue de l'histoire sociale notamment.

On peut alors se demander quel est le régime de responsabilité du romancier lui-même, et ce, d'autant plus que Javier Cercas revendique un statut de 'troisième vérité' pour ses enquêtes documentaires.[25]

Conclusion

Il importe d'identifier l'ampleur de 'l'angle mort' que construit l'œuvre de Cercas sur la question de la justice transitionnelle des crimes de la dictature, car il s'agit d'un imaginaire littéraire de justice littéraire très complexe, qui inverse méthodiquement les rôles historiquement assignés entre les victimes et les coupables. Des figures historiques qui incarnent le fascisme et qui seraient de potentielles accusées dans un procès de justice transitionnelle qui n'a jamais eu lieu, se retrouvent en position de victimes sur la pseudo-scène judiciaire de la non-fiction. Javier Cercas organise ainsi leur réhabilitation par une justice littéraire rétrospective, analeptique, tout en critiquant de manière générale les dérives d'une 'ère de la victime et du témoin'. Cette réversion, ces prises à revers logiques vont jusqu'à l'argumentation sophistique qui nourrit profondément cette pratique d'une forme narrative hybride, le roman sans fiction qui, elle-même, ne cesse de jouer la réversibilité constante entre le factuel et le fictionnel.

La littérature intervient alors dans la production d'un imaginaire collectif qui traverse la société espagnole et les clivages politiques, même si Javier Cercas ne cesse de se revendiquer comme un intellectuel de centre-gauche, européiste convaincu. Il faut rappeler que l'expérience espagnole de démocratie sans justice est devenue depuis longtemps illégitime sur la scène internationale. La CEE, depuis 2006 et l'ONU, depuis 2014, demandent officiellement à l'État espagnol de déroger à la loi d'amnistie de 1977, qui est désormais incompatible avec l'état actuel du droit international et d'engager un processus de judiciarisation des crimes du franquisme. Aucun parti de gouvernement espagnol n'a jamais répondu de manière effective à ces injonctions officielles et très récemment, le 19 mars 2019, le PSOE, avec les partis de droites que sont PP et Ciudadanos, ont voté conjointement contre une proposition de réforme de la loi d'amnistie, portée à l'Assemblée nationale par Podemos et des partis indépendantistes. Le modèle de démocratisation sans justice est donc actuellement impossible à remettre en cause sur le plan national en Espagne, car il ne fait pas l'objet d'une adhésion suffisante, y compris au sein de la gauche espagnole, en dépit des demandes portées par les mouvements citoyens de mémoire, par certains secteurs de la presse ou de l'opinion publique et relayés par des instances internationales.

L'œuvre de Javier Cercas exemplarise donc cette profonde aporie de la social-démocratie sans justice en Espagne qui s'auto-représente toujours comme une démocratisation pleine, en dépit de ses évidentes failles. Le romancier, lorsqu'il met en tension volontaire des régimes narratifs et des responsabilités historiques, revendique une forme littéraire superlativement démocratique, qui ne cesserait de remettre en débat et en délibération publique des versions considérées comme hégémoniques de l'histoire. Javier Cercas a d'ailleurs consacré à cette théorisation de la forme hybride du roman sans fiction comme forme démocratique le cours qu'il a dispensé à Oxford, au St Anne's College en 2014–15 et qu'il a publié sous forme d'essai en 2016 sous le titre *El punto ciego*. Le point aveugle que revendique Javier Cercas pour la fiction documentaire est érigé par lui comme le point de vue démocratique par excellence, celui de la délibération perpétuelle.

On peut cependant construire un point de vue analytique sur ce 'point aveugle' et montrer qu'il s'agit d'un dispositif littéraire d'invisibilisation narrative qui élabore efficacement les conditions discursives d'impossibilité de la justice transitionnelle pour la démocratie espagnole actuelle. Comme le remarque très justement Luisa-Elena Delgado, une partie de la littérature espagnole contemporaine et tout particulièrement l'œuvre de Javier Cercas, participent à un régime général de 'fiction de normalité' de la démocratie espagnole.[26] Pour Javier Cercas, mais aussi pour une partie des auteurs de sa génération, la fiction documentaire sert à autoriser et à valider comme une normalité démocratique l'anomalie profonde d'une absence de justice transitionnelle. Javier Cercas construit ainsi un 'point aveugle', qui rend cette justice toujours majoritairement impensable et irreprésentable en Espagne, car toujours figurée et fantasmée comme une vengeance et donc repoussée perpétuellement comme une apocalypse pouvant faire périr la démocratie actuelle.

Notes to Chapter 10

1. Kathryn Sikkink, *The Justice Cascade: How Human Rights Prosecutions Are Changing World Politics*, The Norton Series in World Politics (New York: W. W. Norton, 2011).
2. Jean-Pierre Massias, 'Politique, politisation et justice transitionnelle', *Les Cahiers de la Justice*, 3.3 (2015), 343–51. Voir également: Rafael Escudero, 'Road to Impunity: The Absence of Transitional Justice Programs in Spain', *Human Rights Quarterly*, 36.1, (2014), 123–46.
3. Anja Mihr, *Regime Consolidation and Transitional Justice: A Comparative Study of Germany, Spain and Turkey* (Cambridge: Cambridge University Press, 2018), p. 339.
4. Javier Álvarez Chinchón, *El tratamiento judicial de los crímenes de la Guerra Civil y el franquismo en España: una visión de conjunto desde el Derecho Internacional*, Cuadernos Deusto de derechos humanos, 67 (Bilbao: Universidad de Deusto, 2012).
5. Javier Cercas, *Anatomía de un instante* (Madrid: Mondadori, 2009).
6. Javier Cercas, *Anatomía de un instante* (Barcelona: Debolsillo, 2011), p. 110.
7. Agnès Delage, *Le Roman historien: littérature, histoire et imaginaires démocratiques dans l'œuvre de Javier Cercas* (mémoire inédit d'Habilitation à Diriger des Recherches, soutenu à l'Université de Grenoble, décembre 2017).
8. Lucía Abellán, 'Javier Cercas recibe el Premio al Libro Europeo por "El impostor"', *El País*, 8 décembre 2016.
9. Kora Andrieu et Geoffroy Lavau, *Quelle justice pour les peuples en transition? Démocratiser, réconcilier, pacifier* (Paris: PUPS, 2014).
10. Paul Preston, *El Holocausto español* (Barcelona: Debate, 2011).
11. Carlos Hernández de Miguel, *Los campos de concentración de Franco: sometimiento, tortura y muerte tras las alambradas* (Madrid: Ediciones B, 2019).
12. David Becerra Mayor, *La guerra civil como moda literaria* (Madrid: Editorial Clave Intelectual, 2015).
13. Javier Cercas, *Anatomía de un instante* (Barcelona: Debolsillo, 2011), p. 432.
14. Javier Cercas, *Anatomía de un instante*, p. 110.
15. Javier Cercas, 'La tiranía de la memoria', *El País*, 2 janvier 2008.
16. Javier Cercas, 'Un respeto', *El País*, 16 octobre 2008.
17. José Saramago, 'La impunidad del franquismo,' *El País*, 16 septembre 2009. Les signataires avec José Saramago étaient des magistrats espagnols: José Jiménez Villarejo, ex presidente de la Sala Segunda del Tribunal Supremo; Enrique Gimbernat Ordeig, catedrático de Derecho Penal; Javier Moscoso del Prado y Muñoz, ex fiscal general del Estado; Luis Guillermo Pérez, secretario general de la Federación Internacional de Derechos Humanos, et Hernán Hormazábal Malaree, catedrático.
18. 'España es una democracia amputada. Ya no tiene sentido discutir quién debía haber ido a la cárcel, pero la gente debe saber que un torturador como Billy el Niño sigue campando y que nunca hubo una comisión de la verdad. Hemos visto en televisión campos de concentración nazis, pero no franquistas, que hubo.' Manuel Rivas, 'España es una democracia amputada', *El País*, 27 novembre 2015.
19. Francisco Casavella, 'Entrevista a Francisco Casavella: "La vida real es un sustituto de lo que tú inventas"', *Revista Quimera*, 303 (2009), 22–29.
20. Javier Tusell, '¿Fue modélica la Transición a la democracia?', *El País*, 2 novembre 2000.
21. Santos Julia, 'Duelo por la República española', *El País*, 25 juin 2010.
22. Javier Cercas, 'La puñetera verdad', *El País*, 6 juin 2009.
23. J'ai abordé le problème que pose le positionnement de Cercas au sujet de la mémoire du fascisme européen dans: Agnès Delage, 'Le Monarque des ombres: Javier Cercas peut-il sauver le soldat fasciste?,' A.O.C. <https://aoc.media/critique/2018/10/17/monarque-ombres-javier-cercas-sauver-soldat-fasciste/>.
24. Javier Cercas, *El monarca de las sombras*.
25. J'ai présenté récemment les résultats de ce questionnement lors du congrès 2019 Memory Studies Associations: session VI Thursday, 27 June, The Construction of the Italian Memory of Fascism through Cultural Representations. Agnès Delage (Universidad Aix Marsella) 'Javier Cercas y la postmemoria del fascismo. ¿Memorialización, invención o falsificación?'

26. Luisa-Elena Delgado, *La nación singular: fantasías de la normalidad democrática española (1996–2011)* (Barcelona: Siglo XXI, 2014).

CHAPTER 11

Transitional Justice and Uses of the Past in Post-authoritarian Portugal

Manuel Loff

Unlike what Tolstoy believed happens with all happy families, not all democratic regimes look alike; nor do democratization processes, as complex as they inevitably are. 'The very process of transition from authoritarian rule, independently of the conditions that generated it, helps not only determine the prospects of democratic consolidation, but also the success of the transition to democracy in the first place'.[1]

Democratization through Revolution...

Unlike most post-authoritarian transitions, the Portuguese was a democratization without transaction with the former authoritarian rule. The process that evolved immediately after the 25 April 1974 Young Captains' movement overthrew the 48-year-old authoritarian regime installed and conceived in the Age of Fascism, included political disruption and anti-capitalistic structural changes in the economic relations. It led to very relevant transformations (through both socialization and nationalization) in the system of property ownership and the removal of entire sections of the political, economic and social elites. During that two-year process (from the April 1974 Revolution to the approval of the Constitution in April 1976),[2] political imagination and ideological discourse were mostly socialist, emancipatory and fundamentally embedded in European antifascist culture. Surely more than other events in history, the Portuguese Revolution was, in fact, a political process of its time, of the post-1968 years. The Portuguese experience was a striking example of that final stage of the progressive and emancipatory swing which won victory after victory worldwide from 1945 until the mid-1970s.

The historical substance of the actual Portuguese mode of transition has been widely discussed. A part of Portuguese and international historiography tried to find in Marcelo Caetano (who had succeeded Salazar in 1968) an equivalent, *avant la lettre*, to Adolfo Suárez, assuming that the Portuguese colonial war (1961–74) in

Angola, Guinea-Bissau and Mozambique and its corollary (the Young Captains' decision to put an end to it by overthrowing the regime) should be taken as the only truly distinctive factor that would have prevented a Spanish kind of transition in Portugal.[3] To a large extent, such an interpretation, widely subscribed to by much of the Portuguese conservative political culture, is based on an overestimation of an interpretative model as equivocal as Samuel Huntington's,[4] who, oversimplifying it, sought to include in a third wave of democratization cases as different as radical democratic transitions such as the Portuguese Revolution, transactional transitions like the Spanish case, in the 1970s, and most of the Latin American and Central and Eastern European cases in the 1980s and 90s. Such historical and political accounts of democratization processes, described as fairly inevitable, tend to find (or rather to look for) among the intentions of social and political ruling elites (especially in Spain and Latin America) the changes that, once effectively put into practice, have made democracy possible. In other words, in these cases we are talking about retroactive accounts of history, deliberately or inadvertently helping to democratize those elites and/or their political behaviour.

The Portuguese Revolution offered a fundamentally different mode of transition, and, from that point of view, was hardly the starting point of a third wave of democratization. To start with, it was a doubly legitimated democratic order, both electoral and military/revolutionary. The Portuguese democratic regime was created by a revolution and fully confirmed by democratic elections. At the end of the transitional process, a very wide constitutional consensus was achieved, including on fundamental economic legislation, ranging from Communists and radical left to Socialists and moderate right, ratified by the wide majority of the Armed Forces Movement (MFA). It was clearly closer to the antifascist and anti-nazi democratization context of 1945 rather than to Polish *Solidarność*, post-Yugoslav and post-Soviet national-democratic, or Chilean post-Pinochet transitional processes in the early 1990s. As in the 1943–47 Liberation of Europe, Portuguese democratization (i) came after a military defeat/dead end and a war effort that had been de-legitimized and had already lost any popular support, (ii) produced a full dismantling of the authoritarian regime by (iii) a wide antifascist coalition taking power, creating a context in which (iv) subaltern social groups felt empowered to put forward social and political radical demands. In other words, what became the last socialist revolution of twentieth-century Europe has hardly any similarity with those other cases of the 1970s, '80s and '90s, like the Spanish, in which transition from dictatorship to democracy was based on a (series of) pact(s) between a part of the authoritarian elites and those democratic leaders they agreed to negotiate with. Nevertheless, the realization that the counter-revolutionary success in Portugal at the end of 1975, freezing and soon reverting most (but not all) of the socialist gains of the previous year a half, eventually produced a liberal-democratic system, may provide what I believe to be the 'third wave illusion' and a fairly superficial view on how democracy emerges from different forms of authoritarian regime crises. Broadly speaking, the Portuguese democratic regime is the outcome of a socialist revolution at the closing moment of the progressive post-1945 cycle, whose political and social regime evolves towards a quasi-classic liberal-democracy, following the neoliberal and neoconservative worldwide swing of the 1980s and '90s.

... But with a Deliberately Limited Transitional Justice

In a democracy emerging through revolution, Portuguese transitional justice and public policies of memory of the authoritarian past were expected to develop a radical critique of dictatorship and war. That would seem coherent with a context in which opposition movements had made no transaction with the authoritarian state elites. But this has not been the case from 1976 onwards. To some, it may seem surprising that what emerges from the study of both transitional justice and public policies of memory in the last four decades is that state policies on the matter offer a very similar picture to those countries in which transition was completely different.[5] At the beginning, in 1974, though, it did not look as if that would be the case. The political and coercive structure put forward by Salazar in the 1930s and '40s was legally and immediately dismantled (the opposite of the Spanish process): President Américo Tomás, the head of the Government, Marcelo Caetano, and several cabinet ministers were all removed from office and arrested in the first forty-eight hours after the military coup, although the new military *Junta de Salvação Nacional* (JSN) appointed by the MFA soon allowed them to go into exile. Every major political entity created by the *Estado Novo* regime was dissolved: the political police (PIDE/DGS), the militia (*Legião Portuguesa*), the youth organizations (*Mocidade Portuguesa* and *Mocidade Portuguesa Feminina*), the single Party (*Ação Nacional Popular*, until 1970 *União Nacional*), the whole corporative system, and the censorship and propaganda departments.[6] Massive demonstrations at the end of the very first day of the military coup forced the JSN, against their early intentions, to release all political prisoners (at least in Portugal — African nationalists had to wait several weeks to be released from civil and military jails in the colonies). As would become usual over the next few months, political power was forced to legalize the situation, as the JSN declared an amnesty on 'political crimes and disciplinary contraventions', desertion from military service and 'military crimes'.[7] Political exiles were immediately allowed to return to Portugal: the Socialist leader, Mário Soares, arrived in Lisbon on the 28th of April, while the Communist leader, Álvaro Cunhal, who had been in exile for thirteen years after escaping from the prison where he had been held for eleven years (1949–60), arrived five days later. Civil servants that had been 'expelled or forced to quit and/or to retire for political reason' under the dictatorship were reintegrated with retroactive effect.[8]

Already under popular pressure, the new military authorities (before the first Provisional Government took office in mid-May 1974) decided to launch a very incipient lustration (*saneamento*) process, aiming to 'purge the Armed Forces ranks' both of military and civil servants,[9] and of the 'State Administration, corporative and economic coordination bodies', as well as of all 'civil service and State companies, local administration and all other public entities'.[10] In the following months, the government and the military established formal procedures, supervised by ministerial committees and a General-Directorate for Re-classification and Purging created within the General-Staff of the Armed Forces.[11] Only on 11 March 1975, the same day a *putsch* organized by former President Spínola (April–September 1974) and his far-right allies was defeated, legislation clearly specified four categories of officials that should be immediately 'dismissed from Civil Service': (i) Presidents and heads of Government between 1926 and 1974; (ii) political police agents and all those who had trained them; (iii) informers of the political police,[12] or all those that 'voluntarily assisted in its repressive activities'; and (iv) the so-called 'vigilantes' acting inside universities, all 'civil servants or agents responsible for any sort of information service for repressive purposes, and members of the 'Militia special forces'.[13]

The impact of these retribution measures was very diverse depending on the departments of the administration and on the specific period in which they were implemented. Generally speaking, 'most affected were the Ministries of Labour and Education'. Student and teacher movements had been at the core of the political protest against the dictatorship in the 1960s and '70s, especially against the war, and demands spread to purge teachers, civil servants and officials in universities and secondary schools who led the repression within these institutions or had reported to the political police on politically engaged teachers and students. 'Least affected was the Ministry of Justice because its ministers promoted very few purges.'[14] On the whole, however, 'huge delays in the legal purging procedures reduced its effect and made possible a speedy reintegration after a short number of years. [...] Most of these high officials would be reintegrated between 1976 and 1980, though most them did not return to the strategic positions they formerly held'.[15] In fact, the social demand for retribution that emerged irrepressibly in the second half of 1974 and until autumn 1975 did not last more than a year. The moderate military–civil coalition that took control of government in September 1975 and of every military command in November 1975 put a swift end to it by revoking most of the punitive legislation, appointing a special committee to evaluate appeals against purges (*Comissão de Análise de Recursos de Saneamentos e de Reclassificação*), created in February 1976 by the Council of the Revolution, a military committee representing the MFA to supervise the whole political process, by that time already having a moderate anti-communist majority. 'Most of those purged had their punishment altered to compulsory retirement. The remainder received a payment in lieu of lost earnings and restoration of their seniority for the purpose of calculating retirement pension entitlements.'[16]The way three of the four last ministers responsible for supervising all the repressive machinery of the dictatorship were treated was particularly enlightening. General Arnaldo Schultz (minister from 1958 to 1961) was released in January 1976 after a year in preventive detention, and was acquitted in 1982. As governor and Chief-Commander in Portuguese Guinea (1964–68), he had reminded the troops, in a general order, that guerrilla fighters were 'terrorists', 'and a terrorist is not a soldier [... and] is closer to a murderer than he is to a military man. [...] According to the Army's ethics, an imprisoned combatant without a regular uniform must be shot'.[17] Alfredo Santos Júnior, who succeeded him in the Home Office (1961–68) and supervised the operation to kill opposition leader Humberto

Delgado (1965), was sentenced in 1979 to ten months imprisonment but released by the court for having already served that time in preventive detention. Lastly, César Moreira Baptista (1973–74) was also acquitted.[18]

On the other hand, it was not until 1997 that the Portuguese state adopted any economic reparatory legislation for former political prisoners, exiles or underground militants. In 1998, special committee representing three different government departments was appointed to deal with individual requests.[19]

A Taboo: Colonial Violence, Veterans, Settlers

Most importantly, no military or civil perpetrator of war crimes against African populations (especially the 1961 massacres in Angola or the 1972 ones in Mozambique)[20] was ever brought to justice. No investigation on pre-war colonial violence was opened. There are several explanations for this, and the military origin of the democratization process is surely one of the most relevant. The military remained until 1976 a central element of the political sphere; they were the same military who had fought in Africa, and had decided to put an end to war by overthrowing the authoritarian regime, but they clearly felt uneasy when forced to face evidence of massacres perpetrated by servicemen (most often special Commando forces) on African populations, ordered by, or with the full knowledge of, commanding officers. In a first stage of post-authoritarian remembrance, while Colonial War massacres perpetrated by the military, mostly in Mozambique,[21] resurfaced, colonial violence as a whole was basically overlooked. In 1975–78, a number of underground publications produced in the last years of dictatorship, especially those prompted by progressive Catholic associations, were republished.[22]Soon after the Revolution and until the early 1990s, the state and the media overlooked these events. In fact, in 1976, Ramalho Eanes, by then the Army's General Chief-of-Staff, and soon to be elected President of the Republic (June 1976), prosecuted one of the publishers for 'abuse of the freedom of the press'.[23] While narratives of the killings (March–April 1961) perpetrated by African nationalists of the Union of Peoples of Angola (UPA) against Portuguese settlers in the northern part of the colony always kept their own space in the public sphere, the reprisal massacres perpetrated by Portuguese settlers in Luanda (starting in February) and in the Dembos area (from March to June 1961) were barely mentioned until the late 1990s.[24] After almost fifty years of democracy, it is still hard to find any reference to Portuguese war crimes in history schoolbooks or in any other sort of educational curriculum. In fact, memory of the war became, at least during the first two decades after it ended, an 'existential and discursive taboo'.[25] As novelist and war veteran António Lobo Antunes asked himself in the late 1970s: 'Porque camandro é que não se fala nisto? Começo a pensar que o milhão e quinhentos mil homens que passaram por África não existiram nunca e lhe estou contando um romance de mau gosto impossível de acreditar' [Why the heck is no one talking about this? I'm starting to think that the one and a half million men that passed through Africa never existed and that I am telling you some tasteless tale it's impossible to believe in].[26]

The whole idea that Portugal had taken a *Sonderweg* [special path] in history (as is often said of Germany),[27] as if it was an obvious exception in the history of colonialism and coloniality — although not a unique case in the European context — remained so evidently hegemonic in post-colonial Portugal, especially after the end of the Revolution, that it helped to silence accounts of colonial violence, perpetrated both during and, more especially, before the Colonial War, and make it invisible. Although this is merely one of the explanatory factors for the pervasive ambiguity in social and political elaboration of the memory of the war, it is central to understanding why there was no major social demand for making the military accountable for serious human rights abuse. In a society in which public memory of colonial violence remains clearly peripheral and where, as even the government acknowledges, denial of racism and racial prejudice, in the past as well as in the present, is part of the mainstream discourses and 'in the last few decades has almost become common-sense',[28] every public denunciation of racism in the police force, in the administration or in social relations becomes controversial and is labelled as merely politically motivated. The same often applies to memory of the sheer colonial nature of the Portuguese rule and of the war waged in Africa.

Already during the political clashes of 1975, a sort of 'memory screen' (as Henry Rousso calls it) was laid on the narratives of Portuguese modern colonialism and the war. Radical political change (revolution, democracy, decolonization) and a whole new cultural and social environment emerged in the years after the Revolution (rise of a post-industrial society, severe adaptation process following the end of corporative controlled economy), allowing anticommunist elites to blame irresponsible revolutionary elements for every problem. This narrative gave Portuguese conservatives the ability, whenever it became impossible to elude the debate on Salazar, Caetano, political repression, corporatism or the war in Africa, to discuss the *negative* legacy of the nineteen-month Revolution rather than the forty-eight years of the *Estado Novo*. By the end of the 1980s, the memory screen had been successfully imposed: before looking into Salazar's dictatorship and the war, debate was redirected to how disastrous the 1974–75 Revolution had been, and how inadequate or dangerous *revolution* itself is as a political/historical tool of democratization. In the new hegemonic narrative, at least until mid-1990s, the Portuguese had suffered under a long right-wing dictatorship until 1974, and then were subjected to a radical Left plot to impose a Communist dictatorship.[29]

In the late 1990s, a quarter-century after the end of the war, when the first generation of war veterans got into a *biographic* age and successfully claimed to have been *victims* of the conflict, memory accounts of it flooded the Portuguese media and bookshelves. According to one of them, a controversial professor of literature, the 'Portuguese combatant is a double victim: victim of a regime who forces him into war and victim of the guerrilla combat. Squeezed between two fires, the serviceman in the frontline is the one who wins the least and suffers the most with the armed struggle.'[30] Before that, autobiographic fiction on the war became a central contribution to set the fundamental terms of a collective narrative described as the memory of a generation. Novels of the 1970s and '80s focused on the sense of estrangement of the Portuguese servicemen, on the physical and psychological violence in combat or during the long wait, and included explicit reference to prisoners being tortured, women raped, non-combatants massacred. This first generation of Portuguese war novelists[31] wrote at the early stages (and even before that) of what Wieviorka called the *ère du témoin*, but in their accounts the perpetrators are also *victims*, sceptical, politically disillusioned and desperate occupying soldiers. Psychiatric as well as social perception of war neurosis changed radically in the late 1960s because of the Vietnam War, which was contemporaneous with the Portuguese Colonial War. Diagnosis of Post-Traumatic Stress Disorder (PTSD) emerged together with the description of the perpetrator 'self traumatized' 'by the extreme violence that they themselves inflicted in morally forbidden ways, such as torturing prisoners, mutilating the dead, and killing civilians and fellow [combatants]';[32] in such cases, the perpetrator emerged as a war victim, or perceived himself as such. It is true that 'the aim was not to exculpate them of any responsibility, nor to consider them not guilty, and especially not to deny the facts; it was simply to say that the Vietnam War had in fact turned these men into killers, although it had not metamorphosed them into monsters. They were still human', because they had been traumatized, and thus 'they all became war victims'.[33]

A somehow similar process happened with the *retornados* (the Portuguese equivalent to the French *pieds-noirs*), settlers who chose to return to Portugal and Africans who chose to leave Africa, portraying themselves as victims of decolonization, Revolution and the national liberation movements, but who hardly felt themselves victims of colonialism and of the dictatorship. Victimization impelled them to talk about their experience, openly asking state and society to empathize with their feelings, their pains, as well as their legal demands.[34] State and media engaged in a condescending discourse on reconciliation and celebration of what was described as the highly positive contribution of the *retornados* to Portuguese modernization. 'Very accommodating to a neoliberal agenda, this narrative often depicts *retornados* as better educated people who had built a modern and prosperous society in the colonies and who have contributed to the modernization of an underdeveloped and backward country after coming to Portugal.'[35] The lack of determination of most of the new African States (except perhaps for Mozambique) to develop specific memorial policies on the war from an African perspective, at least until early this century, left room for Portuguese-centred memorial policies put forward by associations representing the military, veterans and *retornados*. When at the end of the 1980s João de Melo, another veteran and novelist, edited a first anthology of war literature, he considered 'the period ranging from the beginning of the white settlement [in Africa] until the last day of colonization a *long act of war*', contradicting the discourse of most of those associations and the Portuguese Army. According to him, war literature on the '*second* colonial war', i.e. the 1961–74 one, was 'one of the few media that does not silence or deny the huge fraud our colonial past is. [...] today's society, trying to leave behind its war pains, [keeps] producing and rejoicing at the display of their inner violence'.[36]

Settling Accounts with the Political Police: From 'terrorist organization' to 'reconciliation'

Particularly emblematic of the Portuguese transitional justice is the way it dealt with the political police. During the Revolution, the legal definition of the *Estado Novo* as a fascist regime (inscribed in the 1976 Constitution) reflected the clear hegemony of the Left. 'Fascist repression' was the legal definition adopted to describe the activity of the political police (PIDE/DGS) and the oppressive nature of the regime: 'crimes systematically committed against the Portuguese people', 'arbitrary and inhumane action', 'terrorist activities' and 'institutionalized crime'. Criminal procedure against those responsible for such crimes became 'imprescriptible'.[37] In 1974, and especially in 1975, several thousand agents, officials and informers of the PIDE/DGS were arrested; a great number were able to escape from jail, some of whom were eventually recaptured; a significant part of them, however, especially those who served in the African colonies, fled the country. Soon after the 25 November 1975 military movement to get rid of the radical Left military officers, most of the political police agents were released from prison, brought under probation to military courts, and eventually got very light sentences, as the table below demonstrates.

TABLE 1. Political police agents, officials and informers sentenced by Military Courts (1978–86)[38]

Over two years imprisonment (mostly informers and middle-rank; a single top official)	43	(1.6%)
One to two years imprisonment (mostly low-rank agents; only eight top officials)	397	(14.4%)
Six to twelve months imprisonment	172	(6.2%)
One to six months imprisonment	847	(30.7%)
Less than one month imprisonment	1,014	(36.8%)
Suspension of political rights, not sentenced to jail (mostly low-rank agents)	107	(3.9%)
Acquitted	175	(6.4%)
Total: 42 top-rank officials; 274 middle-rank agents; 2,033 low-rank agents; 406 informers	**2,755**	

In short, most of the defendants were convicted to 'jail sentences equivalent to the time of probation already fulfilled', as military courts considered several 'mitigating factors and granted pardons that allowed their immediate and definite release'. Years later, in 1992, those 'mitigating factors' would even justify granting special pensions and honours to former PIDE agents for 'exceptional and relevant deeds for the Motherland' (according to legislation from 1982) carried out during the war in Africa. For Irene Pimentel, there was in fact 'a process of political justice in Portugal, but it was incomplete and even subverted by benevolent and mitigating sentences and pardons'. Therefore, she infers, 'the feeling that no political police agent was arrested, judged or condemned rightly endures in the memory of the Portuguese who lived [under the dictatorship].'[39]

The most symbolic trial on the crimes perpetrated by the political police was the one on the assassination, in 1965, of General Humberto Delgado (the 1958 presidential election opposition candidate) and of his secretary Arajaryr Campos. Delgado was a unique personality among Salazar's victims around whose memory there was a broad consensus after 1974:[40] an ambitious right-wing military officer who had openly collaborated with the regime in the 1930s, with no antifascist background whatsoever, he made a radical break with it in the late 1950s in a way no other Salazarist dissident had done.

The trial lasted for three years (1978–81) and the military court accepted PIDE's main thesis: that the political police aimed only to kidnap and arrest Delgado; his and Campos's killings were merely due to the 'impetuosity and haste' of Casimiro Monteiro, one of the four (out of seven) defendants who were judged *in absentia*, while the court ruled out the prosecution demand to call for their extradition. Those in Spain, France and Brazil who were tried *in absentia* were sentenced to two to nineteen years imprisonment; those who had already spent time in jail on preventive detention were sentenced to 14 to 28 months, and released. Finally, Salazar himself and Santos Júnior (minister for the Home Office) were both exonerated of any responsibility. Evidence of involvement by the Italian extreme-right, French OAS exiled in Portugal, the CIA, and French services were wholly disregarded.

Transitional justice actually carried out after 1974 in Portugal was designed and administered by the military: in July 1975, under pressure from left-wing social movements, they decided to implement a general accountability process of political and legal responsibilities for the abuse of human rights under the authoritarian regime. A few months later (December), in a different political context forced by the military themselves, they reversed that decision and decided to reinstate what they described as the 'rule of law' by administering a swift and benevolent justice, or simply by not accounting for the crimes of the past. Thirty years later, Col. Vítor Alves, one of the leaders of the moderate majority of the MFA and member of the Provisional Government since 1974, still thought that 'to prosecute *pides* [political police agents], the head of the government [Marcelo Caetano] and his ministers [would stir the country for several years] and would lead to a revolutionary state with people's courts and summary justice' and would have meant an 'automatic invasion by NATO. [...] [I]f we had to stick to the legal way, we would still be judging the *pides*.'[41]

As a global assessment of the Portuguese case for transitional justice, (i) reparatory measures were not implemented until a quarter-century after the fall of the authoritarian regime, (ii) punitive procedures started in 1974 were soon interrupted at the end of the Revolution (November 1975), and (iii) public policies on the memory of the authoritarian past, and especially on colonialism and war, can scarcely be taken as 'historical justice'. Out of the five categories set by Ruti Teitel on transitional justice[42] — (i) punitive justice of criminal trials; (ii) historical justice of publicly acknowledging wrongdoing and reconstructing political narratives; (iii) reparatory justice to compensate the injured; (iv) administrative justice involved in restructuring state institutions and removing complicit officials;

and (v) constitutional justice of remaking the juridical foundations of the state — the Portuguese democratic regime fully accomplished only one (v), and partially accomplished two other (iii and iv).

An Ordinarily Ambiguous Transitional Justice

Like in most post-authoritarian societies, the Portuguese new ruling elite assumed that the previous one was useful and/or had a legitimate role in building a new political order, surely different from the authoritarian, but an *order* nonetheless. Post-1976 state policies of memory described the recent past as implying that Revolution had been the final stage of a long civil war that had been going on since 1926 (the military coup overthrowing the liberal Republican regime), continuing throughout Salazar's regime, and also during the Revolution (1974–76). In this sense, the role of the new democratic state would have been to ensure conditions for social and political reconciliation. That is also the mainstream explanation for those who associate the 1974–75 Revolution with 'the outburst of violence by some radical groups'. For them, 'political reconciliation dominated the late 1970s, shaping the government's response to the legacy of the dictatorship.'[43] For Sandrine Lefranc,[44] the idea 'runs obsessively' through every post-authoritarian policy focused on amnesty. This was, in fact, the implicit stance of the Portuguese State after December 1975, very close to the Spanish transitional model.

Justice — in the sense of a politically and morally motivated transitional justice against the crimes of the authoritarian regime — was, therefore, perceived as *disorder*, unsuitable for the new democratic post-revolutionary *order*. In this sense, the Portuguese democracy, although very close to the historical formation of the European post-Liberation democracies, was nearer to the West German example of 'Adenauer's implicit argument that the establishment of a functioning democracy required less memory and justice for the crimes of the Nazi era and more "integration" of those who had astray',[45] i.e. those who had served as officials of the Nazi regime, to whom a 'right to political error' was implicitly acknowledged by Article 131 of the German Basic Law.[46]

Notes to Chapter 11

1. G. L. Munck and C. S. Leff, 'Modes of Transition and Democratization: South America and Eastern Europe in Comparative Perspective', *Comparative Politics*, 29.3 (April 1997), 343–62 (p. 344).
2. What narratives on the transition period commonly call the *revolutionary process* is usually described as having finished on 25 November 1975 with the aborted far-Left military movement, allowing the moderates (those who were allies to the social-democratic and right-wing forces in the process of defeating the radical Left in the final stage of the Revolution) to take full control of the leading military positions and sack every pro-Communist and far-Left military officer. See Maria I. Rezola 'The Portuguese Transition to Democracy', in *The Portuguese Republic at One Hundred*, ed. by R. Herr and A. C. Pinto (Berkeley: University of California, 2012), pp. 83–99.
3. Manuel Loff, '*Marcelismo* (and Late Francoism): Unsuccessful Authoritarian Modernisations', in *From Franco to Freedom: The Roots of the Transition to Democracy in Spain, 1962–1982*, ed. by M. Á. Ruiz Carnicer (Brighton; Chicago; Toronto: Sussex Academic Press, 2018), pp. 137–74.

4. Samuel Huntington, *Third Wave: Democratization in the Late Twentieth Century* (Norman: University of Oklahoma Press, 1991).
5. Manuel Loff, 'Estado, democracia e memória: políticas públicas e batalhas pela memória da ditadura portuguesa (1974–2014)', in *Ditaduras e revolução: democracia e políticas da memória*, ed. by M. Loff et al. (Coimbra: Editorial Almedina), pp. 23–143.
6. Relevant legislation: DL (*Decretos-Lei*) Nos. 171/74 and 172/74 (25 April), 362/74 (17 August), and No. 199/74 (14 May).
7. Respectively, DL Nos. 173/74 (26 April), 180/74 (2 May), 194/74 (10 May), and 202/74 (14 May); my translation. All translations from Portuguese original texts are mine, unless mentioned otherwise.
8. DL No. 304/74 (6 July).
9. The military were mentioned in DL No. 178/74 (30 April), civilians in No. 775/74 (31 December) and 497/75 (12 September).
10. DL Nos. 193/74 (9 May) and 277/74 (25 June). For a global appraisal, see Manuel Loff, 'Coming to Terms with the Dictatorial Past in Portugal after 1974: Silence, Remembrance and Ambiguity', in *Postdiktatorische Geschichtskulturen im Süden und Osten Europas: Bestandsaufnahme und Forschungsperspektiven*, ed. by S. Troebst, and S. Baumgartl (Göttingen: Wallstein Verlag, 2010), pp. 55–121.
11. DL Nos. 366/74 (19 August) and 36/75 (31 January), respectively.
12. Lists of those active in 1974 were burnt by DGS agents before the democratic military took possession of the political police headquarters.
13. DL No. 123/75 (11 March).
14. António C. Pinto, 'Portugal', in *Encyclopedia of Transitional Justice*, ed. by N. Nedelsky and L. Stan, vol. II (Cambridge: Cambridge University Press, 2012), pp. 391–97 (p. 394).
15. António C. Pinto, 'Enfrentando o legado autoritário na transição para a democracia (1974–1976)', in *O país em revolução*, ed. by J. M. B. Brito, Revolução e democracia, 2 (Lisbon: Editorial Notícias, 2001), pp. 359–84 (pp. 369–70).
16. Pinto, *Enfrentando o legado*, p. 395.
17. 'Circular nº 3 do Comando Chefe Português da Guiné', *apud* João P. Guerra, *Memória das guerras coloniais* (Lisbon: Editorial Notícias, 1994), p. 385.
18. Irene F. Pimentel, *O Caso PIDE/DGS: foram julgados os principais agentes da Ditadura portuguesa?* (Lisbon: Temas & Debates/Círculo de Leitores, 2017), pp. 538–39.
19. Respectivley, Law No. 20/97 (19 June) and Decree No. 3/98 (23 February).
20. Dalila C. Mateus, *A PIDE/DGS na Guerra Colonial, 1961–1974* (Lisbon: Terramar, 2004); Dalila C. Mateus, *Angola 61. Guerra Colonial: causas e consequências. O 4 de Fevereiro e o 15 de Março* (Alfragide: Texto, 2011); Felícia Cabrita, *Massacres em África* (Lisbon: A Esfera dos Livros, 2008).
21. The most widely known are the massacres in Wiriyamu and other Mozambican villages in December 1972. See Mustafah Dhada, *The 1972 Wiriyamu Massacre in Mozambique* (London: Bloomsbury, 2014).
22. For a list of these publications, see Manuel Loff, 'Dictatorship and Revolution: Socio-political Reconstructions of Collective Memory in Post-authoritarian Portugal', *Culture & History Digital Journal*, 3.2 (2014).
23. See 'A mentira oficial', in *Expresso-Revista*, Lisbon, 5 December 1992.
24. For a discussion on media reports, documentaries and research, see Loff, *Estado, democracia e memória*.
25. Paulo de Medeiros, 'Hauntings: Memory, Fiction and the Portuguese Colonial Wars', in *Commemorating War: The Politics of Memory*, ed. by T. G. Ashplant and others (New Brunswick, NJ: Transaction, 2006), pp. 201–21.
26. António Lobo Antunes, *Os cus de Judas*, 25th edn (*ne variatur*) [first pub. 1979] (Lisbon: D. Quixote, 2004), p. 69.
27. See Jürgen Kocka, 'German History before Hitler: The Debate about the German Sonderweg', *Journal of Contemporary History*, 23.1 (January 1988), 3–16.
28. Francisca Van Dúnem, Minister of Justice, 9 July 2019. Controversy on the colonial past and its public use was recurrent in the media throughout 2018 and 2019, focusing on Portuguese

responsibilities for modern slavery and deportation, racist police action, the role of the African-Portuguese communities, etc.

29. Manuel Loff, '1989 im Kontext portugiesischer Kontroversen über die jüngste Vergangenheit: Die rechte Rhetorik der zwei Diktaturen', in *Geschichtspolitik in Europa seit 1989: Deutschland, Frankreich und Polen im internationalen Vergleich*, ed. by E. François et al. (Göttingen: Wallstein, 2013), pp. 396–426.
30. Rui A. Teixeira, *A Guerra Colonial e o romance português: agonia e catarse* (Lisbon: Notícias, 1998), p. 311.
31. António Lobo Antunes (born 1942), Álvaro Guerra (1936–2002), João de Melo (b. 1949), Manuel Alegre (b. 1936), Carlos Vale Ferraz (b. 1946), José Martins Garcia (1941–2002), Armor Pires Mota (b. 1939). See Isabel Moutinho, *The Colonial Wars in Contemporary Portuguese Fiction* (Woodbridge: Tamesis, 2008).
32. Allan Young, *The Harmony of Illusions: Inventing Post-Traumatic Stress Disorder* (Princeton, NJ: Princeton University Press, 1997), p. 112.
33. Richard Rechtman, 'Mémoire & Anthropologie: 'Le Traumatisme comme invention sociale', in *Les Chantiers de la mémoire*, ed. by D. Peschanski and D. Maréchal (Bry-sur-Marne: INA, 2013), pp. 98–114 (pp. 109–10).
34. Half a million people fled from the African colonies to Portugal in 1974–76, while several hundred thousand chose to flee to apartheid South-Africa and Ian Smith's Rhodesia. See Rui P. Pires, 'O regresso das colónias', in *História da Expansão Portuguesa*, ed. by F. Bethencourt and K. Chaudhuri, vol. v (Lisbon: Temas & Debates, 2000), pp. 182–96, and M. P. Meneses and C. Gomes, 'Regressos? Os *retornados* na (des)colonização portuguesa', in *As Guerras de Libertação e os sonhos coloniais: alianças secretas, mapas imaginados*, ed. by M. P. Meneses and B. S. Martins (Coimbra: Almedina/CES, 2013), pp. 59–107. In autobiographical fiction, see Isabela Figueiredo, *Notebook of Colonial Memories*, trans. by A. M. Klobucka and P. Rothwell, Luso-Asio-Afro-Brazilian Studies & Theory, 4 (Dartmouth: University of Massachusetts Dartmouth, 2015), and Dulce M. Cardoso, *The Return*, trans. by Á. Gurría-Quintana (London: MacLehose Press, 2017).
35. Elsa Peralta, 'The Return from Africa: Illegitimacy, Concealment, and the Non-memory of Portugal's Imperial Collapse', *Memory Studies* (2019), 1–18 (p. 9); <https://doi.org/10.1177/1750698019849704>.
36. João de Melo, 'A Guerra Colonial e as lutas de libertação nacional nas literaturas de língua portuguesa'. in *Os anos da guerra, 1961–1975. Os portugueses em África. Crónica, ficção e História*, ed. by J. Melo, vol. I, (n.p.: Círculo de Leitores, 1988), pp. 12–13, p. 25, author's italics.
37. Law No. 8/75, 25 July.
38. Sources: Comissão de Extinção da PIDE/DGS e LP; Repartição Judicial, 3ª Secção; data corrected from those collected by Pimentel, *O Caso PIDE/DGS*, p. 595.
39. Pimentel, *O Caso PIDE/DGS*, p. 542.
40. His remains were transferred to the *Panteão Nacional* in 1990 and his name was given to Lisbon airport in 2016.
41. *Apud* Filipa Raimundo, 'Partidos políticos e justiça transicional em Portugal: o caso da polícia política (1974–1976)', in *A sombra das ditaduras: a Europa do Sul em comparação*, ed. by A. C. Pinto (Lisbon: ICS, 2013), pp. 87–119 (p. 96).
42. Ruti Teitel, *Transitional Justice* (New York: Oxford University Press, 2000).
43. Pinto, *Portugal*, p. 395.
44. Sandrine Lefranc, *Politiques du pardon* (Paris: PUF, 2002), p. 296.
45. Jeffrey Herf, *Divided Memory: The Nazi Past in the Two Germanies* (Cambridge, MA, & London: Harvard University Press, 1997), pp. 267, 289.
46. Article 131: Persons formerly in the public service, in 'Basic Law for the Federal Republic of Germany', <https://www.gesetze-im-internet.de/englisch_gg/index.html#gl_p0784>.

CHAPTER 12

❖

Voices of Suffering: Maintaining and Disseminating the Voice of Victims after the ICTY

Christian Axboe Nielsen

In December 2017, the United Nations International Criminal Tribunal for the Former Yugoslavia (ICTY) formally closed its doors after nearly a quarter-century of operations. During its existence, the ICTY indicted 161 individuals for crimes against humanity, war crimes and genocide. Over 4,500 witnesses testified in trials which often lasted for years. Of these witnesses, a considerable number were victims who had not only witnessed atrocities but had themselves suffered grievous physical, sexual and mental harm in the wars in Croatia, Bosnia and Herzegovina, Kosovo and Macedonia. ICTY judge Patricia Wald went so far as to claim that 'victim-witnesses are the soul of war crimes trials at the ICTY'.[1]

From the very first conviction of a low-level perpetrator (Duško Tadić) until the final verdicts against some of the most notorious and highest-ranking perpetrators (Radovan Karadžić and Ratko Mladić), the trial chambers at the ICTY quoted extensively from victims, many of whom had led unremarkable lives as 'ordinary citizens' of Yugoslavia until the violent disintegration of that country. Without their courageous and often harrowing testimony, it would have been impossible to prove many of the crimes. Obviously, therefore, the judges had to rely extensively upon this testimony. However, as has been discussed by Lawrence Douglas and other scholars of Holocaust atrocity trials, the non-linear, 'pathetic', and often overly detailed victim testimonies present challenges and frustrations for judges trying major atrocities.[2]

Functionally construed, the primary purpose of calling any witness — regardless of whether that witness is a victim or not — in a criminal trial is to obtain probative evidence that is relevant for ascertaining the facts necessary to reach a conclusive finding regarding the innocence or guilt of the accused on the charges in the indictment. In principle, the judges at the ICTY could have adopted a narrowly legal and clinical approach in order to achieve the utilitarian minimum goal of proving the guilt of the accused beyond reasonable doubt. In practice, however, in some judgements the trial chamber chose to quote from victims, thereby highlighting their humanity as well as the barbarous nature of the criminal acts which they suffered. As such, the judgements mark an unwitting and limited but important contribution to the 'humanitarian narratives' which have shaped our understanding of the wars of Yugoslav succession. This chapter asks if and how we can help to release these victim narratives from their judicial constraints.

To date little analysis of ICTY judgements has been undertaken from this perspective. After a brief introduction to the topic, this chapter will briefly probe the use of victim testimony in the cases of Galić (Sarajevo siege), Stakić (Prijedor) and Lukić (Višegrad). Subsequently, I will attempt to address the question of the afterlife of ICTY victim testimony. Although much victim testimony is publicly available on the website of the ICTY, the practical accessibility of this testimony leaves much to be desired. The trials at the ICTY often lasted for years, meaning that the affected publics lost interest in the proceedings and rarely paid attention to the content of victim testimony. Journalists and politicians in the former Yugoslavia often displayed much more interest in the accused than in the victims, and victims seemed to be of interest primarily as an abstract or collective whole that could be exploited for the purposes of competitive collective victimhood.[3] When the judgements were finally delivered at the end of the trial, their sheer length proved prohibitive for all but the most dedicated and curious readers. A significant risk therefore exists that victim testimony, so painstakingly collected with the cooperation of the witnesses, will essentially remain buried. It is therefore worth considering what measures can be undertaken to disseminate and (re)vitalize victim testimony so that it does not disappear. The chapter concludes with a presentation of my own recent book about the Yugoslav wars of succession in which I tried to incorporate victim-witness testimony.

Background

The ICTY was established by the UN Security Council in May 1993, at a time when armed conflict was still occurring in Croatia and in Bosnia and Herzegovina. Initially, therefore, great scepticism existed even among the advocates and founders of the Tribunal as to whether any perpetrators at all would actually be apprehended and put on trial. The first person apprehended in February 1994, Duško Tadić, was a minor perpetrator whose arrest allowed the Tribunal to mount its first trial beginning in 1996.

As noted by Robert Jackson, the chief prosecutor at Nuremberg, the challenge in trying mass atrocities was to 'establish incredible events by credible evidence'.[4] Although the Office of the Prosecutor (OTP) followed their ancestors at Nuremberg by placing significant emphasis on the use of documentation as evidence, witness testimony played a much more important role in The Hague than in Nuremberg, where victims were barely heard at all.[5] Several categories of witnesses existed, including expert witnesses — the very first witness was James Gow, a professor of international peace and security — international non-expert witnesses (e.g. military observers), insider witnesses from the conflicting parties and victim-witnesses. It is this last category which I wish to focus on here.

Victim-witnesses are those witnesses who themselves became victims as a result of being present when atrocities were committed, even if they were not personally physically harmed in these atrocities.[6] Without exception, the victim-witnesses stemmed from the former Yugoslavia, although many of them had been resettled to other countries as refugees prior to testifying at the ICTY, while others were resettled after testifying. Often years or even decades had elapsed between the occurrence of the events about which they were testifying and their appearance as witnesses in The Hague, hence creating challenges regarding memory and the reliability of witness testimony.[7]

To date, the most thorough study of witnesses at the ICTY is the book *The Witness Experience: Testimony at the ICTY and Its Impact*. The authors, Kimi Lynn King and James David Meernik of the University of North Texas, used survey methodology with a sample of 300 witnesses in order to gather data about this topic. The book treats many facets of their experience. The authors noted that they 'purposely oversampled' women in their survey, although relatively few women testified at the ICTY, approximately 13% of the total.[8] Unsurprisingly, 'the levels of wartime trauma endured by these witnesses are significant and substantial'.[9]

Eric Stover also produced a book on witnesses and the ICTY. His interviews with them showed that many of them felt a 'moral duty to testify' — 'to ensure that the truth about the death of family members, neighbours, and colleagues was duly recorded and acknowledged. They went to The Hague not on a quest for vengeance [...] but to set the record straight about the suffering of their families and communities in the presence of the accused.'[10]

Framing Victim-Witness Testimony at the ICTY

It bears noting that the victim-witnesses who testified at the ICTY were a subset of a much larger universe of potential victim-witnesses. For a variety of reasons, many witnesses were never approached by investigators, were unavailable, or refused to speak with investigators. Of those who were contacted, ICTY prosecution and defence investigators took statements from considerably more people than the number of those who actually testified at the Tribunal. Many reasons explain why some victims gave statements but never testified. Some of them were assessed to have given statements with little or comparatively less probative value when compared with other victims. Some became unavailable to testify because of health, security or other concerns. And, controversially, amendments to the ICTY's Rules of Procedure and Evidence made it possible to introduce more witness testimony in the form of statements rather than *viva voce* testimony.[11] Even when witnesses were presented in court, the rules meant that the side proffering the witness presented only a brief summary of the statement and then made the witness available for cross-examination and any questions that the judges might have. This effectively mean that some witnesses were left in the emotionally unsatisfactory situation of having their oral testimony be largely restricted to cross-examination, which could be stressful and upsetting for some. Conversely, the resultant relative brevity of the testimony may have benefited some witnesses.

It is neither new nor contentious to observe that the primary objective of criminal trials is to assess the guilt of the individuals accused in the given trial. It follows that a competent and professional trial chamber, including judges, prosecutors and defence attorneys, will duly structure the introduction, presentation and evaluation of evidence so as to achieve this common objective. Already here a tension can be observed between, on the one hand, the desire and need of many if not all victims to unburden themselves and share their stories in as much detail as possible with the economic and time constraints of a criminal court or tribunal on the other. Critics have argued that 'when this tension is resolved in favour of the requirements of collective justice, the needs of individual victims are overlooked so that "justice" is not done to them and to what they have to say.'[12]

The testimony of victim-witnesses at the ICTY was necessarily structured. Witnesses were not permitted to make extemporaneous statements or hold forth at their own volition on topics of their choosing. Rather, they had to respond to the questions posed by the parties to the case: the prosecution, the defence and the judges (the trial chamber). Given the hybrid but predominantly Anglo-Saxon model adopted in the ICTY statute, the questioning of witnesses took place in an adversarial framework of direct examination followed by cross-examination, though with the opportunity for the judges to pose their own supplementary questions. Understandably, this meant that witnesses sometimes ended up having to discuss at length things that they found unpleasant or irrelevant, while some issues or memories which they would have preferred to explore and elucidate remained unspoken.

Quite obviously, the use of cross-examination exposed victims to the risk of retraumatization and undoubtedly proved difficult for many of them. Defence attorneys must diligently and aggressively question the accuracy and veracity of victim-witnesses' accounts. Though legally necessary and important for the rights of the defendants, such interrogation can very quickly appear callous and hurtful, as is vividly illustrated in the recent documentary series 'The Devil Next Door' (2019) on the long trial of Holocaust perpetrator Ivan (John) Demjanjuk in Israel in the 1980s.[13] These challenges exist even for prosecutors who are trying to convict those accused of the crimes committed against these victims. When prosecutors strive to 'take' witnesses as quickly and efficiently as possible, there is often not much time for compassion. But the challenge and the risk become even greater when victim-witnesses are cross-examined in the adversarial system used by international criminal courts and tribunals.

Judges acted to some extent as referees, and prosecutors also objected when defence council's cross-examination of victims appeared to cross the line from reasonable scrutiny of potentially probative evidence to ad hominem attacks on the witnesses themselves. Conversely, judges must remain sceptical and 'check their empathy' in order to respect the rights of the accused. This balancing act does not always succeed. Finally, the victims and witnesses services unit of the Registry worked tirelessly and often with limited resources and under tremendous pressure to ensure the needs of witnesses were properly addressed before, during and after testimony.

The Structure of ICTY Judgements

The judgements of the ICTY are, needless to say, primarily legal documents. As such, their primary purpose is to set forth the trial chamber's verdict of guilt or innocence of those accused in a particular case. Judgements typically introduce the counts of the prosecution's indictment, discuss the applicable law (jurisprudence), review the factual and legal findings based on the evidence presented by the prosecution and the defence, discuss the criminal responsibility of the accused, and then conclude by pronouncing the accused guilty or innocent as regards each point of the indictment and, finally, pronounce the sentence. Judgements range in size from several hundred to several thousand pages — in the cases examined here 260 pages (*Krstić*), 290 pages (*Stakić*), 334 pages (*Galić*), 360 pages (*Lukić*), and 2,615 pages (*Karadžić*).

As will be evident from this overview, there are large sections of the judgements that contain no witness testimony at all. However, all cases relied extensively on witness testimony. For example, in *Galić* 171 witnesses were heard. Of course, only a subset of these were victim-witnesses, and only portions of their testimony were eventually quoted in the judgements, and as already noted these victim-witnesses were themselves a subset of a much larger potential group. Nonetheless, at least for the purposes of the ICTY, it is their testimony that shapes the understanding of victims' experiences.

It was my original intention with this chapter to explore victim-witness testimony that was actually quoted verbatim in ICTY judgements. However, my review of these judgements revealed that the trial chambers only rarely did so at length, choosing instead to summarize and paraphrase the testimony of victim-witnesses.

Galić

Galić was one of two trials focusing exclusively on the siege of Sarajevo. Stanislav Galić commanded the Sarajevo Romanjia Corps of the Bosnian Serbs' army. This corps besieged Sarajevo for nearly the entire duration of the Bosnian war (1992–95), perpetrating nearly daily shelling and sniping attacks. The majority of the trial chamber found that 'Galić was not simply kept abreast of the crimes of his subordinates, he actually controlled the pace and scale of those crimes'.[14] For the crimes committed under his command, Galić was sentenced to life in prison.

In *Galić*, witness testimony was deployed to convey not just the events of the siege — the longest since the Second World War — but also the mood of those enduring it. Witness Tarik Kupusović, a member of the city council, recalled the shock of the beginning of the shelling, while other witnesses referred to disbelief and a 'feeling that something was wrong'.[15] Many of the most poignant descriptions of the harrowing dangers faced by citizens of Sarajevo during the siege came from victim-witnesses: information regarding the shelling or sniping, and the morbid happiness of citizens 'when there was a thick fog in town and around it, when there was no sniping.'[16] One witness stated that she never went out alone during the siege because she was afraid of what would happen to her three children if she were to be wounded or killed without their knowledge.

In addition to the victim-witnesses, the judgment relied heavily upon international witnesses, including journalists such as the Norwegian photographer Morten Hvaal and the Dutch Aernout van Lynden. Their testimony was also quoted in order to corroborate the suffering of Sarajevo's population and the magnitude of the siege and the daily attacks on civilians. Hvaal, who covered the war in Bosnia from September 1992 to August 1994, had attended numerous burials of victims. He recounted how it became necessary to conduct such burials at night in order to avoid those attending these ceremonies themselves becoming victims.[17] This corroborated the testimony of Fuad Šehbajraktarević, a Sarajevo funeral parlour director.[18]

In the judgement, scheduled sniping and shelling incidents function as a way of focusing attention on individuals. As already noted, it is in the nature of the criminal trial that those victims who were selected to testify in the trial represented but a small subset of the total number of potential victims who could have testified. And of these witnesses, not all would find their voices transmitted in the judgements, though some trial chambers tried to list victims and/or incidents in annexes to the judgements. It should also be noted that there were seldom extensive quotations from testimony in the analysis of these incidents. Most of the quotes are brief — albeit sometimes also evocatively dramatic. Thus, the killing of Hatema Mukanović by a sniper on 11 January 1994 was recounted in much detail by her husband, Akif Mukanović. For the fateful moment of her shooting, the trial chamber chose to quote directly the victim's husband's account.[19]

In general, however, the analysis reads like an extended and largely clinical paraphrase of the witnesses' testimony.

Stakić

The case against Milomir Stakić focused on Prijedor, a municipality in north-western Bosnia, and on surrounding municipalities. As one of the leaders of the municipal government, Stakić was instrumental in organizing the persecution of Bosnian Muslims and Croats. 'He actively participated in the establishment of the camps Omarska, Keraterm and Trnopolje where detainees were subjected to serious mistreatment and abuse which amounted to torture on a daily basis: detainees were severely beaten, often with weapons such as cables, batons and chains.'[20] Together with other civilian leaders, the police and the military, Stakić aimed 'to consolidate Serb control over Prijedor municipality at any cost, resulting in widespread killings committed by Serb forces in towns, surrounding areas, and in detention facilities throughout the municipality.'[21] Stakić was sentenced to forty years in prison.

One of the most interesting but least studied aspects of victim-witness testimony in ICTY trials concerns the contingency of Yugoslavia's collapse and the onset of armed conflict. Many victims have testified poignantly how they simply could not come to terms with the fact that their society and state were collapsing around them. This is the primary reason why, for my newly published Danish account of the collapse of Yugoslavia and the ensuing wars, I chose the title 'We didn't think it could happen here.'[22]

Many victims provided detailed accounts not only of the suffering they had endured when crimes were being committed against them, but also about the weeks and months leading up to the outbreak of armed conflict in their area. For example, Mirsad Mujadžić recalled how he had instructed an acquaintance to leave Prijedor as soon as possible for his own safety. The acquaintance had incredulously asked 'But why Mirza? What could possibly happen to me? What did I do wrong? Did I wrong them in any way? We never did anything nor did we plan anything of which we could be accused.' According to the witness, at the time people typically told him 'Why should we run? There is no reason for [anyone] to accuse us of anything, even less arrest us.'[23] Although this part of his testimony touches on no concrete violent or criminal acts, Mujadžić's words poignantly convey the disintegration of a multi-ethnic society and the surreal sense of disbelief of those whose lives would soon be torn apart and lost. Many similar testimonies were elicited from victim witnesses in the trial, but again only portions of their narratives were included in the judgement.

Several of the aforementioned scholars have noted and criticized what they regard as the coarse, unprofessional and inappropriate treatment of some victim-witnesses by judges at the ICTY. Undoubtedly there have been instances in which judges have not treated victim-witnesses in an optimal manner. However, in *Stakić*, presiding judge Wolfgang Schomburg also tried to put a female victim-witness at ease, and also spoke directly to the witness to explain why her testimony was so important. 'You shouldn't be nervous. You should know that the purpose of our work, and we are mandated to find the truth and to hear what the persons in the country, in [the] former Yugoslavia, have experienced. And it's only you, the witnesses, who can tell us what has happened. And I think it could, and can be, of course, also helpful for you if you can tell us what you have experienced in a context.'[24]

Perusing the *Stakić* judgement, the difference with the more clinical treatment of sniping and shelling incidents in *Galić* is apparent. In *Stakić*, the violence was spread chronologically over a shorter period of time than in *Galić*, as the *Stakić* indictment focused solely on crimes committed in 1992. Moreover, the kind of violence perpetrated in *Stakić* was different. In the siege of Sarajevo, the victims were wounded and killed by shells and high velocity bullets fired from artillery positions and snipers' nests hundreds of metres or even kilometres away — in other words without ever seeing the faces of their attackers. In Prijedor, by contrast, the victims of the violence saw their lives and their country disintegrate slowly in front of them, and the victims were often brutally beaten, tortured and killed by perpetrators whom they had previously known personally or professionally. Both kinds of violence were each in their way protracted, but still qualitatively different. A proper understanding of the Bosnian war must encompass both types of stories.

It should be noted that in *Stakić* and in all other ICTY cases, some of the most sensitive testimony was redacted because it occurred in closed sessions, and appears only in summarized form in judgements.

Lukić and Lukić

Moving to the opposite end of Bosnia from Prijedor, the picturesque municipality of Višegrad was made world famous by Ivo Andrić's novel *The Bridge over the River Drina*, which earned him the distinction in 1961 of becoming the only Yugoslav author awarded the Nobel Prize in Literature. Tragically, thirty-one years later the municipality of Višegrad in eastern Bosnia became the scene of some of the worst incidents of the practice euphemistically known as 'ethnic cleansing'.

At the ICTY, Milan Lukić and Sredoje Lukić were charged with committing war crimes and crimes against humanity as leading figures in a paramilitary group known as the 'White Eagles' or 'Avengers'. Even by the appalling standards of the Bosnian conflict, the brutality of these two perpetrators was astounding. Unlike Galić and Stakić, the two accused in *Lukić and Lukić* had participated directly in carrying out crimes. Milan Lukić personally led men to the banks of the Drina River and shot them and participated in numerous similar extrajudicial killings. In one of the most notorious incidents of the war, Lukić 'murdered 53 Bosnian Muslim women, children and elderly men in a house on Pionirska Street in Višegrad by barricading the victims in one room of the house, setting the house on fire and then firing automatic weapons at those people who tried to escape through the windows, killing some and injuring others.'[25] A similar incident in Bikavac near Višegrad cost eighty Bosnian Muslim women, children and elderly men their lives. Sredoje Lukić participated in the Pionirska Street incident. Milan Lukić was sentenced to life imprisonment, while Sredoje Lukić received a sentence of twenty-seven years.

The perpetrators' direct participation in committing crimes meant that a number of witnesses testifying in this case recalled personally encountering the accused and witnessing their violent acts. Perhaps therefore, there seems to be a greater tendency in the judgement to include block quotes of witness testimony and, generally speaking, to rely on such testimony, particularly where mass crimes and sexual crimes are concerned.

A particularly good example of the use of victim-witness testimony in *Lukić and Lukić* is the excruciating testimony of Zehra Turjačanin, a Bosniak woman who was attacked by Milan Lukić and his associates in June 1992 as part of the Bikavac incident. Drawing on the testimony of Turjačanin and several other — mostly protected — witnesses, the trial chamber painstakingly reconstructed the attack. The accounts proffered to the trial chamber clearly left a deep impression on the judges, compelling them to write that

> In the all too long, sad and wretched history of man's inhumanity to man, the Pionirska street and Bikavac fires must rank high. At the close of the 20th century, a century marked by war and bloodshed on a colossal scale, these horrific events remain imprinted on the memory for the viciousness of the incendiary attack, for the obvious premeditation and calculation that defined it, for the sheer callousness, monstrosity and brutality of herding, trapping and locking the victims in the two houses, thereby rendering them helpless in the ensuing inferno and for the degree of pain and suffering inflicted on the victims as they were burnt alive.[26]

A Very Preliminary Conclusion — and a Plea

The eloquence of the above passage in the *Lukić and Lukić* pales when placed next to the courageous full testimonies of victim-witnesses like Zehra Turjačanin. Unfortunately, very few people will read the summaries of the testimonies in the lengthy judgements of the ICTY. And even fewer will take the time to go to the — publicly available — transcripts of their testimony. Hence, for all intents and purposes, these important testimonies that tell us so much about the conflicts in the former Yugoslavia remain buried, lost to all but a few experts working on Yugoslav history and international criminal justice. To give but one example, the English-language transcript in *Stakić* spans 15,362 pages, and that is a trial focusing predominantly on crimes in one north-western Bosnian town, Prijedor, and the surrounding municipalities. Moreover, the transcript is only available in English and French, as astoundingly, no Bosnian-Croatian-Serbian transcripts were made. The original video recordings of testimony exist in the ICTY's archives, but very few of these are publicly available.

An inadvertent irony of judgements serving as the principal texts of international criminal courts and tribunals should also be noted. The main focus of attention in the judgements is necessarily on the accused perpetrator and not the victims. In the case of trials where the perpetrator is defending himself, he is afforded even more agency, and is in some ways able to perpetuate and even increase his role. This focus on the perpetrator also affected reporting about the cases. Quite often, both international journalists and those from the region paid attention to the trials only when the verdicts and sentences were pronounced, which again left the perpetrators and not the victims as the centre of attention.[27] Media outlets in the former Yugoslavia tended to only display interest in their 'own' victims: to the extent that victims' testimony at the ICTY received media coverage at all, Croatian media highlighted the testimony of Croat victims, Serbian media focused on Serb victims, etc. The only agency that consistently covered all the trials and victim-witness testimony was the Sense Agency.[28]

Selma Leydesdorff has argued that even as regards the Srebrenica genocide, all too many stories have been about DutchBat, i.e. the Dutch battalion stationed in the Srebrenica 'safe haven', and very few about the Bosnian Muslim victims.[29] To Leydesdorff, the problem with the testimony of victim-witnesses at the ICTY is that 'the accusatory has become the main form of discourse when talking about the war. Legal witnesses give a different kind of account than what I am interested in.'[30] Yet some of the victims Leydesdorff herself quotes are extremely accusatory. Another problem is presented by the prevalence of journalists who converge upon Srebrenica annually to cover the anniversary of the genocide. 'Every July, journalists arrive in Bosnia looking for instant interviews; many survivors have learned how to give the desired sound bites. This made it difficult for me to explain why they should speak differently to me.'

Another reason to examine more closely victim-witness testimony is to highlight those elements of their stories that were told in court but were not distilled into the judgements because their tales fell outside the scope of the indictment. In the *Lukić* case, for example, the trial chamber specifically mentioned extensive testimonial evidence of rape and other forms of sexual violence that was heard in that case but which was not included in the judgement. The reason for this was that the prosecution had attempted to add additional charges to the indictment after the beginning of the trial, but this motion was denied.[31]

There are many different ways in which victim-witness testimony could be better disseminated. One possibility would be to publish thematically or geographically focused collections of testimony, augmented by annotated commentary. The themes could relate not only to the types of criminal conduct experienced but could also encompass the immediate pre-war period and early war disintegration of normality. In order to speed the process and perhaps facilitate broader dissemination, online avenues of presentation should also be considered. The ICTY's own website has a section entitled 'Voice of the Victims' that provides a potential model, though in practice only very small numbers of witnesses and snippets or summaries of their testimonies are included.[32] A much more ambitious model would be the testimonials gathered and made publicly available by the University of Southern California Shoah Foundation.[33]

This, in turn, leads to a pressing question: is it possible to 'rescue' atrocity testimony from (relative) oblivion and, if so, how can this be accomplished? Besides adapting publicly available victim-witness testimony for publication, another possibility would be to encourage victim-witnesses to publish their own accounts. This should obviously only occur if these witnesses themselves wish to pursue this option. To date, only a very small number have done so. The most notable example is Isak Gaši's book, *Eyewitness: My Journey to The Hague*, which provides a much more detailed and evocative portrait of the war in Brčko in northern Bosnia than his own testimonies at the ICTY already did.[34] Gaši's story is in many respects particularly remarkable, not least because he competed as an athlete for Yugoslavia before the war, but there are many good reasons why similar memoirs should be encouraged. Another option would be to encourage fictionalized accounts, though these are often different from testimonials, even if the authors have personally experienced the wars of Yugoslav dissolution.[35] Such fictionalized accounts also raise the question of whether we would read a victim-witness's testimony differently if we read it from a literary point of view.

Finally, and hopefully needless to say, there is no reason why the dissemination of victim-witness narratives should be limited in the Yugoslav case to those who testified at the ICTY. Many others suffered similar atrocities but never testified at the ICTY. Moreover, not all of those witnesses are available any longer. Some have died, some have been relocated for reasons of witness protection, some would strongly prefer not to have to speak about their experiences again, some simply want to move on and not have their status as victim-witnesses become a 'lifetime sentence'. Secondly, women are as a group for various reasons quite severely underrepresented among ICTY witnesses, and it would be very desirable to have more of their voices recorded and heard.[36] Thirdly — and I recognize here that I have in this chapter focused overwhelmingly on the Bosnian war — there were geographical areas or chronological periods of the wars of Yugoslav succession that were not covered in depth by the ICTY. Stories from these witnesses should also be heard.

That said, the ICTY has assembled a very large number of victim-witness testimonies. I make no claims here that the testimonies of victim-witnesses at the ICTY are *a priori* of higher value than the atrocity stories of the large majority of victims However, the testimonies of ICTY victim-witnesses are identifiable and accessible in a manner that renders them available to interpretation and further dissemination outside the courtroom. They deserve further dissemination, they deserve to be heard by broader audiences, as they contribute in many ways to our understanding of conflict and human misconduct. Historical accounts of the wars of Yugoslav succession still incorporate relatively little victim-witness testimony. In my own modest way, in my 2018 Danish book on the collapse of Yugoslavia and the ensuing wars, I strove to incorporate the voices of the victims.[37] By returning to their testimonies in court and quoting them at length and paraphrasing their experiences, I tried to provide the readers with a better sense of the lives that were shattered by the wars which tore apart a vibrant multi-ethnic society. It is my hope and wish that we will find new ways to honour their courage and their voices.

Notes to Chapter 12

1. Patricia M. Wald, 'The International Criminal Tribunal for the Former Yugoslavia Comes of Age: Some Observations on Day-to-Day Dilemmas of an International Court', *Journal of Law & Policy*, 5 (2001), 87–118 (p. 107).
2. Lawrence Douglas, *The Memory of Judgment: Making Law and History in the Trials of the Holocaust* (New Haven, CT: Yale University Press, 2001).
3. Christian Axboe Nielsen, 'Collective and Competitive Victimhood as Identity in the Former Yugoslavia', in *Understanding the Age of Transitional Justice: Crimes, Courts, Commissions, and Chronicling*, ed. by Nanci Adler (New Brunswick, NJ: Rutgers University Press, 2018), pp. 175–93.
4. This quote was also used by ICTY judge Patricia M. Wald in her own article on affidavit testimony at the ICTY. Patricia M. Wald, 'To "Establish Incredible Events by Credible Evidence": The Use of Affidavit Testimony in Yugoslavia War Crimes Tribunal Proceedings', *Harvard International Law Journal*, 42.2 (Summer 2001), 535–53. See also Patricia M. Wald, 'Dealing with Witnesses in War Crimes Trials: Lessons from the Yugoslav Tribunal', *Yale Human Rights & Development Journal*, 5.1 (2002), 217–39.
5. The trial of Adolf Eichmann in Jerusalem in 1961 marked a breakthrough in the introduction of victim-witnesses into Holocaust trials. See Lawrence Douglas.
6. On victim narratives generally, see Diana Tietjens Meyers, *Victims' Stories and the Advancement of Human Rights* (Oxford: Oxford University Press, 2016).
7. For an incisive critique of the reliance on witness testimony — though based largely on studies of tribunals other than the ICTY — see Nancy Combs, *Fact-Finding without Facts: The Uncertain Evidentiary Foundations of International Criminal Convictions* (Cambridge: Cambridge University Press, 2010).
8. Kimi Lynn King and James David Meernik, *The Witness Experience: Testimony at the ICTY and Its Impact* (Cambridge: Cambridge University Press, 2017), p. 179. Because some trials, including those of Radovan Karadžić and Ratko Mladić were ongoing at the time of their research, King and Meernik were unfortunately unable to speak to witnesses testifying in these trials.
9. King and Meernik, *Testimony at the ICTY*, p. 181.
10. Eric Stover, *The Witnesses: War Crimes and the Promise of Justice in The Hague* (Philadelphia: University of Pennsylvania Press, 2005), pp. 126–27.

11. Eric Stover, *The Witnesses*, pp. 130–31.
12. Marie-Bénédicte Dembour and Emily Haslam, 'Silencing Hearings? Victim-Witnesses at War Crimes Trials', *European Journal of International Law*, 15.1 (2004), 151–77 (p. 154). I would note that I find it quite problematic that these authors castigate other researchers for speaking on behalf of victims when these authors do so themselves — without having interviewed any witnesses.
13. The travails of the victim-witnesses in the Demjanjuk trial is also dealt with in Lawrence Douglas, *The Right Wrong Man: John Demjanjuk and the Last Great Nazi War Crimes Trial* (Princeton, NJ: Princeton University Press, 2016).
14. ICTY, Stanislav Galić, Case Information Sheet (IT-98–29).
15. ICTY, *Galić*, Judgement, para 200.
16. ICTY, *Galić*, Judgement, para 222 and *passim*.
17. ICTY, *Galić*, Judgement, para 220.
18. ICTY *Galić*, Judgement, para 220 and para 524.
19. *Galić*, Judgement, para 278.
20. ICTY, Milomir Stakić Case Information Sheet (IT-97–24).
21. ICTY, Milomir Stakić Case Information Sheet (IT-97–24).
22. A colleague later pointed out a similarity with Sinclair Lewis's *It Can Happen Here*.
23. <http://www.icty.org/x/cases/stakic/trans/en/020528IT.htm>, p. 3710.
24. ICTY, Transcript of *Stakić*, 4 June 2002, 3935–36, <http://www.icty.org/x/cases/stakic/trans/en/020604ED.htm>.
25. ICTY, Milan Lukić and Sredoje Lukić, Case Information Sheet (IT-98–32/1).
26. ICTY, Judgement, *Lukić and Lukić*, para 740.
27. The case of Slobodan Praljak is particularly egregious. By committing suicide in December 2017 when the appeal chamber's sentence was pronounced — the chamber confirmed his sentence — he ensured that the attention of the international media would focus solely on him, and not on his and his co-accused's many victims.
28. The archive of the Senses Agency is available online, <https://sensecentar.org>.
29. Selma Leydesdorff and Kay Richardson, *Surviving the Bosnian Genocide: The Women of Srebrenica Speak* (Bloomington: Indiana University Press, 2011).
30. Leydesdorff, *Surviving*, p. 18.
31. ICTY, Judgement *Lukić and Lukić*, para 36–37.
32. ICTY, 'Voice of the Victims', <http://www.icty.org/en/features/voice-of-the-victims>.
33. USC Shoah Foundation, <https://sfi.usc.edu>. On video testimony, see Aleida Assmann, 'History, Memory, and the Genre of Testimony', *Poetics Today* (Summer 2006), pp. 262–73.
34. Isak Gaši, *Eyewitness: My Journey to The Hague* (Richmond, VA: Brandylane Publishers, 2018).
35. Some notable literary works that would fit into this category are those of Alen Mešković (*Ukulele Jam*, 2011), Pajtim Statovci (*My Cat Yugoslavia*, 2014), Ivana Simić Bodrožić (*The Hotel Tito*, 2010) and Saša Stanišić (*How the Soldier Repairs the Gramophone*, 2006). The short stories of Aleksandar Hemon also deserve mention, though these are more about Yugoslavia than about the wars.
36. On victimhood and gender during and after the Bosnian war, see Elissa Helms, *Innocence and Victimhood: Gender, Nation and Women's Activism in Postwar Bosnia-Herzegovina* (Madison: University of Wisconsin Press, 2013).
37. Christian Axboe Nielsen, *Vi troede ikke, at det kunne ske her: Jugoslaviens sammenbrud, 1991–1999* (Copenhagen: Kristeligt Dagblads Forlag, 2018).

PART IV

Arab World

CHAPTER 13

From Writing in Suffering to Thinking Freedom, or How to 'walk on forgetfulness'

Sonia Zlitni-Fitouri

> Every time our sad societies, in a perpetual crisis of growth, start to doubt themselves, they may be seen wondering if they were right to question their past, or if they have questioned it properly. — Marc Bloch

If there is one recurring feature in the bloody history of humanity other than violence and massacres, it is perhaps the sufferings that go unspoken, and the perpetrators' denial of their deeds. The victims, often devastated and at a loss, have to find the strength to 'think in terms of the possible and the sayable what is often cast as an exception, as the impossible and the unsayable', in the words of Philippe Mesnard.[1]

This chapter does not provide sufficient space to explore all the various characteristics of the accounts written against the backdrop of violence in my corpus, namely: *Cristal* by Gilbert Naccache,[2] about political repression in Tunisia in the 1960s and 1970s, *La Prisonnière* by Malika Oufkir,'[3] about the 'years of lead' in Morocco during the 1970s and 1980s, and *Nos silences* by Wahiba Khiari,[4] which takes us back to the dark decade of 1990s Algeria. The cathartic and therapeutic function of writing being postulated as the starting point of this book, I focus mainly on the important transition from a need to break the silence and say the unqualifiable in a mimetic writing of suffering, to the need to act on a duty to remember and thus bear witness.

I also seek to show that writing and bearing witness thus become a way of 'walking on forgetfulness',[5] of resuscitating a 'pathological memory', of moving towards thoughts of freedom which, according to Nicolas Kovacs, imply 'a dual questioning: first, about the random position of the individual in a period forever torn by social upheaval, and second, on the very meaning of history in a world where freedom and justice are crushed by mechanisms of ideological, bureaucratic, and police oppression'.[6] These questions are, to my mind, essential if we are to transition towards democracy.

Saying the Unqualifiable to 'walk on forgetfulness'

The Moroccan author Malika Oufkir, in her first book, *La Prisonnière*, co-written with the Jewish Tunisian journalist Michèle Fitoussi, offers a deeply moving account of the drama that struck her family. The Oufkir family, who were very closely connected to the Palace, and lived opulently, were detained on 25 December 1972 after the failed coup orchestrated by General Mohamed Oufkir against King Hassan II. The official reason for this was to protect them from the warranted anger of the Moroccan people. They were sent without trial to a secret prison in the Sahara desert, where they were held in extremely harsh conditions, then at Bir Jdid, not far from Casablanca, where Malika Oufkir and her family spent a total of nineteen years in detention in rat- and scorpion-infested cells, hungry, thirsty, and ravaged by illness:

> Barefoot and dressed in rags, we shivered in winter and suffocated in summer. We no longer had a nurse, or medicines [...]. Hunger sometimes drove us to the limit. It was so violent that we would cast envious glances at one of the others who hadn't yet finished their meagre share.[7]

Malika's escape on 19 April 1987, with one of her sisters and her two brothers (by digging a tunnel with a teaspoon), brought their plight to the attention of the French authorities. Although they were recaptured, it led to her mother and other siblings being released.

In *La Prisonnière*, Malika describes in minute detail the degrading conditions in which they lived, their failed attempts at hunger strikes and collective suicide, the violence of certain of their jailers, and the depression caused by solitude and isolation. The royal decision was clear: to strike the Oufkirs off the list of the living. This is conveyed to the reader when they hear the head jailer, Borro, saying to one of his colleagues: 'Don't you understand? It's clear enough. They're going to die. All of them. And they'll be buried here. We'll wait as long as it takes. Those are our orders.'[8] The injustice of this forced disappearance is brought out by Gilles Perrault in his book *Notre ami le Roi*, published in 1990, where he writes: 'in the name of what strange morality is horror inflicted on innocent children for fifteen years? Is there a single criminal code in the world that punishes the crime of descent?'[9]

While the members of the Oufkir family paid for the crime of their father, the Tunisian Gilbert Naccache served an eleven-year prison sentence under the Bourguiba regime because of his political opinions. He had been a communist activist prior even to independence, and a member and leader (in the mid-1960s) of the radical left-wing movement 'Perspectives'. He was given a heavy sentence in March 1968, and jailed in Borj Erroumi, a sordid prison which few ever left alive. He was released in 1979. Naccache's account of this prison experience, written on paper from Cristal cigarettes, emphasizes the repression, torture, and stasis of time.

Cristal provides description after description of the various torture positions, the humiliation of prisoners at the hands of zealous jailers, how they were deprived of everything, the 'stripping away of their sense of self', and the descent into the hellish vaults beneath Borj Roumi:

> Disguised, barefoot, with coarse trousers and a scratchy tunic collar, I found myself sitting on the ground at the foot of the barber who removed what hair I had with three sweeps of his clippers. A corridor, insults from the warders, turn right, a sort of chicane, a door and a cave, a real cave, oval in shape, with bits of rocks and a circular opening for ventilation [...]. Here I was in the infamous vaults beneath Borj Roumi [...] which common prisoners in Tunis spoke of with terror.[10]

In a different register, but also against a backdrop of unspeakable violence, *Nos silences*, by the Algerian writer Wahiba Khiari, follows the fate of two women confronted with the horror of the dark decade of the Algerian civil war. Forced disappearances started with the war in Algeria in 1992, initially targeting certain individuals, but followed by mass kidnappings as of 1994. The victims were snatched at fake roadblocks. At first it was intellectuals, academics, doctors, lawyers, and so on who were taken. Then the terrorists took women to be used as sex slaves. One of the two female characters, an English teacher, who functions as the author's double, manages to leave the country and escape the violence; the other, one of the English teacher's pupils, is snatched from her family and held in the Maquis, where she is exposed to the murderous frenzy of religious fanaticism. These two voices break the silence in a series of confessional monologues — the silence of those who were afraid, of those who mourned, and of those who did not find the courage to denounce or rebel.

The narrator denounces Islamists who, under the guise of 'temporary marriage', rape girls, getting them pregnant with a *bismillah* (in the name of God) or *fatiha*. She describes the girl's bruised and defiled body: 'My body was a battlefield strewn with bruises and bloodied by blows. I had to pick myself up from beneath the wreckage once they had been and gone.'[11] A bit later, she adds:

> Finally one of them managed to sow his seed in me. After having been ploughed so, it was only normal that I germinate. Even though bad seeds are not meant to give life, I am pregnant.[12]

With the passing of the months and years, the context of violence described in *Cristal*, *La Prisonnière*, and *Nos silences* receded, paving the way, by mutual agreement to a kind of respite. History shows us that the aftermaths of conflicts often include amnesty laws, a need to find a way out while remaining aware that it will in any case be unsatisfactory and frustrating. One may, at a pinch, understand that a society needs to turn the page. But by the time of the national reconciliation policy and proposed amnesty of 29 September 2005 in Algeria, of the setting up of the Equity and Reconciliation Commission (Instance d'équité et réconciliation, or IER) on 7 January 2004 in Morocco, and of the Truth and Dignity Commission (Instance de verité et de dignité, or IVD) in 2013 in Tunisia, was it still possible to turn the page and to forgive? Were these reconciliations capable of healing the psychological wounds, of cleansing the stigmata left by the horrors people had undergone? Was it not, in the words of Jacques Commaille, 'a form of abusive political normalization of the victims'?[13] This leads us to the issue of transitional justice.

Clearly, when it is decided to forget, on the pretext of enabling a society to rebuild after an amnesty or national reconciliation law, the victims, representing the core of the collective memory of what happened in the country, are necessarily excluded from the process. Burdened by their experience, about which they have no external knowledge, no truth, they stay stuck in the time of their trauma. They will be unable to move on even when they wish to do so. Theirs is a suspended, immobile time. And while most of the country gradually comes to forget, or repress memories, the victims remain condemned to their suffering and isolation.

As the Algerian journalist and writer Souad Belhadad has observed about Algeria:

> The president requested the forgiveness of all victims in the name of the nation, not of the culprits. Not only were there no apologies to the victims, but they were asked to make an effort. To accept an apology that had not even been voiced to them [...]. But an apology for what? Since, officially, nothing had happened [...]. The term civil war was barred from the language. There was not a trace of a commemorative plaque, not a single street name to mark the slightest memory of these ten years of terror. Knowing was downright forbidden.[14]

Victims risked being trapped in a state of unending resentment, in danger of turning in on their own tragedy, despite aspiring to peace, despite sometimes wishing to give in to forgiveness. But of whom? How? And on the basis of what reality?

When the Oufkir family left prison, far from benefitting from any recognition or any expression of regret by the Palace, they were enjoined to silence by the authorities. Their salvation was bought in exchange for their silence: 'the king does not wish to hear any more about it, but in exchange we must say nothing about what we experienced'.[15] This line in the *La Prisonnière* inevitably sends us to the deceitful speech in Tahar Benjelloun's *Cette aveuglante absence de lumière*:

> Sidna the king has pardoned you. In a few days you'll be with your family. You will doubtless be contacted by foreign journalists, by people wishing to harm our country. The conduct you should adopt is straightforward: do not answer their poisoned questions. Do not cooperate with them. Refuse all contact. If you try any tricks, I'll escort you back to Tazmamart in person.[16]

A vow of silence? Most certainly not. In 1999 Malika Oufkir published the first of a series of books, *La Prisonnière* (which was banned in Morocco), while in 2000 Fatema Oufkir published *Les Jardins du Roi*,[17] in 2005 Raouf Oufkir published *Les Invités: 20 ans dans les prisons de Hassan II*,[18] and in 2008 Soukaina Oufkir *La Vie devant moi: une enfance dans les prisons de Hassan II*.[19] For literature banishes enforced forgetting, reactivates 'atrophied memories', and breaks down the barriers of silence.

In a second book, *L'Etrangère*,[20] published in 2006, Malika Oufkir goes over the psychological traumas and physical consequences of her incarceration. She also goes over what motivated her to write her two accounts, in a chapter with the revealing title 'Ecrire pour témoigner' [Writing to bear witness], which opens with the following lines:

> Surviving. I was guilty of surviving. A strange guilt. My sole prospect was to bear witness, to tell the whole world that Morocco was not the democracy championed by the West, particularly by France. Everyone should know about the barbarism that lay behind the monarchic countenance. In writing *La*

> *prisonnière*, [...] I exorcized the past, partly freed myself of it, but I had to carry the burden of the role assigned to me, that of a victim.[21]

For her part, the Algerian writer Wahiba Khiari sets out an indictment of the law's silence surrounding the crimes of rape committed against several thousand Algerian women during the 1990s, protesting against the banalization of the offence by giving material form to the barbarity and savageness of the rapes and murders, which the government still seeks to erase under the cover of its 'national reconciliation' policy for the Islamist criminals of the GIA. The girl's cynical reaction tinged with irony reveals how absurd the situation is:

> Forgive? Repress my suffering, silence my pain, torture my memory. Harm myself to erase the horror in my head. Resign myself, accept, submit — in short, commit suicide! [...] Forgive? But as far as I know, no one has ever apologized.[22]

The irony in this quotation is insidious. It niggles away at those who, holding the subject to still be taboo, have remained silent. It points the finger of blame at a chauvinist, hence slack and uninterested policy. It injects guilt into sleeping consciences, and denounces the silence held up as a principle by which to live, in the guise of a protective virtue, worse, of a reason of state even. Because: 'Here, supposedly protected, I cry with no voice to whoever will hear me. Here people are afraid of words, especially those which come from elsewhere, we chase them out, burn them, then replace them with silence'.[23]

In her book *Algérie, le prix de l'oubli, 1992–2005*,[24] Souad Belhadad clearly sides with the victims, explaining that the Algerian people, caught between Islamist violence and the abuses stemming from repression, had to confront unaided the massacres, kidnappings, and law of silence. She points out that the women raped by terrorists were traumatically silenced, for 'this silence is all too frequently justified by respect for "*horma*" (female honour) and the state is responsible for this denial of justice'.[25] Yet associations for women and for the victims of terrorism have called repeatedly for the rape of women by terrorists to be recognized as a war crime, for the criminals to be put on trial, and for indemnities; but these calls have gone unheeded. After all, the Charter for Peace and Reconciliation recommends that everything be effaced, everything forgiven.

For the members of the Oufkir family, the idea of forgiveness acquires ironic tones: they were robbed of twenty years of their lives for a crime they did not commit, and the sovereign has not uttered a word of apology. Worse, on being interviewed by the France 2 television channel about the Oufkir family in 1987, King Hassan II spoke of a mere 'incident', and reproached France for supporting the family of a killer. On the king's death, Malika Oufkir allowed her bitterness to show through in *L'Etrangère*:

> I would no doubt have shown joy if Hassan II had recognized his wrongs before dying, if my family's name had been cleared in public, if the public image of the persecutor had been tarnished by the exactions of his regime being revealed. [...] Hassan II leaves me the orphan of my pain, his death takes away my sole reason for hating, fighting, and suffering.[26]

For her part, Malika's sister, Soukaina Oufkir, raises the issue in the following terms in her novel, *La Vie devant moi*:

> I have written my book as a dialogue with Hassan II. It came to me naturally. I ask him why he persecuted us thus, but my question goes unanswered, for Hassan II died without ever explaining his motives, or even apologizing. People often ask me if I am prepared to forgive. The question I am never asked is if anyone has ever said sorry. We suffered at the hands of absolute power and its medieval excesses [...]. But never, not once, did we receive an official apology. It could have allowed me to turn the page, it would have been a way of mourning once and for all, for I feel I have died on several occasions.[27]

The course of transitional justice seems to hit a stumbling block in such cases. It is the duty of commissions of equity and reconciliation to promote justice, to re-establish the truth, and provide full and complete reparation so as to reach reconciliation. Reparation is a legal principle, but its ethical, psychological, and sociological aspects also need recognizing. Yet the status of the IER, as announced by the king of Morocco when it was set up, necessarily implies that no perpetrator's name ever be mentioned. In the absence of any apology by perpetrators, their crime goes unrecognized, impacting on the meaning of truth and justice.

The Oufkirs admittedly received financial indemnity, and have rebuilt their lives in France. But material reparation does not efface the marks left by suffering, nor does it ensure any psychological rehabilitation, as transpires in the following observation by Malika Oufkir:

> Money does not bring reparation. Yet it is with dollars, francs, and dirhams that the world seeks to tend to the wounds of those it has broken. A miscarriage of justice? Twenty years in prison for having been my father's daughter? A cheque will come and repair everything just so. Free men worship money so much they end up imagining, in all good faith, that it can erase everything.[28]

Justice, when it remains a corollary of politics, is hard-pushed to advance down the path towards democracy. Literature has a capacity for catharsis and empathy, in which the emotion it triggers makes it possible to place oneself in another's mind, just as the novelist has entered the life of 'distant others' to apprehend their individuality, as Martha Nussbaum remarks in *Poetic Justice: The Literary Imagination and Public Life*.[29] It thus seems to act as a way of doing justice for Malika Oufkir, enabling her to alert public opinion, view the past, question it, and transmit it to future generations to prevent history repeating itself.

Fate turned out differently for Gilbert Naccache. Unlike in Algeria and in Morocco, where transitional justice was not a corollary of a change in political regime, power was overthrown in Tunisia in 2011, banishing the autocracy of single-party rule and setting the country on the road towards democratization. Gilbert Naccache had the pleasure of living through these changes, and of tasting the wind of freedom blowing over Tunisia. He was heard by the IVD. His speech was even published on the IVD website, under the title 'Gilbert Naccache: my evidence to the IVD, on 17 November 2016'. His speech closed as follows:

> In the face of all the attacks and all the obstacles put in its way, it is possible that the commission may not wholly manage to re-establish the dignity of all those who rose up to reconquer it. But it has already done half its work, that is, it has gathered several tens of thousands of witness statements, and started to re-establish the truth, at least relating to human rights violations. And, as we know, truth is revolutionary.[30]

In addition to reparation in the form of indemnities, and the rehabilitation that truth and reconciliation commissions are meant to provide for victims, one of the crucial conditions for transitional justice is the guarantee that the human rights violations will not be repeated. This literature written in a context of violence functions as the guardian of both individual and collective memory, as a rampart and guarantee against further abuses, and especially against forgetting, for these authors see the weakening or erasure of memories as a threat. As Paul Ricoeur notes, 'it is against this forgetting that we conduct the work of memory in order to slow its course, even hold it at bay'.[31]

Thoughts of Freedom: Towards a Possible Form of Democracy?

The memory revival in Morocco after 1999, the year that Hassan II died, did not stem solely from the king bowing to pressure from human rights organizations. People started to talk. Memories were reactivated. Former victims spoke out and published. Abroad at first; as instanced by Ali Bourequat,[32] then in Morocco. The Tarik publishing house, set up in 1999 in Casablanca, drove this memory revival. They started by publishing a comic script, *On affame bien les rats*,[33] depicting the torture that occurred during the 'years of lead'. In 2001 it brought out *Tazmamart: Cellule 10* by Ahmed Marzouki,[34] in which he recounts his involvement in the Skhirat coup, and his detention in Tazmamart. This renewal in public memory was taken up in historical scholarship. In 2001, the journalist Ignace Dalle published *Maroc 1961–1999: l'Espérance brisée*; this was followed in 2002 by *Histoire du Maroc depuis l'indépendance*, by Maghreb specialist Pierre Vermeren, the same year that Mehdi Bennouna, whose father was a sociologist and insurgent from Atlas, published *Héros sans gloire: echec d'une revolution, 1963–1973*.

In Tunisia, living in fear that the past be forgotten, Gilbert Naccache, in addition to *Cristal*, wrote *Le Ciel par-dessus le toit: nouvelles, contes, poèmes de prison et d'ailleurs*,[35] and *Qu'as-tu fait de ta jeunesse? Itinéraire d'un opposant au régime de Bourguiba*,[36] in which he returns once again to his years of imprisonment. For him, memory is a 'political issue', an ethical obligation towards his fellow detainees, for, as Paul Ricoeur remarks: 'the duty of memory is the duty to do justice, through memories, to another than the self'.[37] It is for this reason that a preoccupation with memory is central to the writings of Naccache, as he explains in Cristal:

> One has to be able to respect oneself in order to live. This self-respect cannot accommodate silence, even less lies. In writing, I have no ambition to change the world. But bearing witness has become of vital necessity to me, and writing is the means, or in any case the one I know.[38]

Mohamed Chagraoui, in his book *La Pensée de la liberté dans les écrits de Gilbert Naccache*,[39] refers to 'memorial justice' capable of bringing about the symbolic rehabilitation of those who suffered repression, of rectifying the 'errors of historical scholarship, or rather of official hagiography', as Naccache notes in *Cristal*.[40] The latter thus devotes an entire chapter of his book to presenting the *Perspectives* movement, an account underpinned by a desire to bear witness, emphasizing interwoven destinies and how politics and personal lives overlapped.

For Malika Oufkir, as for Gilbert Naccache and Wahiba Khiari, setting down in writing a past marked by violence or torture is a way of deriding official history and its falsifications, of keeping collective memory alive, of staging a history 'fashioned of human flesh, blood, and pain',[41] of overcoming the silence, hesitation, and shame which repress, if not the memories, at least the words through which they could be transformed into a memory.

These retrospective texts I have taken as my corpus do not simply break the silence and denounce repressive regimes. They also act as a rampart against the prevailing amnesia, so as to prevent these abuses, these violations against human rights and dignity, the dictatorships and their oppression from falling into oblivion. These writings are thus shaped by a desire to bear witness, with a tendency to emphasize the family group in Malika Oufkir, politics in Gilbert Naccache, and the social dimension in Wahiba Khiari, at times to the detriment of the intimate or individual dimension of the narrator or author. The use of the 'transpersonal I', as Annie Ernaux has termed it,[42] engages an author's responsibility towards a duty of memory, as Ernaux explains in the following terms:

> It is the collective value of the autobiographical 'I' and of the things recounted [...], the collective value of the 'I', of the world of the text, it is moving beyond the singularity of experience, the limits of individual consciousness which are ours in life.[43]

These literary accounts place the violence of the past within a broader discourse about citizenship. The return of the spectres from the past is associated with a form of haunting, an idea developed by Derrida to say the unsayable and restore an individual and collective memory repressed by the ruling powers.[44] Being thus haunted by the past generates new lines to question history, and better understand the present. Pierre Vermeren holds that the question of whether democracy is possible in the Maghreb is inseparable from the urgent need to 'question history and the representations of this history among political and social actors in present-day Maghreb'.[45]

Looking critically at the past epitomizes the idea of the 'spectre' as defined by Derrida.[46] It introduces a new way of relating to the legacy of the past, as well as to the present, and, according to Derrida, makes it possible not only to criticize the present state of affairs, but also to insist on justice being better dispensed:

> No justice [...] seems possible or thinkable without the principle of some responsibility, beyond all living present, within that which disjoins the living present, before the ghosts of those who are not yet born or who are already dead, be they victims of wars, of political or other kinds of violence, of

> nationalist, racist, colonialist, sexist, or other forms of extermination, of the oppressions of capitalist imperialism or of any other forms of totalitarianism.[47]

In the work of Gilbert Naccache, writing about prison provides a way of grounding a social dialogue and raising questions about citizenship, and paves the way to civic awareness and the production of new knowledge about oneself and others. Thus in *Qu'as-tu fait de ta jeunesse?* he examines the possibility of building a national state without authoritarianism and violence against those who contest it, and reflects on the democratic process and the formation of future political citizens. This gymnastics of memory seeks to 'transmit the result, the quintessence of an entire itinerary' as Naccache explains in *Comprendre m'a toujours paru essentiel.*[48]

After examining the functioning of the single-party state — the political structure responsible for his years in prison — in *Vers la démocratie? De l'idéologie du développement à l'idéologie des droits de l'Homme*, published after the Tunisian revolution in January 2011,[49] Naccache returned to this line of thought in 2012, examining the major issues tackled since the beginning of the revolution in Tunisia, 'how to manage society and the state after the end of the single party?', a challenge which resides first and foremost in a thoroughgoing re-founding of the political field. On the basis of his experience of political dissent and his heterodox Marxist political beliefs, Naccache holds that a wish for social change should also embrace fundamental analysis in terms of social class, and be grounded in concrete demands issuing from the base, so as to liberate productive forces and so make genuine development possible. He traces a path which could inspire the young people of Tunisia and elsewhere, since, ultimately, he is speaking to us of real democracy.

Conclusion

'Plotted' memory — the plotting of memory as described by Paul Ricoeur[50] — in the three texts studied here functions as an archive for recording an episode in the respective histories of Tunisia, Morocco, and Algeria. It helps consolidate the chain of transmission, develops a form of critical memory questioning the cultural and geopolitical aspects of civil wars and the use of imprisonment to repress, while envisaging a project of creating a free society. By bringing forth memory, by crossing the threshold of silence, fear, or guilt to speak out, Malika Oufkir, Gilbert Naccache, and Wahiba Khiari, to cite but these three authors, place themselves within the advent of a possible future democracy. I will close with a quotation from Jacques le Goff's *Histoire et mémoire*, which explains that:

> Memory, on which history draws, and which it sustains in its turn, seeks to save the past solely to serve the present and future. Let us ensure that collective memory serves to free men, not to enslave them.[51]

Notes to Chapter 13

1. Philippe Mesnard, *Témoignage en résistance* (Paris: Stock, coll. Un ordre d'idées, 2007), p. 9.
2. Gilbert Naccache, *Cristal* (Tunis: Salammbô, 1982), (republished in 2000 by Editions Chama and in 2011 in Tunisia by Editions Mots-Passants).
3. Malika Oufkir, *La Prisonnière* (Paris: Grasset, 1999).

4. Wahiba Khiari, *Nos silences* (Tunis: Elyzad, coll. Éclats de vie, 2009).
5. The expression is borrowed from the Tunisian poet Tahar Bekri, *Marcher sur l'oubli*, interviews with Olivier Apert (Paris: L'Harmattan, 2000).
6. Nikolas Kovacs, *Le Roman politique: fictions du totalitarisme* (Paris: Michalon, 2002), p. 83.
7. Malika Oufkir, *La Prisonnière*, p. 177.
8. Malika Oufkir, *La Prisonnière*, p. 210.
9. Gilles Perrault, *Notre ami le Roi* (Paris: Gallimard, 1990), p. 65.
10. Naccache, *Cristal*, p. 34.
11. Khiari, *Nos silences*, p. 91.
12. Khiari, *Nos silences*, p. 9.
13. Jacques Commaille and Martine Kaluszynski, *La Fonction politique de la justice* (Paris: PACTE/La Découverte, 2007).
14. Souad Belhadad, 'La Justice pour les victimes', in *Actes du Séminaire Pour la vérité, la paix et la conciliation*, held in Brussels on 18–19 March 2007, p. 109. <https://www.fidh.org/IMG/pdf/Actes_SeminaireAlgerieCVJ_mars2007_FR-2.pdf>.
15. Oufkir, *La Prisonnière*, p. 301.
16. Tahar Benjelloun, *Cette aveuglante absence de lumière* (Paris: Seuil, 2001), p. 241.
17. Fatema Oufkir, *Les Jardins du Roi* (Paris: Michel LAfont, 2000).
18. Raouf Oufkir, *Les Invités: 20 ans dans les prisons de Hassan II* (Paris: Flammarion, 2005).
19. Soukaina Oufkir, *La Vie devant moi: une enfance dans les prisons de Hassan II* (Paris: Calmann-Lévy, 2008).
20. Malika Oufkir, *L'Etrangère* (Paris: Grasset, 2006).
21. Malika Oufkir, *L'Etrangère*, p. 133.
22. Khiari, *Nos silences*, p. 123.
23. Khiari, *Nos silences*, p. 55.
24. Souad Belhadad, *Algérie, le prix de l'oubli, 1992–2005* (Paris: Flammarion, 2005).
25. Belhadad, *Algérie*, p. 28.
26. Malika Oufkir, *L'Etrangère*, p. 241.
27. Soukaina Oufkir, *La Vie devant moi*, p. 56.
28. Malika Oufkir, *L'Etrangère*, p. 255.
29. Martha Nussbaum, *Poetic Justice: The Literary Imagination and Public Life* (Boston, MA: Beacon Press, 1995), p. xix.
30. Gilbert Naccache, 'Mon témoignage à l'IVD, le 17 novembre 2016' [accessed 20 November 2017].
31. Paul Ricoeur, *La Mémoire, l'histoire, l'oubli* (Paris: Seuil, coll. 'Essais', 2000), p. 552.
32. Ali-Auguste Bourequat, *Dix-huit ans de solitude: Tazmamart*, ed. by François Tibaux (Paris: Michel Lafon, 1993).
33. Abdelaziz Mouride, *On affame bien les rats* (Paris: Editions Paris-Méditerranée, 2000).
34. Ahmed Marzouki, *Tazmamart: Cellule 10* (Casablanca, Paris: Tarik Editions, Paris-Méditerranée, 2000).
35. Gilbert Naccache, *Le Ciel par-dessus le toit: nouvelles, contes, poèmes de prison et d'ailleurs* (Paris: Editions du Cerf, 2005).
36. Gilbert Naccache, *Qu'as-tu fait de ta jeunesse? Itinéraire d'un opposant au régime de Bourguiba* (Paris: Le Cerf; Tunis: Mots-Passants, 2009).
37. Paul Ricoeur, *La Mémoire, l'histoire, l'oubli* (Paris: Seuil, 2001), p. 108.
38. Naccache, *Cristal*, p. 316.
39. Mohamed Chagraoui, *La Pensée de la liberté dans les écrits de Gilbert Naccache* (Tunis: Latrech Edition, 2016).
40. Naccache, *Cristal*, p. 312.
41. Hafid Gafaiti, *Boudjedra ou la passion de la modernité* (Paris: Denoël, 1987), p. 35.
42. Annie Ernaux, 'Vers un je transpersonnel' (lecture at Nanterre, 1992), in *Autofictions et Cie*, ed. by Serge Doubrovsky et al., *RITM*, 6 (1993), pp. 219–22.
43. Annie Ernaux, *L'Écriture comme un couteau*, interview with Frédéric-Yves Jeannet (Paris: Stock, 2003), p. 180.

44. Cf. Jacques Derrida, *Le Spectre de Marx* (Paris: Galilée, 1993).
45. Pierre Vermeren, *Maghreb: la démocratie impossible?* (Paris: Fayard, 2004), p. 19.
46. In her article 'Le Retour spectral du passé carcéral dans les écrit de prison d'Abdellatif Lâabi', Safoi Babana-Hampton explains that the importance of the spectre as a conceptual tool resides in its paradoxical nature, affecting both its place of provenance and mode of existence. In other words, in so far as its place of provenance may simultaneously refer to the future and to the past, the spectre thus defined may designate what has happened just as much as what is to come of an event, floating over the present. In *Expressions maghrébines*, Ecritures carcérales dans les littératures maghrébines, 10.2 (2011), 57–72 (p. 60).
47. Jacques Derrida, *Le Spectre de Marx* (Paris: Galilée, 1993), pp. 15–16.
48. Gilbert Naccache, *Comprendre m'a toujours paru essentiel...* Interviews with Mohamed Chagraoui (Neuchâtel: Chama Éditions, 2015), p. 97.
49. Gilbert Naccache, interviews with Alexandre Bisquerra, published on Nawat.org, 12 December 2012.
50. Paul Ricœur, *Temps et récit*, vol. 1 (Paris: Editions du Seuil, 1983), pp. 55–84: plotting entails a complex process of 'construction', of 'organizing facts', of representations 'in the dynamic sense of making representation, of a transposition into representative works'.
51. Jacques le Goff, *Histoire et mémoire* (Paris: Gallimard, 1988), p. 87.

CHAPTER 14

❖

De l'écriture en souffrance à la pensée de la liberté ou comment 'marcher sur l'oubli'

Sonia Zlitni-Fitouri

> Chaque fois que nos tristes sociétés, en perpétuelle crise de croissance, se prennent à douter d'elles-mêmes, on les voit se demander si elles ont eu raison d'interroger leur passé ou si elles l'ont bien interrogé. — MARC BLOCH

S'il y a une continuité autre que celle des violences et des massacres dans l'Histoire sanglante de l'humanité, c'est peut-être aussi celle des souffrances tues, de la dénégation des faits par les bourreaux. Les victimes, souvent anéanties et démunies, doivent trouver la force de 'penser en termes de possible et de dicible ce qui souvent est renvoyé à l'exception, à l'impossible, à l'indicible' selon les termes de Philippe Mesnard.[1]

Dans les limites imparties a ce chapitre, il me serait impossible de rendre compte des différentes caractéristiques du récit écrit en situation de violence dans le corpus littéraire que j'ai retenu en l'occurrence *Cristal* de Gilbert Naccache pour parler de la répression politique dans les années 60–70 en Tunisie,[2] *La Prisonnière* de Malika Oufkir pour parler des années de plomb au Maroc dans les années 70–80,[3] de *Nos silences* de Wahiba Khiari qui nous renvoie à la décennie noire dans les années 90 en Algérie.[4] La fonction cathartique et thérapeutique de l'écriture étant posée comme postulat de départ dans l'argumentaire de ce colloque, nous nous focaliserons essentiellement sur ce passage important du besoin de briser le silence et de dire l'innommable dans une écriture en souffrance et donc mimétique au besoin de témoigner par devoir de mémoire.

Nous tenterons également de montrer que l'écriture et le témoignage deviennent ainsi une manière de 'marcher sur l'oubli',[5] de réactiver 'cette mémoire pathologique', de s'acheminer vers une pensée de la liberté qui impliquerait selon Nicolas Kovacs: 'une double interrogation: d'une part sur la position aléatoire de l'individu dans une époque constamment déchirée par les bouleversements sociaux, d'autre part sur le sens même de l'Histoire, dans un monde où la liberté et la justice sont écrasées par les mécanismes d'oppression idéologique, bureaucratique ou policière',[6] et qui — me semble-t-il — est primordiale pour assurer une transition démocratique.

Dire l'innommable pour 'marcher sur l'oubli'

La marocaine, Malika Oufkir, dans son premier récit, *La Prisonnière*, co-écrit avec la journaliste juive tunisienne Michèle Fitoussi, nous livre un témoignage bouleversant du drame qui a frappé sa famille! Rappelons que la famille Oufkir, très proche du Palais et vivant dans l'opulence, a été enlevée le 25 décembre 1972 suite au coup d'état perpétré contre le roi Hassan II par le général Mohamed Oufkir — au motif officiel qu'il faudrait la protéger contre la légitime colère du peuple marocain, envoyée sans jugement dans une prison secrète dans le désert du Sahara, dans des conditions extrêmement dures, ensuite à Bir Jdid, non loin de Casablanca où Malika Oufkir et sa famille passèrent en tout 19 années de détention dans des cellules au milieu des scorpions et des rats, affamés, assoiffés, anéantis par les maladies:

> Pieds nus, en haillons, nous grelottions l'hiver et suffoquions l'été. Nous n'avons plus d'infirmier ni de médicaments. [...] La faim nous poussait souvent à bout. Elle était si violente qu'il nous arrivait d'avoir des regards d'envie envers celui qui n'avait pas encore terminé sa maigre part.[7]

L'évasion de Malika avec une de ses sœurs et ses deux frères (en creusant un tunnel à la petite cuillère) le 19 avril 1987 réussit à alerter les autorités françaises. Bien qu'ils fussent repris, cela permit à sa mère et au reste de la fratrie d'être relâchés.

Malika s'évertue à décrire minutieusement dans *La Prisonnière*, la dégradation des conditions de vie, leurs tentatives échouées de grève de la faim et de suicide collectif, la violence de certains geôliers, la solitude et l'isolement déprimants. La décision royale était sans équivoque: rayer la famille Oufkir de la liste des vivants. Nous le comprenons au propos de Borro, le chef des geôliers s'adressant à son collègue: 'Tu ne comprends pas? C'est clair pourtant. Ils vont mourir. Tous. Et ils seront enterrés ici. On attendra le temps qu'il faudra. Ce sont les ordres.'[8] L'injustice de cette disparition forcée est rendue par les mots de Gilles Perrault dans son ouvrage *Notre ami le Roi*, paru en 1990: 'Au nom de quelle étrange morale infliger pendant quinze ans l'épouvante à des enfants innocents? Est-il dans le monde un seul code pénal pour punir le crime de descendance?'[9]

Si les membres de la famille Oufkir ont payé pour le crime de leur père, le tunisien Gilbert Naccache va purger une peine de 11 ans de prison sous le Régime de Bourguiba à cause de ses opinions politiques. Militant communiste avant même l'indépendance, membre dirigeant (au milieu des années 60) du mouvement de la gauche radicale 'Perspectives', il a été lourdement condamné en mars 1968, incarcéré à Borj Erroumi, prison sordide où l'on en sort rarement vivant, avant d'être libéré en 1979. De cette expérience carcérale, Naccache a gardé le récit de la répression, de la torture, du temps statique, écrit sur des bouts de papier des paquets de cigarettes Cristal.

C'est ainsi que défilent dans *Cristal*, les descriptions des différentes postures de la torture, de l'humiliation des prisonniers par des geôliers zélés, de la privation de tout, du 'dépouillement de soi', de la descente aux enfers dans les caves de Borj Erroumi:

> Déguisé, pieds nus, le pantalon rêche et le col de la vareuse grattant, je me retrouve assis par terre au pied du coiffeur qui, en trois coups de tondeuse,

> m'enlève ce que j'avais de cheveux. Couloir avec insultes de gardiens, tourne à droite, une sorte de chicane, une porte et une grotte, une véritable grotte à peu près ovale, avec des morceaux de rochers et une ouverture circulaire pour l'aération [...]. Me voici donc à cette fameuse cave de Borj Roumi [...] celle dont les droits-communs parlaient avec terreur à Tunis.[10]

Dans un autre registre différent mais inscrit également dans un contexte de violences ineffables, le récit de l'algérienne Wahiba Khiari retrace, dans *Nos silences* le destin de deux femmes confrontées à l'horreur de la décennie noire. Il faut savoir qu'en Algérie, les disparitions forcées ont commencé en 1992, avec la guerre civile, mais de façon ciblée. Puis, à partir de 1994, les kidnappings de masse ont commencé. Les victimes étaient prises dans de faux barrages. Au début, il s'agissait d'intellectuels, d'universitaires, de médecins, d'avocats, etc. Puis, des femmes ont été enlevées par les terroristes afin d'être utilisées comme esclaves sexuelles. L'un des deux personnages féminins, professeur d'anglais, double de l'auteure, parviendra à quitter son pays et à échapper à la violence; l'autre — qui est l'élève du professeur d'anglais — enlevée à sa famille et retenue dans le Maquis, vivra de plein fouet la folie meurtrière du fanatisme religieux. Sous forme de monologues-confessions, ces deux voix brisent le silence; celui de ceux qui avaient peur, de ceux qui étaient endeuillés et de ceux qui n'ont pas eu le courage de dénoncer ou de se révolter.

La narratrice y dénonce les viols subis par les jeunes filles enlevées par les islamistes sous couvert d'un mariage de jouissance avec des 'maris temporaires', engrossées par un simple *bismillah* et une *fatiha*, y décrit le corps meurtri, avili de la jeune fille: 'Mon corps était un champ de bataille jonché de bleus et de coups ensanglantés. Il me fallait me ramasser de sous les décombres après leur passage.'[11] Elle ajoute plus loin:

> Finalement, l'un deux a réussi à m'ensemencer. Labourée comme je l'ai été, c'est normal que je finisse par germer. Même si les mauvaises graines ne sont pas censées donner la vie, je suis enceinte. [...][12]

Passés les mois et les années et ces contextes de violence décrits dans *Cristal*, la *Prisonnière*, et *Nos silences* débouchent sur une sorte 'd'accalmie à l'amiable' si j'ose dire! L'Histoire nous a montré que très souvent l'issue d'un conflit passe par des lois d'amnistie, par la nécessité de trouver une issue, avec la conscience qu'elle sera de toute façon insatisfaisante et frustrante. L'on peut donc à la limite comprendre le besoin pour une société de tourner la page. Cependant, à l'heure de la politique de réconciliation nationale et du projet d'amnistie du 29 septembre 2005 en Algérie, de la création, le 7 janvier 2004, de l'Instance Equité et Réconciliation (IER) au Maroc, de l'Instance Vérité et Dignité (IVD) en Tunisie en 2013, serait-il toujours possible de tourner la page et de pardonner? Cette réconciliation saurait-elle panser les blessures psychologiques, effacer les stigmates des horreurs vécues? Ne serait-elle pas, selon Jacques Commaille,[13] 'une forme de normalisation politique abusive des victimes'? Se présente alors la difficulté d'une justice transitionnelle!

Force est de constater que lorsque s'organise l'oubli sous prétexte de permettre à une société de se reconstruire suite à une loi de réconciliation nationale ou une amnistie, la victime, elle, représentante du noyau de la mémoire collective de ce qui a eu lieu dans le pays, ne peut que rester exclue de ce processus. En effet, encombrée de son vécu, sur lequel elle n'a aucun élément de savoir, de vérité, elle reste figée dans son temps de traumatisme. Voudrait-elle passer à autre chose qu'elle ne le pourrait pas. C'est un temps suspendu, immobile. Et tandis que la majorité d'un pays tend à l'oubli, voire au refoulement, la victime, elle, reste condamnée à sa souffrance, à son isolement.

En Algérie, selon les propos de Souad Belhadad, journaliste et écrivaine algérienne:

> Le Président a sollicité le pardon de toutes les victimes au nom de la Nation, et non pas au nom des coupables. Non seulement on n'a pas demandé pardon aux victimes, mais on leur a demandé de faire un effort. Accepter un pardon qui ne leur a même pas été exprimé. [...] Et puis, un pardon de quoi? Puisqu'officiellement, il ne s'est rien passé. [...] Dans le langage, le mot de guerre civile est prohibé, dans les rues, pas de trace de la moindre stèle, pas un seul nom de rue ne marque un quelconque souvenir de ces dix ans de terreur. Il y a bel et bien interdiction de savoir.[14]

La victime risque ainsi de s'enfermer dans un ressentiment infini, dans une volonté de repli sur sa propre tragédie alors qu'elle aspire à la paix, qu'elle voudrait même parfois s'adonner au pardon! Mais à qui? Comment? Et autour de quelle réalité?

A leur sortie de prison, loin de bénéficier d'une reconnaissance, de l'expression d'un quelconque regret de la part du Palais, les autorités marocaines ont intimé aux membres de la famille Oufkir le silence. Se taire était donc la monnaie de leur salut: 'le Roi ne veut plus entendre parler de nous, mais en contrepartie nous devons nous taire sur ce que nous avons vécu,[15] lisons-nous dans *La Prisonnière*; réplique qui nous renvoie inéluctablement à cette tirade sournoise dans *Cette aveuglante absence de lumière* de Tahar Benjelloun:

> Sidna le roi t'a gracié. Dans quelques jours, tu retrouveras ta famille. Tu seras certainement contacté par des journalistes étrangers, par des gens qui veulent du mal à notre pays. La conduite à avoir est simple: ne pas répondre à leurs questions empoisonnées. Ne pas collaborer avec eux. Refuser tout contact. Si tu fais le malin, je te ramènerai moi-même à Tazmamart.[16]

Vœu de silence? Certainement pas! Malika Oufkir sort en 1999 un premier livre, *La Prisonnière* qui sera d'ailleurs, interdit au Maroc; Fatema Oufkir publie *Les Jardins du Roi* en 2000,[17] Soukaina Oufkir sort *La Vie devant moi : une enfance dans les prisons de Hassan II* en 2008,[18] Raouf Oufkir écrit *Les Invités: 20 ans dans les prisons de Hassan II* en 2005.[19] C'est que la littérature conjure l'oubli forcé, réactive 'la mémoire atrophiée', casse les barrières du silence!

Dans un deuxième livre, intitulé *l'Etrangère* et publié en 2006,[20] Malika Oufkir revient sur les séquelles et les traumatismes psychologiques et physiques provoqués par son incarcération. Elle revient également sur les motivations qui l'ont poussée à écrire ses deux récits dans un chapitre dont le titre est assez révélateur 'Ecrire pour témoigner' qui commence ainsi:

> Survivre. J'étais coupable de survivre. Une étrange culpabilité. Seule la perspective de témoigner, de dire au monde entier que le Maroc n'était pas la

> démocratie défendue par l'Occident, et particulièrement par la France. Cette barbarie à visage de monarchie devait être connue de tous. En écrivant *La prisonnière*, [...] j'exorcisais le passé, je m'en libérais en partie, mais je subissais aussi le fardeau d'un rôle assigné: celui de la victime.[21]

De son côté, l'écrivaine algérienne Wahiba Khiari, développe en aval un réquisitoire contre le silence de la loi sur les crimes de viol commis sur plusieurs milliers de femmes algériennes au cours de ces années 90, contre aussi la banalisation du corps du délit, l'élément qui matérialise la barbarie et la sauvagerie du viol et du meurtre et que le gouvernement tente, aujourd'hui, encore, d'effacer sous couvert de sa politique de la 'réconciliation nationale' pour les islamistes criminels du GIA. La réaction cynique, teintée d'ironie de la jeune-fille est révélatrice de l'absurde de cette situation:

> Pardonner? Refouler mes souffrances, taire mes douleurs, torturer ma mémoire. M'automutiler pour effacer l'horreur de ma tête. Me résigner, accepter, me soumettre, me suicider quoi! [...] Pardonner? Mais personne ne m'a demandé pardon que je sache?[22]

L'impact de l'ironie contenue dans cette citation est insidieux. Il titille ceux qui se sont tus, considérant encore ce sujet tabou, met en cause une politique laxiste et indifférente parce que machiste, culpabilise les consciences endormies, dénonce le silence érigé en principe de vie sous couvert d'une quelconque vertu protectrice, pire sous couvert de la raison d'Etat! Parce que: 'Ici, soi-disant protégée, je crie sans voix à qui veut bien m'entendre. Ici, on a peur des mots, surtout ceux qui nous viennent d'ailleurs, on les chasse, les brûle, puis on les remplace par le silence.'[23]

Dans son ouvrage intitulé *Algérie, le prix de l'oubli, 1992–2005*,[24] Souad Belhadad se situe clairement du côté des victimes en expliquant qu'entre la violence islamiste et les abus de la répression, le peuple algérien a dû affronter seul les massacres, les enlèvements et la loi du silence. Elle y rappelle que l'on a muré les femmes violées par les terroristes dans un silence traumatisant parce que — souligne-t-elle: 'ce silence (est) trop souvent justifié par le respect de la '*horma*' (l'honneur féminin) et l'Etat est responsable de ce déni de justice.'[25] Pourtant, nombreuses sont les revendications d'associations de femmes et de victimes de terrorisme à appeler à la reconnaissance du viol des femmes par les terroristes comme crime de guerre, la poursuite en justice des criminels, des indemnités, mais qui sont restées sans réponse. La Charte pour la Paix et la Réconciliation ne préconise-t-elle pas de tout gommer et de pardonner!

Chez les membres Oufkir, la notion de pardon prend une connotation ironique: vingt ans de leur vie leur ont été volés pour un crime qu'ils n'ont pas commis et pas le moindre mot d'excuse de la part du souverain. Pis encore! Interrogé en 1987 par une équipe de France 2 sur la famille Oufkir, le roi Hassan II parle d'un simple 'fait divers' et reproche à la France de soutenir la famille d'un tueur! A la mort du monarque, Malika Oufkir laisse exprimer son amertume dans *L'Etrangère*:

> De la joie, j'en aurais sans doute montré si Hassan II avait reconnu ses torts avant de mourir, si le nom de ma famille avait publiquement été lavé, si l'image publique du bourreau avait été ternie par la révélation des exactions du régime.

> [...] Hassan II me laisse orpheline de ma douleur, son décès m'enlève ma seule raison de haïr, de lutter, de souffrir.[26]

De son côté, sa sœur, Soukaina Oufkir s'interroge en ces termes dans son roman *La Vie devant moi:*

> Mon livre a été écrit sous la forme d'un dialogue avec Hassan II. C'est venu naturellement. Je lui demande pourquoi cet acharnement, mais ma question demeure en suspens, car Hassan II est mort sans jamais expliquer ses motivations, ni même s'excuser. On me demande souvent si je suis prête à pardonner. La question qu'on ne me pose jamais, c'est si on m'a déjà demandé pardon. Nous avons souffert d'un pouvoir absolu et de ses dérives moyenâgeuses. [...] Mais jamais, au grand jamais, nous n'avons reçu des excuses officielles. Cela aurait pu me faire tourner la page, ç'aurait été une manière de faire le deuil une bonne fois pour toutes, car j'ai l'impression d'être morte plusieurs fois.[27]

Le cours de la justice transitionnelle semble buter dans de pareils cas. Les commissions d'équité et de réconciliation sont redevables de promouvoir la justice, de rétablir la vérité et d'apporter une réparation pleine et entière pour arriver à la réconciliation. La réparation est un principe de droit mais il faut aussi souligner ses dimensions éthiques, psychologiques et sociologiques. Or le statut de l'IER, tel qu'annoncé par le roi du Maroc à sa création, implique impérativement qu'aucun nom de bourreau ne soit mentionné. Ne pas demander pardon de la part du bourreau suppose une non reconnaissance du crime et altère, par ricochet, le sens de la vérité et de la justice.

Les Oufkir ont certes reçu une indemnisation financière, ont refait leur vie en France mais la réparation matérielle n'efface pas les stigmates de la souffrance et n'assure pas la réhabilitation psychologique tel qu'on le comprend dans les propos de Malika Oufkir:

> L'argent ne répare pas. C'est pourtant à coups de dollars, de francs, de dirhams que le monde panse les blessures de ceux qu'il a brisés. Une erreur judiciaire? Vingt ans de prison pour avoir été la fille de son père? Un chèque viendra tout réparer à point. Les hommes libres vénèrent tant l'argent qu'ils finissent par s'imaginer, en toute bonne foi, qu'il peut tout effacer.[28]

Quand la justice reste corollaire de la politique, dans de pareils cas, elle se fraierait difficilement une voie sur le chemin de la démocratie. La littérature, en ce qu'elle a de pouvoir cathartique et empathique, avec cette capacité que donne l'émotion de se transporter mentalement dans l'esprit d'un autre puisqu'elle permet au romancier d'entrer dans la vie d''autres distants', d'appréhender leur individualité, ainsi que l'explique Martha Nussbaum dans *Poetic Justice: The Literary Imagination and Public Life*,[29] semble rendre justice à Malika Oufkir, lui permettant de sensibiliser l'opinion publique, de poser un regard sur ce passé, de l'interroger, de le transmettre aux générations futures pour que l'Histoire ne se refasse pas!

Le sort en a décidé autrement pour Gilbert Naccache! Contrairement à l'Algérie et au Maroc où la justice transitionnelle n'a pas été corollaire d'un changement de régime politique, la Tunisie a connu, en 2011, un renversement politique qui a banni l'autocratie du pouvoir unique et entamé un processus démocratique. Gilbert

Naccache a eu l'opportunité et le bonheur de vivre et de suivre ces changements, de goûter au vent de liberté qui a soufflé sur la Tunisie. Il est passé en audition publique devant l'Instance de Vérité et de Dignité. Son discours est même publié sur le site de l'IVD sous le titre 'Gilbert Naccache: Mon témoignage à l'IVD, le 17 novembre 2016', un discours qu'il clôture en ces termes:

> Devant toutes les attaques et tous les obstacles mis sur son chemin, il est possible que l'instance ne parvienne pas complètement à rétablir la dignité de tous ceux qui se sont dressés pour la reconquérir. Mais elle a déjà fait la moitié de son travail, c'est-à-dire recueilli plusieurs dizaines de milliers de témoignages et commencé à rétablir la vérité, du moins en matière de violations des droits humains. Et, on le sait bien, la vérité est révolutionnaire.[30]

Outre la réparation par l'indemnisation et la réhabilitation que prévoient les commissions de vérité et de conciliation pour les victimes, l'une des conditions fondamentales de la justice transitionnelle est la garantie de non répétition des violations des droits de l'homme. Aussi la littérature écrite dans un contexte de violence fonctionne-t-elle comme le gardien de la mémoire à la fois individuelle et collective, un garde-fou et un garant contre de nouveaux dérapages et surtout contre l'oubli car l'affaiblissement ou l'effacement des souvenirs est vécu chez ces écrivains comme une menace: 'c'est contre cet oubli-là que nous faisons œuvre de mémoire, afin d'en ralentir le cours, voire de le tenir en échec',[31] précise Paul Ricœur.

La Pensée de la liberté: vers un possible démocratique?

A partir de 1999 — année du décès de Hassan II forcément — le renouveau mémoriel, au Maroc, ne se fait plus simplement par le biais de concessions faites par le roi face à la pression des organisations des droits de l'homme. Désormais, la parole se délie, la mémoire se réactive. Les anciennes victimes parlent, publient. D'abord, à l'étranger, comme pour Ali Bourequat,[32] puis au Maroc. Les éditions Tarik, créées en 1999 à Casablanca, seront le pilier de ce renouveau mémoriel. Ils commencent par publier une bande dessinée, *On affame bien les rats*,[33] témoignage sur la torture pendant les années de plomb. En 2001 paraît *Tazmamart: Cellule 10* d'Ahmed Marzouki,[34] où il relate sa participation au putsch de Skhirat, et sa détention à Tazmamart. Le renouveau mémoriel passe également par un travail historique. En 2001, le journaliste Ignace Dalle publie *Maroc 1961–1999: l'Espérance brisée*, l'historien Pierre Vermeren, spécialiste du Maghreb, sort son *Histoire du Maroc depuis l'indépendance*, et Mehdi Bennouna, fils d'un insurgé de l'Atlas et sociologue, fait paraître *Héros sans gloire: echec d'une révolution, 1963–1973*.

En Tunisie, outre *Cristal* et vivant dans cette hantise de l'oubli, Gilbert Naccache écrira également *Le Ciel par-dessus le toit: nouvelles, contes, poèmes de prison et d'ailleurs*[35] et *Qu'as-tu fait de ta jeunesse? Itinéraire d'un opposant au régime de Bourguiba*,[36] où il reviendra encore sur ses années d'incarcération. Pour lui, la mémoire constitue un 'enjeu politique' et un devoir éthique vis-à-vis de ses camarades de détention car selon Paul Ricœur: 'le devoir de mémoire est le devoir de rendre justice, par le souvenir à un autre que soi'.[37] C'est en cela que la préoccupation mémorielle occupe une place centrale dans les écrits de Naccache ainsi qu'il l'explique dans *Cristal*:

> Il faut pouvoir se respecter pour vivre. Ce respect de soi-même ne s'accommode pas du silence, encore moins du mensonge. Je n'ai pas, en écrivant, l'ambition de changer le monde, mais témoigner est devenu pour moi une exigence vitale, l'écriture en est le moyen, en tout cas celui que je connais.[38]

Mohamed Chagraoui, dans son ouvrage *La Pensée de la liberté dans les écrits de Gilbert Naccache*,[39] parle de 'justice mémorielle' susceptible d'opérer à la fois une réhabilitation symbolique de ceux qui ont subi la répression et une rectification des 'erreurs de l'historiographie, ou plutôt de l'hagiographie officielle' comme le souligne Naccache dans *Cristal*.[40] C'est ainsi qu'il consacre tout un chapitre de son livre à la présentation du mouvement *Perspectives*, récit mémoriel sous tendu par une vocation testimoniale soulignant l'enchevêtrement de plusieurs destinées et l'imbrication de la vie personnelle et de la vie politique.

Chez Malika Oufkir ainsi que chez Gilbert Naccache ou Wahiba Khiari, consigner un passé de violence ou de torture dans des récits reviendrait à narguer l'histoire officielle et ses falsifications, à maintenir vive la mémoire collective, à mettre en scène une histoire 'pétrie de chair humaine, de sang et de douleur',[41] à surmonter le silence, l'hésitation et la honte qui refoulent sinon ce souvenir du moins la parole qui ferait de ce souvenir une mémoire.

Ces textes rétrospectifs de mon corpus servent non seulement à briser le silence ou à dénoncer un pouvoir répressif mais ils servent surtout de rempart contre l'amnésie dominante, pour faire en sorte que les sévices, les atteintes aux droits et à la dignité de l'homme, la dictature et l'oppression ne soient pas oubliés. Ces écrits sont ainsi déterminés par une vocation testimoniale et ont tendance à faire prévaloir le collectif familial chez Malika Oufkir, politique chez Gilbert Naccache et social chez Wahiba Khiari au détriment, parfois, de ce qui relève de l'individuel, de l'intime du narrateur ou de l'auteur. Le recours au 'je transpersonnel', pour reprendre une expression d'Annie Ernaux,[42] engage une responsabilité d'un devoir de mémoire ainsi qu'elle l'explique en ces termes:

> C'est la valeur collective du 'je' autobiographique et des choses racontées [...] la valeur collective du 'je', du monde du texte, c'est le dépassement de la singularité de l'expérience, des limites de la conscience individuelle qui sont les nôtres dans la vie.[43]

Ces récits littéraires inscrivent les violences du passé dans le discours de la citoyenneté. Le retour spectral de ce passé est associé à la hantise, notion derridienne pour dire l'indicible et restituer une mémoire individuelle et collective refoulée par le pouvoir en place.[44] Cette hantise du passé devient génératrice d'un nouveau questionnement de l'Histoire, d'une meilleure compréhension du présent! Pierre Vermeren considère que la question d'une démocratie possible au Maghreb est inséparable de l'urgence de 'questionner l'histoire et les représentations de cette histoire chez les acteurs politiques et sociaux du Maghreb d'aujourd'hui.'[45]

Le regard critique porté sur le passé résume la notion de 'spectre', telle que définie par Derrida.[46] Il introduit une nouvelle relation avec l'héritage du passé ainsi qu'avec le présent et permet, toujours selon Derrida, non seulement de critiquer l'actualité mais aussi d'assurer un meilleur rendement de la justice:

> Aucune justice [...] ne paraît possible ou pensable sans le principe de quelque responsabilité, au-delà de tout présent vivant, dans ce qui disjointe le présent vivant, devant les fantômes de ceux qui ne sont pas encore nés ou qui sont déjà morts, victimes ou non des guerres, des violences, politiques ou autres, des exterminations nationales, racistes, colonialistes, sexistes ou autres, des oppressions de l'impérialisme capitaliste ou de toutes les formes du totalitarisme.[47]

Le récit carcéral accède, chez Gilbert Naccache, à la possibilité d'asseoir un dialogue social et un questionnement sur la citoyenneté, à une prise de conscience civique et la production d'une nouvelle connaissance de soi et de l'autre. Aussi s'interroge-t-il dans *Qu'as-tu fait de ta jeunesse?* sur les possibilités de construire un Etat national sans autoritarisme et violence contre les contestataires et de réfléchir sur le processus démocratique et la formation d'un futur citoyen politique. Cette gymnastique de la mémoire cherche à 'transmettre le résultat, la quintessence de tout un itinéraire' explique Naccache dans *Comprendre m'a toujours paru essentiel.*[48]

Après avoir tenté de réfléchir sur le fonctionnement de l'État de parti unique, cette structure politique à laquelle il devait ses années de prison dans son ouvrage, *Vers la démocratie? De l'idéologie du développement à l'idéologie des droits de l'Homme*, publié après la Révolution tunisienne de janvier 2011,[49] Gilbert Naccache reprend, en 2012, le fil de sa réflexion en abordant une des grandes questions affrontées depuis les débuts de la révolution en Tunisie: 'comment gérer la société et l'État après la fin du parti unique?'; un défi qui repose d'abord sur une refondation totale du champ politique. Parti de son expérience de la contestation politique et de ses convictions politiques marxistes hétérodoxes, Gilbert Naccache pense qu'une volonté de changement social doit également s'inscrire dans une réflexion de fonds en termes de classes sociales, s'appuyer sur des revendications concrètes, issues de la base, et qui permettront de libérer les forces productives afin de rendre possible un véritable développement. Il trace dans ses réflexions un chemin qui pourrait inspirer les jeunes de Tunisie et d'au-delà, puisqu'au fond, il nous parle de démocratie réelle.

Conclusion

La mémoire 'mise en intrigue' — encore une expression de Paul Ricoeur[50] — dans ces trois textes étudiés, sert ainsi d'archive pour consigner un pan de l'Histoire de la Tunisie, du Maroc et de l'Algérie, participe à consolider la chaine des transmissions, développe une sorte de mémoire critique qui interroge les aspects géopolitiques, culturels des guerres civiles, des répressions carcérales, qui envisage un projet de création pour l'individu d'une société libre. En faisant advenir la mémoire, sortir la parole du seuil du silence, de la peur ou de la culpabilité, Malika Oufkir, Gilbert Naccache et Wahiba Khiari — pour ne citer qu'eux — s'inscrivent dans l'avènement d'un possible démocratique. Je finirai sur une citation de Jacques le Goff qui explique dans *Histoire et mémoire* que:

> La mémoire, où puise l'histoire qui l'alimente à son tour, ne cherche à sauver le passé que pour servir au présent et à l'avenir. Faisons en sorte que la mémoire collective serve à la libération et non à l'asservissement des hommes.[51]

Notes to Chapter 14

1. Philippe Mesnard, *Témoignage en résistance* (Paris: Stock, coll. Un ordre d'idées, 2007), p. 9.
2. Gilbert Naccache, *Cristal* (Tunis: Salammbô, 1982), (réédité en 2000 aux Editions Chama et en 2011 à Tunis aux éditions Mots-Passants).
3. Malika Oufkir, *La Prisonnière* (Paris: Grasset, 1999).
4. Wahiba Khiari, *Nos silences* (Tunis : Elyzad, coll. Éclats de vie, 2009).
5. Expression empruntée au poète tunisien Tahar Bekri in *Marcher sur l'oubli*, entretiens avec Olivier Apert (Paris: L'Harmattan, 2000).
6. Nikolas Kovacs, *Le Roman politique : fictions du totalitarisme* (Paris: Michalon, 2002), p. 83.
7. Malika Oufkir, *La Prisonnière*, p. 177.
8. Malika Oufkir, *La Prisonnière*, p. 210.
9. Gilles Perrault, *Notre ami le Roi* (Paris: Gallimard, 1990), p. 65.
10. Naccache, *Cristal*, p. 34.
11. Khiari, *Nos silences*, p. 91.
12. Khiari, *Nos silences*, p. 9.
13. Jacques Commaille et Martine Kaluszynski, *La Fonction politique de la justice* (Paris: PACTE/La Découverte, 2007).
14. Souad Belhadad, 'La Justice pour les victimes', in *Actes du Séminaire Pour la vérité, la paix et la conciliation*, tenu à Bruxelles, les 18–19 mars 2007, p. 109. <https://www.fidh.org/IMG/pdf/Actes_SeminaireAlgerieCVJ_mars2007_FR-2.pdf>.
15. Oufkir, *La Prisonnière*, p. 301.
16. Tahar Benjelloun, *Cette aveuglante absence de lumière* (Paris: Seuil, 2001), p. 241.
17. Fatema Oufkir, *Les Jardins du Roi* (Paris: Michel Lafont, 2000).
18. Soukaina Oufkir, *La Vie devant moi une enfance dans les prisons de Hassan II* (Paris: Calmann-Lévy, 2008).
19. Raouf Oufkir, *Les Invités: 20 ans dans les prisons de Hassan II* (Paris: Flammarion, 2005).
20. Malika Oufkir, *L'Etrangère* (Paris: Grasset, 2006).
21. Malika Oufkir, *L'Etrangère*, p. 133.
22. Khiari, *Nos silences*, p. 123.
23. Khiari, *Nos silences*, p. 55.
24. Souad Belhadad, *Algérie, le prix de l'oubli, 1992–2005* (Paris: Flammarion, 2005).
25. Belhadad, *Algérie*, p. 28.
26. Malika Oufkir, *L'Etrangère*, p. 241.
27. Soukaina Oufkir, *La Vie devant moi*, p. 56.
28. Malika Oufkir, *L'Etrangère*, p. 255.
29. Martha Nussbaum, *Poetic Justice: The Literary Imagination and Public Life* (Boston, MA: Beacon Press, 1995), p. xix.
30. Gilbert Naccache, 'Mon témoignage à l'IVD, le 17 novembre 2016' (dernière consultation 20 novembre 2017).
31. Paul Ricoeur, *La Mémoire, l'histoire, l'oubli* (Paris: Seuil, coll. 'Essais', 2000), p. 552.
32. Ali-Auguste Bourequat, *Dix-huit ans de solitude: Tazmamart*, récit recueilli par François Tibaux (Paris: Michel Lafon, 1993).
33. Abdelaziz Mouride, *On affame bien les rats* (bande dessinée) (Paris: Editions Paris-Méditerranée, 2000).
34. Ahmed Marzouki, *Tazmamart: Cellule 10* (Casablanca: Tarik Editions; Paris: Paris-Méditerranée, 2000).
35. Gilbert Naccache, *Le Ciel par-dessus le toit : nouvelles, contes, poèmes de prison et d'ailleurs* (Paris: Editions du Cerf, 2005).
36. Gilbert Naccache, *Qu'as-tu fait de ta jeunesse? Itinéraire d'un opposant au régime de Bourguiba* (Paris: Le Cerf; Tunis: Mots-passants, 2009).
37. Paul Ricoeur, *La Mémoire, l'histoire, l'oubli* (Paris: Seuil, 2001), p. 108.
38. Naccache, *Cristal*, p. 316.
39. Mohamed Chagraoui, *La Pensée de la liberté dans les écrits de Gilbert Naccache* (Tunis: Latrech Edition, 2016).

40. Naccache, *Cristal*, p. 312.
41. Hafid Gafaiti, *Boudjedra ou la passion de la modernité*, (Paris: Denoël, 1987), p. 35.
42. Annie Ernaux, 'Vers un je transpersonnel', in *Autofictions et Cie*, colloque de Nanterre, 1992, ed. by Serge Doubrovsky et al, *RITM*, 6 (1993), pp. 219–22.
43. Annie Ernaux, *L'Ecriture comme un couteau*, entretien avec Frédéric-Yves Jeannet (Paris: Stock, 2003), p. 180.
44. Cf. Jacques Derrida, *Le Spectre de Marx* (Paris: Galilée, 1993).
45. Pierre Vermeren, *Maghreb: la démocratie impossible?* (Paris: Fayard, 2004), p. 19.
46. Safoi Babana-Hampton explique dans son article 'Le retour spectral du passé carcéral dans les écrit de prison d'Abdellatif Lâabi' que l'importance du spectre en tant qu'outil conceptuel réside dans son caractère paradoxal, touchant autant son lieu de provenance que son mode d'être. Autrement dit, dans la mesure où son lieu de provenance peut renvoyer simultanément au futur comme au passé, le spectre ainsi défini peut désigner le 'revenir', ce qui s'est passé tout autant que l'à 'venir' d'un événement, planant sur le présent.' In *Expressions maghrébines*, Ecritures carcérales dans les littératures maghrébines, 10.2 (2011), 57–72 (p. 60).
47. Jacques Derrida, *Le Spectre de Marx* (Paris: Galilée, 1993), pp. 15–16.
48. Gilbert Naccache, *Comprendre m'a toujours paru essentiel...* Entretiens avec Mohamed Chagraoui, (Neuchâtel: Chama Éditions, 2015), p. 97.
49. Gilbert Naccache, Entretiens avec Alexandre Bisquerra, publiés sur Nawat.org, 12 décembre 2012.
50. Paul Ricœur, *Temps et récit*, T1 (Paris: Editions du Seuil, 1983), pp. 55–84: la mise en intrigue implique un processus complexe de 'construction', d''agencement des faits', de 'représentations dans son sens dynamique de mise en représentation dans des œuvres représentatives.'
51. Jacques le Goff, *Histoire et mémoire* (Paris: Gallimard, 1988), p. 87.

CHAPTER 15

❖

Testimonies and Literature as Alternative Transitional Justice in Algeria

Anissa Daoudi

> I am here to tell my story for you to write and it is what will help me die in peace, as I know that you will make sure that my voice is heard.
>
> Survivor 'Khalti Zohra' (1 November 2017)

> Most of what has been written in literature on the 1990s in Algeria was based on secondary witnesses. I don't think there are novels which are based on first-hand witnesses. This is the first time the victim becomes a partner in the writing process. In this writing workshop, we didn't only retell the stories, but through those stories, we transferred feelings... My writing is about counter history, it is about filling the gaps...and what more do we have than the gaps in the Algerian contemporary history
>
> Interview with Said Khatibi (2 November 2018)

> At one point I was for the Amnesty Law, I was for applying the law. However, I have always asked questions about the feelings of those hit in their hearts, whether they can one day forgive... We have listened in the workshop to the young girl who lost her leg, her sister... Worse for these women is to know the perpetrator and to see him day in day out over years and to see how his ideas changed, he no longer has a beard and a kameez, he even became wedding photographer.
>
> Interview with Fadhila Al Farouq (2 November 2018)

Introduction[1]

The direct cause of Algerian Civil War was the unexpected victory of the *Front Islamique du Salut* (FIS) at the National Assembly elections in December 1991. The military abruptly halted the process and cancelled the elections. The indirect causes were mainly socio-economic, like unemployment, shortage of housing, and decline of oil revenues, which preceded the 1990s. For example, in the 1980s, there were protests like the ones in Kabylia or protests by women against the 1984 Family Code, in which Islamists called for a total implementation of the Shari'a and the institution of an Islamic State in Algeria. The country slipped into bloodshed for more than a decade. The Civil War[2] cost the lives of thousands of people and the disappearance of thousands more, and cost the country billions of dollars.[3] After Abdelaziz Bouteflika won the presidency in April 1999, he launched a programme to promote peace and national reconciliation through the adoption of amnesty actions.

The Charter for Peace and National Reconciliation (CNPR) was adopted in 2005. It was an amnesty that allowed most guerrillas to return to normal life in exchange for giving up politics and surrendering to the state. In practical terms, this has meant that it was almost impossible, for example, for women to denounce the acts they suffered, both for fear of retaliation by the perpetrators and because of the Amnesty Law. Furthermore, the law forbids Algerians from, as article 46 states clearly, 'instrumentalizing the wounds of the national tragedy in order to detract from its institutions and weaken the state, to harm the honourability of its agents [...] or to tarnish internationally the image of Algeria', under the legal threat of a hefty fine and up to five-years' imprisonment.[4] This meant that a state of denial was imposed on the people; including criminals who were allowed back to their homes, often living at close proximity to their victims. It also means that to date, narratives related to the 1990s in Algeria are scarce, fragmented and controlled by the state. Amnesties by default may suggest a need to forget. But this has been unacceptable for Algerian survivors as we will explore through first-hand testimonies as well as through the novel *Hatab Sarajevo* [Firewood of Sarajevo] (2019). Through the two types of testimonies (first-hand testimonies as well as the testimonies in the novel), a further form of transitional justice which exists outside the judicial and political spheres might be achieved, as will be argued in this chapter.

The first quotation at the head of this chapter is a first-hand/eye-witness testimony by Khalti Zohra,[5] a name given to one of the survivors, a woman in her late eighties who survived the Civil War. The second is by Said Khatibi, an Algerian Arabophone writer who lived through the Civil War as a journalist, at a time when journalists were assassinated nearly every day. The third is by Fadhila Al Farouq, a female Algerian Arabophone writer and journalist who was forced to leave Algeria in the 1990s to live in Lebanon. She was the first person who dared to write a novel in Arabic about rape in the Civil War. The three testimonies powerfully convey ideas of what it felt like living in Algeria in the 1990s, but most importantly, they are concerned with different issues. The first quotation asserts the importance of making the voice heard and most importantly, put in a written form, as a mode of resistance. Khalti Zohra's first-hand testimony acts like a verbal will (*wasiyya*), which has the same importance as a written legal document. The survivor chose to present her will publicly, which is uncommon, as it is in the nature of a will that it is usually something to be done privately. By disclosing her will publicly, the responsibility moves to the addressee's side and becomes a duty to be fulfilled. She is aware that the will can be oral or written and by asking for the inclusion of her story in the written form of history, implicitly, she aims for her story to be included in the re-writing of the history of her country. The re-writing of history testifies to refusing the version provided by the authorities or the official narratives.

The second quotation is a related example by Khatibi, who argues that his novel is 'not only about the stories, but also about capturing the detail, like the smells, the background voices and so on' (interview, 2 November 2018). Khatibi hopes to contribute to the re-writing of history too, by performing it through literature, through making available the untold stories of the Civil War, as a way of what he calls 'counter history' (ibid.). The last quotation is about the Amnesty Law (1999, 2015), its application on the ground and its impact on victims' daily lives. It is a form of translation of what the Amnesty Law means on the ground. All of the examples are forms of democratization of memory, of knowledge, of literature and opportunities that show that sentiments have been mobilized as justifications for what Bevernage calls 'truth telling'.[6] He considers the latter productive and a significant factor in securing social peace and in the restoration of civic trust in wounded nations, in a manner which could never be realized by tribunals (ibid.). The aim of the overall project is truth telling. The researcher, the participants and the survivors are collaboratively engaged in the project with the goal of inviting the readers to participate in a project of social justice, as will be shown in this chapter. The methodological concerns of this practice-led research have been designed specially to achieve this aim.

The testimonies have been collected as part of a practice-led research in the form of a 'writing workshop' co-organized on 1 November 2018 by the researcher and Ms. Cherifa Kheddar, director of an Algerian NGO called *Djazairouna*. Among the participants was Said Khatibi, mentioned above, who put into practice his 'translation' or his re-narration of first-hand testimonies in his creative and the innovative novel *Hatab Sarajevo*,[7] discussed in this chapter. Khatibi's novel is an original collection of testimonies, bringing together the writer, the survivors and the researcher in one project. Moreover, in the workshop, the researcher collected first-hand testimonies from journalists Hmeida Layachi and Malika Bousouf and artists like Denis Martinez, who experienced the Black Decade first-hand. Some of what they said resonates with the novel, as I will show in due course. The workshop itself represented an act of resistance against an official process of Transitional Justice of which little information is known. Most importantly, it highlights its failures in achieving justice and democracy in the country. The gap in literature about the Civil War in Algeria as a whole makes the writing workshop a unique opportunity to collect first-hand testimonies of survivors, and to gather Algerian intellectuals who share a similar mission of unravelling untold stories of Algerian women survivors, but also to confirm the idea of resistance, discussed in this chapter. Furthermore, this chapter engages directly with the daily lives of survivors and attempts to represent them through different mediums, including literature, which is considered an alternative form of Transitional Justice. This is in line with what Omri refers to as 'poetic transitional Justice'[8] and what Clarkson calls the 'aesthetics of Transitional Justice'.[9]

Empirical Study: Practice-led Research

Methodology

The project started in 2017, and in 2018 I co-organized a writing workshop in collaboration with an association called *Djazairouna* [Our Algeria] in Blida, Algeria. Its director, Ms Cherifa Kheddar, is one of the survivors who refused to give in.[10] After the assassination of her brother and sister, in the same year, she set up the association, through which she and families of other victims set up a support network.[11] Their work included accompanying families of the victims to funerals, at a time when this action could result in their names being put on the death list. They offered counselling, psychological and financial support and legal advice. In 2016 and 2017, I participated in their two-day commemorative event, for which the date 1 November was purposefully chosen due to its symbolic significance and because traditionally the state enjoyed the role of remembrance and had always sponsored related events.[12] The date was chosen consciously to remember the eruption of the Algerian revolution against French colonialism in 1954. It symbolizes the will of Algerians to fight against French brutalities and the inhuman ways in which they were subjugated. The date also coincides with the International Remembrance Day. Given that individuals do not live in isolation, and that most of their actions take place within a societal setting, remembering never occurs in a vacuum, but it is a social and collective phenomenon, with individual memory being filtered through emotions and group experiences.

The workshop gathered thirty women survivors, some of whom came accompanied by members of their families. The various experts whom I call 'participants' were divided into four groups. In each group, there was a writer, two journalists (one Arabophone and one Francophone), a Berberophone (as translator), a psychologist known to the survivors, an artist and a film maker. The interviews were semi-structured and were video recorded. Each participant was asked to listen to the eye-witness testimonies and translate them into the medium she/he saw as appropriate. *Hatab Sarajevo* [Sarajevo Firewood] is the 're-narration' or the outcome of that workshop. In 2013, Said Khatibi decided to write on the Bosnian war and moved to live in the country and to learn its language. This decision was taken after discovering, in one of his visits to a war museum in Sarajevo, the names of Algerians who came to fight for what was framed as the holy war, 'jihad' (interview with Khatibi: 20 May 2017). The names of the Algerians were the start of the journey Khatibi undertook to unravel two similar histories. It is noteworthy that the 1990s the writer lived in Algeria, working as a journalist and a writer at a time when his colleagues were being assassinated nearly every day. In 2017, I met Khatibi and discussed the writing workshop project on women survivors of the Algerian Civil War. Testimonies of the Civil War survivors at that time, and even today, are not an easy matter, due to the policy (Amnesty Law) of clamping down on any attempt to 'deal' with the 1990s. The workshop was an opportunity for both projects, as we both agreed that re-narrating the stories of how people lived the wars in the two countries was one way of dismantling the official narratives of the wars.

One of the dilemmas I faced was differentiating between the various testimonies I was working with. In other words, differentiating between the survivors' first-hand testimonies, collected at the writing workshop from the writer's testimonies in their two forms, i.e., in interviews and in Khatibi's re-narration of testimonies in the novel, which includes fictional and non-fictional elements. Jones argues that using testimony in other media invites what is known as secondary or tertiary witnessing, which comprises those who did not experience an event first-hand, but who have heard and bear witness to the testimony of those who did.[13] Jones adds: 'Secondary witnesses in this understanding did not "witness" that event in the passive sense, but they can "witness" the mediation of that event and consider themselves to have knowledge of the event through that mediation. Moreover, they can bear witness in the active sense by recounting/presenting this knowledge to an audience.'[14]

The word 'testimony' has been used to mean different things. For example, as Winter argues, under the term '*testimonio*' different research had been conducted and yet the concepts covered by these terms are diverse.[15] She gives some examples: 'Latin-Americanists (e.g., Beverley 2004; Sklodowska 1996; Sommer 1996; Yúdice 1996) refer to the literary genre of testimonial literature. Holocaust researchers also use to speak of testimony predominantly referring to written documents (e.g., Waxman 2006)'. She adds that in some cases, the term is also used to describe survivors' video or audio testimony, like the ones collected by the Fortunoff Video Archive (Winter, 2009). The term has also been used by human rights organizations, which 'have also begun to collect video- and audio testimony from survivors of violent conflicts, e.g., the project IDP Voices, led in Colombia by the Norwegian Refugee Council in cooperation with the Internal Displacement Monitoring Center'.[16]

The use of the term 'testimony' in this chapter refers to two types of testimonies: a) the 'data' collected in the form of video-recording of 30 female survivors, which I call 'eye-witness testimonies; and b) the novel *Hatab Sarajevo* containing the data processed by the author/mediator, which cannot be called 'fictional testimonies' because most of it consists of facts and is not fictional. Therefore, I decided to consider *Hatab Sarajevo* as a *testimonio*, as per Beverley's definition: 'the word *testimonio* in Spanish carries the connotation of an act of truth-telling in a religious or legal sense — *dar testimonio* means to testify, to bear truthful witness. Testimonio's ethical and epistemological authority derives from the fact that we are meant to presume that the narrator is someone who has lived in his or her person, or indirectly through the experiences of friends, family, neighbors, or significant others, the events and experiences that he or she narrates'.[17] The fact that Khatibi lived the atrocities of the Civil War in Algeria gives him that ethical permission to report on what he lived and what he listened to. 'Testimonio is implicitly or explicitly a component of what Barbara Harlow has called "resistance literature"'.[18] Furthermore, Beverley clearly states: 'because in many cases the narrator is someone who either functionally illiterate or, if literate, not a professional writer, the production of a testimonio generally involves the tape-recording and then the transcription and editing of an oral account by an interlocutor who is an intellectual, often a journalist or a writer.'[19] The only difference is that *Hatab Sarajevo* contains some elements of fiction. One important element this research takes into consideration is the use of word 'testimony' rather than 'oral history' to refer to the fact that, as Beverley states, the difference between the two relates to the issue of intentionality:[20]

> In oral history it is the intentionality of the recorder [...] that is dominant, and the resulting text is in some sense 'data.' In testimonio, by contrast, it is the intentionality of the narrator that is paramount. The situation of the narration in testimonio has to involve an urgency to communicate, a problem of repression, poverty, subalternity, imprisonment, struggle for survival, implicated in the act of narration itself. The position of the reader of testimonio is akin to that of a jury member in a courtroom.[21]

The conscious decision to consider the book as *testimonio* is linked to its purpose, its mission, its audience and its context, which is similar to Latin American countries coming to terms with a violent past, as is the case in Algeria. It is certainly different from the novels discussed below in the nature of its writing process.

How Different is Khatibi's *Hatab Sarajevo*?

Literature has historically played a crucial role as witness-bearer to massacres and incidents of mass violence, especially when other forms of documentation have been missing. In Algeria, in particular, literature has been, with no exaggeration, the only way to document the two wars (the Algerian War of Liberation (1954–62) and the Civil War of the 1990s). What is original in this research is the practice-led nature of the novel under study. What makes Khatibi's *Hatab Sarajevo* different is the use of testimonies of real people which represents a primary source of knowledge about the crimes of the Civil War, on to which the government tries to impose an amnesia. The difference lies in the writing process, the data collection and the research included which, as mentioned, is part of a writing workshop from a larger project titled 'Narrating and Translating Sexual Violence against Women in Conflict' with emphasis on the Civil War of the 1990s, on which little is known. It is important to say that literature has often been used as a medium where Arab writers can express their views without facing their authoritarian regimes. Amine Zaoui and many other Algerian writers (both Arabophone, e.g., Bachir Mufti, H'meida Layachi, Fadhila al Farouq, Mourad Boukerzaza, and Francophone, e.g., Rachid Boudjedra, Assia Djebar, Yasmina Khadra, Maissa Bey, Adlene Meddi, Wahiba Khiari, Hafsa Zinaï-Koudil and Leila Marouane) have used literature as the only vehicle to challenge official narratives. Most importantly, their aim was to document the atrocities that took place, at a time where the regime actively confiscated any form of archive on the Civil War. This literature is known in Francophone studies as 'l'écriture d'urgence'.[22] In 'Literature d'urgence', the important aspect to remember is that it reflects a society which has undergone extreme violence and its writers use literature as a medium to give us a glimpse of what happened and at the same time to document and seek justice.

Hatab Sarajevo by Khatibi is proposed as a case of an alternative way of 'doing' Transitional Justice through the medium of *testimonios*. The Civil War is remembered as well as communicated and represented in the novel through various forms of testimonies by victims and specialists, as I mentioned earlier. The purpose of combining testimonies and comparing them is to see whether or not writing testimonial literature in this practice-led research reveals anything that other forms of bearing witness cannot do? This question preoccupies the minds of the three parties involved in this project, namely the researcher, the writer and the witnesses. It is of particular interest to the researcher whose aim is not only to compare recorded video testimonies by first-hand survivors with those of the writer's, but also to dig deeper into what kind of Transitional Justice may be appropriate in Algeria. What and how does Khatibi re-narrate the untold stories? How does he deal with concepts of 'justice' and 'transition'? Furthermore, as the researcher listened to survivors' testimonies over the three years (2016, 2017 and 2018), the interest became to investigate how they relate to the past and present; more importantly, how do they conceive concepts of reconciliation and justice at both individual and collective levels? What motivates the survivors to testify, other than generating empathy,[23] and/or being heard?[24] What is the author's motivation other than testifying to the trauma he has gone through, as a journalist, at a time when his colleagues were killed? One answer may be in taking an interdisciplinary approach which bridges the gap in the research literature by bringing together discussions on the role of memory in transitional justice with theoretical approaches to social and cultural memory studies.

Memory Studies and Transitional Justice

As this research is about a community of marginalized Algerian women survivors of the Civil War, the concept of 'mnemonic communities' is specifically relevant.[25] The concept highlights 'the fact that people do not act only according to strategic calculations, but in the light of the memories and narratives they have adopted and that make sense to them as members of a particular "memory group".'[26] Transitional justice is seen as an aspect of the 'politics of memory' which is used by different mnemonic communities and which is part of 'much broader processes of socialisation and identity formation' than the temporally limited policies and actions that constitute the focus of political science approaches.[27] However, what is missing from this approach, which is relevant to this study, is an understanding of the dynamic nature of memory, including personal memories; they are constituted not only by past events, but also by contemporary context. 'As Halbwachs observed as early as 1925, while mnemonic communities are formed on the basis of shared memories, the meaning ascribed to these memories is constructed through their narration and representation in the present moment'.[28] This is particularly relevant to this research about victims' narratives of the 1990s in Algeria. Halbwachs argued that 'while the collective memory endures and draws strength from its base in a coherent body of people, it is individuals as group members who remember'.[29]

Furthermore, memory is always connected to the present.[30] Every time a particular past is evoked, it goes through the filters of the present. Memory is therefore as much about the present and the future as it is about the past.[31] In other words, as Francesca Lessa argues, 'Memories are not simple recollections but rather their meanings are fiercely contested. Both public and private memories make claims about the past that are not acceptable to everybody.'[32] It is about taking the past forward and appropriating it, as Lazzara states, 'a flexible process of composition and recomposition, of casting and recasting the past in its relation to present circumstances and future expectations'.[33]

'Memory narratives', a concept developed by Francesca Lessa for the understanding the links between memory and transitional justice can be of use. By 'memory narratives', Lessa refers to 'a blend of individual and collective memory'. She adds that 'memory narratives set out specific interpretations and understandings of the facts, and they acquire different levels of legitimacy and appeal within society depending on how compellingly such narratives present a contested past'.[34] Certainly, 'the power of collective memory does not lie in its accurate, systematic, or sophisticated mapping of the past, but in establishing basic images that articulate and reinforce a particular ideological stance'.[35] What is important to remember is that 'memory narratives are likely to go on over generations'. Lessa emphasizes that 'several memory narratives are likely to emerge, and they will continue to evolve into the present and future, across decades, for as long as events remain subject to contestation, even affecting several generations. Therefore, it is necessary to trace memory narratives both at the time at which they originated and their later articulations.'[36] It is important to mention that analysing 'memory narratives' helps shed light on the range of motivations driving Transitional Justice choices, allowing us to see beyond political decisions in order to comprehend the reason behind specific Transitional Justice policy choices.[37]

Hatab Sarajevo

Hatab Sarajevo is about two countries separated geographically but united in traumas; Bosnia and Algeria went through similar civil wars in the 1990s. Both cost the lives of hundreds of thousands of people and numerous disappearances. The novel narrates the lives of two characters, Salim, an Algerian journalist, and Ivanka, a Bosnian young woman who has run away from the war in search of a place where she can write her dream play. The two characters' testimonies meet through trauma, destruction, death and writing. Ivanka lost her father to the war and Salim lived through the Civil War where death was around the corner, particularly for journalists and intellectuals whose names and dates of death he makes sure to insert in his narrative in an attempt to archive their history, as I detail in the coming sections. The narration of the stories of their lives reconstructs and performs the historicity of the two countries and brings to life a theme which was threatened by institutionalized amnesia.

Since I have chosen to look at the relationship between memory and Transitional Justice and how it is communicated through literature, I focus on how the problematic issue of 'rape' in wartime, which is the overarching theme of the project as a whole, is represented in the novel. The theme is indeed present when the plot is problematized as Salim encounters one of the War Veterans, Al Hadj Lazrag, who was suspected of torturing Si Ahmed during the war of liberation. Salim learns about Si Ahmed's betrayal of the *khawa* (the brothers, a word used to refer war veterans) by denouncing one of them, called Boualem, which led to his death under torture by the French. As a form of local justice, Si Ahmed was forced to marry Boualem's only daughter, Zohra, who turns out to be Salim's biological mother. 'Zohra died of a bullet in her head, from my father's gun, who wanted to get rid of her and to live a new life. He invented the story of her suicide, after spreading rumours about her rape by Mudjahideen (war veterans) during the War of Liberation'.[38] The quote is complex since it claims that rape was perpetrated not only by the colonizer but also by the so-called 'brother', the Algerian war veteran who is seen as a 'living legend'. The glorification of War Veterans is enshrined into a law, which forbids Algerians from saying anything negative that might tarnish their reputation.[39] The sacredness of the War Veteran figure is part of the glorified official history of Algeria. The first-hand testimonies collected during the writing workshop reveal a form of silence around the theme of sexual violence, which is in line with what Clark argues above.[40] One of the survivors, whom I shall call Amina in order to protect her identity, insisted on narrating her story without any hint towards sexual violence. She says: 'the neighbours told me that "they" (referring to the Islamists) were for 15 days waiting for you to come. You were lucky because they usually came only minutes after you had left'. She adds: 'once, I went to an army officer and asked to be accompanied to my house, after I had told them that I am the widow of the university employee whose head was thrown in the market...'. Her narrative was constructed in such a way as to leave no room for the possibility of sexual violence. The only reference to rape was made by one of the survivors, whom I shall call Zakia, who said: 'the cases of rape we heard about were done among the Islamists. They were cases of revenge'.

Khatibi's reference to the War of Liberation is part of a new movement by Algerians to re-write history, a community of intellectuals who challenge official narrative. This is a mnemonic community which is part of 'much broader processes of socialisation and identity formation'.[41] The reference to rape in the novel as something that happened in the War of Liberation shows that rape is a recurrent issue. Khatibi's use of 'memory narratives' highlights, as mentioned above, that 'the power of collective memory does not lie in its accurate, systematic, or sophisticated mapping of the past, but in establishing basic images that articulate and reinforce a particular ideological stance'.[42] By using the war of Liberation instead of the Civil War the novel reinforces the idea of re-emergence of violence over generations.[43]

Khatibi's reference to Zohra's case confirms Francesca Lessa argument, when she writes: 'Memories are not simple recollections but rather their meanings are fiercely contested. Both public and private memories make claims about the past that are not acceptable to everybody'.[44] Khatibi is basically taking the past forward and appropriating it since the process is about 'composition and recomposition, of casting and recasting the past in its relation to present circumstances and future expectations'.[45] In the same vein, the marriage of Si Ahmed in the novel with his victim's daughter is perceived as part of practising 'justice'. This is of course a common, if controversial, practice in most of the Arab world, as there are countries (e.g., Algeria) where the crime of rape is dismissed if the perpetrator agrees to marry the victim. Here again, it is a case of re-appropriating the past to serve the present.

Aleida Assmann's concept of 'active memory' in relation to the theme of 'rape at wartime' has been associated with the Algerian collective memory in relation to the colonial period.[46] It is a topic that keeps re-emerging in different forms. As recently as June 2000 (forty years after Algerian independence), the testimony of the iconic war veteran Louisette Ighilahriz's came to light through the article written by Florence Beauge titled 'Torturée par l'armée Française, "Lila" cherche l'homme qui l'a sauvée'.[47] 'Memory narratives', mixing Ighilahriz's individual story about her rape by a French soldier is a story which resonates with Algerian collective narratives in relation to the French colonial era. However, the taboo of rape becomes worse when the rapist is the 'brother', either the Algerian Mudjahid (war veteran) or the Islamist, who could be a neighbour. From the video-interviews, as I discuss below, the word 'brother' was mentioned only in reference to the cases of revenge rape.

Hatab Sarajevo is divided into equal chapters, alternating between Salim (the Civil War in Algeria) and Ivanka (the Civil War in Bosnia). I argue that Khatibi's novel can be read as a performative example of testimony, as a text which, through fictional accounts, provides testimonial evidence of the trauma experienced by the characters and by the broader Algerian society. By *performative history*, I am referring to what Austin calls 'doing' something as opposed to just saying something,[48] which is what Khatibi is doing by bringing up the 'rape' case of the War Veterans. He challenges the 'sacredness' of the Algerian War and puts it under scrutiny. Khatibi is aware that literature is a more or less safe platform where ideas, ideologies, concepts and, in this case, laws can be contested, debated and it can participate in the changing of discourses. Khatibi adds fictional elements in order to problematize the story of 'rape' but finishes the chapter 'Like an Old Pair of Shoes'[49] with an open-ended question about the extent of truth of the whole story. He asks: what proves that what I heard from Hadj Razk is the truth? As far as first-hand testimonies went, there was no mentioning of the War of Independence and certainly nothing related to the War Veterans. The fictional side is clear and shows that the writer's invention of the story was intended to raise the issue of the sacredness of war veterans as well as to inject some doubts in the discourses around the War of Liberation. The story is narrated in a coherent pattern that makes it difficult to distinguish truth from fiction.

This hybridization of the genre we are dealing with, between what was actually testified by the eyewitnesses and the fictional side, is at the core of this experiment. Going back to the data collected, in the thirteen hours recorded, the stories of rape were not spoken about in a clear way, which is something we had anticipated.[50] When we asked the survivors whether members of the army had had any links to incidents of sexual violence, unanimously, they denied any wrongdoing. The stories about rape were an opportunity for the survivors to detach themselves from the issue, by the othering of the perpetrators as Islamists, and they were used to discredit the Islamists' propaganda as being pious. It is in a way similar to Khatibi's attempt to take away the 'sacredness' of the War Veterans and to demonstrate that sexual violence in wars is a global phenomenon throughout history.

When describing what it was like living in Algeria during the 1990s, Khatibi was more direct. Salim, the main character in the novel, for example, is an Algerian journalist, through whom we get to sense of what it felt like to be living in Algeria during the 1990s. Through him, we get to know the life of Said Khatibi, the author and journalist who comes from Bousaada, one of the cities of the Algerian interior. Both Salim and Khatibi move to live in Algiers, in one of the popular neighbourhoods, and to archive the daily lives of Algerians. Through both characters (the main character and the author), the history of Algerian journalists is performed. During the workshop, Khatibi testified about his life as a journalist coming from the South of Algeria, giving details of both cities, the capital Algiers and Bousaada, which might differ in terms of military presence, which was much less visible in Bousaada than in Algiers, but were both affected by the state of fear imposed on the country. In his chapter titled 'Heading South' (sawba al-janub), Khatibi describes the ways people live their everyday lives, in the practical side of history,[51] in a way that historians would not do. He says: 'features of "a normal" life change as soon as you leave Algiers; the concrete, which changed the capital into a human barracks disappears and is replaced by forest and mountains'. This does not mean that the rest of the country is unaffected. He describes the scene of taking a taxi going to Bousaada, where the driver warns the passengers that he will not stop until he reaches his final destination, bearing in mind that it is a four-hour journey.[52] He then describes a discussion between the driver and a passenger who asks about Bousaada. The driver says: 'the acorn was trilling between the military and the others, but now things are calmer'. The acorn is part of a coded language referring to bullets. This performative use of language[53] gives the narrative a local flavour, which distinguishes it from other parts of Algeria and which Modern Standard Arabic will miss out. Two major incidents happened in Bousaada which Khatibi deliberately wanted to use in his performative representation of the city. They are the burning down of the oldest hotel in the region, the Hotel Caid, and of 'Etienne Dinet's Museum'. These two incidents are minor events and might be missed out by a historian writing on the Algerian Civil War. Khatibi's aim is to document the history of his town Bousaada and at the same time communicate and represent the state of fear throughout the country. After describing another small town on the way to Bousaada, called Sidi Aissa, which for him looked grim, he says: 'fear is not restricted in the capital only, it grows and matures higher than carob trees, which decorate those empty roads'. One might argue that Khatibi did not need fiction to discuss the Civil War; as a journalist, he could have used other media. I argue that unlike Aleida Assmann's idea that 'Nation-states produce narrative versions of their past which are taught, embraced, and referred to as their collective autobiography',[54] it is in fact, through this hybrid genre, which includes autobiographical elements (as the case of Khatibi), that collective memory is challenged.

Furthermore, through Salim, we are introduced to other minor characters like his girlfriend Malika, a teacher who was forced to wear the veil out of fear of being killed. She embodies the life of the majority of Algerian women who were unveiled, who feared for their lives and opted to wear the veil in the public spaces. Malika's story resonates with a first-hand eye-witness testimony given by Malika Bousouf, a Francophone journalist, who took part in the workshop and who provided testimonies about how she used to disguise herself in public spaces, particularly at the time when her male colleagues were being assassinated. Bousouf said: "I received my letter condemning me to death issued by the MEI (Movement pour l'État Islamique) at home, because the other death threats I used to receive through the radio... After authentication of the letter by the Algerians and the French, I was offered refugee status in France, which I rejected, as it meant not coming back to Algeria for ten years. I also believed that the combat should take place here in Algeria' (Interview, 1 November 2017). She adds that after the infamous massacre, she went to Bentalha to investigate the state of children, where she found herself talking to women survivors who have never set foot in their lives in the capital Algiers. The problematization of the traumatic experiences that Algerian women went through during the 1990s makes the participant (as the case of Malika Bousouf, the journalist) becomes eyewitnesses. In other words, the articulation of traumatic experience helps the process of developing recognition of the suffering of others, as well as generating empathy,[55] which is the purpose of *testimonios* in the first place.[56] More importantly, Khatibi's performative usage of stories is a means to archive women's stories in a country which denied women the re-narration of their contribution to the War of Independence. For example, when he dedicates the first few pages (p. 11) of the novel to list of the names of the journalists and intellectuals assassinated during the Black Decade, it is his way of fighting against amnesia. In the novel, Khatibi invests in naming each person with the date of his assassination, he says:

> I don't forget the years that writers, intellectuals, journalists, artists, friends or colleagues I liked left us: Mouloud Mammeri, 1989. Jillali Elyabess and Tahar Djaout, 1993. Abdelkader Alloula and Chab Hasni, 1994. Rachid Mimouni, Bakhti Benouda and Rabah Belamri, 1995. Chab Aziz, 1996. Mustapha Belgharbi also left us in the same year.

Fascinatingly, at the writing workshop, Denis Martinez, the Algerian artist who took part as an eyewitness started by listing the same names:

> Hamza Assla, directeur de l'Institut des Beaux Arts, who was assassinated in 1994 as well as other friends and comrades like Alloula and Tahar Djaout. I was a member of the committee looking into Djaout's assassination. A day later, a list of members of the same committee to be assassinated was published. The first on the list was Doctor Boucebsi [...] We had to find ways of hiding. I used to change route [...] I was asked by Ahmed Assla to leave and to go into exile [...] A few months later, he was assassinated. (Interview 1 November 2017)

In the same vein, Malika Bousouf says: 'it is difficult to remember colleagues mentioned in the workshop, like Djaout who was a friend and a colleague,

Boucebsi, in whose house I dined, a few days before his assassination…'. The pattern of naming those assassinated during the Civil War seems like a deliberate act by the eyewitnesses participating in the workshop. The act is a form of 'naming', an act against amnesia and for bringing their perpetrators to justice.[57] Naming in this case is an act of defiance of the Amnesty Law, which forbids naming and bringing the perpetrators to justice.

Khatibi's survivor-centred approach goes beyond the traditional way of representing the past or searching for the truth. Re-narrating their stories gives the opportunity to survivors to perform their side of reality, using their own language. For example, the story of the young flower-vendor in the novel has been taken as it has been narrated by the eyewitness. Khatibi did not add any fiction to the story; the fictional side is in the development of the narratives through the fictional characters. For example, the vendor's story has been narrated by Malika (a fictional character) who tells Salim how her uncle's wife Battoul left her house in the morning to go to the market, leaving her four daughters (fictional), carrying an empty basket, hoping to buy sweets for her youngest daughter. The story is knitted in a way that leaves the boundaries between truth and fiction fluid. Khatibi then inserts the story of how the daughters were not able to recognize their mother's corpse in the hospital, as the bodies were burned to ashes and it was only the eldest daughter who identified her from her long soft legs.[58] Furthermore, the language used by the young flower-vendor in the market, who discovered a bomb, shouting in Algerian dialect: 'Bumba Bumba' (a bomb…a bomb), is exactly how the mother (an eyewitness) narrated the story. The language used is not very far from the everyday one used throughout the novel. Khatibi's proficiency in various Algerian regional dialects added to the authenticity of the story. His contribution to the survivors' narratives through his use of language, combining factual and fictional events, performs a version among other versions of history. This is in line with Ruth Franklin, who argues that 'to consider any text "pure testimony", completely free from aestheticizing influences and narrative conventions, is naïve'.[59] However, Khatibi's emphasis 'is not factual or forensic truth but its social construction through testimonies and witness accounts'.[60] Khatibi's rendering of women's narratives is a form of psychosocial justice, as its aim is not to achieve legal justice, but is a way of healing.

Conclusion

This chapter seeks to answer whether or not literature can play a role (or roles) in the provision of a remedy for historical injustice. In answering this particular question and other related ones, the chapter puts forward an original practice-led research where the researcher as well as the author, along with first-hand eyewitnesses, create together new narratives that contradict the official ones and can be a form of justice. In this way *Hatab Sarajevo* represents first-hand testimonies mediated and communicated through literature. Through the medium of *testimonio*, as a genre, through the language in its literal and figurative forms, and through culture in general, the reader is exposed to a different discourse than the official one. More importantly, the reader becomes a witness and shares the survivors' wishes to make their voices heard. As Franklin argues: 'literature, by virtue of its ability to make difficult ideas easier to contemplate, also increases the possibility of the listener's or reader's empathetic response'.[61] To strengthen this argument, Franklin uses Jorge Semprum, the author of *The Long Goodbye*, who advocates for the use of literature to communicate the experiences of the others, saying 'only artifice of masterly narrative will prove capable of such testimony'.[62] Franklin adds: 'Semprum does not believe naively in the power of literature as a humanizing impulse [...] Semprum also recognizes that literature, while not perfect, is the best chance survivors have'. This raises other issues relevant to Algerian women survivors, such as creating a platform where they can be heard. While the chapter highlights the different types of testimonies, it equally puts forward the importance of the workshop, organized by the researcher, as a platform where the Civil War was discussed at length. This is just as important as the provision of the testimonies in forms where they will be heard.

The importance of the study is that it addresses the process of testifying and the importance of narratives through different media. The empowerment and the agency that survivors achieved in having their narratives archived in what I call an 'alternative history of Algeria' is part of the survivor-centred approach, which is the focus of the novel and the project as a whole. Mnemonic communities are empowered through collaborative work like this and are the way forward to defying the Amnesty Law (1999, 2005). By this I mean, that the motive of research initiated is a move towards challenging the Amnesty Law and emptying it of its content. It was a move to declare to the world that the 'cooked up' transitional process that the regime imposed is ineffective.

Throughout the project, the collection of first-hand testimonies at a time when a fine and imprisonment might be a possibility, is in line with other alternative projects, run by citizens as well as civil society organization to deter the regime's move towards amnesia of the Civil War. The novel, *Hatab Sarajevo* is a practical move towards empowering survivors to own their narratives, while being given the opportunity to be heard does not conflict with, but rather furthers, the objectives of Transitional Justice in post-conflict settings. Analysing the data which includes the videos of first-hand testimonies as well as secondary ones through the novel, exposes how testimonies in their different forms have lives of their own, and a complex relationship between them. They bring to light different aspects, which provide coherence of narratives about a difficult past and are part of Transitional Justice. *Hatab Sarajevo* is a concrete example of the agency of literature used by mnemonic community 'doing' an alternative Transitional Justice.

Notes to Chapter 15

1. Many thanks to Professor Sara Jones for her critical reading of early drafts of this chapter and for her useful comments.
2. Naming the 1990s in Algeria as a 'Civil War' remains contested. For more information, see Jacob Mundy, *Imagining Geographies of Algerian Violence* (Palo Alto, CA: Stanford University Press, 2015), p. 31.

3. Anissa Daoudi, 'Algerian Women and the Traumatic Decade: Literary Interventions', *Journal of Literature and Trauma Studies*, 5.1 (2017), 41–63; Anissa Daoudi, 'Introduction: Narrating and Translating Sexual Violence at Wartime in the Middle East and North Africa (MENA region)', *Boundary 2 O*, 13 July 2018 <http://www.boundary2.org/2018/07/anissa-daoudi-narrating-and-translating-sexual-violence-at-wartime-in-the-middle-east-and-north-africa-mena-region-english/>; Anissa Daoudi, 'Untranslatability of Algeria in "The Black Decade"', *Boundary 2 O*, 5 July 2018, <www.boundary2.org/2018/07/anissa-daoudi-untranslatability-of-algeria-in-the-black-decade-2/>.
4. Article 46: 'anyone who, by speech, writing, or any other act, uses or exploits the wounds of the National Tragedy to harm the institutions of the Democratic and Popular Republic of Algeria, to weaken the state, or to undermine the good reputation of its agents who honourably served it, or to tarnish the image of Algeria internationally, shall be punished by three to five years in prison and a fine of 250,000 to 500,000 dinars.' See: <https://www.hrw.org/news/2006/02/28/algeria-new-amnesty-law-will-ensure-atrocities-go-unpunished>.
5. *Khalti*: in English 'auntie' is a polite form of addressing an older woman.
6. Berber Bevernage, 'Writing the Past Out of the Present: History and the Politics of Time in Transitional Justice', *History Workshop Journal*, 69.1 (Spring 2010), 111–31.
7. Said Khatibi, *Hatab Sarajevo* [Firewood of Sarajevo War] (Algiers: Editions El-Ihktilef and Editions Difaf, 2019).
8. Mohamed-Salah Omri, 'Écriture et liberté en Tunisie', in *Escribir la democracia*, ed. by Anne-Laure Bonvalot, Anne-Laure Rebreyend and Philippe Roussin (Madrid: Casa de Velázquez, 2018), pp. 247–58.
9. Carrol Clarkson, *Drawing the Lines: Towards an Aesthetics of Transitional Justice* (New York: Fordham University Press, 2014).
10. Jessica Ayesha Northley, *Civil Society in Algeria: Activism, Identity and the Democratic Process* (London and New York: I. B. Tauris, 2019), p. 1.
11. Northley, *Civil Society in Algeria*, p. 1.
12. Francesca Lessa, *Memory and Transitional Justice in Argentina and Uruguay: Against Impunity* (Basingstoke: Palgrave Macmillan, 2013), p. 21.
13. Sara Jones, *The Media of Testimony: Remembering the East German Stasi in the Berlin Republic* (Basingstoke: Palgrave Macmillan, 2014), p. 187.
14. Sara Jones, 'Testimony through Culture: Towards a Theoretical Framework', *Rethinking History*, 23.3 (2019), 257–78.
15. Franka Winter, 'Giving Voice to the Voiceless? Second Thoughts on Testimony in Transitional Justice', *A Contracorriente: Revista de Historia Social y Literatura en América Latina*, 6.3 (Winter 2009), 90–107.
16. Franka Winter, 'Giving Voice to the Voiceless?', pp. 91–92.
17. John Beverley, *Testimonio: On the Politics of Truth* (Minneapolis: University of Minnesota Press, 2004), p. 3.
18. Beverley, *Testimonio*, p. 31.
19. Beverley, *Testimonio*, p. 31
20. Beverley, *Testimonio*, p. 32.
21. Beverley, *Testimonio*, p. 32.
22. Tristan Leperlier, *Algérie: les écrivains de la décennie noire* (Paris: CNRS Editions, 2018); Jeffrey K. Olick, *The Politics of Regret: On Collective Memory and Historical Responsibility* (London: Routledge, 2007); Charles Bonn and Farida Boualit, *Paysages littéraires algériens des années 90: témoigner d'une tragédie?* (Paris: L'Harmattan, 1999).
23. Aleida Assmann and Ines Detmers, *Empathy and its Limits* (Basingstoke: Palgrave Macmillan, 2016).
24. Shoshana Felman and Dori Laub, *Testimony: Crises of Witnessing in Literature, Psychoanalysis and History* (New York: Routledge, 1992).
25. Sara Jones, '"Simply a little piece of GDR history"? The Role of Memorialization in Post-Socialist Transitional Justice in Germany', *History & Memory*, 27.1 (2015), 154–81.
26. Barahona de Brito cited in Jones, *The Role of Memorialization*, p. 158.

27. Jones, *The Role of Memorialization*, p. 158.
28. Ibid.
29. Maurice Halbwachs, 'From *The Collective Memory*', in *The Collective Memory Reader*, ed. by Jeffrey K. Olick, Vered Vinitzky-Seroussi and Daniel Levy (Oxford: Oxford University Press, 2011), p. 142.
30. Andreas Huyssen, *Twilight Memories: Marking Time in a Culture of Amnesia* (Oxford: Routledge, 1995).
31. *Collective Memory of Political Events: Social Psychological Perspectives*, ed. by James W. Pennebaker, Darío Páez and Bernard Rimé (Mahwah, NJ: Lawrence Erlbaum, 1997).
32. Lessa, *Memory and Transitional Justice*, p. 17.
33. Michael J. Lazzara, *Chile in Transition: The Poetics and Politics of Memory* (Gainesville: University of Florida, 2006), p. 2.
34. Lessa, *Memory and Transitional Justice*, p. 19.
35. Yael Zerubavel, *Recovered Roots: Collective Memory and the Making of Israeli National Tradition* (Chicago, IL: University of Chicago Press, 1995), p. 8.
36. Lessa, *Memory and Transitional Justice*, p. 19.
37. Ibid.
38. Khatibi, *Hatab Sarajevo*, p. 288.
39. For reference on the Law, see <http://www.majliselouma.dz/index.php/ar/2016-07-19-12-56-20/2016-07-19-13-25-03/1013-08-19-17-1429-15-2008>.
40. Janine Natalya Clark, 'Finding a Voice: Silence and its Significance for Transitional Justice', *Social and Legal Studies*, 29.3 (2019), 355–78.
41. Jones, *The Role of Memorialization*, p. 158.
42. Zerubavel, *Recovered Roots*, p. 8.
43. Lessa, *Memory and Transitional Justice*, p. 19.
44. Lessa, *Memory and Transitional Justice*, p. 17.
45. Lessa, *Memory and Transitional Justice*, p. 2.
46. Aleida Assmann, 'History, Memory, and the Genre of Testimony', *Poetics Today*, 27.2 (2006), 261–73.
47. See Florence Beauge's article <https://www.lemonde.fr/afrique/article/2000/06/20/torturee-par-l-armee-francaise-en-algerie-lila-recherche-l-homme-qui-l-a-sauvee_1671125_3212.html>.
48. J. L. Austin, *How to Do Things with Words* (Oxford: Oxford University Press, 1962), p. 47.
49. The chapter in Arabic is called مثل نعل مهترى.
50. Clark, 'Finding a Voice.'
51. Hayden White, 'Figural Realism in Witness Literature', *Parallax*, 10.1 (2004), 113–24.
52. Khatibi, *Hatab Sarajevo*, p. 78
53. White, 'Figural Realism'.
54. Aleida Assmann, 'Canon and Archive', in *Cultural Memory Studies: An International and Interdisciplinary Handbook*, ed. by Astrid Erll and Ansgar Nünning (Berlin: Walter de Gruyter, 2008), pp. 97–107 (p. 101).
55. Assmann and Detmers, *Empathy and its Limits*.
56. Beverley, *Testimonio*.
57. For more information, see Lazhari Labter, *Journalistes algériens, 1988–1998: chronique des années d'espoir et de terreur* (Algiers: Chihab Editions, 2018).
58. Khatibi, *Hatab Sarajevo*, p. 160.
59. Ruth Franklin, *A Thousand Darknesses: Lies and Truth in Holocaust Fiction* (Oxford: Oxford University Press, 2011), p. 11.
60. Susanne Buckley-Zistel, 'Narrative Truths: On the Construction of the Past in Truth Commissions', in *Transnational Justice Theories*, ed. by Susanne Buckley-Zistel et al. (Cambridge: Routledge, 2014), pp. 144–62 (p. 144).
61. Franklin, *A Thousand Darknesses*, p. 13.
62. Franklin, *A Thousand Darknesses*, p. 13.

CHAPTER 16

Writing, Law and Transitional Justice in Tunisia

Mohamed-Salah Omri

> '[The revolution was] beautiful because it was just and just because it was beautiful.'[1]
>
> 'By writing, I don't have the ambition to change the world. Yet, to testify has become for me a vital need (*exigence vitale*). Writing is the means to it; or, in any case, the one means I know.'[2]

The 2010–11 revolution in Tunisia presents us with a telling paradox. History teaches us that revolutions and law are not exactly soulmates. How can we explain, then, that the first instinct after 2011 in Tunisia was what I will be calling legalism: how to have a legal transition, how to set the legal bases for new institutions; in essence, how to regulate what is inherently beyond or against regulation and normative control — a revolution? This may be explained, in part, by what the President of the Lawyers Association at the time, Chawki Tabib, saw as an alignment between law and justice. He wrote: 'On the 14th of January, law was put in its place: it was no longer the law of the most powerful but that of the most just.'[3] But there is a long history to this turn of events, which this chapter seeks to uncover. Most importantly, though, in response to the denial of justice perpetrated by successive governments in the country, prisoners of conscience have been writing their side of the story and putting forth the case for justice since the 1970s. In this chapter, I zero in on a particular corpus through which I single out three broad areas where the convergence between law and writing is tested. They also highlight tensions and zones of shade for law, and for transitional justice specifically, which writing seeks to enlighten or fill. While this literature contests and protests, it is also lucid about the pitfalls of individual memory, the allure of style and the limitations of language in expressing, for example, bodily pain resulting from torture and coercion. Why and in what ways do writers resort to collective remembering and collective writing? To what extent are we able to say that these writers have produced collective counter-knowledge or collective resistance against unjust knowledge? What kind of justice is this? How does it relate to concepts like proleptic forgiveness and epistemic justice? How does the writing of the incarceration experience handle the seeming contradiction between the literary and the legalistic?

State Tutelage and the Nature of the Revolution

As early as the first day of freedom from Ben Ali's rule, Tunisia triggered the existing constitutional mechanisms for transfer of power in case of vacancy. Soon afterwards, I would argue, the revolution itself was turned over to lawyers.[4] The three main commissions created in February 2011 were all chaired by lawyers or jurists: The National Commission for Investigating Abuses and Acts Committed during the Revolution was chaired by Maitre Taoufik Bouderbala; the National Commission for Investigating Corruption and Unlawful Money Transfers by Law Professor Abdelfattah Omar; and the most powerful one of all, the High Commission for Realizing the Objectives of the Revolution, Political Reform and Democratic Transition, was headed by jurist Yadh Ben Achour.[5] There are at least two explanations for this legal turn in the revolution. One is historical while the other is political. I start with what I call the pedagogical state. As early as the late 1950s, the first president of independent Tunisia, Habib Bourguiba, and labour and cultural leaders contemporary to him, saw themselves as educators.[6] The people needed tutelage into modern life, including respect for the law. Therefore, these leaders set about teaching and preaching, leaving no issue off limits. Bourguiba famously moved around the country and dominated local radio and television, talking about family planning, clothing and smart dress, disease, treatment of wives, health, education, religion, sex... His government set in motion the legal framework for a 'modern' nation. The strategy was a top-down approach by which laws preceded, rather than reflected or followed people's expectations. The Personal Status Code of 1956, which ended the rule of Islamic jurisprudence in family matters and the rights of women, is a case in point. Emboldened by his overwhelming popularity as nationalist leader, Bourguiba would mobilize his rhetorical prowess and acting skills to mould a population into his own image. However, in time that moulding came to serve his own vanity and cause his paranoia. For what he came to fear most were challenges to his place in the collective memory of Tunisians and dissidence from his line of thought by those he considered his sons. He thought of the protesting youth in the late 1960s as prodigal sons.[7]

The story of legalism in Tunisia is, therefore, rather long. However, come 2010–11, Tunisians were trained to obey a law designed from above, to both dominate and enable citizens, a law manipulated and corrupted by Bourguiba's successor, Zin al-Abidin Ben Ali. It is worth bearing in mind that Bourguiba was a lawyer and so was his main rival, Salah Ben Youssef. In fact, lawyers have played determining roles across the history of Tunisia, both as foundational figures and as voices of dissent.[8] The early opposition practised a form of dissent from the state's policies, not an outright rejection of it. Dissidents noted a separation between law and justice. In fact, they saw law as specifically being at the service of injustice, particularly in the areas of social justice and freedom of expression and association.

The Perspectives group, a left-wing association of young activists most active between 1963 and 1975, were jailed for claiming their right to full citizenship, and argued that the project of the independent state was unfinished or inconsistent with its own aims. Gilbert Naccache, to whom I will return, found the arbitrariness and cruelty of his imprisonment unlawful:

> I am in prison, innocent of any action against the law (for the ideas and intentions, yes, but these are not punishable by law). Without a judge's order, without sentence, in the name of empty accusations, which would be abandoned upon a decision from President Bourguiba, in a letter handed to me 14 years later![9]

The legalism, which influenced the development of a popular constitutionalist culture in the country over a long period of its history, may have led to what Yadh Ben Achour calls a 'constitutionalist revolution'.[10] In his recent book, *Tunisie: une révolution en pays d'Islam* (2016), Ben Achour claims that 'In Tunisia, the primacy of the political imposed itself by the fact that the power was affected only in part, the highest part, by the Revolution'.[11] This allowed levels of continuity between the old and the new orders, and, eventually, proponents of reconciliation won the day. 'We have here one of the fundamental paradoxes of the Tunisian revolution: the revolution took place: one must try and punish. The revolution must continue without risking war: one must compromise (*pactiser*).'[12] This would give priority to political order without sacrificing responsibility. In a word, 'What we call transitional justice is, in a sense, a transactional justice.'[13] For these transactions to occur and succeed, respect for the law, or at least legality, must be maintained.

In Tunisia, the transitional period was the subject of intense political and social debate and pressure.[14] It was chaotic and piecemeal, and reflected, in many ways, the balance of political power in place.[15] Yet, it enjoyed constitutional backing. Chapter X of the 2014 Constitution stipulates in Article 148, paragraph 9: 'The State undertakes to apply the transitional justice system in all its domains and according to the deadlines prescribed by the relevant legislation.' This was reflected in the 2013–53 Organic Law of 25 December 2013, which details the Commission for Truth and Dignity (French acronym, IVD).[16]

Ben Achour sees in its fate the character of the Tunisian revolution itself. He concludes:

> In reality, the great debate around transitional justice, as well as the conflicts resulting from them, bring to light the specificities — some would say, the weaknesses — of the Tunisian revolution. Neither ideological nor partisan nor belligerent, it is situated in a half-tinted zone, marked by half-measures, lack of clarity and the hesitations between more or less radical solutions.[17] In fact, the crisis of transitional justice is revealing of a more general political choice, between exclusion and reconciliation.[18]

It is amidst this debate that a new constitution was constructed. The making of the new constitution served as the best training for full citizenship. It revealed what Ghazi Ghrairi, constitutional lawyer and spokesperson for the High Commission on Reform, calls 'a society anxious about its rights, conscious of its force and able, in effect, to compel the political class to act under its control.'[19] Ben Achour concludes that the real impact of the Revolution was this: 'The Society is no longer under tutelage, as it was in the time of Bourguiba.'[20]

If we accept this assessment, we can understand that while the revolution reopened old wounds and revived an appetite for revenge, it also restrained, some would say manipulated, the public mood by mobilizing a local tradition of legality, compounded by international pressure, to contain this first all-out revolution in the region since the wars for independence. As the struggle against impunity continued with varying degrees of intensity but limited success, memory battles raged on, waged by all sides, along with battles to preserve the spaces of freedom necessary to wage them. Yet, whatever the outcome, local history became available for construction and revision, and people felt entitled to their narratives and empowered to put their cases within a liberated field, one which quickly grew crowded with competing claims. It is to this corpus of accounts and testimonies that I now turn.

Prison Literature Reconsidered

The corpus in question is restricted to writings by prisoners, during and after their incarceration experience. Two key points must be borne in mind in this selection. Aleida Assman argues in 'Memory, Individual and Collective' that autobiographical memory of events experienced in one's lifetime has a powerful impact and provides higher status (e.g., to victims of events). The second element is the age of these writers when events took place.[21] A study shows how 'events occurring in a generation's early adulthood seem to have particularly powerful impact on their collective memory and political outlook for the rest of their lives.'[22] In Tunisia, the 200 people tried in the aftermath of student protests in the summer of 1973 were aged between 19 and 32.[23] One of them was the poet Ammar Mansour, who was incarcerated at the age of 23. He distinguishes between two moments of writing, which give us two types of writing by prisoners: 'My prison memoirs are only the poems I have written in prison. My memories written after jail are a different matter, which concerns the consciousness of that moment historically, culturally and philosophically...' [24] In line with this view, he intended to publish his prison papers 'without changing a comma or a period.'[25]

'The person I was at age 20 or 30 is not me at age 60'. He adds: 'that person may not be me or is another: I feel protective of him but I don't own that person. He reflects a specific consciousness at a specific period of history, which we should neither embellish nor manipulate.'[26] One reason this writing is perhaps closer to the incarceration experience has to do with the body. Mansour makes a key link between body and writing during incarceration: 'I considered writing inseparable from the body, and this is perhaps what made me continue writing in prison because this was an act of resistance, faith and truthfulness.' Zemzmi, the poet's fellow prisoner who gathered the poems and published them, writes in a different book that he considers prison literature to be part of resistance literature, insisting on the 'literary value' of texts on the one hand, and the need for them to be 'an

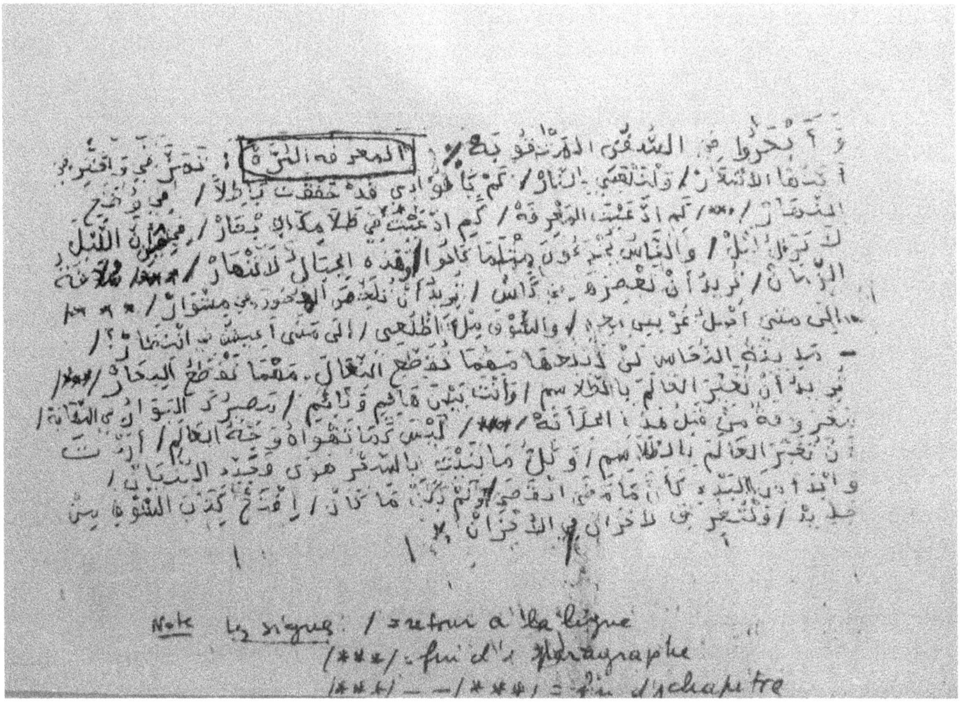

FIG. 16.1. Poem by Ammar Mansour written on cigarette paper, using ash and water as ink.

expression of a prison experience endured by the writer or at least inspired by it'.[27] For him, Mansour's poetry is the prototype of the genre because it describes a prison experience and is written by the prisoner entirely in prison.[28] How do these two considerations translate into methodology, into ways of approaching this literature?

Much of course has been said about representing one's pain and trauma and representing the pain of another, notably the debate instigated in literature by J. M. Coetzee and carried further by Judith Butler.[29] However, my focus on these types of accounts is also motivated by what I consider specific ethical considerations and epistemological ones. At the heart of it is a rethinking of the status and situation of the knower, who is in this case the prisoner and more specifically the prisoner as a producer of knowledge about their own condition. In this regard, what philosopher Miranda Fricker called 'epistemic injustice' is relevant. She famously distinguished between two major forms of epistemic injustice, namely 'testimonial injustice' and 'hermeneutic injustice'.[30] Both are linked to situations of power relations and degrees of access to knowledge. Testimonial injustice occurs where a speaker is given less credibility than they otherwise deserve to get. In the case of the prisoner, he or she suffers two forms or degrees of cognitive injustice. The first is related to the prejudice or assumption that what a prisoner says is not true or is misleading within the context of trials and investigation. Their testimony is not to be trusted. The second is the assumption that the prisoner's testimony is as credible as second-hand testimony. There may be a third kind, related to the genre or form of testimony itself, whether it is a novel, a memoir etc., or what Wertsch called 'instrumental memory'.[31]

My argument is that in a situation where injustice is to be repaired, a prisoner's knowledge needs to be acknowledged and given the status it deserves. From an epistemological angle, then, Mansour must be read along Butler, Coetzee and others in accounts of pain. This leads to implications on methodology, or ways in which prisoners' accounts are to be read and utilized, including in an academic setting such as this one.

Positioning becomes important. I see my role as that of solidarity, which prevents me from participating in perpetuating censorship through certain discursive academic practices, which obscure and often seek to replace those it should enable.[32] Therefore, my work here is conceived, in part, as a forum and an expression of moral solidarity. It is a form of alignment with victims against what Fricker calls 'normative abandonment'.[33] In the Tunisian case, and more widely, these people liberated my voice, and I feel the need to express my gratitude. That gratitude should not, of course, preclude critique and rigour; but neither should it fall into the traps of privilege and narcissism of the kind we see all too often in academic practice, in this case, in my own Western academic situation. For, if anything, the lesson of these prison narratives and testimonies should be humility, including in the area of knowledge. In the end, every little scratch on a prison cell wall was yet one more statement in a counter-narrative, and thereby, one more nail in the coffin of repression. In addition, these people have reflected on, and produced knowledge about, not only their societies, but also the incarceration experience, writing, and humanity. Epistemic justice requires a recognition of the credibility of this knowledge.

Collaborative Testimony: The Uses and the Limitations

Members of the Leftist Perspectives movement in particular offer the most complete case study of collaborative writing and collective remembering, ever since Gilbert Naccache's pioneering account in *Cristal* (1982) which advocates and practises it.[34] In fact, collaborative writing is so prevalent among the members of the group that it is almost a rite of passage in their testimonies.[35] Why do they insist on this collective writing and remembering? How much of it has to do with their specific, and perhaps unique, prison experience, of group incarceration, learning and solidarity?[36] Zemzmi's testimony, corroborated by many fellow prisoners, demonstrates how writing and reading were the hallmark of the political incarceration experience in Tunisia at the time. Zemzmi called this a 'cultural revolution',[37] while Naccache credits it with turning him into a writer. (The prison liberated me completely, says Ben Mhenni; Naccahe considered prison a school; Fliss credits prison with becoming human in the wider sense; Belhaj Yahia speaks of it almost as an aesthetic experience...). One significant moment for them was the autumn of 1974 in Borj Roumi prison. Members of the group produced cartoons and newsletters, *Romien malgré lui* by Rachid Belallouna and *Canards déchainés* by Nouri Bouzid. In fact,

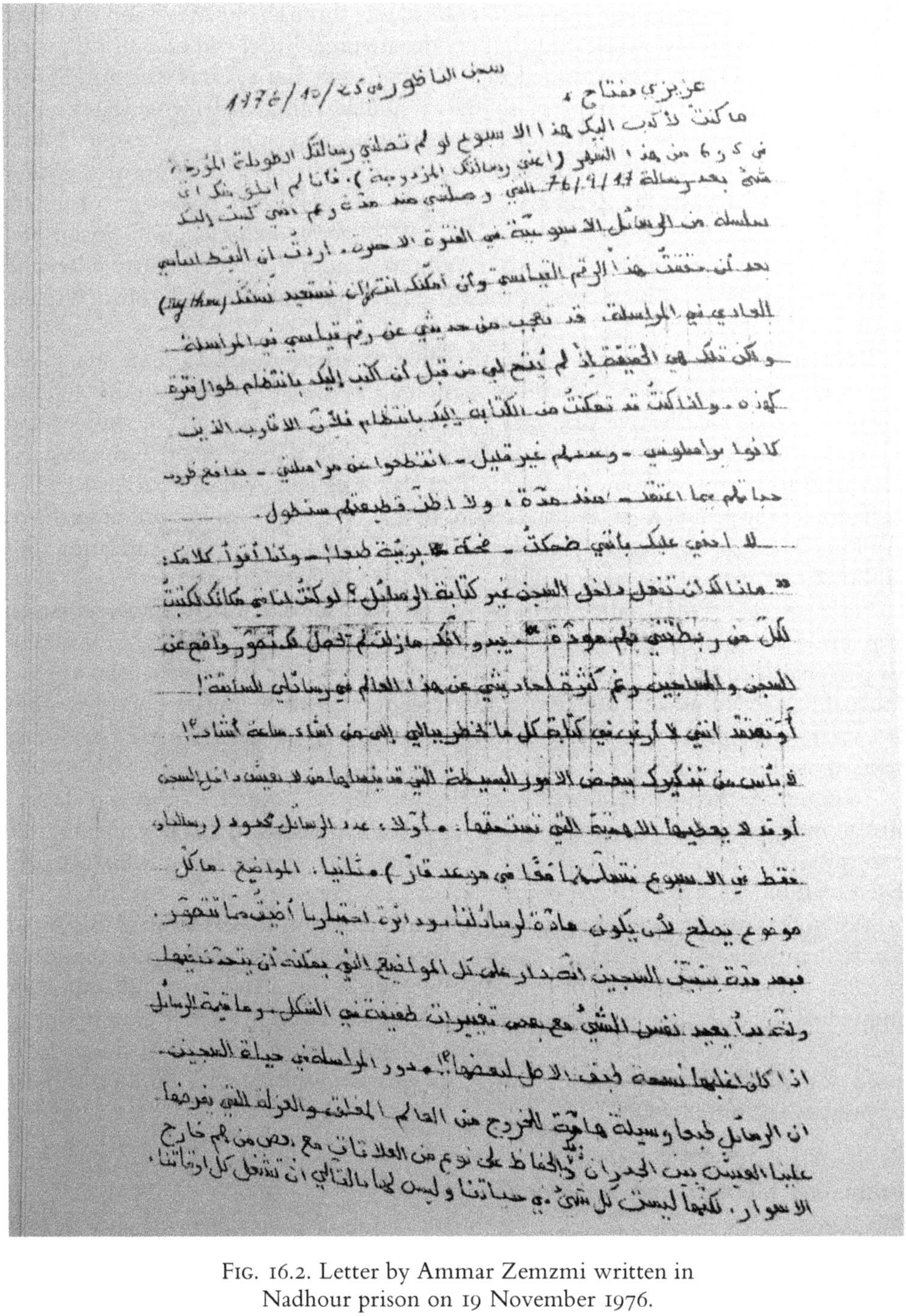

سجن الناظور في 1976/10/25

عزيزي مفتاح ،

ما كنت لأكتب اليك هذا الاسبوع لو لم تصلني رسالتك الطويلة المؤرخة
في 5 و 6 من هذا الشهر (أعني رسالتك المزدوجة). فأنا لم أتلق منك أي
شيء بعد رسالة 76/9/17 التي وصلتني منذ مدة رغم أني كتبت اليك
سلسلة من الرسائل الاسبوعية في الفترة الاخيرة. أردت أن التزم
بعد أن حققت هذا الرقم القياسي وأن أمكنك انتظاري نستعيد نسقنا (say three)
العادي في المراسلة. قد تعجب من حديثي عن رقم قياسي في المراسلة
ولكن تلك هي الحقيقة إذ لم يتح لي من قبل أن أكتب اليك بانتظام طوال فترة
كهذه. ولئن كنت قد تمكنت من الكتابة اليك بانتظام فلأن الاقارب الذين
كانوا يراسلونني - وعددهم غير قليل - انقطعوا عن مراسلتي - بدافع فتور
حماسهم بما اعتقد - منذ مدة، ولا أظن قطيعتهم ستطول.

لا أخفي عليك بأني ضحكت - ضحكة بريئة طبعا! - وأنا أقرأ كلامك:
"ماذا عساك تفعل داخل السجن غير كتابة الرسائل؟ لو كنت مكانك لكتبت
لكل من ربطتني بهم مودة" [illegible] وأنك ما زلت تحمل تصورا واضحا عن
السجن والمساجين رغم كثرة أحاديثي عن هذا العالم في رسائلي السابقة!
أو تعتقد أنني لا أرغب في كتابة كل ما يخطر ببالي الى من أشاء ساعة أشاء؟!
فلا بأس من تذكيرك ببعض الامور البسيطة التي قد ينساها من لا يعيش داخل السجن
أو قد لا يعطيها الاهمية التي تستحقها. أولا: عدد الرسائل محدود (رسالتان
فقط في الاسبوع نسلمهما معا في موعد قار). ثانيا: المواضيع. ما كل
موضوع يصلح لأن يكون مادة لرسائلنا بود أنه اختياريا أضيف ما تتصور.
فبعد مدة يشعر السجين بالاندثار على كل المواضيع التي يمكنه أن يتحدث فيها
ولذا يبدأ يعيد نفس الشيء مع بعض تغييرات طفيفة في الشكل. وما قيمة الرسائل
إذا كان أغلبها نسخة طبق الاصل لبعضها؟! دور المراسلة في حياة السجين.
ان الرسائل طبعا وسيلة هامة للخروج من العالم المغلق والعزلة التي يفرضها
علينا العيش بين الجدران والحفاظ على نوع من العلاقات مع بعض من هم خارج
الاسوار. لكنها ليست كل شيء في حياتنا وليس لها بالتالي أن تشغل كل أوقاتنا.

FIG. 16.2. Letter by Ammar Zemzmi written in Nadhour prison on 19 November 1976.

Zemzmi confirms that their entry into politics was through culture,[38] and therefore prison cells were transformed into a hub of debate on cultural and theoretical issues. The atmosphere in prison was such that leaving it was not easy, as Zemzmi agrees with Naccache. A community of solidarity and learning had formed and made the place familiar. The list of books Zemzmi read in prison is impressive.[39] And it is perhaps significant that most of the reading was literary in nature since other books were restricted, as Zemzmi explains in his published collection of letters from Bourj Erroumi prison.[40] In a word, the collective experience in prison was such that testimonies and recollections sought to honour it and perpetuate it beyond incarceration, even as members of the group set out on their individual writing paths.

Beyond the individual and group therapeutic functions of writing, the stated aims in these texts are often to achieve accuracy and impact. There is in this activity a care to build a collective case and a unified record by multiplying sources and making a conscious crosschecking of facts. This is, in a sense, a legalistic activity, aimed at the corroboration of accounts, fact checking and evidence gathering. The cohesion of the group, or at least the record of that cohesion, was important to them. And they set about doing that, motivated by the breakup of their organization, the authoritarian turn of the state and the rise of Islamist opposition.

For Zemzmi (b. 1951), jailed from November 1973 to March 1979, documentation was made more urgent by the deaths of several first-hand witnesses. In addition to personal memories of events, he relied on a number of sources: entries from a journal he kept in prison from 1969 to 1971; letters sent to relatives; poetry written between 1969 and 1971; official correspondence with authorities; and occasional texts written after leaving prison.[41]

To complete the picture, he calls on others to 'check, correct, enrich and clarify' his account as they see necessary.[42] There is an obvious archival value to this enterprise. There is even a legal force to it, although I am not aware it has actually been used in legal cases. It also comes closest to expressing collective pain.

Yet, collective writing leaves part of the incarceration experience unaccounted for. Belhaj Yahia speaks of prison, particularly solitary confinement, as an experience situated beyond the capacity of collective writing or even solidarity: 'Prison is an individual solitary experience impossible to write collectively no matter how strong the unity and the solidarity of the group. For pain, loneliness, sexual misery, the need of the body for warmth, are things for which you can accept no substitutions or postponing inside yourself.'[43]

Embodied Memory and Unattainable Justice

In 'Forgetting the Embodied Past: Body Memory in Transitional Justice', Teresa Koloma Beck recognizes that torture, being violence directed to the body (as well as the psyche), defies representation in the sense that representational memory remembers the past from the starting point of the present. Body memory is about the effect of the past on the body itself, and how it is in the present — e.g., bodily habits acquired during a period of repressive rule, prison, etc., such as sleeping with a door open at all times. It enacts the past in the present.[44] Invariably, it is in talking about torture that language and narrative seem to lose their capacity, not only to articulate pain but also to convey an argument for justice. Elaine Scarry has argued the case: 'Physical pain does not only resist language but actively destroys it, bringing about an immediate reversion to a state anterior to language, to the sounds and cries a human being makes before language is learned.'[45] In literature, as in visual arts, the distance between the experience of torture and representation is impossible to bridge.[46] J. M. Coetzee, Solomon-Godeau and others, mentioned earlier, have written persuasively about this. Yet, it is this untranslatability which should compel us to speak about torture. And, indeed, it is precisely what incarceration writing by Perspectivist Mohamed Salah Fliss and many others does. They may describe their ordeals in excruciating detail, or simply gloss over their pain, or even shrug it off. Yet, what they insist on naming is their torturers. They resist grief and show how they managed to overcome, but they do not resist the urgency to accuse: Fliss names those who tortured him in one session which left him unable to stand on his feet for 92 days: Abdessalem Darghouth, known as Skaba; Mohamed al-Bohli; Abdelmajid Khemiri, and Hassen Abid, their boss.[47] Yet, Fliss, on recall, and at a distance from his ordeal, still thought in terms of law: 'They were a bunch of people who transgressed law, morality and values in the name of an institution which was theoretically accountable to law, but was in reality governed by the deep fear which haunted them.'[48]

Fliss's prison mate, Sadok Ben Mhenni, comments on how his tortured body was transformed in fact into the site of empathy for his torturers: 'I resisted and everything in me supported me, even my tortured body [...] I loved my body. I loved myself. I loved myself to the point that I did not hate my torturers. I did not resent them. I pitied them and felt angry on their behalf against their masters.'[49] Torture becomes an inaugural moment of body awareness. 'I had no relationship with my body before, neither love nor hate.'[50] Because of this, torture becomes the script in which body memory is built. It must be noted that these and other torturers were never held to account. They have not asked for forgiveness, either. But there is a sense in which their victims felt they had to forgive them. The wider case against the authoritarian system depended on it. Equally, so did the reconstruction of the self. Belhaj Yahia explains: 'If one overcame the experience of isolation and uncommunicable personal pain, they would find in themselves a type of internal solidity and reconstitution of the self because it breaks inside him or them the walls of fear, not fear of the other, authority, guards or watchmen, but fear of oneself.'[51]

Proleptic Forgiveness

There is a particular kind of forgiveness in Ben Mhenni, which is also developed in Naccache's reflective meditations, a liberating gesture, regardless of the processes of transitional justice, or indeed of public justice. Naccache's novel, *Cristal*, partly written in prison, was conceived as a 'work of reflection, understanding, sympathy towards others despite everything, of reconstitution of the self.'[52] Once the reconstitution is done, 'one is no longer the same, one is almost ready to leave [prison], reunite with the others, without hate, without grudges and even without blame.'[53]

In a sense, he forgives ahead, and regardless of transitional justice or even justice *tout court*. This seems to me an important intervention in the writing of justice under unjust, authoritarian, rule.[54] What Naccache recognizes as a liberating moment, which authorizes the reconstitution of the self, is equally liberating of the forgiven, as Hannah Arendt points out. She says: 'Forgiving, in other words, is the only reaction which does not merely re-act but acts anew and unexpectedly, unconditioned by the act which provoked it and therefore freeing from its consequences both the one who forgives and the one who is forgiven.'[55] Arendt spoke of the liberating nature of forgiveness and of its alignment with action rather than reaction.

Is this the sense in which Miranda Fricker uses the term 'proleptic forgiving'?[56] For her, 'communicative blame' is key to forgiveness, whether the blame is acknowledged, shared or not. 'Gifted forgiveness' is not dependent on remorse or shared blame-feeling. Fricker calls this 'Proleptic Gifted Forgiveness', which works on the premise that the wrongdoer will eventually experience remorse or shared moral understanding with the victim/the forgiver.[57]

In light of the foregoing discussion of writing under the condition of an absence of justice or the prospect of justice, I am tempted by some questions: What happens, then, when we put *poiesis* and *prolepsis* together in the context of justice? The first is a work of construction, of reinvention and representation of the world — in this case, injustice — whereas the second works with anticipation and prefiguration of the future. In other words, what happens when we put Naccache in dialogue with Fricker? What does the moment of writing has to do with this? How does it affect proleptic forgiveness? Does it depend on, or is it affected by, whether or not there is a hope of justice at the time of writing?[58] The two moments are, I would argue, radically different, and so are the poetics and the politics of writing associated with them. The poet Ammar Mansour, as I explain above, is quite clear that only one of these moments is 'authentic' or faithful to the experience.

After 2011 in Tunisia, testimonial writing has become — like everything else, I must stress — a form of positioning and part of discourses competing for legitimacy, part of the jostling for a place in a history which has become available for construction. In addition, we are witnessing the beginnings of what we might describe as memory as a market or memory as a label. The current period is in many ways a struggle for narrative, for reclaiming a history of resistance. For Islamists, the political clout and gains have not been matched by cultural and literary presence. They are conscious of the risk that their public perception would remain frozen in the image of the Islamist as politician, ideologue, traditionalist and anti-humanist, even violent militant. Therefore, writing could temper that image or change it. In other words, this is writing within a transitional justice process, authorized by it, or enabled by it.

One such project is the planned trilogy by the prominent Islamist former prisoner and leading figure in the Ennahda Party, Abdelhamid Jelassi, the first volume of which appeared in 2016, and which bears a strong affinity with these concerns. Nevertheless, there are also key differences between the two projects. Unlike all the other prisoners cited here, Jelassi was sentenced to life for political activity, spending sixteen years in prison before he was released in 2006. His story reached spectacular heights after 2011 when he became one of the most influential figures in the Ennahda Party. In *Hasad al-Ghiyab* [The Harvest of Absence], Jelassi places writing high in the roles it plays for prisoners of conscience in particular, despite restrictions on writing and self-censorship — writing fills an 'existential need'[59] and allows a 'vicarious life'.[60] Like several other writers, he dwells on the practice of writing letters, hiding them, smuggling them out, the scarcity of pens.[61] Yet letters, sanitized as they are, do not reveal the prison experience.[62] In order to achieve this, the author 'played with time and space',[63] keeping the overall chronological line but opening up windows on the outside world. The overall structure of Jelassi's book consists of a long introduction about arrest and interrogation; information about practices in jail; a review of what was going on in Tunisia and in the world (usually in the form of dates and events); surviving letters from relatives; petitions and letters sent by his wife; and reflections on readings. In addition, there are testimonies written by his wife, brothers and sisters specifically solicited by him in order to complete the picture. 'This book is then a type of collective creation' from different perspectives,[64] but not by fellow prisoners as is the case with Perspectivists. In sum, 'The book is a museum, a family book, the book of a generation, but one which aspires to be a page from the story of a community.'[65] Jelassi's text is generically difficult to classify, just like the books published by Zemzmi, Fliss and others. In his own words: 'It is a text which intrudes on literature, history, politics and thought [...] and does so unashamedly. It is "my museum".'[66]

Jelassi is conscious of the wider implications of this type of writing: it serves a wider effort, namely, to 'free the past from unitary reading, and save it from forgetting'. The Islamists' reticence to write is due, according to Jelassi, to a 'modesty which prevents religious people from talking about themselves'.[67] He advocates more writing by his fellow Islamists in order to 'clarify the image' of what Islamists are, at the 'human level'.[68] Writing five years after the revolution, Jelassi urges others to publish their sides of the story in 'order to *contribute to the process of transitional justice*' which he considers necessary for the country.[69] Reconciliation is needed, he argues. 'But confession, knowing the truth, admitting wrongdoing, asking for forgiveness are more necessary, so that treatment can be made on solid foundations which would prevent the return of the past and its atrocities.'[70] The specific reference to transitional justice is indicative of a new element in Tunisian, and indeed Arab, prison literature. Jelassi's work is a future-oriented account, by someone who is clearly looking ahead, who feels suffering has been rewarded and resistance vindicated ('Those who will look in this book for mourning [...] and resorting to the past as refuge [...] will be disappointed.')[71] There has been a shift in the balance of power, which needs to be seized since 'history is not written by justice or by morality but by the balance of power.'[72] These reflections are, in a sense, born of a post-revolutionary situation in which it has become possible to think of a future written from the point of view of former victims and survivors but also to take part in partisan politics of memory.

Conclusion

I conclude by reflecting on the oscillation of the testimonies discussed so far between the urgency to testify, in the historical as well as legal senses, and the allure of style, or between law and literature, in other words by linking aesthetic justice and epistemic justice. Survivors have taken different approaches to the problem of representation. Ben Mhenni debates his choices thus: 'I hesitated between several entry points: to tell the story starting from the end, starting from the present days and moving backwards until birth; or start with the moment of arrest and move back and forth as my pen pleases.'[73] He also mentions pages he wrote and then destroyed for fear of causing offence, hurt or division (among his comrades in prison).[74] Zemzmi expresses this anxiety: he is keen to steer clear of 'the rules of autobiography' in order to avoid 'creating heroism' and appearing as a writer, preferring instead 'expression to impression.'[75] His desire to document and reject the 'censorship of memory' led him to 'sacrifice literary craft', he explains. Samir Sassi describes known torture techniques he was subjected to — beating (*falqa*); hanging (*ta'liqa*); water boarding; whipping — as follows:

> When I woke up from the sting of a rod, *like one of the pillars of 'Ad*, I found myself hanging from one leg like a sheep hang up for skinning. [...] I was brought back down on the ground, a whip *caressed* my body turning it into a *canvas on which the torturer painted his creation* up and down; the torturers legs would kick me to *the rhythm of insults played by tongues incapable of finding another tune.*[76]

It could be argued that through metaphor and simile, oblique expression, ironic tone and researched register, the force of Sassi's account is watered down rather than sharpened. But it seems to me that in writing 'political' pain and prison trauma, there must be some giving in to metaphor, to the allure of style and the temptation to exceed the testimony. Or, put differently, writing is perhaps guided by the desire and will to make one *last*, and hopefully *lasting*, stand against the law. It is also an attempt to say that truth is more than 'factual' accounts of it. Otherwise, why write a memoir when you can get a good lawyer?[77] We might call this the quest for aesthetic justice, to link up with epistemic justice, in the sense that writers work on correcting and, in many cases, founding knowledge about their experiences and about themselves (including putting forward their side of the story in public) in order to counter the hegemonic knowledge held against them and what they stand for by the state. (And, lest we forget, the very concepts of hegemony and counterhegemony were developed under conditions of incarceration and duress in *The Prison Notebooks* by Antonio Gramsci.)

At the same time, Tunisian prison writing has not taken place in a cultural and literary vacuum. In fact, it joins a long tradition in the region. For so much of 'political' pain and prison trauma has been expressed in poetry and song that narrative testimonies feel compelled to lean on this long tradition. In some cases, this was to be the trigger which inspired them into politics, as well as into writing, in the first place. Fliss is not an exception when he evokes numerous precedents that inspired him to resist and to write in equal measure. Among these, he cites a colloquial poem by the Egyptian Mahmud Shadhili:

> If they strung a rope
> Or even a million ropes
> Around my neck,
> I will untie them.
> And from the ropes,
> I will braid a pen
> Which writes letters
> Longing for the moment of salvation.[78]

In prison, Fliss and his fellow prisoners would have heard, rather than read, the poem because it was a song by Shaykh Imam and because they did not always have access to writing. Indeed, we are reminded that writing, for all it enables, may silence the sounds of incarceration and fail to translate them. In this, it seems that the prison experience, once again, exceeds the sum of its expressions. These forms of aesthetic justice may not have had the legal force to bring about justice, but they have surely outlasted, and exceeded, law itself. Herein, perhaps, lies the gist and paradox of prison writing: it falls short of the experience and exceeds the normativity of law.

This paper is dedicated to the memory of Chokri Belaid, Tunisian lawyer, activist and poet who was assassinated by fundamentalists on 6 February 2013.

Notes to Chapter 16

1. Abdelwahab Meddeb, 'La "révolution du jasmin", signe de la métamorphose de l'histoire', *Le Monde*, 17 January 2011, available at <https://www.lemonde.fr/idees/article/2011/01/17/la-revolution-du-jasmin-signe-de-la-metamorphose-de-l-histoire_1466684_3232.html> [accessed 2 May 2020]. All translations from Arabic and French are mine, unless indicated otherwise.
2. Gilbert Naccache, *Cristal* (Tunis: Mots Passants, 2011; 1st edn, Tunis, Salammbo, 1982), p. 340.
3. Chawki Tabib, *Avocats et politique en Tunisie, 1887–2011* (Tunis: Editions SPA, 2015), p. 19.
4. The term legitimacy dominated to the extent that we witnessed the emergence of a conflict of legitimacies: revolutionary legitimacy, historical legitimacy, constitutional legitimacy, people's legitimacy, etc.
5. The latter commission would go on to frame and nurse the birth of new lawmakers in the form of the National Constituent Assembly. Internationally, there was a lot of interest and involvement, not least in the area of transitional justice.
6. Unions have a lot to do with this, making contestation occur within norms and regulations set by the law. In the long run, trade unionism created what I call a ceiling of dissent which tempered — and 'legalized' — otherwise revolutionary demands and expectations. See Mohamed-Salah Omri, *Confluency (Tarafud) between Trade Unionism, Culture and Revolution in Tunisia* (Tunis: Tunisian General Union of Labour Information and Publishing Section, 2016).
7. Several accounts by Leftist militants, in particular, dwell on a meeting with Bourguiba in 1974 and his insistence that they ask for forgiveness. Naccache and his comrades in prison adamantly

refused to ask for pardon from 'The father of the nation', insisting that the state owed *them* an apology, not the other way around. See Gilbert Naccache, *Qu'as-tu fais de ta jeunesse? Itinéraire d'un opposant au régime de Bourguiba (1954–1979)*, suivi de: récits de prison (Tunis & Paris: Mots Passants, 2009), p. 181. In the end, 'there was neither pardon nor request for pardon', Ben Mhenni concludes. Sadok Ben Mhenni, *Sariq al-Tamatim* [The Tomato Thief] (Tunis: CERES, 2017), p. 130.

8. See Chawki Tabib, *Avocats et politique en Tunisie, 1887–2011*. See also *Juges et avocats entre dépendance et autonomie (1956–2010)*, ed. by Abdeljelil Temimi (Tunis: FTERSI, 2012).
9. Naccache, *Cristal*, p. 274. Also note the chapter on the trial by Zemzmi, 'Who is trying whom?', where he details the defence strategy and preparation by prisoners and the court proceedings. Ammar Zemzmi, *Azizi Miftah: ras'il min borj Erroumi* (Tunis: Nadhar, 2019), pp. 47–52. The lawyer Mohamed Cherfi goes into detail about these trials and elements of defence in his memoir, *Mon combat pour les lumières* (Paris: Zellig2, 2009; repub. Algiers: Elyzad, 2015), pp. 113–21.
10. On constitutionalisms, see Mohamed-Salah Omri, 'The Tunisian Constitution: The Process and the Outcomes', *Jadaliyya*, 12 February 2012, <https://www.jadaliyya.com/Details/30221/The-Tunisian-Constitution-The-Process-and-the-Outcome> [accessed 10 June 2020].
11. Yadh Ben Achour, *Tunisie: une révolution en pays d'Islam* (Tunis: Cérès, 2016), p. 181.
12. Ben Achour argues that while revolution is necessarily against the law, it is in the direction of rights. 'In other words, in transitional situations, the main objective is no longer an objective of morality, dissuasion or retribution but a political objective of pacification.' Ben Achour, *Tunisie*, p. 181. Hence, truth comes to be at the service of consolidating pacification and facilitating reconciliation. That is the context within which truth commissions emerged in Bolivia (1982), Argentina (1983), Chile (1990), and Rwanda (1999). See Ben Achour, *Tunisie*, p. 181.
13. Ben Achour, *Tunisie*, p. 182.
14. Tunisia was seen, almost immediately, as a test case for implementing transitional justice in the Arab world. The International Centre for Transitional Justice paid special attention to Tunisia immediately after the revolution. See a review of its international conference held in Tunis in April 2011, only three months after the revolution. 'Conference Wrap-up: Justice in Times of Transition', 15 April 2011, <http://tjtunis.blogspot.co.uk/> [accessed 10 June 2020].
15. The chaos came in the form of multiplicity and dysregulation of venues for the expression of grievances. Reparations and restitution for victims of the Ben Ali era in particular became a pressing issue, leading to the focus being limited to financial compensation and finding employment for those who were dismissed or excluded for political reasons. In addition, Tunisia did not have a unifying figure around whom the entire nation could unite and reconcile as was the case for South Africa and Nelson Mandela.
16. 'Loi organique n° 2013–53 du 24 décembre 2013, relative à l'instauration de la justice transitionnelle et à son organisation', *Journal Officiel de la République Tunisienne, 105: 3655–3665.* 31 décembre 2013. <http://www.legislation.tn/sites/default/files/journal-officiel/2013/2013F/Jo1052013.pdf> [accessed 10 June 2020].
17. 'By its very nature, the Tunisian Revolution could not go that far. It lacked, fortunately (*providentiellement*), the doctrinal density of ideological revolutions, the structuration of partisan revolutions and the violence of belligerent revolutions.' Ben Achour, *Tunisie*, p. 189.
18. Ben Achour, *Tunisie*, p. 192. The idea of compromise would not only set up a mechanism for solving knotty issues and smoothing out divergences; it would also help foster a favourable climate for reconciliation and inclusion. In the context of a revolution, these are not necessarily aligned with the will of large segments of the people who saw, and still see, justice in the shape of inclusion and accountability.
19. Ben Achour, *Tunisie*, p. 354.
20. Ben Achour, *Tunisie*, p. 355.
21. Aleida Assmann, 'Memory, Individual and Collective', in *The Oxford Handbook of Contextual Political Analysis*, ed. by Robert E. Goodin and Charles Tilly (Oxford: Oxford University Press, 2006), pp. 210–24. There are arguably three types of memory: *individual memory*, which is embodied and raises questions of reliability, narrativity or representation; *collective memory*, where

a shared identity is based on a shared past — some call it a-historical; and *instrumental memory*, a concept promoted by Wertsch, which asks questions such as how does a literary genre or even a language affects the way we remember. See James V. Wertsch, *Voices of Collective Remembering* (Cambridge: Cambridge University Press, 2002), p. 51 ff.

22. Study by Schuman and Scott (1989) in Wertsch, *Voices*, p. 38.
23. Naccache and Kamel Cherni devote some attention to the issue of age, albeit from different age perspectives, with predictably different accounts of the effects of incarceration. Cherni was 17 while Naccache was 29 when they were first arrested. On the ages of those put on trial in 1973, see the appendix to Karoud's book *Min durus al-shaykh Khalil bi masjid al-Qayrawan, ila al-yasar al-mawi* [From the Lessons of Shaykh Khalil at a Qayrawn Mosque to the Maoist Left] (Tunis: Dar Afaq, 2018).
24. Neji Kachnaoui, 'Inteview with Ammar Mansout', *Manarat*, supplement of *al-Sh'ab*, 17 April 2010.
25. The motivation was to keep the text as it was smuggled (two sets of poems, one smuggled out within Tunisia by Noureddine ben Khidhr and the other to Paris through Ahmed Othman).
26. He argues that prison experience may lead to good prison literature, or may not. 'Therefore we should not sanctify everything that is written in prison or about prison.' This is done out of respect and dignity: 'I care about that person I was, and if I embellished or betrayed him, this means I assaulted his dignity as a being who is related to me and is separate from me at the same time.' Mansour points to the dangers of falsifying the experience. 'I personally denounce and hate *post facto* consciousness, which is built on the logic of justification, such as inserting or imposing the consciousness of a sixty- or seventy-year-old man upon a youth in their twenties who is still finding their way.' Neji Kachnaoui, Inteview with Ammar Mansour.
27. Ammar Zemzmi, *Fi adab al-Sujun* [On Prison Literature] (Gabes: Hamma International Festival, 2018), p. 7.
28. Zemzmi, *Fi adab al-Sujun*, p. 10.
29. See, for example, J. M. Coetzee, *Waiting for the Barbarians* (1980) and Judith Butler's *Frames of War: When is Life Grievable?* (London: Verso, 2009).
30. Miranda Fricker, *Epistemic Injustice: Power and the Ethics of Knowing* (Oxford: Oxford University Press, 2007).
31. Wertsch, *Voices*.
32. 'The novelist must struggle to articulate torture without falsifying it, to understand and to depict oppression without unconsciously aiding the oppressor, to find texts transparent enough to carry meaning.' Susan van Zanten Gallagher and J. M. Coetzee, 'Torture and the Novel: J. M. Coetzee's *Waiting for the Barbarians*', *Contemporary Literature*, 29.2 (1988), 277–85 (p. 280). Coetzee argues: 'If the ethics and politics of representation turn on the responsibility of the image maker to resist the lure of spectacle as well as that of aestheticism, this requires some form of reckoning with the complex attributes of the spectatorial gaze, its elements of eroticism, mastery, projection, and fantasy.' Abigail-Soloman Godeau, 'Torture and Representation: the Art of Détournement', in *Speaking about Torture*, ed. by Julia Carlson and Elisabeth Weber (New York: Fordham University Press, 2012), pp. 115–28 (p. 123).
33. Miranda Fricker, 'Forgiveness: An Ordered Pluralism', *CUNY Academic Works* (2018), <https://academicworks.cuny.edu/gc_pubs/564>, p. 16.
34. The Groupe d'études et d'action socialiste en Tunisie (GEAST) was a Leftist organization that was active from 1963 to the end of the 1970s; it was better known by the name of its journal, *Perspectives*.
35. Gilbert Naccache, *Prison et liberté: parcours d'un opposant de gauche dans la Tunisie indépendante* (Tunis: Mots passants, 2014), p. 6.
36. Ben Mhenni, Mohamed Salah Fliss, and Mohamed Cherif Ferjani discuss submitting their work to one another for feedback, comment and critique. Zemzmi discusses doing justice to fellow prisoners.
37. Ammar Zemzmi, *Dhakirah ta'ba al-musadarah* [A Memory which Refuses Confiscation] (Sfax: Matba'at Sujik, 2013), p. 7.
38. Zemzmi, *Dhakira ta'ba al-nisyan*, p. 276.

39. Zemzmi, *Dhakira ta'ba al-nisyan*, pp. 298–300.
40. Ammar Zemzmi, *Azizi Miftah: ras'il min borj Erroumi* (Tunis: Nadhar, 2019), p. 55.
41. Ammar Zemzmi, *Dhakirah ta'ba al-musadarah*, p. 13.
42. See Ammar Zamzmi, 'hal ataka hadith al-ta^c^widhat?' [Did you hear about compensation?], *al-Hayat al-Thaqafiyya*, no. 225, January 2012, pp. 78–82.
43. Fethi Belhaj Yahia, *Al Habs kadhab wa al-hay yrawwih: awraq min malaf la-yasar al-tunisi* [Prisons Lie, and Survivors Will Return Home: Leaves from the File of the Left during Bourguiba's Reign] (Tunis: Klaimat 'abirah, 2009), p. 84. The same applies, even more so, to the experience of torture, as I explain in a separate essay: Mohamed-Salah Omri, 'New Humanism in Times of Torture', in *University and Society within the Context of Arab Revolutions and New Humanism*, ed. by Mohsen ElKhouni, Moulid Guessoumi and Mohamed-Salah Omri (Tunis: Rosa Luxemburg Foundation, 2016), pp. 83–98.
44. See Teresa Koloma Beck, 'Forgetting the Embodied Past: Body Memory in Transitional Justice', in *Transitional Justice Theories*, ed. by Susanne Buckley-Zistel, Teresa Koloma Beck, Christian Braun and Friederike Mieth (London: Routledge, 2014), pp. 184–201. Beck distinguishes between discursive transitional justice (telling the past, etc.) and experiential transitional justice. The latter is transformative in two respects: by implementing social justice one changes conditions and therefore changes body memory; likewise, local and cultural rituals (funerals, cleansing etc.) do the same. Both are future-oriented, not past-orientated.
45. Scarry in Solomon-Godeau, 'Torture and Representation', p. 118. On the perils, limits and history of representation of torture in visual arts, see Solomon-Godeau, 'Torture and Representation'.
46. Discussing the photographs of Abu Ghraib, Solomon-Godeau notes: 'When we confront the actual photographic representation of acts of torture that emerged from Abu Ghraib prison, there is obviously an unbridgeable gulf between our reception of these fifteen hundred-odd pictures as spectators and those acts as they were experienced by the victims, or for that matter, by the perpetrators.' Solomon-Godeau, 'Torture and Representation', p. 118.
47. Mohamed Salah Fliss, *Sajinun fi watani* (Tunis: Nuqush Arabiyya, 2016), p. 409. These same names and a full list were published in a court case within the context of transitional justice in Tunisia, held on 16 December 2019. It includes the extensive list of the accused with their positions during the trials of 1973, 1974 and 1975. Ref. post by Tah^a^r Chargouche (11 December 2019) [accessed 11 December 2019]. On Abid's death and secret burial on 12 June 2019, see Hassan Salman, 'Tunis: Wafat ashhar "jaladi" Ben Ali tuthir mawjat istinkar li'adam muhakamatihi', *al-Quds al-Arabi*, 19 June 2019. <https://www.alquds.co.uk/تونس-وفاة-أشهر-جلادي-بن-علي-تثير-موجة/> [accessed 10 June 2020].
48. Fliss, *Sajinun fi watani*, p. 410.
49. Ben Mhenni, *Sariq al-Tamatim*, p. 28.
50. Ben Mhenni, *Sariq al-Tamatim*, p. 28.
51. Belhaj Yahia, *Al Habs kadhab wa al-hay yrawwih*, p. 85.
52. Naccache, *Qu'as-tu fais de ta jeunesse?* p. 275.
53. Naccache, *Qu'as-tu fais de ta jeunesse?* p. 275.
54. Naccache's *Qu'as-tu fais de ta jeunesse?* details life in prison, including reflections on writing, torture, sports, group dynamics; a calm irony is characteristic of Naccache's self-deprecating humour and understatement, such as an entry on the various prisons he had been in referenced as 'My addresses from 1968 to 1979'. It also includes exact dates of incarceration and trials, meditations on understanding and generosity. *Le Ciel est par-dessus le toit: nouvelles, contes et poèmes de prison et d'ailleurs* (Paris: Editions du Cerf, 2005) gathers his creative writings in prison except for *Cristal*, which was published earlier. He plays down and rationalizes the effect of prison: 'It took barely 13.5% of my lifetime', he observes. *Le Ciel est par-dessus le toit*, p. 199.
55. Hannah Arendt, *The Human Condition* (New York: Double Day Anchor Books, 1958), p. 216. Other writers are perhaps more concerned with setting the record straight, telling their side of the story, staking claims to truth, contributing to an archive... They are no longer seeking shared understanding with their oppressors but a share in the discourse on memory and a say in it.
56. I am grateful to Miranda Fricker for sharing with me her essay in question, Miranda Fricker,

'Forgiveness: An Ordered Pluralism', *CUNY Academic Works* (2018), <https://academicworks.cuny.edu/gc_pubs/564>.

57. She says: 'Forgiveness is the exact opposite of vengeance, which acts in the form of re-acting against an original trespassing, whereby far from putting an end to the consequences of the first misdeed, everybody remains bound to the process, permitting the chain reaction contained in every action to take its unhindered course.' Hannah Arendt, *The Human Condition* (New York: Double Day Anchor Books, 1958), p. 216.
58. cf. Naccache and Bel Haj Yhiya, Cherni, writing before 2011, vs testimonies and reflections written after the revolution, e.g., Jelassi, Keroud, Fliss, Hazgui and several other testimonies and novels.
59. Abdelhamid Jelassi, *Hasad al-Ghiyab* [The Harvest of Absence], vol. 1: *The Small Hand Does Not Lie* (Tunis: maktabat Tunis, 2016), p. 26.
60. Jelassi, *Hasad al-Ghiyab*, p. 27.
61. See the section of Jelassi, *Hasad al-Gh'yab* entitled 'I fear for you from the mountain wolves', pp. 267–80.
62. Jelassi, *Hasad al-Ghuyab*, p. 47.
63. Jelassi, *Hasad al-Ghuyab*, p. 47.
64. Jelassi, *Hasad al-Ghuyab*, p. 49.
65. Jelassi, *Hasad al-Ghuyab*, p. 50.
66. Jelassi, *Hasad al-Ghuyab*, p. 51.
67. Jelassi, *Hasad al-Ghuyab*, p. 62.
68. Jelassi, *Hasad al-Ghuyab*, pp. 64–65.
69. Jelassi, *Hasad al-Ghuyab*, p. 67, my emphasis.
70. Jelassi, *Hasad al-Ghuyab*, p. 67.
71. Jelassi, *Hasad al-Ghuyab*, p. 61.
72. Jelassi, *Hasad al-Ghuyab*, p. 61.
73. Ben Mhenni, *Sariq al-Tamatim*, p. 15.
74. Ben Mhenni, *Sariq al-Tamatim*, p. 15.
75. Zemzmi, *Dhakira*, p. 12.
76. Samir Sassi, *Borj al-Rumi: abwab al mawt* [Borj al-Rumi: The Gates of Death] (Tunis: Karem Sherif, 2011), p. 35, my emphasis."
77. The poet Awlad Ahmad called what happened in Tunisia a 'revolution-poem', while Abdelwahab Meddeb wrote: 'Cet événement inouï nous fit voir, comme par surprise, la réalisation du désir de tout un peuple sur la scène de l'histoire, laquelle s'est avérée belle parce que juste, et juste parce que belle'. Meddeb, 'La "révolution du jasmin"', <https://www.lemonde.fr/idees/article/2011/01/17/la-revolution-du-jasmin-signe-de-la-metamorphose-de-l-histoire_1466684_3232.html>.
78. Fliss, *Sajinun fi watani*, p. 421. The poem was written by Mahmoud Shadhili and sung by the legendary Egyptian singer Shaikh Imam Issa.

CHAPTER 17

Tolerance in Arab Muslim Thought from the Arab Renaissance to the Present Day

Mohsen Elkhouni

Introduction

The question of tolerance lies at the heart of the topic of transitional justice in those Arab countries which experienced revolutions, commonly referred to as 'Arab Spring' countries. The adjective 'transitional', adjoined to the term 'justice', seems to deprive the latter of the universality and abstraction characterizing concepts, making it dependent on technical commissions and judicial experts.

And indeed the context — setting up bodies, establishing facts and offences (dictatorships, civil wars, etc.) committed during the preceding period, and enacting transitional justice laws — circumscribes reflection within the limits of the particular.[1] In becoming transitional, justice is no longer a matter for jurists or philosophers, and instead becomes an objective for managing a country in a state of crisis, thus more a matter for international experts and local politicians.

Like transitional justice, tolerance is always linked to a context of conflict, making it a highly problematic concept. Without reference to the socio-historical contexts giving rise to it, the concept remains void, as argued by many philosophers such as Locke, Voltaire, Rousseau, Mill, Walzer, and Forst. The latter, in reconstructing a theory of tolerance, is careful not to dissociate the concept from the circumstances in which it emerged.[2]

We are thus obliged to advance on uncertain ground, causing the concept of tolerance to be ill-defined. The difficulty only increases when we examine tolerance within a transition towards a state grounded in justice. But the issue at stake makes the effort worthwhile.

In a globalized world rocked by crises, it is both necessary and urgent to summon values of tolerance. Among the various facets of this crisis, one may cite the preoccupying rise in religious fanaticism, in terrorism, and in xenophobia. Locally (speaking as a Tunisian citizen), tolerance is integral to reconciliation, one of the 'non-judicial' mechanisms for administering transitional justice.

To set out a comprehensive and contextual approach to tolerance (in the past and in the present day), we must first clarify the historical framework specific to the Arab world. It is true that the process of transitional justice seems to be steered by political actors and international experts who take tolerance and reconciliation as necessary components thereof. However, reconciliation in fact emanates from mentalities, predispositions, and traditions which were forged over the course of historical experience as part of a cumulative and conflictual process.

Tolerance in the Context of the Arab Muslim Tradition

Most Arabic writings on the theme of tolerance date from the Arab Renaissance in the nineteenth century (*al Nahda*). They faced a lexical obstacle, needing to find an Arabic word adhering as closely as possible to the word of Latin origin. It was in the wake of the reception of modern liberal thought that the pioneers of the Arab Renaissance suggested the word *tasahol*, meaning facilitation, indulgence, permissiveness, laxity even. Subsequently the word *tasamoh* came to prevail, being semantically richer. The transitive verb (*samaha*), in addition to meaning facilitation, also covers ideas of generosity, kindness, care, incursion, gift, permission, and obedience.[3]

The search for an Arabic word that would correspond perfectly to the Latin term is not simply a matter of terminology. It is also a problem in the Arab world's translation and reception of Western culture. The issue of tolerance arose when the pioneers of the Arab Renaissance came into contact with the literature, philosophy, sciences, and arts of the West. This occurred against the backdrop of a complex crisis in the nineteenth-century Arab world, which, under Ottoman domination, was sapped by colossal problems and became easy prey for the European great colonial powers. It was governed by despotic regimes and ravaged by social crises aggravated by ignorance and religious fanaticism.

Amidst this crisis, two currents of thought emerged. Though opposing, they both sustained an identitarian conceptualization, and were both a reaction to the severe civilization clash between a declining Arab world and the West. On the one hand was a fairly conservative current, and on the other a more modernizing current.

For the first current, tolerance was a value specific to the West. Institutionalizing this 'pernicious' value would lead to the disappearance of the religious heritage specific to the original identity of Arab Muslim countries. According to this current, it was to be feared that in adopting a new non-religious identity (like the West), the Muslim *ummah* would thereby alienate its own religious identity.

The second current also considered tolerance to be a specifically Western creation, but held that defending and promoting it had favoured modernity. Consequently, it would be judicious to adapt it to the context of the Arab world, if the latter truly wished to start down the path towards its own modernization.

At this stage of the analysis, however, and prior to briefly presenting a few of the emblematic figures in each current, it is important to note the lack of rigour, common to both currents, in certain theses about tolerance which sought to ground them in ideological beliefs. These theoretical shortcomings may be found in two diametrically opposed positions.

Certain writers held that there was no Arabic equivalent for the term 'tolerance', and hence by extension for its conceptual content, in order to prove that the idea and its practice had no place in the Arab tradition. The notion was therefore a mere artefact, both recent and unwelcome.[4] Advocates of this position failed to take into account that any concept is linked to a historic context and thus necessarily relative.

Then there were those (such as Radhouan Essayed) who held that tolerance had a more subtle meaning in the Arab tradition than its modern Western equivalent. Since tolerance is necessarily linked to a particular context and experience, each period gives rise to a tolerance and a fanaticism which is its and its alone. Unbiased study of the use of the term tolerance in philosophical, legal, literary, mystical, and even theological writings from well before the Arab Renaissance shows it to embrace a wealth of meanings specific to each period. But this semantic wealth in no way makes up for the institutional deficit in the social existence of Arab Muslim peoples since the *Nahda* (Renaissance) period. Let us now briefly examine the two currents mentioned above.

The Conservative Current in the Arab Renaissance

This current is represented primarily by Sheikh Rifa'al Tahtawi, Sheikh Jamel Eddin El Afghani, and Sheikh Mohamed Abdu.

Sheikh Rafa'al Tahtawi (1801–1873)

In 1826, Tahtawi, an Egyptian imam, was sent by the pasha to Paris at the head of a group of students for a five-year period of study. While there, he wrote *The Gold of Paris: A Travel Account*,[5] going over the main points of the author's experience in France and offering a critical description of the French way of life. During his time in Paris he learnt French, enabling him to read many works in various disciplines (philosophy, logic, geography, mathematics, literature), and to familiarize himself with the thought of Voltaire, Rousseau, and Montesquieu.

Although Tahtawi followed the classical approach in developing his ideas, tackling all questions by referring to the Prophet and his companions, and though his vision of political power differed little from classic Islamic thought, he pursued an in-depth and innovative enquiry into certain questions.[6]

Believing the practice of *Ijtihad* [interpretation] could underpin tolerance, he concluded that Islamic and liberal thought were compatible. He thus described tolerance as the condition for progress and prosperity. But some passages in his book disclose the limits in his understanding of the notion. In the foreword, he presents his book as a guide for travellers and as a means to expand Arab readers' awareness. He adds: 'I do not approve anything which goes contrary to Mohammed's sharia'. And right from the first sentence of the introduction, he describes France as 'the country of unbelief and heathenism'. During his time in Paris he was custodian of the religious faith of a group of Egyptian students sent by Emir Mohamed Ali Pacha.

Sheikh Jamel Eddin El Afghani (1838–1897)

El Afghani belonged to the same fundamentalist current. He held tolerance to be extraneous to Islamic culture. By encouraging fundamental freedoms, any adoption of tolerance would undermine the unity of the Islamic community. He also suspected it of being used to cloak the hegemonic ambitions of the West. Conversely, he held the capacity for religious solidarity to be guaranteed by fanaticism. He wrote:

> Admittedly, Arabs are persuaded that the religious tie is stronger between Muslims, and they are convinced that their strength may only be attributed to the 'Assabia' (spirit of kinship) of belief; and Europeans have designs on Muslim territories and homelands so have started spreading their confused idea amongst the masters of these countries to embellish the breaking of this holy tie and so enfeeble the constitution of the Islamic community and divide it into sects and parties.[7]

El Afghani was in fact opposed to tolerance for pragmatic reasons. Religious fanaticism could mobilize the faithful, unite them under the banner of a single belief, and help them resist the hegemonic ambitions of the colonial powers. At the end of his life he sought a rapprochement between Sunnis and Shi'ites under a single Islamic belief. He combated the modernizing (or as contemporaries called it the naturalist) movement led by Sayed Ahmad Khan. The latter taught that the order of nature as deduced by reason was the basis of all interpretation of Islam and all appraisal of human actions, considering the Koran, not sharia, to be the essential component of Islam. In El Afghani's eyes, the writings of Sayed Ahmad Khan not only represented an immediate threat to Islam, but were in fact a British plot against the Muslim world.

Sheikh Jamel Eddin El Afghani crossed swords with Ernest Renan and his thesis that Islam was incompatible with science. While conceding that Islam had become decadent, he held that society could only advance within the framework of religious reform. He spent much of his life seeking a just Muslim king capable of restoring Islam, a quest in which he was repeatedly disappointed.

His refusal of tolerance towards laypeople and non-Muslims is grounded in strategic reasons, a conditional refusal also found among certain pioneers in the Arab Renaissance. El Afghani's position within the ideological landscape of his period raises once again — in the wake of Rousseau — the issue of the ambiguous relationship between fanaticism and patriotism. For El Afghani, the ideal was a just king who would recognize the sovereignty of sharia and thus be able to reform Islam.

Sheikh Mohamed Abdu (1849–1905)

Sheikh Mohamed Abdu was the author of *Islam and Christianity between Science and Civility*. He started from the same identity-centred vision as his master El Afghani, but pursued a different line of argument against Ernest Renan. He sought to show that Muslims were tolerant towards adepts of other religions. He illustrated this with examples taken from history, the appointment of non-Muslims to political and academic posts, and the peaceful coexistence during the Andalusian period.

Abdu used these examples to confute his contemporary, the lay intellectual Farah Antūn, and to contest any separation of politics from religion. He postulated that Islam is more tolerant than Christianity.

Like El Afghani, he started from the dual observation of the decadence of the Islamic world and the growing influence of the Western (British) way of life on Egyptian society. He recognized the existence of a traditional religious education guided by the El Azhar mosque and of a modern, European-style education introduced by the government and missionaries. Abdu's critique spares neither, castigating the traditionalism and stagnation of El Azhar education while denouncing the blind reproduction of government-provided education and the dangers of Muslims being Christianized by missionaries, thereby weakening their ties to religion. Abdu portrays Egyptian society as torn between a Westernized lifestyle receptive to all changes coming from Europe and a traditionalist lifestyle hostile to renewal. His purpose is to foster change within Islam.

Religious conservatives continue to make privileged use of Abdu. Their strategy consists in drawing on Islam itself to criticize Muslims (particularly those who govern in its name), holding them to blame for any exegetic or behavioural imperfection that might harm the Text. This is the approach adopted by the various factions of what is known as Political Islam. Their objectives consist in placing what they regard as the true Islam above all criticism and cleansing it of any bad actions committed in its name. But conservatives are themselves rent by infighting, with each sect seeking to impose its own interpretation as the only one to be faithful to the letter of Text.

The Modernizing Current in the Arab Renaissance

This current, once again sustaining a certain sense of identity, sowed the seeds of secular Arab nationalism. Most of its members came from Christian minorities. In addition to many figures from the Arab Renaissance, its exponents included eminent modern thinkers such as Ishaq and Antun.

Adīb Ishāq (1856–1886)

Ishāq came from a Christian Armenian family saved from the 1860 massacres by Emir Abd Elkader. While living in exile in Damas, he met El Afghani in Cairo and worked alongside him as his disciple. Adib Ishāq 'removed religion wholly from the picture: for him, this unity [of the ummah] was based solely on race and language'.[8]

Ishāq was a poet, and made a career for himself as a journalist and politician. He wrote a utopia called *The New Era* (al-ʿṣr al-jadīd) in which he sets out his political ideas inspired by the French Revolution and by theories of modern natural law. In his conclusion he notes: 'Such is the manifesto of the new era [...] inspired by Western wisdom; I have presented it to herald good, and to act as a model in our current efforts to reform laws and organize political affairs'.[9]

His championing of the French Revolution, praise for Emile Littré and Léon Gambetta, and friendship with Victor Hugo did not prevent him from pointing out the contradiction characterizing Western democracies' internal and especially external policies in the nineteenth century: 'Can you not see that the West, on the pretext of liberating you, has enslaved you? That the instruction it gives you is a way of demeaning you? Then finding you unworthy of being its equal, it allows itself to do what it forbids you.'[10] Thus Ishāq raised the question of tolerance correctly: he succeeded in criticizing colonial policy without falling back on religious fanaticism. Any examination of the idea of tolerance needs to include discussion of the principles of freedom and justice.

Ishāq was also one of the first to work on conceptualizing tolerance. Influenced by nineteenth-century evolutionism, he noted that Muslim societies were still in their infancy and needed an 'educator' to guide them towards political maturity. For him, tolerance in the religious sphere is grounded in the positive acceptance of difference and recognition of the other within the framework of mutual respect. Starting from a study of the history of various nations, Ishāq shows, in the wake of Rousseau, that fanaticism, though not a natural form of behaviour to man, may be found at all periods of history, and results from corruption and political oppression.

What is Ishāq's stance on identity? Despite belonging to a minority whose existence was threatened by increasing fanaticism, he did not call for the partition of the Arab nation. On the contrary, he defended the unity of a democratized Ottoman Empire, that is, pluralism in unity. Ishāq's approach demonstrates that solutions to the problems raised by fanaticism involve taking the situation of ethnic and religious minorities into account, in order to attain a pluralistic society.

Farah Antūn (1874–1922)

Farah Antūn was an Orthodox Greek. He defended tolerance in his polemic with Abdu, marking a turning point in the history of this topic. He approached it from the viewpoint of the relationship between Islam and Christianity, though without going along with Abdu's line of reasoning, which only compared the two reasons in order to better cherish Islam. Antūn examined tolerance in light of the foundations making it possible, writing:

> I hold that in Islam, civil power and religious power are linked by law, and this because the sovereign is both governor and Caliph. Consequently, tolerance becomes harder in Islam than in Christianity: the Christian religion has separated the two powers magnificently, and paved the way before the whole world to true civilization. [...] Another consideration: science and philosophy have hitherto managed to overcome Christian oppression, and have thus grown on European soil, engendering modern civism; but they have been unable to overcome Islamic oppression, offering real proof in return that Christianity is more tolerant with philosophy.[11]

The last sentence in this quotation alludes to the condemnation and humiliation of Ibn Rushd by his contemporary theologians in the twelfth century. Antūn was well-informed about scholarly culture in modern Europe. And taking up Ernest Renan's famous interpretation, he viewed Ibn Rushd as a radical rationalist and victim of the fanaticism spawned by collusion between princely power and the religious power of jurisconsults ('*Foukaha*', plural of '*Fakih*'). Antūn's interpretation still acts as a source of inspiration for certain writers supporting the transition to democracy and modernity within the Arab world.[12] Thus his formulation of the principle of secularity and the independence of science and philosophy no doubt fed into the following definition of tolerance:

> In its general definition, tolerance is accepting the existence of what is contrary to you. In its particular definition, it is permitting the existence of religious rites and beliefs differing from habitual rites and beliefs. This is a definition which does not correspond to present circumstances. Here is a definition which meets our requirements: religious tolerance is the consideration and respect we owe to doctrines produced by other humans even if they are contrary to ours.[13]

This analysis shows that the modernizing current managed to link tolerance to justice. The repression of religious minorities due to misrecognition of their fundamental rights was indeed a major obstacle to social justice. Calling for secularity was a matter of pointing the way towards lasting social justice. Thus the Arab world was materially unable to attain justice until it secularized the political and cultural spheres. Taking this path therefore came across as radical resistance to the rise in various expressions of fundamentalism and Salafism. Rawls argues (in *Political Liberalism*) that tolerance is a virtue, in that it makes it necessary to justify principles (including that of justice). In other words, it is a virtue of political philosophy in societies or political communities that are religiously and culturally pluralistic.

The Arab world has been torn between the conservative and the modernizing currents since the nineteenth century, and is still going through a transitional phase. It may even be safely said that the signs of regress have been more marked than those of progress, particularly over the past two decades, characterized by disputes between the fundamentalist-Salafist current and the secular-civic current. Recent tragic events have only awoken the destructive dimension of the more radical movements within Political Islam.[14]

The Transition to Literary Fiction

Thus far, I have privileged a historical-political approach to the treatment of the idea of tolerance. But I wish to signal that the questions bound up with this idea have led certain authors to use it as the basis for their fiction. Antūn himself wrote several novels deploring the fact that novels remained a mere entertainment in the Arab world, whereas in the West they had been taken up for activist purposes. In the introduction to his novel *Religion, Science, and Money*, he emphasizes the importance of novels, which may be compared to 'research in social philosophy' and which treat social relationships against the background of tolerance or intolerance. He writes for example:

> Certain novels are written for humour and entertainment, while others are for interested reasons and to disseminate principles and ideas. In the West, those who have written novels for interested reasons are among the most famous authors, such as Tolstoy, Zola, Kipling, and many others. None of these authors

> saw the writing of novels as decadent or scorn for narration, on the contrary, each considered the novel as a platform to publish his opinions and his ideas in a way that was easy for readers to apprehend. We in the east are deprived of this style of writing because of its unpopularity, for reasons which cannot be explored here. Consequently, the sole purpose of most novels published here is humour.[15]

This paragraph clearly announces a turning point in the history of literary narration by the pioneers of the Arab Renaissance, attributing social content to novels and a practical role to novelists. The task of novelists would thus be enhanced by the obligation to teach their readers tolerance via the dynamic established between the events, characters, and conversations between them. Finally the author (the novelist) brings various representations of tolerance to life via the characters and events he chooses. By orchestrating the events he invents and giving them a certain slant, he presents himself as a judge wielding influence over his readers, his narrative enabling them to follow situations of conflict and 'unbearable' scenarios in everyday life, thereby accustoming them to situations of tolerance.

Antūn's comments quoted in the previous paragraph also apply to literary currents which use fiction to create an environment conducive to tolerance.

Religious beliefs have always been a source of conflict and fanaticism, and are often treated in novels. In *Urachlim al-jadida*,[16] a dialogue between Elie (a young Christian man) and Esther (a young Jewish woman), the characters expound the following views:

- Religions are not mutually exclusive: 'you are a Jew, and I am a Christian, but you are not prevented by your religion from recognizing truth, no more than I am forbidden from admitting it by my religion'.[17]
- Respect is described as a higher degree of tolerance: 'I respect your doctrine and all doctrines in which the adept finds comfort and peace, truth and virtue, but I intended to teach you to respect the doctrines of others'.[18]
- Morality must be an ideal common to all religions: 'Let us set human religions to one side, in a sacred and respectful place, and meet in a new religion which accepts all virtuous religions and rejects none of them; and this religion is that of justice, mentioned earlier, of right, of love, and of pardon for all. We underlings and underdogs have a very urgent need to establish 'right, justice, and love' in the place of all. Place your hand in mine to live in peace on this earth and with this new religion which respects all other religions'.[19]

Realizing an ideal of tolerance such as this in the Arab world is out of reach, to varying degrees depending on the country. Critical literature, a feature stretching far back into the past of Arab Islamic civilization, is forever condemned to fight censorship — as exemplified by Naguib Mahfouz's *Children of Gebelawi* (1959) and Salman Rushdie's *The Satanic Verses* (1988). Mahfouz received threats after the publication of his novel and was attacked by a fanatic who had not read his novels, while Rushdie was censored and threatened with death. There are numerous other examples once one expands the field of enquiry to include poetry, theatre, cinema, printing, caricature, and so on.

In her novels, Ahlam Mustaghanmi draws her readers' attention to the disasters of the bloody 1990s in Algeria. In one of her books, she describes the scene after a massacre:

> What was this child doing sitting dumbstruck on the pavement? Everybody neglected him for they were busy burying the dead. Forty-five corpses. As there were more than the cemetery could take, people had had to use the neighbouring cemetery. After the 'Ibn Talha' massacre three cemeteries had been needed, spread over three villages, to bury over 300 corpses. Was death more tender this time? Had it allowed a few souls, by dint of cogitating, to escape its jaws?[20]

A bit further on she adds: 'The child was sitting as if still dumbstruck and stupefied. I was told they had found him under the narrow iron bed on which his father slept'.[21]

Mustaghanmi places the following words in the mouth of another character, a journalist who has fled the massacres in which his colleagues died: 'in the season when they were picking heads and collecting pens, we journalists failed to find borrowed names behind which to hide from the murderers. "Each chose a new name at random".'[22]

She has one of her characters enquire bitterly: 'we were once a people who mastered irony, so how have we lost the desire to laugh? And how did we get these closed faces, this hostile behaviour, these strange clothes which have never been ours?'[23]

Along with religion, politics is another fertile subject for literature. Literature acts as the guardian of a people's memory. Through the voice of one of her characters, an Algerian artist sitting in front of the River Seine, Mustaghanmi develops thoughts combining tolerance with matters of remembrance:

> I understand Khalid's inability in this novel to establish friendly relations with this fine view. I have no blame towards this river, nor am I in disagreement with it. The memory of the water through the ages, bearing the corpses of all races, is unable to distinguish identities, unable to distinguish the corpses of the French thrown into the river in 1789 in the name of the Revolution. The bodies of the Algerians thrown into it for the same reason two centuries later.[24]

Memory lies at the heart of the great transition which, since the Arab Renaissance, has been in continuous gestation, and under perpetual threat.

Arab Tolerance: From Tolerance as Acceptance to Tolerance as Respect

In light of the above, it may be seen that Arab Muslim tolerance is an embryonic concept, which has in practice scarcely moved beyond the principle of acceptance. To elucidate this, I shall now address the question of how to conceive of a form of tolerance that could be defended over time.

In Arab Muslim literature, the issue of tolerance has hitherto been circumscribed by two primitive ways of thinking about it: the conception based on permission (meaning the majority allows the minority to live according to their set of values, principles, and specific modes of thought) and the conception of coexistence (stipulating a context in which a preliminary agreement is reached between a dominant majority and a minority, with the goal of mutual recognition to ward off all sorts of potential ulterior conflict). Why are things thus?

It stems mainly from the fact that Arab thought functions primarily, and at times excessively, in terms of duality (alterity/identity), always invoking, whether implicitly or explicitly, the historical conflict which prevailed between Islam and Christianity, or that which took place during the colonial period (in which Arab countries were the victims). Consequently, a permanent internal conflict is at work within Arab thought: do we need a rationality that explores our identity, or else should we turn towards alterity (which has historically brought injustice and submission)? There is no consensus on these points. Thus while the thought of Albert Hourani purports to be conservative (it is important, to his mind, that Arab thought be grounded in identity in matters of religion, value, and culture), that of Fahmi Jadaan or Wajih Khoutharani is more liberal and universalist. The latter two call on Arab Muslim thought to reconcile itself with the universalism reaching us via the channel of world values. To their minds, this would make it possible to found a new Arab world defending tolerance, freedom, justice, liberalism, and cultural identity (both ancient and modern).

It is this latter cognitive approach which provides an underpinning for a tolerance based on respect, stipulating that individuals mutually tolerate and respect each other, with each being aware of his or her autonomy and equality vis-à-vis others before the law and justice.

This tolerance is that which is most compatible with modern democracies for it summons other values (as signalled by Habermas and Rawls), first among which are justice and freedom. In the context of Arab transitions, reaching the stage of this latter form of tolerance is nevertheless difficult in both the short and the medium term, though far more possible in the long term once democracy becomes a strongly anchored social conviction and no longer a mere formula of language deployed by politicians and interest groups.

Conclusion

As a conclusion we may say that the question of tolerance, far from being recent, has been present in the Arab Muslim world since the advent of Islam, either as a maxim of value expressing the capacity to accept other religions, or as practices approved by Muslims towards 'religious difference'. Arab thought about tolerance may nevertheless be considered as relatively dependent when identified primarily with the colonial era, and with the two currents of thought which emerged at that time: the conservative current (Tahtaoui, Al Afghani, and Abdu) holding that tolerance is a condition for accepting the other without resulting in a substantive change to Muslim society (it is thus a tolerance based on permission); and the modernizing current (Ishāq and Antūn) holding that tolerance is not just a value of permission but one of existence. I would suggest that the value of tolerance is nowadays unbalanced, given the virtual absence of democracy. The risk is that ideals, forged over the course of a long history of dictatorship (religious, political, etc.), be maintained in a state of suspended animation. Nevertheless, in Arab Spring countries, and specifically in Tunisia, things may follow a different course, especially if the democratic process holds on to the objectives it has set itself. It may thus be hoped that tolerance be founded on respect and — why not? — esteem for that which is different. Great effort will be required to reach this point. Critical reconciliation with our memory, and cultural heritage even, is a precondition for reconstructing and appropriating the value of tolerance, while ensuring that we are indeed fully situated within a modernity aware of its limits. This effort is required not only of those involved in science and culture but, above all, by political actors in a globalized world.

The value of tolerance founded on the principles of respect and esteem is no longer foreign to our shared history which has long embraced heterogeneous components. Philosophy and religious Sufism have concurred in their treatment of this value.

The philosophical position is represented primarily by Ibn Rushd, who lived in a pluralistic society and sought to reach a compromise between philosophy and sharia on the grounds that reality is one, even if the paths leading there are many (revelation and reason). When, for whatever reason, an individual no longer manages to apprehend or see reality, then we should tolerate them irrespective of their religion or belief.

Ibn Arabi, for his part, calls on a universal religion in which divine, 'historical' religions are merely specific examples. Finally, he perceives that we should not blindly examine the certitude and absolutism of religious texts, but always refer to reason via hermeneutics (through contextualizing texts properly so as to understand them) and good interpretation (Al Ijtihad).

Notes to Chapter 17

1. Sandrine Lefranc, 'La Justice transitionnelle n'est pas un concept', *Mouvements*, 1 (2008), 61–69. See too Kora Adrieu, *La Justice transitionnelle* (Paris: Gallimard, Collection Folio Essais, 2012).
2. Rainer Forst, *Toleration in Conflict: Past and Present* (Cambridge: Cambridge University Press, 2013).
3. Razwān al-Sayed, 'Al-tasāmoḥ fī ktābāt al-ʿrab al-moḥdaṯīn wālmoāṣrīn', *Revue al-Tasāmoḥ*, 1 (2003).
4. Samīr al-Khalil, 'Al-Tasāmoḥ fī al-loġhah al-arabīa', in *altasāmoḥ bayna sharq wa Gharb* (multi-authored), trans. by Ibrahim Alaris (Beirut: Dar Alsaqui, 1992).
5. Rafaa Tahtaoui, *Takhlis et ibriz Fi talkhis bariz* (Cairo: wizarat althakafa wal irched alkawmi, 1958).
6. Albert Hourani, *Al Fikr al arabi fi 'asr al-nahda (1798–1939)*, 3rd edn (Beirut: Dar al-Nahar Linnachr, 1977), p. 96 (1st edn 1968).
7. Jamel Eddin El Afghani and Mohamed Abdu, *Al-orwah el-wouthka* (Cairo: Fondation Hindawi, 2012), p. 76.
8. Jean Fontaine, *La Crise religieuse des écrivains syro-libanais chrétiens de 1825 à 1940* (Tunis: IBLA, 1996), p. 77.
9. Adīb Ishāq, *Al-kitabat al-siyasiyya wa-l-ijtimâ'iyya*, 2nd edn (Beirut: Dar Talia, 1982), p. 120.
10. Ishāq, *Al-kitabat*, p. 146.
11. Farah Antun, *Ibn Roshd wa Falsafatoho* (Beirut: Dar Talia, 1981), p. 126.

12. 'In this category may be placed Abd al- Rahmân Badawî, Mâdjid Fakhrî, Murâd Wahba, 'Atif al-'Irâqî, and Tayyib Tizinnî. All are supporters of an enlightened theology, and receptive to varying degrees to progress, democracy, modernity, etc.; each takes up and extend in their own manner the interpretation developed at the beginning of the century by 'Abduh, Sheikh Tâhir al-Djazâ'irî, and Mustafâ Qabbânî. Among the representatives of this current one may cite Mahmûd Qâsim, Hasan Hanafî, 'Âbid al-Djâbirî, and all those in the Maghreb and the Mashreq who dismiss as equally misguided the supporters of an Islam closed to progress and the adepts of a modernity relegating religious matters, if not to outmoded forms of thought, at least to the private sphere.' Mohamed-Chérif Ferjani, 'Le Devenir de l'œuvre d'Ibn Rosh dans le monde arabe', in *Averroès et l'averroïsme (XIIe-XVe siècle): un itinéraire historique du Haut Atlas à Paris et à Padoue*, ed. by André Bazzana, Nicole Bériou and Pierre Guichard (Lyon: Presses Universitaires de Lyon, 2005), pp. 239–48.
13. Amin Rayhānī, *Arrayhaniet* (Cairo: Fondation Hindawi, 2012), pp. 35–36.
14. The events of 11 September, then the worrying increase in religious fundamentalism (Al-Qaida, Nosra, Daesh, etc.).
15. Farah Antūn, *al-Dīn wa L-'ilm wa L-māl aw al-mudun al-thalāth* (Cairo: Fondation Hindawi, 2012), p. 7.
16. Farah Antūn, *Urachlim al-jadida aw Fath al-Árab bayt al-maqdas* (Cairo: Fondation Hindawi, 2012) (first published in 1904).
17. Antūn, *al-Dīn*, p. 19.
18. Antūn, *al-Dīn*, p.118.
19. Antūn, *al-Dīn*, p. 117.
20. Ahlem Mustaghanmi, *Ábiru Sarir*, 11th edn (Beirut: *Dar al-Adeb Li-Lnachr Wattawziá*, 2012), p. 31.
21. Mustaghanmi, *Ábiru Sarir*, p. 31.
22. Mustaghanmi, *Ábiru Sarir*, p. 28.
23. Mustaghanmi, *Ábiru Sarir*, p. 25.
24. Mustaghanmi, *Ábiru Sarir*, p. 78.

CHAPTER 18

❖

La Tolérance dans la pensée arabo-musulmane, de la Renaissance à nos jours

Mohsen Elkhouni

Introduction

La question de la tolérance se situe au cœur du thème de la justice transitionnelle dans les pays arabes qui ont vécu des révolutions et qui sont communément appelés pays du *printemps arabe.* L'adjectif *transitionnelle* accolé au terme de *justice* semble priver celle-ci du caractère universel et abstrait des concepts et la rend dépendante des commissions techniques et des experts de la justice.

En effet, le contexte, la création des instances, l'établissement des faits et des abus (dictature, guerre civile, etc.) de la période précédente et la promulgation des lois de la justice transitionnelle cantonnent la réflexion dans les limites du particulier.[1] La justice, en devenant transitionnelle, n'est plus du ressort des juristes ni des philosophes mais se présente plutôt comme un objectif de gestion d'un pays en état de crise et relève davantage des compétences des experts internationaux et des acteurs politiques locaux.

Comme la justice transitionnelle, la tolérance est toujours liée à un contexte conflictuel, ce qui rend le concept hautement problématique. En d'autres termes, le concept resterait vide, sans référence aux contextes socio-historiques qui l'ont vu naître, comme l'affirment maints philosophes à l'instar de Locke, Voltaire, Rousseau, Mill, Walzer et Forst. Ce dernier, dans sa reconstruction d'une théorie de la tolérance, ne dissocie pas le concept de ses contextes d'émergence.[2]

Nous sommes alors condamnés à évoluer sur un terrain instable qui rend flou le concept de tolérance. La difficulté croît lorsqu'il s'agit d'examiner la tolérance par rapport à la transition vers un Etat de justice. Mais l'enjeu vaut l'effort requis.

Dans un monde globalisé et secoué par des crises, la mobilisation des valeurs de la tolérance est à la fois nécessaire et urgente. Parmi les aspects de cette crise, nous pouvons citer la montée préoccupante du fanatisme religieux, du terrorisme et de la xénophobie. Au plan local (je parle ici en tant que citoyen tunisien), la tolérance fait partie intégrante de la réconciliation, l'un des mécanismes 'non judiciaires' pour administrer la justice transitionnelle.

Afin de formuler une approche compréhensive et contextuelle de la tolérance (hier et aujourd'hui), il est impératif de commencer par clarifier le cadre historique propre au monde arabe. Il est vrai que le processus de justice transitionnelle est, en apparence, dirigé par les acteurs politiques et par les experts internationaux qui font de la tolérance ou de la réconciliation une étape nécessaire de ce processus. Cependant, cette dernière valeur, émane, en vérité, de mentalités, de prédispositions et de traditions qui se sont forgées au cours d'expériences historiques et à travers un processus cumulatif et conflictuel.

La Tolérance dans le contexte de la tradition arabo-musulmane

La plupart des écrits arabes qui ont traité du thème de la tolérance remontent à la Renaissance arabe du 19ème siècle (*al Nahda*). Ils ont été confrontés à un écueil lexical, celui qui consiste à trouver un mot arabe qui puisse correspondre au mieux au terme d'origine latine. C'est à partir de la réception de la pensée libérale moderne que les pionniers de la Renaissance arabe ont proposé le mot *tasahol* qui veut dire facilitation, indulgence, permissivité et même laxisme. Par la suite, c'est l'usage du mot *tasamoh* qui a prévalu parce qu'il est sémantiquement plus riche. Le verbe transitif (*samaha*) possède, en effet, outre le sens de facilitation, ceux de générosité, de gentillesse, de suivi, d'incursion, de don, de permission et d'obéissance.[3]

La recherche d'un mot arabe qui puisse parfaitement correspondre au terme latin n'est pas une simple question de terminologie. C'est aussi un problème de traduction et de réception de la culture occidentale par le monde arabe. La problématique de la tolérance s'est imposée à l'occasion du contact des pionniers de la Renaissance arabe avec la littérature, la philosophie, les sciences et les arts de l'Occident et ce dans un contexte de crise complexe. Le monde arabe, au 19ème siècle, était miné par des problèmes colossaux: alors sous domination ottomane, il constituait une proie facile pour les grandes puissances coloniales européennes. Il était gouverné par des régimes despotiques et traversait des crises sociales aggravées par l'ignorance et le fanatisme religieux.

Dans ce contexte de crise, deux courants de pensée qui, quoique opposés, nourrissaient tous deux une même conception identitaire et réagissaient au grave choc civilisationnel d'un monde arabe en déclin face à l'Occident ont émergé: d'un côté, un courant plutôt conservateur et, de l'autre, un courant plus moderniste.

Pour le premier courant, la tolérance est une valeur propre à l'Occident. L'institutionnalisation de cette valeur 'pernicieuse' aurait comme conséquence la disparition de l'héritage religieux propre à l'identité d'origine des pays arabo-musulmans. D'après ce même courant, il était à craindre qu'en adoptant une nouvelle identité non religieuse (à l'instar de l'Occident), la 'Oumma' musulmane aliène aussi son identité religieuse propre.

Le second courant considère également que la tolérance est une création propre à l'Occident mais il juge que sa défense et sa promotion y ont favorisé la modernité. Par conséquent, il serait judicieux de l'adapter au contexte du monde arabe, si celui-ci veut réellement amorcer son propre processus de modernisation.

A ce stade de l'analyse, et avant de présenter, brièvement, quelques une des figures emblématiques des deux courants, il convient, cependant, de souligner le manque de rigueur scientifique de certaines thèses de la tolérance communes aux deux courants de pensée qui ont essayé de les soutenir à partir de convictions idéologiques. On retrouve cette insuffisance théorique dans deux prises de position diamétralement opposées.

Il y a, ceux qui croient que l'absence d'un équivalent arabe du terme de tolérance et, donc, de son contenu conceptuel, prouve l'absence de l'idée et de sa pratique dans notre tradition arabe. La notion ne serait, par conséquent, qu'un artefact, récent et malvenu.[4] Ceux qui défendent cette position ne tiennent pas compte du fait que toute conception est liée à un contexte historique et que, par conséquent, elle est nécessairement relative.

Il y a ensuite, ceux (dont Radhouan Essayed) qui affirment que, dans la tradition arabe, la tolérance a un sens plus subtil que son équivalent occidental moderne. Puisque la tolérance est toujours liée à une expérience et à un contexte particuliers, chaque époque vivrait une tolérance et un fanatisme qui n'appartiennent qu'à elle. Lorsque l'on étudie — sans préjugés — l'usage du terme de tolérance dans les écrits philosophiques, juridiques, littéraires, mystiques et, même, théologiques bien antérieurs à la Renaissance arabe, on retrouve une richesse sémantique spécifique, propre à chaque époque. Mais la richesse du champ lexical ne peut en aucun cas combler le déficit institutionnel existant dans la vie sociale des peuples arabo musulmans à partir de l'époque de Nahda (la Renaissance). Examinons maintenant sommairement les deux courants évoqués plus haut.

Le Courant conservateur de la Renaissance arabe

Ce courant est principalement représenté par Cheikh Rafa'al Tahtawi, Cheikh Jamel Eddin El Afghani et Cheikh Mohamed Abdu.

Cheikh Rafa'al Tahtawi (1801–1873)

Auteur d'un livre célèbre intitulé *L'Or de Paris: relation de voyage*,[5] (traduisant l'essentiel de l'expérience que l'auteur a vécue en France, c'est une description critique du mode de vie des Français), cet imam égyptien a été envoyé par le Pacha à Paris en 1826 à la tête d'un groupe d'étudiants pour un séjour d'étude de cinq ans. Durant cette période, l'auteur a appris la langue française, ce qui lui a permis de lire nombre d'ouvrages de diverses disciplines (philosophie, logique, géographie, mathématique et littérature), de côtoyer et de se familiariser avec les pensées de Voltaire, Rousseau et Montesquieu.

Bien que, pour le développement de ses idées, il suive la démarche classique qui consiste à approuver toute question en se référant au prophète et à ses compagnons, et en dépit du fait que sa vision du pouvoir politique, ne diffère guère de la pensée islamique classique, l'auteur a pu et a su, pour certaines questions, mener une importante approche réflexive, innovante et approfondie (Albert Hourani).[6]

Croyant trouver dans la pratique de l'*Ijtihad* (Interprétation) le fondement même de la tolérance, il conclut à la compatibilité et à l'harmonie entre pensées islamique et libérale. Il décrit ainsi la tolérance comme la condition du progrès et de la prospérité. Mais quelques passages du livre trahissent les limites de sa compréhension de la notion. Dans la préface, il présente son livre comme un guide pour les voyageurs et pour la conscience des lecteurs arabes. Il ajoute: 'Je n'approuve rien qui soit contraire à la charia de Mohamed'. Et dès la première phrase de l'introduction, il décrit la France comme 'le pays de l'incrédulité et de la mécréance'. Durant son séjour, il sera le gardien de la foi du groupe des étudiants égyptiens envoyés à Paris par l'émir Mohamed Ali Pacha.

Cheikh Jamel Eddin El Afghani (1838–1897)

Cet auteur appartient au même courant fondamentaliste et soutient que la tolérance est intruse dans la culture islamique. Son adoption viserait, en favorisant les libertés fondamentales, à saper l'unité de la communauté islamique. Il la soupçonnait, également de servir à dissimuler les ambitions hégémoniques de l'Occident. Inversement, c'est au fanatisme qu'il reconnaissait la capacité de garantir la solidarité religieuse. Il écrit:

> Certes, les Arabes sont persuadés que le lien religieux est le plus fort entre les musulmans, et ils sont convaincus que leur force ne peut être que grâce à la 'Assabia' (esprit de clan) de croyance, et les Européens ont des vues sur les territoires et les patries des musulmans, alors, ils se sont mis à diffuser leurs idées confuses parmi les maîtres de ces pays, à embellir la rupture avec ce lien sacré en vue d'affaiblir la constitution de la communauté islamique et de la diviser en sectes et partis.[7]

En fait, El Afghani s'est opposé à la tolérance pour une raison pragmatique. Le fanatisme religieux peut mobiliser les fidèles, les unir sous la bannière d'une seule croyance et les aider à résister aux ambitions hégémoniques des puissances coloniales. Il a essayé, à la fin de sa vie, de faire se rapprocher les sunnites et les chiites sous la bannière d'une seule croyance islamique. Il a lutté contre le mouvement moderniste conduit par Syed Ahmad Khan (appelé par ses contemporains naturaliste) prônant l'ordre de la nature, déduit de la raison, comme base de toute interprétation de l'Islam et de toute évaluation des actions humaines et qui considère que l'essentiel de l'Islam est le Coran et non la chariaa. A ses yeux, les écrits de Syed Ahmad Khan constituent autant un danger imminent pour l'Islam qu'une conspiration britannique contre le monde islamique.

Cheikh Jamel Eddin El Afghani a ferraillé avec Ernest Renan et sa thèse de l'incompatibilité entre l'Islam et la science. Tout en concédant la décadence de l'Islam, il considérait que le développement de la société ne pourrait se réaliser que dans le cadre d'une réforme de la religion. Il a passé un long moment de sa vie à la recherche d'un roi musulman juste et ayant la capacité de restaurer l'Islam, mais chaque fois, il fut déçu.

Son refus de la tolérance envers les laïcs et les non musulmans est fondé sur des raisons stratégiques. Il s'agit d'un refus conditionnel qu'on retrouve également chez certains des pionniers laïcs de la Renaissance arabe. La position d'El Afghani dans le paysage idéologique de son époque soulève de nouveau — à la suite de Rousseau

— le problème du rapport ambigu entre fanatisme et patriotisme. L'idéal pour El Afghani est, en effet, d'avoir un roi juste qui reconnaisse la souveraineté de la chariaa afin de pouvoir réformer l'Islam.

Cheikh Mohamed Abdu (1849–1905)

Cheikh Mohamed Abdu est l'auteur de *L'Islam et le Christianisme entre la science et le civisme.* Disciple d'El Afghani, il est parti, comme son maître, de la même vision identitaire, tout en polémiquant autrement avec Ernest Renan. Il a voulu montrer que les musulmans étaient tolérants envers les adeptes des autres religions. Il illustre son propos par des exemples pris dans l'Histoire, ainsi la nomination de non musulmans à des fonctions politiques et scientifiques et la coexistence pacifique avec eux à l'époque andalouse.

Abdu use de ces exemples pour confondre son contemporain, le laïc Farah Antūn, et pour contester toute séparation de la politique et de la religion. Son postulat est que l'Islam est plus tolérant que le Christianisme.

Comme El Afghani, il part du double constat de la décadence du monde islamique et de l'influence croissante du mode de vie occidental (britannique) dans la société égyptienne. Il a reconnu l'existence d'une éducation religieuse traditionnelle polarisée par la mosquée d'El Azhar et d'une éducation moderne à l'européenne instaurée par le gouvernement ou les missionnaires. La critique d'Abdu ne ménage aucune de ces deux orientations; il critique le traditionalisme et la stagnation de l'éducation d'El Azhar, aussi bien que la reproduction aveugle de l'éducation gouvernementale et le danger d'une christianisation des musulmans par les missionnaires et d'un affaiblissement de leur lien à la religion. Abdu est le témoin d'une société égyptienne écartelée entre un mode de vie occidentalisé et ouvert à tous les changements venus de l'Europe et un mode de vie traditionnaliste et hostile à la rénovation. L'objectif d'Abdu est de favoriser le changement au sein de l'Islam.

L'usage préférentiel de M. Abdu est aujourd'hui encore reconduit par les conservateurs religieux. Leur stratégie consiste à critiquer — au moyen de l'Islam même — les musulmans (notamment ceux qui gouvernent en son nom) et à leur imputer toute imperfection comportementale ou exégétique qui nuirait au Texte. Telle est la démarche des différentes fractions de ce qu'on appelle l'Islam politique. Leurs objectifs consistent à placer ce qu'elles croient être le véritable Islam au-dessus de toute critique et à le laver de toute mauvaise action commise en son nom. Les conservateurs sont, cependant, eux-mêmes déchirés par des guerres intestines et chaque secte tente d'ériger et d'imposer son interprétation comme étant la seule fidèle à la lettre du Texte.

Le Courant moderniste de la Renaissance arabe

Ce courant, également identitaire, a semé les germes du nationalisme arabe laïc. Ses membres appartenaient, pour la plupart, à des minorités chrétiennes. Il est aussi bien représenté par de nombreuses figures de la Renaissance que par d'éminents penseurs modernes comme A. Ishāq et F. Antūn.

Adīb Ishāq (1856–1886)

Issu d'une famille arménienne chrétienne sauvée des massacres de 1860 par l'Emir Abd Elkader pendant son exil à Damas, il a rencontré El Afghani au Caire et il est devenu son collaborateur et son disciple. Adib Ishāq a 'totalement [fait] abstraction de la religion: pour lui, cette unité (de la Oumma) n'est basée que sur la race et sur la langue'.[8]

Ishāq était poète. Il a fait une carrière de journaliste et de politicien. Il a écrit une utopie intitulée *L'Ere nouvelle* (al-ʿṣr al-ğdīd) dans laquelle il a développé des idées politiques inspirées par la Révolution Française et les théories du droit naturel moderne. Dans sa conclusion, il écrit: 'Tel est le manifeste de l'ère nouvelle [...] inspiré de l'émanation de la sagesse occidentale; nous l'avons exposé pour présager le bien, et afin qu'il nous serve de modèle dans notre effort actuel pour réformer les lois et organiser les affaires politiques.'[9]

Sa défense de la Révolution française, ses éloges d'Emile Littré et de Léon Gambetta, son amitié avec Victor Hugo ne l'ont pas empêché de pointer la contradiction qui caractérise la politique intérieure et surtout extérieure des démocraties occidentales du 19ème siècle: 'Ne vois-tu pas, que l'Occident t'a asservi sous prétexte de te libérer, et qu'il a fait de l'instruction qu'il te donne un moyen pour t'avilir? Puis ne te trouvant pas digne d'être son égal, il se permet ce qu'il t'interdit.'[10] Ishāq a, ainsi, su poser correctement le problème de la tolérance: il a su conduire une critique de la politique coloniale, sans se replier sur le fanatisme religieux. Tout examen de la notion de tolérance, en effet, doit inclure la discussion des principes de liberté et de justice.

Ishāq est aussi parmi les premiers à avoir entrepris une conceptualisation de la tolérance. Influencé par l'évolutionnisme du 19ème siècle, il fait le constat que les sociétés musulmanes sont encore dans l'enfance de l'humanité et qu'elles ont besoin d'un *éducateur* pour les guider vers la maturité politique. La tolérance est, selon lui, conçue dans la sphère religieuse et sur la base de l'acceptation positive de la différence et de la reconnaissance d'autrui dans le cadre d'un respect mutuel. Partant d'une étude de l'histoire des différentes nations, Ishāq montre, dans un esprit rousseauiste, que le fanatisme, sans être pour autant un comportement naturel de l'homme, est présent à toutes les époques de l'histoire et qu'il est le résultat de la corruption et de l'oppression politique.

En quoi consiste l'attitude identitaire d'Ishāq?

Bien qu'il ait appartenu à une minorité menacée dans son existence par la montée du fanatisme, il ne réclame pas la partition de la nation arabe. Bien au contraire, il défend l'unité d'un empire ottoman démocratisé, c'est-à-dire un pluralisme dans l'unité. L'approche d'Ishāq prouve que les solutions des problèmes posés par le fanatisme doivent tenir compte de la situation des minorités, ethniques ou religieuses, en vue de parvenir à une société pluraliste.

Farah Antūn (1874–1922)

Farah Antūn est un grec orthodoxe. Il a défendu la tolérance lors de sa polémique avec Abdu, qui a marqué un tournant dans l'histoire de cette question. Il l'a abordée sous l'angle des relations entre l'Islam et le Christianisme, sans toutefois tomber dans la logique d'Abdu qui ne compare les deux religions que pour mieux chérir l'Islam. Antūn étudie la tolérance à partir des fondements qui la rendent possible. Il écrit:

> Nous pensons que dans l'Islam, le pouvoir civil et le pouvoir religieux sont liés par la loi et ce, parce que le souverain est à la fois gouverneur et Calife. Par conséquent, la tolérance devient plus difficile dans l'Islam qu'elle ne l'est dans le Christianisme: la religion chrétienne a séparé les deux pouvoirs d'une manière magnifique et a ouvert devant le monde entier la voie de la vraie civilisation. [...] Autre considération: la science et la philosophie ont, jusqu'ici, réussi à vaincre l'oppression chrétienne et ont, donc, grandi sur le sol européen et engendré le civisme moderne, mais elles n'ont pas pu vaincre l'oppression islamique et c'est, en retour, une preuve réelle que le Christianisme était plus tolérant avec la philosophie.[11]

La dernière phrase de la citation fait allusion à la condamnation et à l'humiliation d'Ibn Roshd, par ses contemporains théologiens au 12ème siècle. Antūn, a une bonne connaissance de la culture savante de l'Europe moderne. Et, à la suite de la célèbre interprétation d'Ernest Renan, il voit en Ibn Roshd un rationaliste radical et une victime du fanatisme né de la collusion entre le pouvoir religieux des jurisconsultes (*Foukaha*, pluriel de *Fakih*) et le pouvoir princier. Cette lecture d'Antūn continue aujourd'hui encore à inspirer certains des écrivains engagés dans le soutien de la transition démocratique et moderniste du monde arabe.[12] Ainsi, la formulation du principe de laïcité et l'indépendance de la science et de la philosophie ont, sans aucun doute, contribué à introduire la définition suivante de la tolérance:

> La tolérance est, dans sa définition générale, l'acceptation de l'existence de ce qui vous est contraire. Dans sa définition particulière, c'est la permission de l'existence des croyances et rites religieux différents des croyances et des rites habituels. C'est une définition qui ne correspond pas aux circonstances actuelles. Voici une définition qui répond positivement à nos attentes: La tolérance religieuse est la considération et le respect que nous devons aux doctrines produites par d'autres humains même si elles sont contraires aux nôtres.[13]

Il ressort de notre analyse que le courant moderniste a pu articuler la tolérance avec la justice. L'oppression des minorités religieuses due à la méconnaissance de leurs droits fondamentaux est, en effet, un obstacle majeur à la justice sociale. Réclamer la laïcité, c'est indiquer la voie vers une justice sociale permanente. Ainsi, le monde arabe ne peut, concrètement accéder à la justice tant qu'il n'a pas sécularisé les sphères politique et culturelle. De ce fait, l'engagement dans cette voie apparait aujourd'hui comme une résistance radicale à la montée des différentes expressions du fondamentalisme et du salafisme. La tolérance est, selon Rawls (*Political Liberalism*) une vertu, dans la mesure où elle oblige à la justification des principes (même celle de la justice). Autrement dit, elle est une vertu de la philosophie politique, dans des sociétés ou des communautés politiques qui sont religieusement et culturellement pluralistes.

Le monde arabe est tiraillé entre ces deux courants, conservateur et moderniste, depuis le 19ème siècle et il reste, à ce jour, dans une phase de transition. Nous pouvons même dire, sans trop nous risquer, que les signes de régression sont plus marqués que les signes de progrès et ce, notamment depuis les deux dernières décennies, qui ont été caractérisées par des différends entre les deux courants fondamentaliste-salafiste et laïc-civique. Les récents évènements tragiques ne font que réveiller la dimension destructrice des mouvements les plus radicaux de l'islam politique.[14]

La Transition vers la fiction littéraire

Jusqu'ici, j'ai privilégié l'approche historico-politique du traitement de la notion de tolérance. Mais, je voudrais signaler que les questions que la notion charrie ont poussé certains à en faire la trame de leur œuvre de fiction. F. Antūn lui-même lui a consacré plusieurs romans, déplorant que, dans le monde arabe, la fiction romanesque soit demeurée un simple motif de divertissement là où, en Occident, le genre avait été mobilisé dans une perspective militante. Dans l'introduction de son roman *Religion, Science et Argent*, il souligne l'importance des romans qui s'apparentent à une 'recherche de philosophie sociale' et qui traitent des relations sociales sur fond de tolérance ou d'intolérance. Il écrit par exemple:

> Certains romans sont écrits pour l'humour et le divertissement, tandis que d'autres le sont à des fins intéressées et pour diffuser des principes et des idées. En Occident, ceux qui ont écrit des romans à des fins intéressées sont considérés parmi les plus célèbres comme Tolstoï, Zola, Kipling et bien d'autres. Chacun de ces écrivains ne voit dans la rédaction des romans aucune décadence ou mépris de la narration, bien au contraire, il considère le roman comme une plate-forme pour publier ses opinions et ses idées d'une manière facile à saisir par les lecteurs. Nous, en Orient, sommes privés de ce style d'écriture à cause de son impopularité pour des raisons qui ne peuvent pas être mentionnées ici. Par conséquent, la plupart des romans publiés chez nous n'ont aucun but sauf l'humour.'[15]

Force est de constater que ce paragraphe annonce un tournant dans l'histoire de la narration littéraire des pionniers de la Renaissance arabe: il attribue au roman un contenu social et au romancier un rôle pratique. Ainsi, la tâche de ce dernier sera accrue par l'obligation d'enseigner à son public la tolérance et ce, *via* la dynamique créée entre les évènements, les personnages, et les discours qu'ils échangent entre eux. Finalement, l'auteur (le romancier) attribue une vie à ses différentes représentations de la tolérance à travers les personnages et les événements qu'il choisit et se montre, par le biais de la mobilisation et de l'orientation des événements qu'il invente, sous les traits d'un juge, qui exerce son influence sur le lecteur en lui permettant de suivre, à travers les récits, des situations de conflit et des scénarios 'intolérables' dans la vie ordinaire, l'accoutumant ainsi à des situations de tolérance.

Les remarques d'Antūn citées dans le paragraphe précédent valent pour les courants littéraires utilisant la fiction en vue de créer un environnement favorable à la tolérance.

Les croyances religieuses sont, depuis toujours, objet de conflit et source de fanatisme. Le genre romanesque s'en empare très souvent. Dans *Urachlim al-jadida*,[16] un dialogue entre Elie (un jeune chrétien) et Esther (une jeune juive), les personnages tiennent les discours suivants:

- Les religions ne sont pas exclusives l'une de l'autre: 'Vous êtes juive et moi je suis chrétien, mais vous n'êtes pas empêchée par votre religion de reconnaître la vérité, moi non plus ma religion ne m'interdit pas de l'admettre.'[17]
- Le respect est décrit comme un degré supérieur de la tolérance: 'je respecte votre doctrine et toute doctrine dans laquelle l'adepte trouve le confort et la paix, la vérité et la vertu, mais j'avais l'intention de vous apprendre à respecter les doctrines des autres.'[18]
- La morale doit être un idéal commun aux religions: 'Mettons les religions des humains de côté, dans un lieu sacré et respectueux, et rencontrons-nous dans une nouvelle religion qui accepte toutes les religions vertueuses et ne rejette aucune d'entre elles et cette religion est celle de la justice, mentionnée ci-dessus, du droit, de l'amour et du pardon pour tous. Nous, petits subalternes et opprimés dans cette vie, avons un besoin très urgent d'établir "le droit, la justice et l'amour" à la place de tout. Mets ma main dans la tienne pour vivre en paix sur cette terre et avec cette nouvelle religion qui respecte toutes les autres religions.'[19]

La réalisation d'un tel idéal de tolérance demeure, à des degrés divers selon les pays, hors de portée dans le monde arabe. La littérature critique dont l'existence remonte loin dans le passé de la civilisation arabo-islamique est, en permanence, condamnée à lutter contre la censure. *Les Fils de la Medina* (1952) de Naguib Mahfouz et *Les Versets sataniques* de Salman Rushdie (1988) en sont des témoins. Le premier a subi des menaces depuis la publication en 1959 de sa fiction *Awlad haratina*. Il a été victime d'une agression par un fanatique, qui n'avait pas lu ses romans. Le second a été l'objet de la censure et de menaces de mort. Les exemples abondent lorsqu'on élargit le champ d'investigation pour y inclure la poésie, le théâtre, le cinéma, la peinture, la caricature, etc.

Dans ses romans, A. Mustaghanmi a attiré, l'attention du lecteur sur les désastres de la décennie sanglante en Algérie. Dans l'un d'entre eux, elle décrit une scène qui fait suite à un massacre:

> Que faisait là ce petit qui était assis seul sur le trottoir de la stupeur? Tous le négligeaient car occupés à inhumer les morts. Quarante-cinq cadavres. Le nombre ayant excédé la capacité du cimetière, les gens ont dû recourir au cimetière voisin. Lors du massacre d''Ibn Talha', il fallait trois cimetières répartis sur trois villages pour enterrer plus de trois cents cadavres. Est-ce que la mort était, cette fois-ci, plus tendre, et — à force de cogiter — aurait permis à quelques âmes d'échapper à ses mâchoires?[20]

Un peu plus loin, elle ajoute: 'L'enfant était assis comme s'il était encore étourdi et stupéfait. On m'apprit qu'ils l'ont retrouvé sous l'étroit lit de fer sur lequel dormait son père.'[21]

La romancière place les mots suivants dans la bouche d'un autre personnage — celui d'un journaliste qui a fui les massacres dont ses collègues ont été les victimes: 'Dans la saison de la cueillette des têtes et de la récolte des stylos, nous, les journalistes, avons échoué à trouver des noms d'emprunt derrière lesquels nous cacher des meurtriers. "Chacun a choisi au hasard son nouveau nom".'[22]

Elle fait amèrement s'interroger l'un de ses personnages: 'Il est arrivé que nous fûmes une fois un peuple maîtrisant l'ironie, alors comment avons-nous perdu l'envie de rire? Et comment avons-nous eu ces visages fermés, ces comportements hostiles, et ces habits étranges qui n'ont jamais été les nôtres?'[23]

A côté de la religion, la politique est aussi un sujet propice à l'écriture littéraire. La littérature est gardienne des souvenirs des peuples. Par la voix de son personnage, algérien et artiste peintre, assis devant la Scène, A. Mustaghanmi développe ces réflexions qui mêlent tolérance et travail de la mémoire:

> Je comprends l'incapacité de Khalid dans ce roman à établir une relation amicale avec cette belle vue. Je n'ai pas de regrets envers le fleuve et je ne suis pas non plus en désaccord avec lui. La mémoire de l'eau chargée à travers les âges des cadavres de toutes races, ne peut pas distinguer entre les identités, elle ne peut pas distinguer entre les cadavres des Français qui ont été jetés en 1789 dans cette rivière au nom de la Révolution et les corps des Algériens qui y ont été jetés pour la même raison il y a deux siècles.[24]

La mémoire est au cœur de la grande transition qui demeure, depuis la Renaissance arabe, toujours menacée et en gestation continue.

La Tolérance arabe: de la tolérance d'acceptation à la tolérance de respect

Il ressort de ce qui précède que la tolérance arabo-musulmane est un concept embryonnaire qui n'a, actuellement, guère dépassé, dans la pratique, le principe d'acceptation. Pour élucider cette idée, nous allons essayer de nous demander-comment on peut concevoir une forme de tolérance que l'on puisse durablement défendre.

Dans la littérature arabo-musulmane, la question de la tolérance a été jusqu'ici enclavée dans deux conceptions primitives: la conception permissive (qui signifie que la majorité autorise les minorités à vivre selon leurs échelles de valeurs, principes et modes propres de pensée) et la conception de coexistence (stipulant un contexte dans lequel un accord préliminaire entre une majorité dominante et une minorité est établi, qui a pour but la reconnaissance mutuelle visant à prévenir-toutes sortes de conflits ultérieurs éventuels). Pourquoi en est-il ainsi?

Ceci traduit essentiellement le fait que la pensée arabe fonctionne essentiellement et parfois, de manière excessive, selon la dualité (Altérité/Identité) qui évoque toujours, implicitement ou explicitement, le conflit historique qui a prévalu entre l'Islam et le Christianisme ou celui qui a eu lieu lors de l'époque coloniale (et dont les pays arabes ont été les victimes). Par conséquent, la pensée arabe est, *a priori* contrainte par un conflit interne permanent: faut-il disposer d'une raison qui se penche sur notre identité ou bien se tourner vers l'altérité (qui nous a historiquement apporté injustice et soumission)? Aucun consensus n'existe sur ce point. Ainsi, tandis que la pensée d'Albert Hourani se veut conservatrice (il est, selon lui, important que la pensée arabe soit de nature identitaire en matière de religion, de valeur et de culture), celles de Fahmi Jadaan et de Wajih Khoutharani sont plus libérales et plus universalistes. Ces auteurs invitent la pensée arabo-musulmane à se réconcilier avec l'universalisme qui nous parvient via le canal des valeurs mondiales. Ceci permettrait de fonder, selon eux, un nouveau monde arabe qui défende la tolérance, la liberté, la justice, le libéralisme et l'identité culturelle (ancienne et moderne).

C'est cette dernière approche cognitive qui permet de fonder une tolérance de respect, stipulant que les individus se tolèrent et se respectent mutuellement et que chacun d'entre eux est conscient de son autonomie, et de son égalité face aux autres devant la loi et la justice.

Cette tolérance est celle qui est la plus compatible avec les démocraties modernes car elle appelle d'autres valeurs (comme le signalent Habermas et Rawls) dont, principalement, la justice et la liberté. Dans le contexte des transitions arabes, atteindre le stade de cette dernière forme de tolérance s'avère, néanmoins, difficile à court et à moyen termes mais bien plus possible à long terme, lorsque la démocratie devient une conviction sociale forte et n'est plus un simple stéréotype langagier dont usent les politiciens et les groupes d'intérêts.

Conclusion

En guise de conclusion nous pouvons dire que, loin d'être récente, la question de la tolérance a été présente dans le monde arabo-musulman depuis l'avènement de l'Islam, soit en tant que maxime ou valeur exprimant la capacité à accepter les autres religions, soit en tant que pratiques approuvées par les musulmans envers le 'différent religieux'. La pensée arabe de la tolérance peut, toutefois, être considérée comme relativement dépendante si on la rapporte essentiellement à l'ère coloniale, et aux deux courants de pensée qui ont alors émergé: le courant conservateur (Tahtaoui, Al Afgani, Abdu), qui considère que la tolérance est une condition pour accepter l'autre, sans qu'elle aboutisse à un changement substantiel de la société musulmane (il s'agit d'une tolérance permissive); le courant moderniste (A. Ishāq et F. Antūn) qui considère que la tolérance est, plus qu'une valeur permissive une valeur d'existence. A l'époque contemporaine, la valeur de la tolérance est, à notre sens, une notion déséquilibrée, étant donné la quasi absence de démocratie, qui risque de figer et de maintenir en vie les idéaux forgés au cours d'une longue histoire de dictature (religieuse, politique etc.). Toutefois, dans les pays du printemps arabe, et spécifiquement en Tunisie, les choses peuvent se développer autrement, surtout si le processus démocratique atteint les objectifs qu'il s'est assignés. On peut ainsi, espérer que la tolérance soit fondée sur le respect et, pourquoi pas, sur l'estime du différent. Pour ce faire, un grand effort reste à fournir (un travail de réconciliation critique avec notre mémoire, voire avec notre héritage culturel, est un préalable si l'on veut reconstruire et se réapproprier la valeur de la tolérance, tout en veillant à nous situer, bel et bien et pleinement, dans une modernité consciente de ses limites) non seulement de la part de ceux qui s'occupent des sciences et des cultures mais, aussi et surtout, de la part des acteurs politiques d'un monde globalisé.

La valeur de la tolérance, fondée sur les principes du respect et de l'estime n'est plus étrangère à notre histoire commune qui a, durant longtemps, regroupé des composantes hétérogènes. Cette valeur a suscité l'unanimité entre la philosophie et le soufisme religieux.

La position philosophique est représentée essentiellement par Ibn Rushd, qui a vécu dans une société plurielle et essayé de dégager un compromis entre la philosophie et la chariaa, au motif que la réalité est une, même si les chemins qui y ramènent sont multiples (la révélation et la raison). Lorsque l'individu, pour une raison ou une autre, ne parvient plus à saisir ou à voir la réalité, alors on doit le tolérer, et ce abstraction faite de sa religion ou de sa croyance.

De son côté, Ibn Arabi a fait appel à une religion universelle dans laquelle les religions divines dites historiques ne sont que des exemples spécifiques. Finalement, il perçoit qu'on ne doit pas se pencher à l'aveuglette sur la certitude et l'absolutisme des textes religieux mais que l'on doit toujours se référer à la raison via l'herméneutique (bien contextualiser et comprendre les textes) et la bonne interprétation (Al Ijtihad).

Notes to Chapter 18

1. Sandrine Lefranc, 'La Justice transitionnelle n'est pas un concept', *Mouvements*, 1 (2008), 61–69. Voir aussi Kora Adrieu, *La Justice transitionnelle* (Paris: Gallimard, Collection Folio Essais, 2012).
2. Rainer Forst, *Toleration in Conflict: Past and Present* (Cambridge: Cambridge University Press, 2013).
3. Razwān al-Sayed, 'Al-tasāmoḥ fī kitābāt al-ʿrab al-moḥdaṯīn wālmoāṣirīn', *Revue al-Tasāmoḥ*, 1 (2003).
4. Samīr al-Khalil, 'Al-Tasāmoḥ fī loġha alarabīa', in *altasāmoḥ bayna sharq wa Gharb* (collectif), trad. par Ibrahim Alaris (Beyrouth: Dar Alsaqui, 1992).
5. Rafaa Tahtaoui, *Takhlis et ibriz Fi talkhisi bariz* (Caire: wizarat althakafa wal irched alkawmi 1958).
6. Albert Hourani, *Al Fikr al arabi fi 'asr al-nahda (1798–1939)*, 3ème édition (Beyrouth: Dar al-Nahar Linnachr, 1977), p. 96 (1ère édition 1968).
7. Jamel Eddin El Afghani and Mohamed Abdu, *Al-orwatu el-wouthka* (Caire: Fondation Hindawi, 2012), p. 76.
8. Jean Fontaine, *La Crise religieuse des écrivains syro-libanais chrétiens de 1825 à 1940* (Tunis: IBLA, 1996), p. 77.
9. Adīb Ishāq, *Al-kitabat al-siyasiyya wa-l-ijtimaâ'iyya*, 2ème édition (Beyrouth: Dar Talia, 1982), p. 120.
10. Ishāq, *Al-kitabat*, p. 146.
11. Farah Antun, *Ibn Roshd wa Falsafatoho* (Beyrouth: Dar Talia, 1981), p. 126.
12. 'On peut ranger dans cette catégorie Abd al- Rahmân Badawî, Mâdjid Fakhrî, Murâd Wahba, 'Atif al-'Irâqî, Tayyib Tîzinnî. Les partisans d'une théologie éclairée, plus ou moins ouverte sur le progrès, la démocratie, la modernité, etc., prolongent, chacun à sa manière, l'interprétation développée au début du siècle par 'Abduh, le sheikh Tâhir al-Djazâ'irî ou Mustafâ Qabbânî. Parmi les représentant de ce courant on peut citer, à titre d'exemple, Mahmûd Qâsim, Hasan Hanafî, 'Âbid al-Djâbirî et tous ceux qui, au Maghreb comme au Mashreq, renvoient dos à dos les partisans d'un islam fermé au progrès et les adeptes d'une modernité reléguant le religieux sinon parmi les formes de pensée désuète du moins dans la sphère privée.' Mohamed-Chérif Ferjani, 'Le Devenir de l'œuvre d'Ibn Rosh dans le monde arabe', in *Averroès et l'averroïsme* (XIIe–XVe siècle): *un itinéraire historique du Haut Atlas à Paris et à Padoue*, ed. par André Bazzana, Nicole Bériou and Pierre Guichard (Lyon: Presses Universitaires de Lyon, 2005), pp. 239–48.
13. Amin Rayhānī, *Arrayhaniet* (Caire: Fondation Hindawi, 2012), pp. 35–36.

14. Evénements du 11 septembre, puis inquiétante montée du fondamentalisme religieux (Al-Qaida, Nosra, Daech, etc.).
15. Farah Antūn, *al-Dīn wa L-'ilm wa L-māL aw al-mudun al-thalāth* (Caire: Fondation Hindawi, 2012), p. 7.
16. Farah Antūn, *Urachlim al-jadida aw Fath al-Árab bayt al-maqdas* (paru pour la première fois en 1904), (Caire: Fondation Hindawi, 2012).
17. Antūn, *al-Dīn*, p. 19.
18. Antūn, *al-Dīn*, p. 118.
19. Antūn, *al-Dīn*, p. 117.
20. Ahlem Mustaghanmi, *Ábiru Sarir*, ed 11 (Beyrouth: *Dar al-Adeb Li-Lnachr Wattawziá*, 2012), p. 31.
21. Mustaghanmi, *Ábiru Sarir*, p. 31.
22. Mustaghanmi, *Ábiru Sarir*, p. 28.
23. Mustaghanmi, *Ábiru Sarir*, p. 25.
24. Mustaghanmi, *Ábiru Sarir*, p. 78.

CHAPTER 19

A Conversation with Zakaria Tamer

Ali Souleman and Robin Ostle

Introduction by Ali Souleman

Zakaria Tamer is one of the most prominent Syrian writers, the father of the Syrian short story and one of the most influential living Arab writers. Born in Damascus in 1931, he has played a major role in creating the modern literary scene in the Arab world, and in forming the cultural and moral sensibility for generations of Syrian writers since the late 1950s.

For most Syrians from all generations, the long and often difficult voyage of enlightenment in the context of the ongoing political and social struggle for freedom, democracy and justice in the region starts by reading books by Zakaria Tamer such as *al-Numur fi al-Yawm al-'Ashir* [The Tigers on the Tenth Day] (1978), *Dimashq al-Hara'iq* [Damascus of Fires] (1973) and *Rabi' fi al-Ramad* [Spring in the Ashes] (1963). Today, new generations are once again reading their own Damascus of Fires and witnessing how the war is turning the long-awaited dream of spring into ashes. Zakaria Tamer is for Syria the guardian of the cross-generational dreams of freedom, social progress and justice. He is the storyteller of the epic struggle for emancipation from political repression, patriarchy and religious traditions.

He acquired a leading position in modernist writing in the literary life of the Arab World since the late 1950s and constitutes a unique literary school. He is often called by Syrian critics 'the poet of the Arabic short story'. Unlike the majority of the pioneers of modern Arabic literature, he devoted his life and career solely to one form of literature, namely the short story. Tamer began his literary career in 1957, when he published a number of stories in literary journals in Syria and Lebanon. His extraordinarily poetical prose in these stories brought him considerable attention and aroused particular critical interest. They were followed in 1960 by the publication of his first collection of short stories *Sahil al-Jawad al-'Abyad* [The Neighing of the White Steed]. He has been experimental in his style, pioneering the evolving and developments of the Very Short Story (al-qissa al-qasira jiddan), a form which characterized his writing, notably in his collection *Taksir Rukab* [Breaking Knees] (2002).

Tamer has published eleven collections of stories, two collections of satirical articles and dozens of children's books. In his writing over six decades, he has developed his own style and techniques, and created a fictional world where he blurs the borders between reality and imagination, the rational and the irrational, and the contemporary and the historical to allow a space for the voices of the marginalized and the victims. This is the unique world of Tamer who stayed faithful to his visions, free from all ideologies and political trends. Through all the political upheavals, destructive wars and human tragedies which the Arab region has endured over the last sixty years, Tamer has stayed faithful to his only commitment: to be a dissident writer in a country torn apart by the struggle for the very central two themes in his work over more than half a century, democracy and justice.

What puts Tamer's work in a unique position with regard to freedom and justice in the context of the intellectual life in Syria in general, and in the development of modernist Syrian fiction in particular, is his ontological, existential obsession with those two questions of social justice. He is one of a few Syrian writers, like the late poet Muhammad al-Maghut, who upheld a deeply rooted vision of democracy and justice, independent from an over-politicized, often ideologically driven commitment to those issues.

The conjunction between the crisis of the modernist cultural project of the 1960s generation and the rupture of the nationalist/socialist narrative took until the turn of the century to be fully grasped, and consequently manifested itself starting from the early 1990s as a shift in aesthetic and artistic sensibility in contemporary Syrian fictional writing, where 'a more personal, anti-ideological or non-ideological art, an art evolving outside the space of consensus, has been taking shape and acquiring prominence'.[1] But the short stories of Tamer had been, to use his own fictional metaphor, that tiger that has never been tamed.

The question of social justice in particular has been central in Tamer's approach to the fundamental theme of his work, freedom. During the 1980s, a sense of disillusionment started to grow amongst Syrian intellectuals. It was primarily concerned with what was often described as the failure, the insufficiency or the defeat of a generation of Arab intellectuals and modernists in addressing the real questions and issues concerning Arab societies, especially in the post-1967 era. Some Syrian writers, such Sa'dallah Wannus, admitted that it had been an illusion, in the 1960s and '70s, to believe that it was possible to expand the marginal space of dialogue in society, and, consequently, be able to 'do something about the oppressive instrument of power by implicating it in dialogue'.[2] It had equally been an illusion to think that the solution to the problems in Arab societies was just a question of changing the political regime.[3] The problems were more complex and structural, and deeply rooted in the social structure and in the individual psyche.[4]

Zakaria Tamer, however, from an early stage in his career, has been more aware of the depth of that structural problem, and he was precocious in liberating his work from illusions with regard to the ruling political power in the Arab World. As portrayed in his short stories, those regimes were grotesquely tyrannical, absurdly oppressive and totally unchangeable entities. All the authorities in his stories, be they political, religious or social, are like a unified evil, a corrupted power of oppression and cruelty. The individual in that sphere of fear and intimidation is always subject to terrorization by the police state and the traditional social powers, all united within a deep structural amalgamation of deceptively contradictory powers, but functionally interdependent and collaborative. Hisham Sharabi relates that to a unique structural characteristic of Arab societies, which he calls the neo-patriarchal structure. This structure is neither traditional nor modern; it is unique in that it has its own particular patterns of doing and thinking.[5]

That bizarre, abnormal socio-political reality which engulfed almost all Arab societies in the second half of the twentieth century is fictionalized by Tamer in his short stories as he employs a variety of literary devices and modes of expressions such as irony, dark-humour, the grotesque, surrealism, satire, and symbolism. In every story he writes, the question for Tamer seems to be: how to write in such a world where the boundaries between reality and nightmare are blurred, the world of that socio-political system, where the newly emerging militarized states malformed into dictatorships, create a history of suffering and repression beyond imagination, and cultivate violence and violation of basic human rights to an absurd degree. That question always locates Tamer on the opposition side, not only against the ruling powers, but also against the literary and intellectual establishment.

It is relevant here to point to an example of his contribution to one of the most controversial debates in the literary life of Syria. In his response to the debate created by the publication in 1974 of *al-Adab wa al-Idiulujiyya fi Suriyya* [Literature and Ideology in Syria] by Nabil Suliman and Bu Ali Yasin, he mocks the two notions promoted by the book as the pillars of any literature seeking modernity and real change, namely Literature of Commitment (*Adab al-Iltizam*) and Socialist Realism.[6] He argues that literature cannot liberate Palestine, free slaves, eliminate illiteracy, create a conscientious citizenry, or abolish apartheid.[7]

With his unique personal experience, a blacksmith in his early adult life and, later, the poet of the modern Arabic short story, Tamer wrote with the resolve of a blacksmith and the language of a poet. He charts the long voyage to freedom and justice for generations from the early stage of the totalitarian states in the region up to the Arab Spring and its still unfolding consequences. He even contributes to the cultural exchanges of the post-2011 revolutionary generation in writing on social media as a new platform. This is typical of the unique nature of his style in terms of its flexibility and its deep-rooted connection to the real life of his people.

Interview conducted in Arabic by Ali Souleman and Robin Ostle, translated by Robin Ostle

Your stories have been since the late 1950s a space, or spaces, for all types of marginalized voices in society — the poor, the underprivileged, the unknown. In the age of social media and 24-hour news, how does literature, your literature, bear witness to the unfolding tragedies in Syria and the Middle East?

All the literature and all the stories which I have written are the practical embodiment of my theory of literature and the responsibility of literature. But at the same time I was always aware that literature cannot really change a bad situation. However, it can mobilize for change and create within people the desire for change, and that desire will one day surely become a desire for action.

I believe in the right of the writers to write whatever they wish. But when they can see the fires around them, then writing at that time cannot ignore these fires, their causes and their victims.

There are two types of writers: 'tourist' writers — their relationship with the people around them is very limited. They may also side with those who steal people's rights, and they may do that to protect and preserve their own security and to gain benefits for themselves. The other type is those writers who are linked to their environment, and that link is conscious. This type of writer aspires to make people's pains their own personal pains.

Does your literature, or can literature, play any role in transitional justice and social reconciliation by creating spaces, or imaginary spaces, for the voices of the victims?

This is an important and perplexing question which contains elements that are contradictory — justice, reconciliation, victims. The conflict in the Arab World is not a conflict between social groups who are divided into oppressors and oppressed, but the conflict is between authoritarian states and the peoples who long for democracy and freedom. In my view there is no room for reconciliation between the killer and the killed. Justice will not be achieved until the killer is punished. Any reconciliation between the two is illusory and actually impossible. Especially given that the Arab-Islamic religious and cultural tradition believes in a life for a life, an eye for an eye, and a tooth for a tooth.

(The following question refers to one of the author's famous short stories, 'The Tigers on the Tenth Day' in which a number of caged Tigers are subjected to a process of taming and by the tenth day they are tamed. This is usually interpreted as a political allegory.)

After eight years of the so-called Arab Spring, can we say that the Tigers of Zakaria Tamer have been finally liberated from the cage, and did you anticipate what would happen to the tigers after that tenth day?

'The Tigers on the Tenth Day' is a story about an experiment on the part of the rulers to tame their people, and the verdict is that the experiment failed. Success in taming tigers can only be temporary and tigers will return to being tigers and will escape from their cages. But now I confess that the story neglected to think about what happens to the tigers once they have escaped from their cages. Any real tiger who tries to get rid of its tamer and its cage is killed immediately. This is precisely what happened to the Arab tigers when they sought to escape from their cages. They were killed in the most atrocious manner and with unlimited savagery.

During the past seven years there has been a great deal of fictional writing by Syrians, both inside and outside Syria. The majority of these works have been novels and most of them have memorialized the victims of the war. Where does the short story stand in this situation?

I am not a great follower of the publication scene in the Arab World, but the current flow of novel writing does not necessarily mean that novelists are more prolific and that short story writers are not. It could simply mean that Arab publishing houses prefer novels rather than short story or poetry collections. The fashion now in the Arab world is for the novel. Short story writers and poets are like orphans, and the publishing houses run away from them and what they produce.

In your short stories, one of the striking stylistic features is the frequent tendency to blur the borders between reality and imagination, the rational and the irrational, the contemporary and the historical and so forth. Have these borders or dividing lines changed in your vision and your writing over the past seven or eight years?

This is a very difficult question for me to answer just now, because the development in my writing does not follow a mental or rational process, nor does it occur as a result of a decision or a particular intellectual conviction. So I continue writing and then I am surprised that there is a change or development in my writing. I am not really sure that what is happening in Syria is affecting my writing. I have no choice but to continue writing, but I would like to point out that the blurring of the borders between different worlds in my writing is not a technical or artistic feature designed to surprise. Rather it is an attempt to portray what is happening inside the depths of the Arab individual, and to present a portrait of what these depths may look like. My experience has led me to believe that the Arab individual does not differentiate between the world of imagination and reality, or of life and death, but deals with them as if they are one world.

You have been extremely active on social media over the past seven years. Has this interaction with your readers via social media affected your writing style or your vision of the role of literature? And has this experience via social media in your opinion made you an activist in this new space for writing?

I have to confess at the outset that Facebook has given us Arabs a freedom that doesn't exist in the Arab countries themselves and it has created a democratic society and a world which guarantee for everyone the right to express their ideas, opinions and feelings. It has allowed each to have their own newspaper which speaks for them and speaks on their behalf. In short, Facebook provides a daily training in freedom, and I chose Facebook in order to reach out to readers instead of newspapers and magazines. This has been a very successful means of doing this. It allowed me to reach more readers than those of newspapers and magazines, and it gave me thousands of readers from all over the world.

But Facebook has no influence in in developing or changing the way I write. It is actually completely in harmony with my love of condensing and conciseness. My use of Facebook was a mere attempt to harness it in a serious and useful manner, especially as many Arabs use Facebook for chattering, exchanging greetings or insults, or to show the latest photographs of themselves.

I come from Denmark where we are having a big debate about social media and the negative impact which they may have on democracy and social discourse. In multi-ethnic and multi-cultural situations, are social media ultimately helpful or do they unleash hatred and vitriol in ways more harmful than helpful to dialogue?

When I spoke about Facebook, I did so in the specific context and environment of the Arab World. Danish people can easily criticize any of their readers or politicians without fear of being fired from their job, or being imprisoned, or simply disappearing from the register of the living. An Arab is deprived of this particular advantage. When I look at Facebook, it is full of insults and criticisms, and I think that this is a very healthy thing. Yes, Facebook gives freedom and democracy to the ignorant as well as to the knowledgeable, but for us Arabs at this particular stage in the Arab World, Facebook is very useful.

I don't read Arabic, so could you explain what kind of textual postings you place on Facebook — literary pieces or pieces about political events: who are your readers and how do you interact?

I publish different types of text on Facebook — children's stories, stories for adults, intellectual or political comments, and some of these comments include severe criticism of phenomena in the Arab World. In fact Facebook is particularly appropriate for short texts, but I have been able to publish a number of long texts and these have been read very widely.

You talked about the Arab World, or maybe the Arab Mind. How do you think of the notion of the Arab Nation? How would you define it? Would you define it in terms of language and literature, and where does Syria fit it?

This is a very difficult question. Fifty years ago the response was easy, and I would have said that there was one Arab nation. But that Arab nation has been torn apart. Subsequently I have written many articles predicting that every single street in the Arab World is going to be an independent nation, with its own flag and its own army.

To return to the issue of Facebook, first of all the numbers of readers or 'likes' can be misleading, but when you find comments from specific readers and you respond to them, presumably that takes you from your role as a writer to a different role?

I don't enter into that type of game. I think that my page consists of genuine readers. I could almost say that I know them one by one. Of course there are ways of getting a large number of readers, but I avoid those methods. For example, I have a beautiful friend from Syria: she posted her picture and simply said 'Ah, Aleppo!', and immediately got 1500 likes.

For example, if you raise the sectarian issue, then you get lots of readers. My page is completely free of any racism or sectarianism. My page is directed towards serious readers and if they are that kind of reader, they are welcome. I also don't enter into conversations with readers, as I don't believe in that sort of exchange. I only say what I think and I listen to what others say.

Being concise sounds like it requires a lot of work. Could you tell us about your writing as a process and a practice?

To this particular question I have no particular answer, but I say to my wife that it's as if I have a factory inside me or something more like a kitchen. Someone actually cuts the vegetables and cooks. Or it's like being in a bank when you need a secret code: I merely need one key word, then the kitchen will provide me with hundreds of words. I start writing stories in a strange way. I may open the dictionary, close my eyes and put my finger on a page, and that can be the secret key word for that short story. I write stories that I think are beautiful, but usually I do not write at home. I write when I am on the move, and the best place for me to write is on the train. For example, I choose a quiet place, take a pen and start thinking about perhaps the three key words. By the time I get to London, the story is ready both as a draft and as a clean copy.

Notes to Chapter 19

1. Kamal Abu Deeb, 'The Collapse of Totalizing Discourse and the Rise of Marginalized/ Minority Discourses', in *Tradition, Modernity, and Postmodernity in Arabic Literature: Essays in Honor of Professor Issa J. Boullata*, ed. by Kamal Abdel-Malek and Wael B. Hallaq (Leiden: Brill, 2000), p. 336.
2. Mari Ilyas, 'Ḥiwar: Wannus 'an kitabatih al-jadidah', *al-Ṭariq*, 1 (Jan–Feb 1996), p. 101.
3. Ilyas, 'Ḥiwar', p. 99.
4. Ilyas, 'Ḥiwar', p. 99.
5. Hisham Sharabi, 'Patriarchy and Dependency and the Future of Arab Society', in *The Next Arab Decade: Alternative Futures*, ed. by Hisham Sharabi (Boulder, CO: Westview; London: Mansell, 1988), p. 2.
6. Nabil Suliman and Yasin Bu Ali, *Al-adab wa-al-idiyulujiyya fi Suriyya 1967–1973* [Literature and Ideology in Syria] (Al-Ladhiqiyyah: Dar al-Hiwar, 1974).
7. Alexa Firat, 'Cultural Battles on the Literary Field: From the Syrian Writers' Collective to the Last Days of Socialist Realism in Syria', *Middle Eastern Literatures*, 18.2 (2015), 153–76.

PART V

Asia

CHAPTER 20

❖

Alternative Account, Mourning Family and Transformation into Life: Three Contemporary Artworks Related to the Event of 28 February 1947 in Taiwan

Chi-Ming Lin

Background Stories

The 'February 28 incident', also known as the 228 or 2/28 event, was a massacre of participants in an uprising against the Kuomintang government which had taken over Taiwan after the surrender of Japan at the end of World War II. The killing of thousands of civilians began on 28 February 1947, with the number of Taiwanese deaths in this traumatic event estimated to be between 5,000 and 28,000.[1] This massacre was followed by the 'White Terror' period, dating from the declaration of Martial Law on 20 May 1949 to the end of the anti-rebellion legislation on 22 May 1991 (though Martial Law itself was not lifted until 15 July 1987). Tens of thousands more Taiwanese people disappeared, or were imprisoned, tortured or executed.

The 228 event is therefore one of the most important in Taiwan's modern history. It is nevertheless a tragedy in which we know more about the victims than the perpetrators. One reason for this, in the eyes of most scholars, is that democratization in Taiwan was a relatively peaceful and gradual process, so that many of the 228 event's perpetrators were still in power, and it was politically difficult to probe all the responsibilities. Another reason is that during the subsequent White Terror period, the perpetrators and victims of the 228 event became entangled in a complicated relationship, and many perpetrators themselves became victims.

The other background to this chapter is an exhibition titled 'The Aftermath' that I curated at Liang Gallery in Taipei in 2017, which tries to depict the course of the development of visual arts in Taiwan over the three decades following the lifting of Martial Law in 1987.[2] The exhibition not only provides a look at the past but also proposes a starting point to consider the future of Taiwanese contemporary art related to these past thirty years. The exhibition explores different generations of Taiwanese contemporary artists over those decades, as well as their reflections and responses to the declaration and abolition of Martial Law.

Based on the liberating and pluralistic spirit that came with the lifting of the Martial Law, the exhibition adopts a curatorial gesture that is different from most exhibitions. 'The Aftermath' was co-organized with some participant artists. In a first step, the curator invited representative artists from different generations to submit their works. Following this, they were asked to recommend another artist and suggest some of their artworks. In this process of working together to select works for the exhibition, in-depth interviews with the artists were also conducted in order to understand the reasoning behind each artist's submission, as well as gather suggestions or recommendations. In the course of these interviews, one artist labelled this method as 'Lifting the Martial Law of a Curated Exhibition'. There could be a theoretical problem with this label because it is difficult to say whether the curation had observed a kind of Martial Law. Nevertheless, to grasp the spirit of diversity and not fall into a politically correct pattern, this was indeed the core principle behind this exhibition.

By holding diverse views towards the lifting of Martial Law, the exhibition 'The Aftermath' investigates the declaration and abolition of the Martial Law of Taiwan through the perspective of artists from different generations. Artists' views include questions about repression and liberation, trauma and healing, historical reconstruction, a thorough understanding of the abolition of Martial Law, and the relation between consumerism and pleasure in the period that followed.

An Alternative Account of the History

In chronological order, the first artwork that I would like to discuss in this chapter is a sculpture created in 2003 by the Taiwanese artist Mei Dean-E (b. 1954). This sculpture, titled *The Brilliant Post*, is a small stainless-steel pillar placed upon a stainless-steel square. The pillar reflects, in a kind of anamorphic game, an image of the reproduction of a woodcut print on the square. The woodcut print itself was made by Huang Rong-Can, an artist who was himself a victim of the White Terror, and titled *The Terrible Inspection — Taiwan's 28 February 1947 Incident*. This print work is generally considered the iconic image of the event, especially because of the date of its creation, 1947, shortly after the massacre broke out.

Huang Rong-Can and 228

For a better understanding of this work, one has to know who Huang is and what his relationship with the 228 event is. Huang Rong-Can came to Taiwan from Nanking via Hong Kong as a teacher in the winter of 1945. On the 1 January 1946, he held his first solo show in Taipei. He then worked on the magazine *People's Report* as their deputy chief editor, and collaborated with several publishing companies to introduce the new woodcut print art and new realism art from China.

After the 228 event Huang Rong-Can, by then editor of *People's Report*, created in secret the woodcut print *The Terrible Inspection*, which was published two months

FIG. 20.1. 梅丁衍: 燦柱 2003, 不銹鋼, Mei Dean-E (b. 1954),
The Brilliant Post, 2003, stainless steel

FIG. 20.2. 黃榮燦《恐怖的檢查——台灣二二八事件》1947年
Huang Rong-Can, *The Terrible Inspection — Taiwan's 28 February 1947 Incident*,
1947, woodcut print

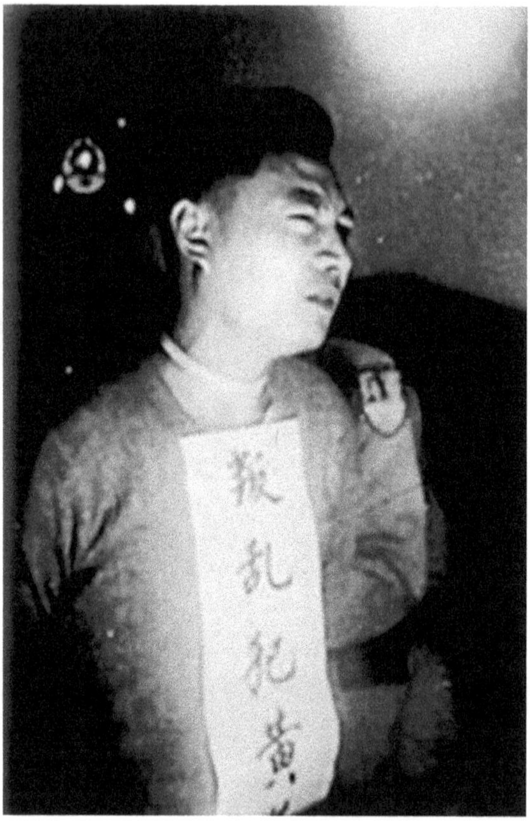

Fig. 20.3. The final picture of Haung Rong-Can before his execution

later in the left-wing newspaper *Wenwei Po* of Shanghai. Huang then gave the work to Kakitsu Uchiyama, a brother of Kanzō Uchiyama, a Japanese friend of Lu Xun, the famous Chinese left-wing writer, and it finally entered the collection of the Kanagawa Museum of Modern Art. This picture is generally regarded as the most powerful icon for the tragic event of 228.

During the White Terror, Huang was arrested on 1 December 1951, because of his connection with a friend, Wu Naikuang, who was denounced and arrested as a communist. Huang was accused of rebellion against the nation on 8 September 1952, sentenced to death on 11 November, and executed on 19 December of the same year. He was just thirty-six years old.

Mei Dean-E and Haung Rong-Can

The artist who made *The Brilliant Post*, Mei Dean-E, recalled recently: 'On 28 February 1991, several Taiwanese associations held a commemoration of the victims of the 228 event and those of the White Terror in the concert hall of the Youth Park of Taipei. The catalogue of the commemoration included this picture titled *The 228 Event* but its author is marked as "unknown".'

Mei insists that *The 228 Event* print by Huang was first reported by the mass media and only later caught the attention of historians of art. Mei recalled that when he came back from New York to Taiwan, in 1993, he discovered this phenomenon of 'disruption', so he decided to do some research into Huang. He ended up publishing a research paper running to 50,000 Chinese characters in the *Modern Art* journal of the Taipei Fine Arts Museum in 1996. In the 228 commemoration exhibition held the same year in that museum, Mei exhibited an installation, *Homage to Huang Ron-Can*, declaring that his intention was to restore Huang's reputation as an artist.

In 1998, Mei helped the reporter Hsu Tsong-mao to hold an exhibition of early Chinese woodcut prints, for which he borrowed the original of Huang's *228 Event* from the Kanagawa Museum of Modern Art where it is preserved. This was the first time, after 50 years, that the work had returned to Taiwan. Even recently, when Mei recalled this return, he still felt 'very excited, like having a roaring ocean inside'.[3]

Artist as researcher offering an alternative account of history

From Mei's relationship with Huang's print, one may perceive his role as a researcher who has integrated this research into his artistic creation. His double role as researcher and creator at the same time transforms his research as an art action, and makes him able to offer an alternative account of history. To understand this more deeply, Mei invites people to put the artwork by Huang back into the context of the history of the modern woodcut print in Taiwan, especially in the period after the Second World War.

Mei reports that Chen Yi, then chief administrator of Taiwan sent by the central government under the control of Chiang Kai-shek, had recruited teachers chiefly from Fuchien where he had been governor. In Chen Yi's team, one finds, surprisingly for a contemporary reader, a lot of 'left-wing' personages and that is why the woodcut print artists of Fuchien area had more opportunities to come to Taiwan. Among these woodcut print artists, Chu Ming-kang was the most renowned. He came to Taiwan in January 1946 and was responsible for the editing of a KMT Party magazine.

Chu Ming-kang wrote in 1947 that the National Association of Woodcut Print of China started up its Taiwanese branch. From this one may deduce that this important woodcut group planned to develop woodcut print in Taiwan. The artists of the Association used newspapers and magazines as their first and most important places for publication and held occasional exhibitions. Their activities were chiefly to express their attitude towards the war but at the same time they promoted the 'New Realism'. These 'left-wing' woodcut prints formed the first wave of the post-war print art movement in Taiwan.

According to Mei, Huang was the first to publish woodcut prints in Taiwan. The date was the 1 January 1946. Huang later became the editor-in-chief of the 'South Rainbow' pages in the *People's Report* and published articles in it and in other newspapers to present Chinese woodcut prints of the war period. Huang was not only a creator but also an active promoter of the woodcut prints movement in Taiwan.

FIG. 20.4. 朱鳴岡～<迫害>, *Repression*, by Chu Ming-kang, 1948

In that period, several woodcut print artists came to Taiwan from China, but left after the 228 Event. One such was Chu Ming-kang, who had been arrested and interrogated by the Taiwan Garrison Command, and decided to leave Taiwan. He recommended Huang to replace him in his newly appointed position in the Department of Art of the Normal College of Taipei. Huang thus entered officially into the Normal College in 1948 and taught there until his arrest in 1951. Chu went back to China through Hong Kong and created the famous wood print *Repression* during his travel. After the founding of the People's Republic of China, he lectured in Lu Xun Art Academy.[4]

Mei comments that Realism is a convenient style to serve the politics, in which the signs in the work and their narrative function are easily connected to the verbal language, allowing the purpose of communication and education to be quickly achieved. For Mei, Realism does not put emphasis on style because the style is idealistic and an over-emphasis on it could lead to its being over-subjective, while any style that does not transgress political correctness could be acceptable.[5]

For Mei, Huang Ron-Can's woodcut prints have their own style which could be reconstructed. But since he died young and left just a few works, one cannot really assert his artistic achievement. In his Taiwanese period, the most representative work of Huang is the *Terrible Inspection*, in which he treats his subject realistically but also takes others' styles as references. Together with his early works, one could make out the style he is searching for — the rhythm in the composition and the exaggerated movement of the figures. For Mei it is an attempt to preserve Romanticism in Realism.

Mei's research led him to ask the question of when Huang had made this print. This kind of question is typical in art history. Mei found the answer to this question in the testimony given by one of Huang's friends. In the memoir left by his friend Wu Ke-tai, who was a direct witness to the raid on illegal cigarette selling which sparked the uprising,[6] it was stated that Huang had no personal experience of the precise event but he knew quite well what had happened and managed to express the anger of people in his picture the *Terrible Inspection*.

Mei wrote years later about the intention of his own works: the *Homage to Huang Ron-Can* is an installation which groups together works by Huang and related documents. Besides the commemoration of the victims (the souls murdered by political repression according to Mei), it intends also to investigate the true history. In contrast, The *Brilliant Post* is a work of reflection: it is cold, simple and clear. It commemorates the premature death of the artist Huang Ron-Can and reminds people that the tragedy must never be repeated.

To understand better Mei's idea of the true history better, one may refer to an early interview of 2003. In this interview, Mei said:

> The 228 Event's becoming a national trauma is not a historical necessity. Now it is part of the political struggle while the historical lessons and the humanitarian topics became secondary. When I was doing research on the life of Huang Ron-can, numerous warm-hearted people have helped me. But they clearly had their own ideology. A person with a different political position would have a quite different interpretation of Huang's role.
>
> In the movement of the rehabilitation of the 228 Event, the question of who could be rehabilitated and become part of the history and cultural memory is highly related to power relations in the real world and to the political appeals of the family of the victims. I think it is necessary to rehabilitate Huang Ron-can, not only because he has done many works with serious messages which were critical of the actual politics, but also because he was one of the single and non-native persons coming from China and who had no family to take care of their funeral or to make an appeal to justice after their death. Nevertheless, the most important thing to remember is that Huang has contributed to the art sphere after the War and was a politically repressed artist; he was executed just for having a different political tendency from the government. Moreover, I believe that the unknown victims who were as neglected as Huang could be many.[7]

More recently in my own interview with Mei during the summer of 2017, he confirmed that his investigation into Huang's life and creation is an integral concept in his art, and that means if there is no real understanding of this history there could be no real lifting of Martial Law.[8]

To conclude, Mei, as an artist-researcher, actually plays several roles. Firstly, he researches like an art historian and offers an alternative account of art and culture history, and this in itself has a political implication. Secondly, he sometimes writes like an art critic and makes his own judgments. Finally, as an artist he skilfully utilizes the connotation of brilliance — the name of Huang Ron-Can implies the idea of brilliance — and that of the restoration of the original (symbol of the rehabilitation) implied in the anamorphic game.

The Mourning of the Family

The second Taiwanese contemporary artwork related to transitional justice I would like to discuss is a work dated from 1987 to 2010. The dates of the work have an important message in itself: it means that the work was conceived close to the moment of the lifting of the martial law and was finished more than twenty years later, during which time the artist could think deeply on the meaning of his own work.

Fig. 20.5. 謝春德：淡水河的眼淚, Hsieh Chun-te (b. 1949), *The Tears of Dan Shuei River*, 1987–2010, 200 × 150 cm

History and Mind[9]

Taiwan experienced rapid economic development in the 1980s and '90s. During this period, in the political sphere, the end of martial law and the transition to democracy were accompanied by an increase in civil awareness. The suburban situation that Hsieh wanted to depict in his original project of the 1980s became progressively a thing of the past.

For Hsieh, while the changes in the appearance of the city of Taipei may be more visible, the transformations in the minds of people are much less so. In line with his own history of artistic development (from his *Home*, which more closely approximated photojournalism, to the more deeply introspective scenes of *Borderless Floating*), the *Raw* series of which *The Tears of Dan Shuei River* is part spans two decades, beginning with observational reportage and gradually shifting toward an application of the method of staged photography to craft a series of metaphors. In this series, Hsieh Chun-te provides his own perspective on Taiwan's process of development as well as his personal spiritual landscape.

His solo exhibition, *Le Festin de Chun-te*, which was held at the historical Scoletta dell'arte dei battioro e tiraoro in Venice (2011), fully exemplifies the cross-disciplinary and time-consuming aspects, two defining qualities of Hsieh Chun-te's work. The photographic portion of the exhibition is a series of 21 large-scale images taken and post-produced digitally over a period of 24 years (1987–2011). The making of these large-scale photographic pictures accompanies the history of the development of the Taiwanese society.

Originally titled *Sanchong*, the series was renamed *Raw*, referring to a sense of life stripped of its skin (*la vie écorchée*). The source of inspiration for this series was the community of Sanchong and the daily life of its people. A satellite of Taiwan's capital, Taipei, Sanchong was originally a place of transition: people from other areas of Taiwan came to Taipei looking for job opportunities and means for advancement in society. In the early period, when they had few economic resources, they would choose to live in areas on the periphery of the city such as Sanchong.

In the 1980s Hsieh Chun-te himself set up his studio in Sanchong to get deep into the community in order to observe the place and the daily life of its people, but he gradually discovered that, in contrast to the dwelling place of temporary transition it had originally been, Sanchong had become in his mind a microcosm of a period of Taiwanese history.

Firstly, he discovered that many people had lived there for longer periods of time than in the hometowns from which they originally came, yet they were still unable to identify with the place, always feeling that their original city was their family's true home. This made people feel no concern whatsoever for their surrounding environment, tossing garbage and setting down junk when and wherever they pleased.

Several years later, when I myself went with Hsieh Chun-te on a trip through Sanchong visiting the places he had originally photographed, he related the scene at the time: some people lived in clusters of illegal shacks, while others lived in modern apartments. A large group of illegal factories could be found nearby, and next door to residential dwellings stood little hills of piled-up garbage. Perhaps the interiors of people's homes were nicely decorated, but outdoors, the public spaces were in a state of neglect and abandonment.

Sanchong is situated next to the Tamsui River, the major river flowing through the Taipei area. Taiwan's climate includes occasional typhoons, which cause water levels to rise, leading to flooding along the banks of big rivers like the Tamsui. The repeated inundation of low-lying areas exacerbated the temporary nature of the residential areas, because if the temporary, illegal dwelling one built was always destined to be flooded, then there seemed to be no need to make the building particularly sturdy or stately. Because of difficulties encountered in dredging the river, the first method used early on to control the waters was to build a floodwall, and this tall structure separated the people from the river, which had originally served to nourish civilization. So for a period of time, the lives of the people became disconnected from the river, even though the growth of Taipei had originally relied on the river that ran through it. This lofty floodwall symbolizing humanity's segregation from nature became a source of inspiration for Hsieh Chun-te. He wrote a film script about this place, describing how children used a rundown house and a mountain of garbage at the riverside to make the paradise of their dreams, where they could live and play, but in the end it was destroyed in a sudden fire.

Allegory of the traces of history

Evolving from the original *Sanchong* to the later series *Raw*, the traces of history can still be seen everywhere. For example, *The Tears of Tamsui River* is an image that blends together the themes of nearly the entire series.

Its inspiration comes from the February 28 massacre. During the bloody oppression that the Chinese Nationalist government launched to establish their rule soon after arriving in Taiwan, many of the torture victims were paraded before the public with coarse metal wires running through their hands, or they were drowned in the river. *The Tears of Tamsui River* revisits the banks of the river at the town of Bali, where one of the execution grounds may have been at the time, creating a photographic image with greater metaphorical meaning.

In this picture one sees that a small pier extending out into a river is covered with iron spikes, arranged in an orderly fashion and pointing up like a bed of nails. On this brambly stretch — the surface is rough as well — is a nude woman with her hands and feet bound together. Because of the camera angle and the position of her body, her limbs seem to have been cut off, and we can see an expression of pain so extreme that she has entered a kind of trance. In an interview done by Monique Sicard with Hsieh, the artist said that the woman in the picture represents for him the family of the victims of 228. For Hsieh, they could not even express their grief and that's why the woman in the picture is depicted in this position. The direct victims of the 228 event are represented instead by the swimmers floating on the river, where they symbolize the corpses dropped by the perpetrators of the massacre.[10]

In the background of the photo is the Tamsui River, exuding a gloomy, sombre feeling, a faint trace of ambiguity arising from the mountains in the distance and the effect of the light above them, glimmering yet indistinct at dusk or dawn.

Fig. 20.6. 觀音山下的渡船人, *Ferry Voyagers at the Guan-yin-shan*, 1987–2010, 200 × 150 cm

The scenery around the town of Tamsui, located in the vicinity of Taipei, has long been a favourite subject of Taiwanese painters. The reason that artists of the past were fond of painting scenes here was because Western traders and missionaries had been active in the area from early times, and therefore buildings of local and Western styles were pleasingly interspersed here. In addition, the area offers many scenic features considered worth including in a painting: the river widening as it approaches the sea, and the mountains on either side of the river, each with its own distinct character.

The Tamsui that Hsieh Chun-te portrays this time is considerably different from the traditional treatment: firstly, it is photographed from Bali, on the left bank of the river, looking toward Tamsui. Furthermore, the scenery at the water's edge is no longer dominated by traditional houses that accentuate the harmonious integration of nature and humanity, but modern high-rises towering above the riverbank. These high-rises bear witness to the new way in which Taipei has developed: because of the construction of the mass rapid transit system, Taipei's middle class can easily relocate to the city's periphery, but Tamsui's rapidly increasing population has produced pressure on the riverside ecosystem.

Consequently, in addition to the historical tragedy of more than sixty years ago, the *Tears of the Tamsui* encompass the harm that rivers have suffered from the selfish exploitation of humankind and the suffering of the river like that of the family of the victims, could not be expressed, but only symbolized by this gloomy scenery.

The allegorical nature of *Raw* is also expressed in a different image related to the Tamsui River.[11] Titled *Ferry Voyagers at the Guan-yin-shan*, we see in it an 'extended version' of a scene often glimpsed on the streets of Taiwan. A whole family is squeezed onto a single motorcycle, two children seated in front of the father, the mother seated behind him, and two pairs of children in front and in back of her, making a total of two adults and six kids, packed together on the same motorbike. To this peculiar family scene is added a dog, acting as navigator in the front of the boat (which holds the motorcycle). But in addition to the familiar scene of family members, some geese are on the boat as well (one at the front and two at the back), quite possibly symbolizing the remnants of the agrarian age (because in the former days families often raised poultry to supplement their resources). This little boat is paradoxically both crowded and lonely, traversing forward in this not particularly formal way. The arrangement of the human figures and the overall sense of direction give the impression that the family is crossing the river by motorbike.

Employing the family as a metaphor for the nation is a common device, and even at a theoretical dimension, 'a nation [...] is a spiritual family' (Ernest Renan). The artist left a thin protective film unremoved from portions of the negative, resulting in an unstable, vague sensation, and thus the nation metaphorically represented by this family is like a temporary, informal, pieced-together vehicle aboard a boat sailing toward the unknown.

Transformation by Art

The film and its background

The last of the three works by contemporary Taiwanese artists that I would like to discuss in this chapter is the *Transformation into Life*, a short film of 32 minutes,[12] by the renowned film maker Tsai Ming-liang. This film was shot in 2012 to participate in the 'Prelude exhibition' of the Museum of National Taipei University of Education.

The film *Transformation into Life* is quite simple in its scenario: in the typical long take which marked the style of Tsai as *auteur*, it shows firstly the making-up process of Li Kang-shen, his usual leading actor, then that of Yang Guei-mei, his regular leading actress. After these sequences, one sees Li lying down and dressed like the dead body of Chen Cheng-po, a famous painter who was massacred in the 228 event. Yang, in a red robe, then appears and walks to the bedside to watch the dead body for long time. After she leaves, the face of Li, who represents Chen, fades out and the face of Chen in his last photo fades in; the process is made very slow, so that the two faces superimpose. This photo is in itself a famous relic of the event because it was made after Chen's body was brought back home and his widow had asked a photographer to take it in secret.

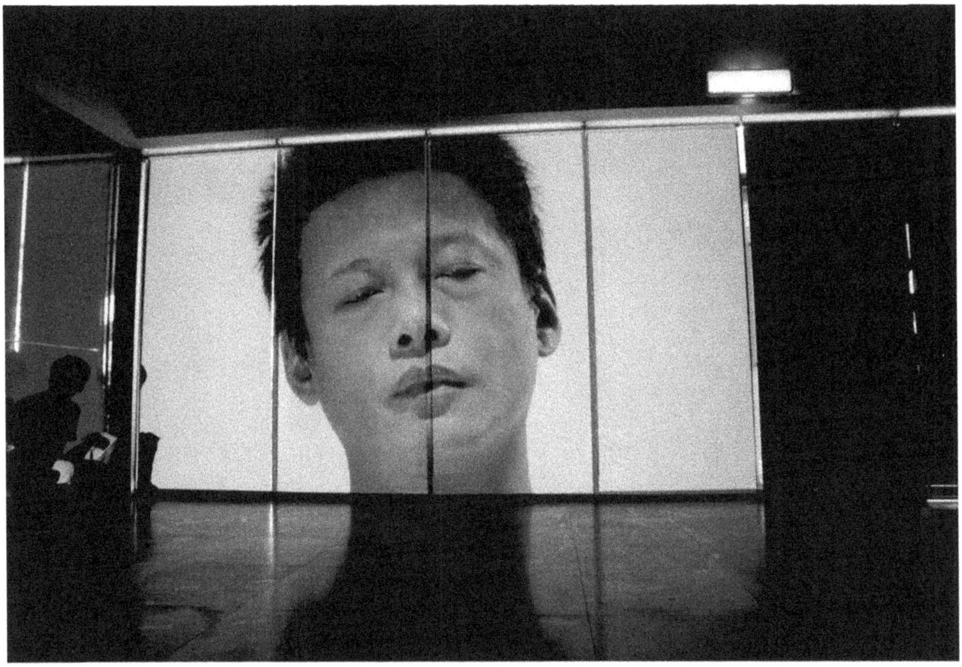

Fig. 20.7. The actor Li Kang-shen in the process of making up (1).

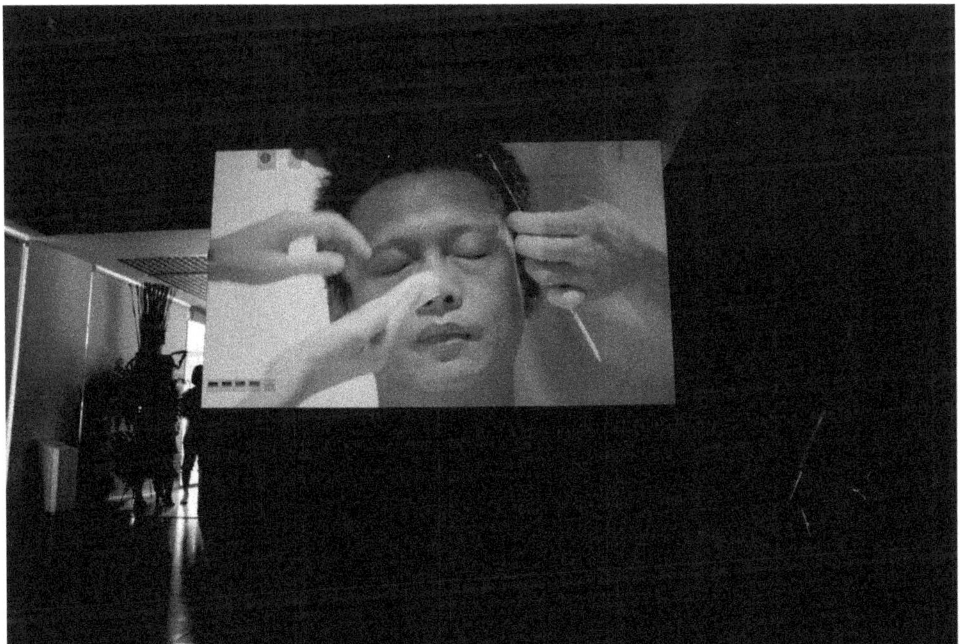

Fig. 20.8. The actor Li Kang-shen in the process of making up (2).

FIG. 20.9. The actress in the process of making up (1).

FIG. 20.10. The photo of the dead body of the painter Chen Cheng-po, victim of the 228 Event.

FIG. 20.11. The actress in the process of making up (2).

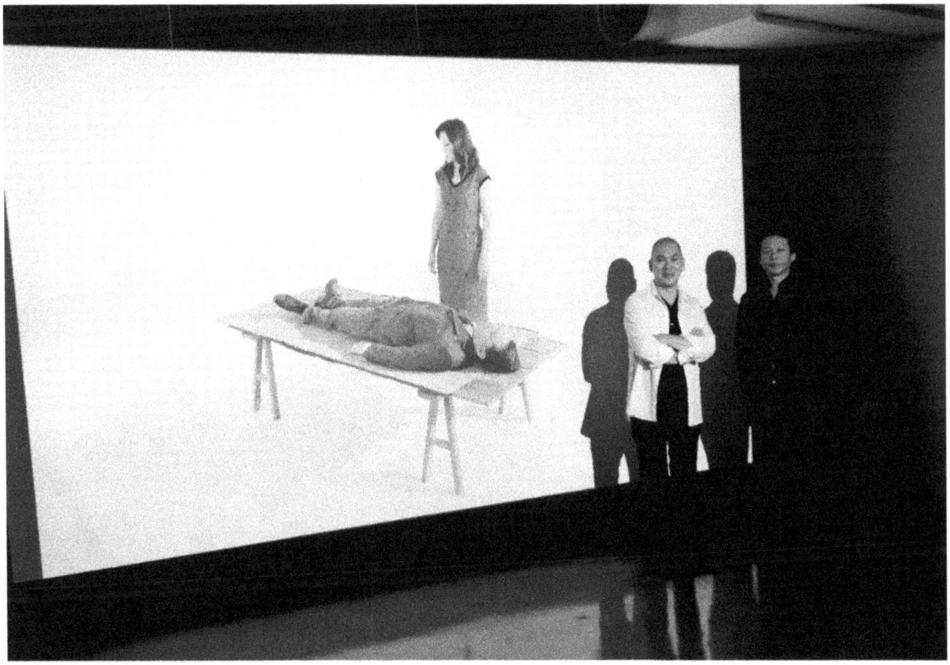

FIG. 20.12. The director Tsai Ming-liang and the actor Lee Kang-shen before the screening in which the red-clad woman appears.

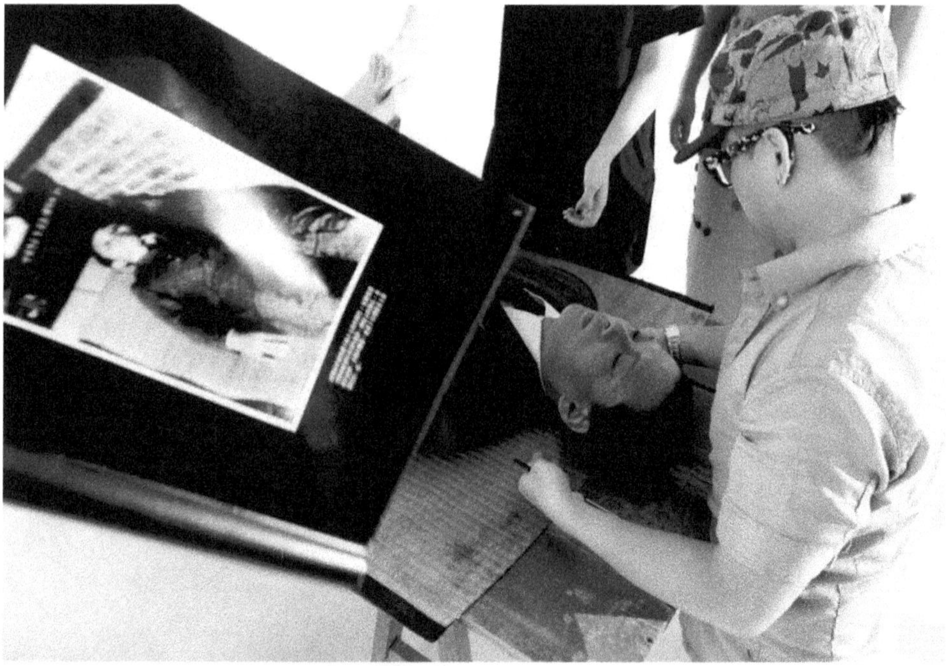

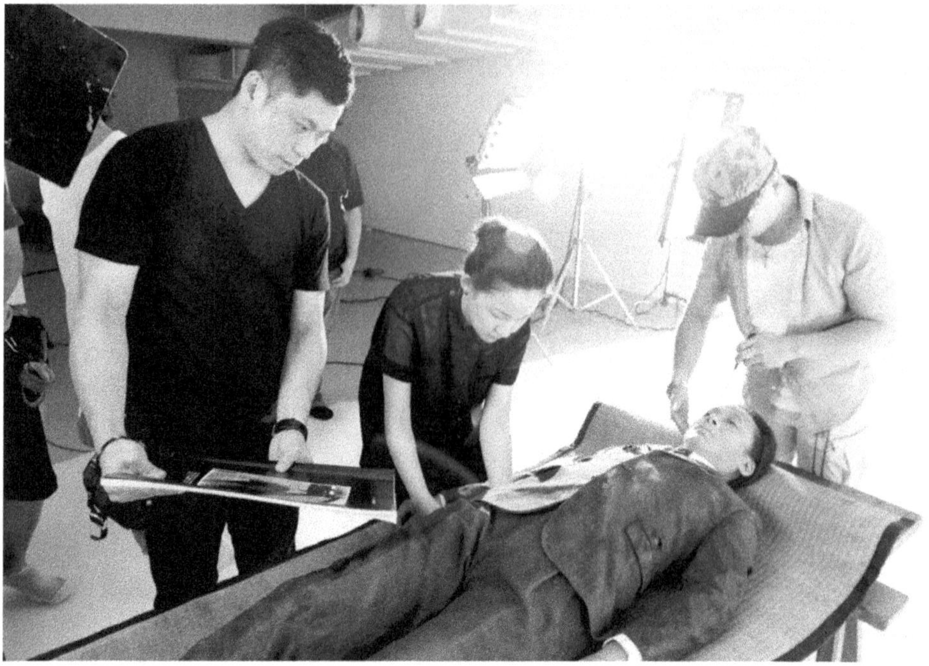

FIG. 20.13, 20.14. The making of '*Transformation into Life*'.

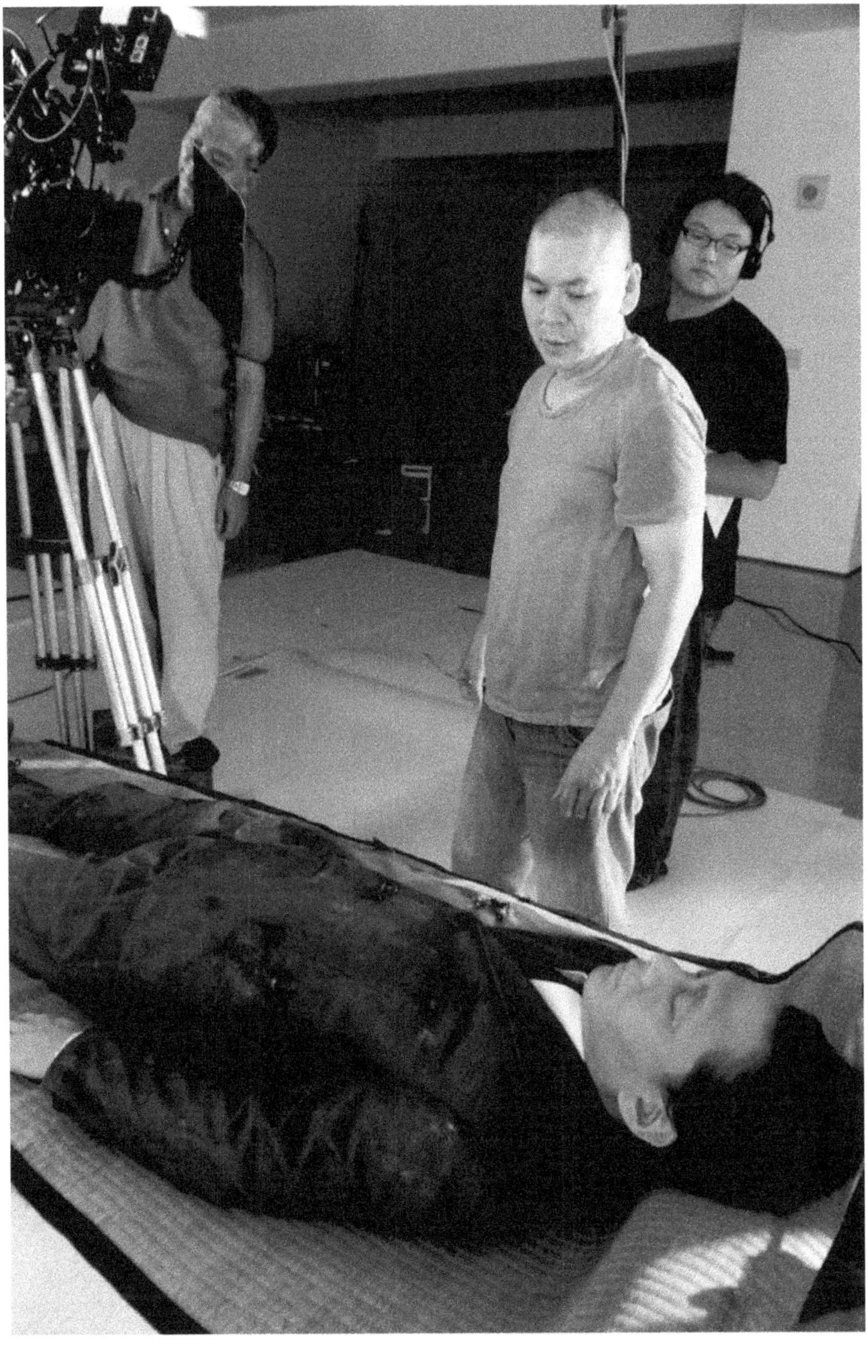

Fig. 20.15. The making of '*Transformation into Life*'.

FIG. 20.16. Chen Cheng-Po, *Woman*, 1931
(a possible source of inspiration of the film).

Possible interpretations of the film

The director Tsai Ming-liang has titled the film *Transformation into Life*. As a Buddhist term its meaning should be understood in contrast with Ovipara (reproduction by laying eggs) and Viviparity (reproduction via embryos), it means thus birth via the fusion of the cold and the hot.

The red-clad woman in the film, played by the actress Yang, is inspired by a portrait of a woman wearing red cloth made by Chen. The possible interpretations of the film could be firstly transformation (rehabilitation) through art. If transformational justice in Taiwan is a delayed process,[13] the transformation or the rehabilitation could be still done symbolically through art. The scenario of the film seems very simple but each shot speaks of a transformational process, those of the actors, of the woman in the picture becoming alive. Finally, the superposition of the image of the actor and the painter in the photo refers also to an appropriate incarnation. Secondly the coming to life of the woman in the picture symbolizes also the afterlife of art which transcends the fortune of the common human and functions as a kind of poetic justice. Because of the particularity of the subject matter, the Death and Life trope for the actor is particularly prominent in this film. Li, the favourite actor of Tsai, plays the dead painter and he has, in a way, to pass through the process of the sacrifice (from life to death) to incarnate his role well (to bring the painter and his picture back to our memory). Finally, the film, in its very slow pace, makes one see more clearly the contrast between different media deployed in this film — cinema, photography and painting — while only cinema could show directly the process of transformation.

Conclusion

Contemporary art about 28 February is not limited to the representation of the event. Through the research-based art project, through staged photography and through the very long takes allowed by the digital camera, these three contemporary artists of Taiwan give not only their personal reflections and insights on Taiwan's traumatic modern history but also develop their own problematics in the vanguard of artistic trends. The encounter between art and history, concerning transitional justice, has still a long and interesting chapter to write.

Notes to Chapter 20

1. Michael Forsythe, 'Taiwan Turns Light on 1947 Slaughter by Chiang Kai-shek's Troops', *The New York Times*, 14 July 2015.
2. About 'The Aftermath' exhibition, please consult <http://www.lianggallery.com/en/?p=16335>.
3. Quoted from Mei's Facebook page, 4 August 2017.
4. Quoted from Mei's Facebook page, 31 July 2017.
5. From commentaries on Mei's Facebook page, 8 August 2017.
6. The event's catalyst was a brutal crackdown on the sale of contraband cigarettes that took place in Taipei on 27 February 1947, when a woman seller was severely hurt by agents, provoking the rage of the surrounding crowd, and a bystander was fatally wounded by gunfire. The following day a crowd made its way to the Governor General's office, where there were further fatalities, and a call for uprisings across the island led later to the imposition of Martial Law. For further

details see the following Wikipedia page: <https://en.wikipedia.org/wiki/February_28_incident>.

7. Interview of Mei by Chen Shian-chun, 1997–2003.
8. A brief sound recording of this interview could be found at <https://www.youtube.com/watch?v=Awv-OAhPlbQ>.
9. An early version of this section has been previously published in Lin Chi-ming, 'The Flux of Desire', in *Le Festin de Chun-te, Collateral Event of the Biennale Arte 2011* (Taipei: A-TE-A Cultural Creative Enterprise Ltd, 2011), pp. 81–89.
10. Please refer to the 2014 documentary by Monique Sicard, *Scènes et rêves de Hsieh Chun-te* (from 26:26) <http://www.item.ens.fr/film-scenes-et-reves-de-hsieh-chun-te/>. Réalisation: Monique Sicard, ITEM (ENS/ CNRS), Genèse des arts visuels. Montage: Arghyro Paouri, Cellule audiovisuelle du Centre Edgar Morin, IIAC (EHESS/CNRS).
11. For the Image of the river in the works of Martial Law period artists, cf. the catalogue of the above mentioned 2017 exhibition 'Aftermath', <https://issuu.com/lianggallery/docs/the_aftermath-the_lift_of_martial_l>.
12. 蔡明亮：化生, 2012, 32min Tsai Ming-liang (b. 1957), *Transformation into Life*, 2012, 32 min., produced by MoNTUE.
13. The central governmental 'Transformational Justice Commission' of Taiwan started to function on 31 May 2018.

INDEX

www.ingramcontent.com/pod-product-compliance
Lightning Source LLC
Chambersburg PA
CBHW080402270326
41927CB00015B/3319
* 9 7 8 1 7 8 1 8 8 3 7 7 8 *